THE GLOBAL JUSTICE MOVEMENT

THE GLOBAL JUSTICE MOVEMENT

Cross-national and Transnational Perspectives

edited by Donatella della Porta

Paradigm Publishers
Boulder • London

green press
INITIATIVE

Paradigm Publishers is committed to preserving ancient forests and natural resources. We elected to print *The Global Justice Movement* on 50% post consumer recycled paper, processed chlorine free. As a result, for this printing, we have saved:

7 Trees (40' tall and 6-8" diameter)
3,074 Gallons of Wastewater
1,236 Kilowatt Hours of Electricity
339 Pounds of Solid Waste
666 Pounds of Greenhouse Gases

Paradigm Publishers made this paper choice because our printer, Thomson-Shore, Inc., is a member of Green Press Initiative, a nonprofit program dedicated to supporting authors, publishers, and suppliers in their efforts to reduce their use of fiber obtained from endangered forests.

For more information, visit www.greenpressinitiative.org

Copyright © 2007 Paradigm Publishers

Published in the United States by Paradigm Publishers, 3360 Mitchell Lane Suite E, Boulder, Colorado 80301 USA.

Paradigm Publishers is the trade name of Birkenkamp & Company, LLC, Dean Birkenkamp, President and Publisher.

Library of Congress Cataloging-in-Publication Data

The global justice movement : cross-national and transnational perspectives / edited by Donatella della Porta.
     p. cm.
   Includes bibliographical references and index.
   ISBN-13: 978-1-59451-304-6 (hc)
   ISBN 10: 1-59451-304-X (hc)
   1. Social movements—International Cooperation.
2. Protest movements—International cooperation.   3. Anti-globalization movement—International cooperation.   I. della Porta, Donatella, 1956–.   II. Title.
   HM881.G553 2007
303.48'4—dc22   2006035794

Printed and bound in the United States of America on acid-free paper that meets the standards of the American National Standard for Permanence of Paper for Printed Library Materials.

Designed and Typeset by Straight Creek Bookmakers.

11   10   09   08   07   1   2   3   4   5

Contents

Figures and Tables

Figures

Tables

Acknowledgments

This book reports the first results of the comparative research project Democracy in Europe and the Mobilization of Society—Demos (http://demos.iue.it). The Demos project is financed by the European Commission, 6th FP Priority 7, Citizens and Governance in a Knowledge Based Society, and (for the Swiss case) the Federal Office for Education and Science, Switzerland. It is coordinated by Donatella della Porta (European University Institute); partners are University of Kent at Canterbury, UK, Christopher C. Rootes; Wissenschaftszentrum Berlin fuer Sozialforschung, Germany, Dieter Rucht; Università di Urbino, Italy, Mario Pianta; Centre de recherches politiques de la Sorbonne (CRPS), Université Panthéon-Sorbonne, France, Isabelle Sommier; Instituto de Estudios Sociales de Andalucia, Centro Superior de Investigaciones Cientificas (IESA-CSIC), Spain, Manuel Jimenez; and Laboratoire de recherches sociales et politiques appliquees (resop), Universite de Geneve, Switzerland, Marco Giugni. We are especially grateful for their time and their trust of the thousands of activists who helped our understanding of the global justice movement. We also wish to express our deep gratitude to Sidney Tarrow for his many suggestions, and to Sarah Tarrow, for a careful editing of the manuscript.

Chapter One

The Global Justice Movement

An Introduction

Donatella della Porta

The Global Justice Movement in Context

When some fifty thousand demonstrators protested against the third World Trade Organization (WTO) conference in Seattle in November 1999, social scientists still focused on explaining the institutionalization of social movements. Only gradually did intense international mobilization—in counter-summits, Global Days of Action, European Marches against Unemployment, Intergalactic Meetings of the Zapatistas, and World Social Forums—start to build awareness of and interest in the emergence of a new cycle of protest. In subsequent years, hundreds of thousands marched against the International Monetary Fund (IMF) and World Bank meetings in Washington and Prague in 2000 and 2001 and against the European Union (EU) summits in Amsterdam in 1997, Nice in 2000, and Gothenburg in 2001. They protested the World Economic Forum in yearly demonstrations in Davos, the G8 summit in Genoa in 2001, and (following the call issued by the first European Social Forum) the Iraq war in hundreds of cities on February 15, 2003. That cycles of protest emerge unexpectedly is certainly not new. On the eve of 1968, social scientists and politicians alike lamented the "end of ideologies," the institutionalization of the labor movement and consumption

1

society, and, above all, the decline of interest in politics. At the turn of the millennium, the debate focused on the disappearance of a sense of community, the institutionalization of the "new" social movement, the antipolitical stance of new generations. Surely, the emergence of a new cycle testifies to a rupture in the prevailing forms of collective action and organizational strategy as well as collective identities. In this sense, the perception of a sudden break reflects the challenges that cycles of protest pose to existing repertoires of collective action. During protest cycles, new organizational structures emerge with new styles of activism (Tarrow 1989; della Porta 2005a). What seemed established is once again in movement.

Waves of protest do not, however, emerge from nowhere. In the sociology of social movements, various concepts have been used to depict movement survival beyond protest mobilization: Melucci (1996) described the alternate stages of visibility and latency; Verta Taylor (1989) analyzed the functioning of organizations in periods of movement "doldrums." It was observed that, even in low ebbs, social movement organizations do not invariably transform themselves into interest groups or charities (della Porta 2003a and 2003b). Social movement organizations from previous waves of mobilization often participate in the rise of new cycles of protest, ensuring continuity with the past.

Although often unexpected, the emergence of a protest cycle is not as sudden as it appears. Protest requires existing organizational structures able to mobilize resources, as well as less visible processes of networking and construction of justifications for collective action. It involves institutional actors and arenas: For instance, in some countries, the 1968 movements also developed inside student unions as well as in parties' structures (Tarrow 1989). The emerging movements are often influenced by the characteristics of the organizations that "host" them in their infancy, and their evolution is the product of a mix of traditions and challenges to those traditions. The perception of a sudden rupture is in part an outcome of the natural conformism in the social sciences, where the confirmation of general trends (such as the bureaucratization of labor unions or the institutionalization of social movement organizations) is often facilitated by the choice of some objects of study (such as the union leadership or the more visible and better structured nongovernmental organizations [NGOs]) and not others. Conversely, the singling out of countertrends seems to be discouraged by their lack of visibility or relevance within the dominant paradigm.

In this volume, we pay attention to the way in which the protest on global justice developed, singling out the less visible steps of "remobilization," as well as the innovations introduced in the action repertoires, structures, and frames during the protest cycle.

The protests we have just mentioned developed, as we will see, from a number of campaigns that networked existing organizations against the

North American Free Trade Agreements (NAFTA); against the Multilateral Agreement on Investment; for the cancellation of poor countries' foreign debt (in the Jubilee 2000 campaign); and for a more social Europe (in the European Marches against Unemployment and Exclusion).[1] Within these campaigns, new frames of action developed, symbolically constructing a global self, but also producing structural effects in the form of new movement networks. After some preliminary experiences in the 1980s, countersummits multiplied over the succeeding decade, simultaneous with large-scale UN Conferences (Pianta 2001b) and supported by frenetic Transnational Social Movement Organizations and NGO activity that claimed to represent not only their hundreds of thousands of members, but more generally the interests of millions of citizens without a public voice. Mobilizations at the transnational level have also been linked to (more traditional) local and national protests such as the mobilization of the "have-nots" in France, the anti-road protests in the UK, the labor action of critical, grassroots unions in Italy, and the environmental campaigns against large infrastructures in Spain. Local and national organizations interact transnationally, reacting to supranational institutions of governance, but they are also embedded in national traditions and opportunities.

Although the Global Justice Movement (GJM) acquired notoriety in Seattle, United States, it seems to have had a larger impact in Europe. Although September 11 and, especially, the Iraq war did in fact bring about a redomestication of activism in the United States (or, as Jennifer Hadden and Sidney Tarrow argue in their chapter, a process of internalization), in Europe transnational protest remains very dynamic. The process of the Europeanization of social movements not only intensified with the building of Europe-wide networks and campaigns, but is also spreading to Eastern Europe and Turkey.

On the Old Continent, the extraordinary capacity of transnational networking in the GJM is visible in the European Social Forum (ESF), the regional version of the World Social Forum, which provides an arena for encounters and debates to large numbers of organizations and activists from different countries. The first ESF, held in Florence in 2002, involved 60,000 participants—more than three times the expected number—taking part in the 30 plenary conferences, 160 seminars, and 180 workshops as well as 75 cultural events in various parts of the city. More than 20,000 delegates of 426 associations arrived from 105 countries, and about one million took part in the march that closed the forum. Although the number of registered participants declined in the two following meetings (about 40,000 in Paris in 2003 and 20,000 in London the succeeding year), the capacity of the events to involve activists from heterogeneous backgrounds and different countries remained high. The effects of increasingly broader networking were even more visible in the fourth ESF in Athens in May 2006, where not only did

Table 1.1 Opinions on the Global Justice Movement

	Trust	Do Not Trust	Don't Know/ No Answer
France	51%	45%	5%
Italy	33%	64%	3%
Germany	36%	56%	8%
Spain	47%	42%	11%
United Kingdom	41%	49%	10%

Source: Adapted from "Flash Eurobarometer" on "Globalization" (2003).

the number of registered participants again almost double (36,000), but the event attracted numerous delegations from Eastern Europe and the Mediterranean area.

Additionally, if social movements are usually carriers of minoritarian challenges, the global justice movement seems to be an exception: According to a Eurobarometer Survey concluded in 2003, as many as 51 percent of citizens in France, 47 percent in Spain, 41 percent in the UK, 36 percent in Germany, and 33 percent in Italy claim to trust the movement (see table 1.1). In addition, many citizens think that the global justice movement should have more influence on the process of globalization: Sixty-one percent of respondents in Italy, 55 percent in Spain, 48 percent in Germany, 47 percent in France (but only 36 percent in the UK) state, in fact, that the global justice movement does not have enough influence on globalization (table 1.2). More than 70 percent of citizens in each country think that the global justice movement raises points that deserve to be debated; more than 60 percent (except for the Spanish: 49 percent) believe that it raises awareness of certain aspects of globalization, whereas between 47 percent (France) and 32 percent (Italy) think that it proposes concrete solutions to globalization (table 1.3). Additionally, between 41 percent (France) and 29 percent (Spain) believe that

Table 1.2 Opinions on the Global Justice Movement

	Too Much Influence	The Right Level of Influence	Not Enough Influence	Don't Know/ No Answer
France	18%	29%	47%	7%
Italy	16%	18%	61%	5%
Germany	11%	27%	48%	14%
Spain	10%	22%	55%	13%
United Kingdom	19%	29%	36%	16%

Source: Adapted from "Flash Eurobarometer" on "Globalization" (2003).

Table 1.3 Opinions on the Global Justice Movement

	Raise Points That Deserve To Be Debated (Yes %)	Raise Your Awareness of Certain Aspects of Globalization (Yes %)	Propose Concrete Solutions to Globalization (Yes %)	Decision Makers Succeed in Influencing National Political (Yes %)	Manage to Slow Down the Process of Globalization (Yes %)
France	88%	69%	47%	41%	47%
Italy	78%	62%	32%	30%	32%
Germany	84%	61%	44%	33%	44%
Spain	72%	49%	40%	29%	40%
United Kingdom	75%	68%	33%	37%	33%

Source: Adapted from "Flash Eurobarometer" on "Globalization" (2003).

the global justice movement is successful in influencing national political decision makers, and more than 31 percent of citizens in all countries even see it as successful in slowing down the process of globalization.

Addressing the analysis of this cycle of protest at the turn of the millennium, we want to describe the emergence and evolution of the GJM, with its blending of tradition and innovation, national roots and cosmopolitan visions in six European countries, in the United States, and at the transnational level. As we will see, the mobilizations on global justice issues in France, Germany, Great Britain, Italy, Spain, and Switzerland, as well as in the United States, have much in common. Not only do they remobilize people on the street, but they also cast a broad net that covers organizations and groupings active on different issues and with heterogeneous initial concerns. They all focus attention on issues of global justice and "globalization from below." They link local, national, and global issues, as well as local, national, and global organizational structures, mobilizing against a multilevel system of governance. If wide differences exist within each national context (with groups animated by moderate and radical repertoires and frames competing with each other), we also stress national specificities in our cross-national comparison—different densities in the networks of protest, different blends of protest repertoires, and different master frames—that are forged by national opportunities and movement traditions.

This chapter introduces this comparative endeavor by proposing, first of all, a definition of our object of analysis (section 2), and then by singling out common characteristics as well as different typologies in the movement networks (section 3), action strategies (section 4), and frames of action (section

5). Furthermore, we present some possible explanations for the emergence of the movement and its various national characteristics (section 6).

Defining the Global Justice Movement

This volume focuses on contemporary social movements, in particular on the mobilizations on issues of global justice and a "globalization from below." The first question we want to address in this introduction refers to the definition of our object of research: the global justice movement. We can consider *social movements* as interactions of mainly informal networks based on common beliefs and solidarity, which mobilize on conflictual issues by frequent recourse to various forms of protest (della Porta and Diani 2006, chap. 1). In Sidney Tarrow's definition (2001, 11), *transnational* social movements are "socially mobilised groups with constituents in at least two states, engaged in sustained contentious interactions with power-holders in at least one state other than their own, or against an international institution, or a multinational economic actor." *Global* social movements can be defined as transnational networks of actors that define their causes as global and organize protest campaigns and other forms of action that target more than one state and/or international governmental organization (IGO).

Although these are all analytic definitions, useful for identifying abstract concepts, in our book we want to focus on an empirical actor, the *global justice movement,* which we define as the loose network of organizations (with varying degrees of formality and even including political parties) and other actors engaged in collective action of various kinds, on the basis of the shared goal of advancing the cause of justice (economic, social, political, and environmental) among and between peoples across the globe. This means that we focus on an empirical form of transnational activism, without implying that this covers all the existing manifestations of that abstract concept. We operationalize our definition by looking at collective identity, nonconventional action repertoires, and organizational networks.

A fundamental characteristic of a social movement is its ability to develop a *common interpretation of reality* able to nurture solidarity and collective identifications, as well as a collective attempt to change or resist changes in the external environment. Outside the political routine, the movements develop visions of the world alternative to the dominant ones. New conflicts emerge on new values. In particular, from the 1970s onward, "new social movements" began to be seen as actors in new conflicts, in contrast to the "old" workers' movement that was by then perceived as not only institutionalized, but also focusing on materialistic issues. Gender difference, defense of the environment, and cohabitation among different cultures are some of the issues around which social movements have formed. The establishment of a global movement requires the development of a discourse that identifies both a *common identity—the "us"—and the target of the protest—the "other"—at the transnational level.* As far as the framing of the action is concerned, we are interested in those groups/individual activists who frame their action in terms of *global identity and concerns*: They identify themselves as part of a "global movement," targeting "global enemies" within a global *enjeu*/field of action. Operationally, we focus on groups/activists that have been identified, in different countries, as alter-global, no global, new global, global justice, *Globalisierungskritiker, altermondialists,* globalizers from below, and so on. The individual chapters will discuss to which extent a common global concern spread during transnational protests.

Social movements are characterized by the use of *protest* as a means of pressure on institutions (e.g., Rucht 1994). Those who protest address the public even before they approach elected representatives or public bureaucracy. Just as protest actions were concentrated at the national level with the creation of the nation-state, globalization may be expected to generate protest at the transnational level against international actors. In our operational definition, we consider organizations and individuals who have participated in contentious actions organized by groups/activists with a global concern, as defined above. In parallel to past research that focused on those groups/actors taking part in protest activities, we look at organizations and individuals taking part in protest campaigns focusing on poverty in the South, taxation of capital, debt relief, fair trade, global rights, and reform of international intergovernmental organizations. In our contributions, we shall discuss to what extent mobilizations on these various issues have been linked in a common wave of protest.

Social movements are *informal networks* linking a plurality of individuals and groups, more or less structured from an organizational point of view. Whereas parties or pressure groups have somewhat well-defined organizational boundaries, with participation normally verified by a membership card, social movements are instead composed of loose, weakly linked networks of individuals who feel part of a collective effort. Although there are organizations that refer back to movements, movements are not organizations but rather nets, linking various actors who encompass (also but not only) organizations with a formal structure. One distinctive characteristic of a social movement is the possibility of belonging and feeling involved in collective action without necessarily being a member of a specific organization. It follows, therefore, that a global movement should involve organizational networks active in different countries. Operationally, with our focus on the global justice movement, we are interested in the individuals, groups, and organizations in each country that have built and/or participated in one or more networks on the global issues mentioned previously and acted via protest. Especially since we are dealing with movement(s) that address different specific issues (labor rights, genetically modified organisms [GMOs], women's liberation, etc.), their belonging to networks that address these issues within global frames has a relevant, discriminating value. Participation in European social forums (or national/local social forums) and/or similar/parallel events or umbrella organizations is covered by our operational definition. In our research, we shall indeed address the role (frequency and importance) of participation in transnational events for local and national social movement organizations. The various chapters will discuss how dense the movement networks are in each of the analyzed countries and at the transnational level.

To summarize, we aim to analyze the presence of a social movement, defined by the presence of networks of individuals, groups, and organizations that, based on common beliefs and a collective identity, seek to change society (or resist such a change) mainly by the use of protest (Rucht 1994, 77; della Porta and Diani 1999, 16). We focus in particular on movement(s) as networks participating in protest campaigns on the issue of global justice. For our movement(s), the ultimate frame of reference is indeed the globe: Although specific actions often have a narrower scope, solutions are sought at the global level, and/or specific claims are embedded in visions of global change. Within these global dimensions, the main aim of the movement(s) is the struggle for *justice*—a general term that encompasses more specific domains of intervention such as human rights, citizens' rights, social rights, peace, the environment, and similar concerns. Our empirical research will also address the issue of the degree of transnationalization in the movement discourse and the extent to which a scale shift (Tarrow 2005) has occurred.

Looking at trans-issue and transnational networking, as well as the degree of strategic and ideological diversity within the GJM, we shall discuss to what extent, in the different countries, we can speak of one or more movements focusing on global justice.

The Movement as a Network—and Network Types

According to our definition, we are interested in organizations acting within transnational networks. Social scientists have emphasized the growing number of transnational organizations linked to social movements (often "global" not in the sense of covering the whole globe, but of involving membership from various countries) (Sikkink and Smith 2002), a trend that is particularly vigorous in the South of the world (see also Smith and Johnston 2002). The greater influence wielded by these organizations is beyond doubt, but opinions vary on the extent to which they are able to engage in stable networks (e.g., Fox and Brown 1998; on immigration, see Guiraudon 2002). The highly flexible organizational structure, with demonstrations organized via the Internet by ad hoc coordination committees, is seen by some as the best solution for adapting to global trends, by others as a sign of the inability to build a durable organization.

Our research addresses the network of the global justice movement by looking at the linkages among transnational, national, and local groups that have mobilized on global issues. As all the chapters indicate, the new cycle of protest has mobilized in each country a plurality of networks active on various issues. Differently from that of the labor movement, but also from many social movements that followed it—which tended to have a homogeneous basis in terms of generation (the student movement), gender (the women's or gay liberation movements), or social position (chiefly involving the middle classes)—the global justice movement, as we will see, is instead heterogeneous from the generational viewpoint, while seeking to help diverse, distant national cultures to communicate. More than in recent movements, the presence of a large number of organizations compensates for the weakness in terms of categorical homogeneity. Membership in a movement is favored by incorporation into informal networks of individuals sharing an interest in particular causes: It is through these links that potential activists develop their worldview and acquire mobilization skills (della Porta and Diani 1999, chap. 5).

The inclusive structure already typical of other movements (especially the women's and peace movements) appears in the global justice movement in a more highly networked version. The new communication technologies—primarily the Internet—have not only steadily reduced the costs of mobilization, allowing slim, flexible structures, but also facilitated transversal interaction among different areas and movements (della Porta and Mosca 2005a). Trans-issue as well as transnational attention constitutes a novelty in a panorama that seemed typified by specialization in single-issue movements (from women to the environment, from peace to AIDS).

In all the countries we cover, organizations from different movements have converged in a series of roundtables, nets, and coalitions that were very often not limited to one national state. *Netzwerke, reti, redes, coordinadoras, tavoli, nets, forums,* even *movements* are all terms that we shall find in the following chapters in the names of new organizations that usually allowed not only for overlapping membership by individual activists, but also for the convergence of collective members. The local social forums, in all their variations, represent an attempt to create open spaces for the interactions of different individuals and groups.

In the individual countries, as well as at the transnational level, the density of the network, as well as its format, tends to vary (see also chapter 10). At the transnational level, vertical and horizontal networks adapt their strategies to the characteristics of the international governmental organizations they target. There are loose, rank-and-file movement networks involving mainly grassroots groups, and there are movement coalitions with larger influence by more structured associations.

At the national level, variations abound with (softer or harder) tensions between rank-and-file, grassroots, direct-action groupings and well-structured and institutionalized unions and large associations. In Germany, there is a tension between the more institutionalized human rights and development NGOs allied with environmental associations and unions, on the one hand, with the net of autonomous and antiracist groups on the other. Local forums vary significantly in the composition of the actors involved, with participation mainly of grassroots-oriented activists with previous experiences in "new social movements," religious groups, unions, and also the more radical Left (e.g., in Berlin or Cologne). The constellations of subnetworks is similar in Switzerland, with an institutional branch composed of formalized ecological, solidarity, and labor associations, on the one hand, and autonomous, anarchist, and squatters' groups on the other. In the UK, the movement sees the (difficult) coexistence of a well-established coalition of aid, trade, and development NGOs, environmental movement organizations, religious groups, and unions alongside informal nets of anarchists, squatters, and radical ecologists supporting direct action. Similar tensions exist also in other countries, but they seem to have been less disruptive in terms of competition within the movement. In Spain, decentralized and grassroots tendencies dominate, resonating with libertarian traditions as well as with the mobilization of ethnic and national territorial minorities. In Italy, the three main nodes present in the global justice movement—the ecopacifists, the anti-neoliberals and the (inheritor of the) Disobedients—have interacted in the local social forums that flowered before and after the anti-G8 protest in Genoa. Even after the demise of most of them, occasions for collaboration have been frequent. In France, tensions around the conception of internal democracy have punctuated the story of Attac, although they have not polarized the movement.

As we will see in the following chapters, national movement networks in Europe show different formats (cliqued in France, Italy, and Spain; polarized in Germany and Switzerland and, to a lesser extent, in the UK) and organizational structures (more horizontal in the first case, vertical in the second). In the United States, with the spread of single-issue and pragmatic movement organizations, the alliance between "turtles and teamsters," proclaimed in Seattle, was hard to consolidate.

Protest Campaigns and Multiple Repertoires

Our definition includes a focus on mobilization targeting multilevel governance. Protest event research has stressed the rarity of transnational protest.

Protests—at least those that get national press coverage—still mainly target the state or substate level of government (Imig and Tarrow 2002; Rucht 2002a), as has been confirmed for various types of movements from environmental (Rootes 2003a) to antiracist (Giugni and Passy 2002). Furthermore, it has often been emphasized that organizations active at the transnational level adopt conventional types of action oriented more toward discreet lobbying than street protest. On that basis, some have suggested that mobilizations such as Seattle or Genoa are to be considered as episodic events, with collective action still firmly anchored at the national level and dominated by increasingly institutionalized NGOs and "normalized" action repertoires. In our research we shall first stress the extremely relevant effects of transnational events. Even when few in number, transnational protests further the development of new networks and frames.

As the chapter by Pianta and Marchetti thoughtfully describes, in the last decade transnational protest events have intensified over time in terms of numbers of events, organizations, and activists involved. They have also become more cross-issue and autonomous from political institutions. In the 1990s, the end of the Cold War opened opportunities for movements in the form of UN-sponsored conferences but also autonomous networking, especially against the war in Iraq and former Yugoslavia, and in solidarity with the Zapatistas movement. The tactics of confrontational counter-summits also developed with the contestation of IGOs such as the World Bank, the IMF, the WTO, the G8, and even the EU. In the first decade of the new millennium, counter-summits were accompanied by global days of action, as well as world and macro-regional social forums as autonomous spaces for a growing global civil society.

Additionally, transnational events reverberate at the local and national levels with protest campaigns that simultaneously address several territorial levels of governance (Diani 2005; Rootes 2005; della Porta and Mosca 2005b). Our country chapters indicate that not only have transnational events increased in frequency, in the forms of both the transnational convergence of protesters in a symbolic place and global days of action with large demonstrations staged at the same time in dozens of cities all around the world; they have also constituted founding events for a new cycle of protest that has developed at the national and subnational levels on the issue of global justice.

Transnational protest has reflected transnational links and also fueled them. Research in the 1980s and 1990s described a progressive institutionalization of social movements, at least in Western democracies (della Porta 2003a). Some movement organizations had become better structured at the national or even the transnational level, had acquired substantial material resources and a certain public recognition, had set up paid staffs thanks to mass membership drives, and tended to replace protest by lobbying or contentious actions. They had become interest groups, albeit of a public interest type. Other groups involved in the process of contracting out social services had entered the third sector, acquiring professional skills and often administering public resources, here, too, with little recourse to unconventional political action. Protest had in the meantime become the domain of local campaigns and citizen committees, often fragmented down to the street or neighborhood level, with the pragmatic objective of protecting limited territories. Even the social centers, at least in some countries, seemed caught between commercialization in administering spaces for alternative culture and radicalization of forms of action.

If the global justice movement (re)mobilized disillusioned activists who had used (and often continued to use) lobbying and consultation tactics, it also brought about a return of *direct action*—rehabilitating protest, as our German authors frame it. Although the movement became visible with the Black Bloc smashing windows in Seattle, violence is criticized within the movement on both ethical and instrumental grounds (della Porta et al. 2006). Direct nonviolent action and civil disobedience are instead welcomed as forms of action capable of simultaneously drawing the attention of public opinion and testifying to the activists' commitment.

In addition, such types of repertoire aim at combining conflict and consensus on the example of the Zapatista movement. The symbolic penetration of no-go areas for demonstrators (red zones) represented a widespread tactic during counter-summits. The destruction of transgenetic fields as well as the dismantling of McDonald's belong to the early story of the French global justice movement. The nonviolent roadblocks (or street reclaiming) migrated from the British anti-road protests to other European countries and then to Seattle, together with the "spectacularization" of marches in ways that emphasized individual creativity (carnivals, critical mass). In Italy, the "train-stopping" Disobedients and Catholic groups supported the blockades of trains transporting arms for the Iraq war. In the more radical wing of the movement, squatting for housing as well as for the development of "free space" is quite widespread. Symbolic forms of free-consumption or price-reduction also spread to protest precarious jobs and cuts in the welfare state. Harsh confrontations with police in Geneva in 1998 as well as in Davos testify to an increasing use of disruptive tactics in a country otherwise characterized by moderation of action repertoires. Ecotage had developed (already before the global justice movement) in the (traditionally moderate) British environmental movement. Break-ins hit the offices of big corporations and public agencies.

The Seattle demonstrations also started a new wave of "politics on the street," with large marches that had seemed just a memory of the past. *Mass demonstrations* are in fact often organized during counter-summits, defined as arenas of international-level initiatives during official summits and on the same issues but from a critical standpoint, heightening awareness through protest and information with or without contacts with the official summit (Pianta 2001b and 2003). Millions of people joined the international day of protest against the Iraq war on February 15, 2003 (della Porta and Diani 2004b; Walgrave and Rucht forthcoming).

In each of the countries we have analyzed, some of these counter-summits and global days of action represented the founding events (or at least a symbolic reference) for the emerging protest: in Germany, especially the protest against the IMF and World Bank summit in Berlin in 1988, followed by those (less successful) against the G7 and EU summit in 1992 in Munich and then against the EU in Cologne; in France, the European Marches against Unemployment and Exclusion; in Switzerland, the 1998 summit against the WTO in Geneva and the subsequent anti–World Economic Forum demonstrations; in Italy, the demonstration against the Organization for Security and Co-operation in Europe (OSCE) meeting on new technology in Naples in 2001 and later the Genoa anti-G8 protest; in Spain, the protests in Madrid during the "50 years are enough" campaign in 1994, and then in Barcelona against the World Bank (2001), as well as the campaign against the Spanish presidency of the EU; in the UK the anti-G8 protest in Birmingham in 1998; in the United States, the anti-WTO protests in Seattle in 1999.

During counter-summits, protest is also linked to the construction and exchange of knowledge. In its strategies, the global justice movement attaches high value to alternative knowledge and skills, aiming to build up a global public sphere. The relevance of communication is further confirmed by the importance assumed not only by the Internet, but also by issues connected with it, from copyright to censorship of telecommunications. Professional skills and counter-expertise are important characteristics of many more formal German associations and of the French movement's think tanks and alternative media. Everywhere, a leading organization of the global justice movement such as Attac presents itself as a movement for people's self-education oriented to action—and the relevant role of scientific committees testifies to this attention to alternative knowledge.

The spread of information is also central in actions that seek to mobilize, in addition to the citizen, the consumer (through boycotts and political consumerism) or the saver (through ethical banks). Transnational campaigns against multinational corporations such as De Beers, Microsoft, Monsanto, and Nike favored transnational networking and the building of global frames of action. The underlying logic of many movement campaigns is the "naming and shaming," which, especially when targeting multinationals, aims at increasing public awareness of especially glaring cases of ignoring human rights—spreading detailed information and often asking people to punish the companies involved by boycotting their products. The boycotts, producing direct damage to the targeted economic enterprises, adapt action repertoire to a situation in which multinational companies have growing power (according to the activists, even more power than many nation-states). They also exploit the particular need for a "clean image" of corporations that rely more on their logo than on the quality of their products.

The global justice movement in fact developed actions oriented to sensitize citizens to *alternative* values and culture. This logic is especially expressed in the *consumer activism* that "challenges our sense that money and morality cannot be mixed" (Micheletti 2003, 3). Presenting consumption as a potential political act, ethical consumerism stresses the central role of individuals in taking responsibility for the common goods in their everyday life. Boycotts of bad products, but also *buy*cotts of fair ones (environmental-friendly and solidaristic) as well as socially responsible investment are ways not only of resocializing wrongdoers and changing business activities, but also of practicing certain values (Follesdal 2004). Fair trade is indeed mentioned in all our cases as an innovation on protest repertoires: Although it predated the global justice movement, it spread widely after Seattle.

Our research confirms that cycles of protest not only revitalize street action, but also make changes in protest repertoires. The campaigns against land mines or NAFTA and the Multilateral Agreement on Investments (MAI), the UN-sponsored world conferences, and Jubilee 2000 emerge as main occasions for organizational networking, aggregating the more institutionalized organizations: development and human rights NGOs, religious and nonreligious charities, labor unions and large environmental associations that had already collaborated, among others, in the previous waves of pacifist mobilization. On the other hand, the European Marches against Unemployment and Exclusion (Chabanet 2002), the actions in solidarity with the Zapatistas and the Intergalactic meetings (in 1996 in Chiapas and 1997 in Spain), as well the later demonstrations in Prague against the IMF and World Bank and in Nice and Gothenburg against the EU, constituted moments of interaction among the more radical groups as well as the critical unions.

In all our countries as well as at the transnational level, protest campaigns facilitated (and were facilitated by) organizational networking. Large associations frustrated by ineffective lobbying and unions in search of new mobilization models met with rank-and-file, decentralized groupings of squatters, cross-fertilizing one another's repertoires (della Porta and Mosca 2005b). Here, as well, we will also note cross-national differences, with more radical and mass-oriented repertoires dominating in some countries, more moderate and communication-oriented ones in others. In Italy and Spain (and to some extent France), direct action became more central, in the form of both mass demonstrations and civil disobedience. In Germany, Switzerland, the UK, and to a lesser extent in the United States, more radical sectors advocating direct action competed with associations much more resourceful in terms of channels for lobbying and access to public decision making as well as contacts in the institutional mass media.

How Much Justice, and What Type of Democracy?

We mentioned the development of global issues as a definitional character-istic of global movements. On the understanding of "global issues," however, observers' opinions differ: Some see the beginnings of global identities, whereas others speak of an (almost opportunistic) adjustment by mainly na-tional actors to territorially multilevel governance. If the symbolic reference to the globe is considered by some as nothing really new—referencing the traditional internationalism of the workers' movement or the transnational campaigns against slavery—others instead stress the centrality of the global dimension today (for a discussion of these definitional issues, see della Porta 2005b; Rucht 2005). If for some the mobilization on globalization is a leftover from the past, for others it is the movement of the future.

In this volume, we will address these topics, describing the processes of connection (or frame bridging) at both the transnational and the "trans-issue" levels (Gerhards and Rucht 1992; Andretta 2005). In the 1980s, so-cial movements had undergone a process of specialization on single issues. Not only did new social movements seem to develop apart from the labor unions, but, notwithstanding some mentioned countertrends, organizations also seemed to specialize within these "new social movements," developing specific knowledge and competences on particular sub-issues.

All of our contributors stress the multi-issue nature of the global justice movement. Concerns with the environment, women's rights, peace, and social inequalities remain as characteristics of subgroups or networks in the mobi-lization on globalization. The definition of the "movement of movements" stresses the survival of these specific concerns and the non-subordination of one conflict to another: If in the socialist ideology women's emancipation was subordinated to workers' emancipation, most GJM organizations deny a hierarchy of conflicts. The multiplicity of reference bases in terms of class, gender, generation, race, and religion seems to have developed in the direc-tion of not weak, but certainly composite identities.

As we will see, in different countries the different concerns of different movements were bridged in a lengthy, although not very visible, process of mobilization. The global justice movement developed from protest campaigns around "broker issues" that tied together concerns of differ-ent movements and organizations. In Switzerland, the campaign against the WTO brought together squatters, human rights activists, and labor unionists. In France, the struggle against genetically modified (GM) food linked peasants and ecologists; the *mouvements de sans* involved the critical unions with organizations of the unemployed, sans-papiers, and homeless. Jubilee 2000 linked development NGOs with rank-and-file religious groups. In the anti-Maastricht movement in Spain (and later in the "50 years are enough" campaign), ecologists and pacifists met with critical unionists. In

Great Britain, opposition to the Criminal Justice and Public Order Act was perceived as a catalyst for the interaction of travelers, squatters, "ravers," and environmentalists (and in the campaign against dismissals, dockers encountered—even if occasionally—the Reclaim the Street direct action network).

In all these campaigns, to different degrees, fragments of diverse cultures—secular and religious, radical and reformist, of younger and older generations—have been linked to a broader discourse with the theme of social (and global) injustice as an adhesive, while still leaving broad margins for separate developments. At the transnational level, local and global concerns were connected around values such as equality, justice, human rights, and environmental protection. Platforms, forums, coalitions, and networks allowed for reciprocal knowledge and often mutual understanding among different cultures. Although emphasizing pluralism and diversity, in the discourse of the movement, a common master frame developed upon a definition of the self around a global dimension.

In parallel, the enemy is singled out as neoliberal globalization, which activists perceive as characterizing not only the policies of the international financial organizations (the WB, IMF, and WTO), but also the policy choices of national right-wing and even some center-left governments. These policies are considered to be responsible for growing social injustice and its negative effects on women, the environment, the South, and other groups. Alongside social justice, the meta-discourse of the search for new forms of democracy has emerged as a common basis. The traditional legitimation of democracy through electoral accountability was challenged by the development of global governance and also by the perceived decline in state intervention faced with the increasing influence of (private) global economic actors. The various demonstrations solidified a strong demand for political participation to which parties no longer seemed able to respond. As in subsequent mobilizations, protest not only developed outside the parties, but also expressed strong criticism of the existing forms of representative democracy. In this process, an action frame was created around the belief that "another world is possible."

Also on identities, however, we shall see a new emphasis on rather different frames, both within and across countries. The definitions of global issues vary: Some groups target poverty and others capitalism; some advocate social justice, others socialism or anarchism; some are mainly concerned with workers' rights, others with environmental disasters. As for the definition of the problem, solidarity frames can be distinguished from anti-neoliberal (or even anticapitalist) ones. On the other hand, on the issue of democracy, more radical proposals of participatory democracy can be distinguished from associational ones, with some conceptions that resonate more in some transnational networks and countries than in others. In Germany, the North-South cleavage (human rights as well as development) is presented as the main theme for the emergence of the movement, although national issues—such as the reform of unemployment compensation and the appeal for a social Europe—develop later. Solidarity with the South plays a main role in the convergence of religious groups, unions, women's groups, and developmental NGOs in the Jubilee 2000 campaigns in Switzerland, where national social issues were late to develop, and in the UK. Conversely, in France, the larger part of the movement developed from a concern with social justice issues at the national level, emerging from the 1997 protest against cuts in the welfare state and the *mouvement de sans* in the second half of the 1990s. Also in Spain and Italy, issues of social justice at home are central in a movement characterized by the presence of critical unions and later of traditional ones as well. More in general, the chapters on North-European countries stress the role of the (institutionalized) new social movement organizations, and the influence of the Old Left remains more visible in Southern Europe. If the new social movement component is strong in Germany, Switzerland, and the UK (with both environmentalist and solidarity organizations), it is much weaker in southern Europe. In France, decentralized critical unions and organizations of the "have-nots" have allied with peasants and ecologists active in the anti-GMO campaigns, extending the net to groups active on human rights and solidarity. The new social movement component is also weak in Spain and Italy, where, respectively, radical ecological groups and pacifists play a visible role. In both countries, squatted youth social centers represent an important, although quite scattered component—with a resonance in similar milieus in other countries.

Social Movement Theory: Explaining the Global Justice Movement

Summarizing, the mobilizations on global justice issues seem to be taking on many features typical of the preceding generations of social movements, but also new ones, above all a further marked supranational dimension. They express a conflict defined as "global," allowing new collective identities to emerge; they employ protest repertoires in transnational campaigns innovating on the margins of forms already widespread in the past; and they construct transnational networks. In this sense, they impel a rethinking of some concepts and hypotheses present in research on political participation. The concepts and approaches of social movement studies provide useful insights for understanding the movements of the new millennium; they should, however, be adapted and specified to account for emerging phenomena.

Which Resources for the Global Justice Movement?

Until the 1960s, studies in social movements had been dominated by a functionalist approach interpreting them as responses to systemic dysfunctions (Smelser 1962). Against this representation, during the 1970s a trend of studies developed that regarded them as part of the normal political process, concentrating analysis on the mobilization of resources needed for collective action. According to this approach, social movements act in a rational, proactive, organized fashion. Protest actions are the outcome of a cost-benefit calculation influenced by the presence not only of conflicts, but also of resources necessary for mobilizing these conflicts. In a historical situation where deprivation, contrasts, clashes of interest, and conflicting ideologies seem ever present, the rise of collective action cannot be explained by these factors alone. It is not enough to discover the existence of clashing interests; it is also necessary to study the conditions that allow the transformation of discontent into action. In fact, the movement organizations investigated using this approach in the 1980s and 1990s proved rather rich in both symbolic and material resources, and were often invested in creating more or less powerful movement organizations active on such single issues as defending the environment or women's liberation. Accordingly, the analysis focused on the resources available to relatively well-endowed groups, to the exclusion of more marginal groups regarded as incapable of mobilization. Additionally, the moral motivations of the protest remained hidden (but see Rootes 1980; Jasper 1997).

The important role of organizational networks in mobilizing resources is confirmed in our research. The accounts presented in the next chapters all point at the relevance of the remobilization of previously existing networks (or movements) with (often long) historical traditions in the global protest campaigns of the 1990s and the early 2000s. Global (or at least transnational) resources emerge as more and more relevant, and not only for movements in poor and nondemocratic countries. In this process, the symbolic work oriented to the building of common master frames between different cultures is increasingly important (Andretta 2005).

In the mobilization of the protest, national (cultural and structural) movement traditions play an important role. Organizations with different characteristics, strategies, and ideologies interact with the emerging movement and are challenged by the new waves of protest, but also contribute with their histories to the new mobilization. The specific dynamics—the richness but also the tensions—within these "movements of movements" are, however, still to be investigated. As we will see in the following chapters, in some countries the social capital for the movement includes wide nets of associations with large memberships, in others it has a more scattered basis with more militant propensity; in some cases unions are well connected and influential, but less prone to ally with movements; in others, less powerful unions are still more closely linked with their social bases and capable of mobilizing activism through overlapping membership (Moody 1997; Silver 2003; della Porta and Mosca 2005b).

Which Opportunities for the Global Justice Movement?

Another challenge for the literature on social movements comes from the interactions between the global movement and national and transnational political opportunities. Social movement studies have traditionally focused on the analysis of the nation-state and representative democracy; they therefore need to address challenges linked to both the development of international governmental organizations as well as the decline of the (identifying functions of) national political parties. Without implying a demise of the nation-state or the end of representative democracy, the transformations in both the boundaries of the polity and the main political actors have affected the traditional functioning of the democratic state. The increasing number of international institutions has facilitated the creation of transnational social movement organizations as well as experiences of international and inter-issue collaboration, fostering the emergence of infrastructures that facilitate global movement campaigns. As Sidney Tarrow has pointed out, "international institutions serve as a kind of 'coral reef,' helping to form horizontal connections among activists with similar claims across boundaries. This leads to the paradox that international institutions—created by states, and usually powerful ones—can be the arenas in which transnational contention is most likely to form against states" (2001, 15). So "international institutions are not only the targets of national state and non-state actors; they are the fulcrum around which they may turn their attention and their activities" (ibid.).

With weakening parties and the growing importance of a supranational level of governance, the alliance strategies of social movements must change accordingly. In IGOs, they can still sometimes find support in the institutional Left, as represented by some states with social democratic traditions. Movement activists can even enter supranational institutions by taking part in the national delegations of sympathetic states. Support by left-wing governments seems, however, more effective on some of the movement concerns, less on others: Complex internationalism requires complex strategies (Fox and Brown 1998: O'Brien et al. 2000; Boli and Thomas 1999; della Porta and Tarrow 2005; Sikkink 2005).

The traditional questions of alliances in the political and institutional system must also be reformulated at the domestic level. While emphasizing the differences between the two types of actors, the political process approach to social movements has regarded openness and alliances among institutional political actors as decisive for collective mobilization and its success. Although the interactions between institutional politics and politics from below—between *routine* and *contentious politics* (McAdam, Tarrow, and Tilly 2001)—continue to be important, the image of a sort of division of labor between parties and movements, especially on the Left, is becoming more and more problematic. Additionally, even if the movement stresses the need for political governance of the economy, there is nonetheless an increasing tension between a representative and a participatory conception of politics—a separation symbolically expressed in the opening slogan for the international parade at Genoa: "You G8, we 6 billion." In the first conception, in a modern representative democracy, politics becomes an activity for professionals (G8 leaders and other professional politicians) who take decisions legitimated by electoral investiture. The second conception not only articulates a demand for politics but also advances a proposal for "different politics," that is, for participatory politics carried out in areas open to citizens regarded as subjects and actors of politics. If the global justice movement represents a return to politics, it is also a challenge to the traditional understanding of politics.

In the following chapters, we shall see that the mentioned transformations had different consequences in the various countries. Notwithstanding the increasing influence of global institutions, national opportunities still play a key role. If in general the movement seems to mobilize more often on the street against right-wing governments (as in Italy and in Spain), left-wing governments are still far from being considered natural allies by the global justice movement. Moreover, the Left in government can have different reactions to the movement, ranging from greater emphasis on co-optation (as the socialists in Spain) to containment of at least the direct action wing (as Great Britain's New Labour). Also, if the traditional parties of the Left distrust the global justice movement, even though they try to incorporate some more moderate sectors of the movement, other political parties (the Greens in the UK, Rifondazione Comunista in Italy, the League Communiste Revolutionnaire in France, or Izquerda Unida in Spain) are part of the movement. In particular, we will notice that where the Left is electorally divided (as in Italy, France, and Spain) the more radical left-wing parties will ally with the global justice movement; moreover, their potential competition will push the more moderate left-wing parties toward some openings to the protesters' demands.

Which Conflicts for the Global Justice Movement?

The global justice movement also challenges some hypotheses about the structural bases for conflict in our societies. Scholars who analyzed social changes started out, beginning in the 1960s, by speaking of new social movements (Touraine 1977) and post-materialistic values (Inglehart 1977), stressing the pacification of conflicts about economic inequality and the emergence of new demands tied to the defense of individual freedoms against the new technological society. The new middle classes were regarded as the main social basis for the new movements (but see Rootes 1995), based not on appeals to a "class," but on the sharing of new values—or "other codes" (Melucci 1996).

By extending to (or in some cases starting from) the world's South, the global justice movement involves the poorest classes like the Brazilian *Sem Terra* or the Argentine *piqueteros*; but also, in the world's North, it seems to mobilize—at least in some countries—groups described as poor in collective resources (like the unemployed or precariously employed) or lacking the most basic rights (like migrants). Even there, the end of the "midcentury compromise" between capitalism and the welfare state (Crouch 2001) brought to center stage the conflicts on social rights underlined in the definition "movement for a globalization of rights"—albeit not without attention to new themes (like environmental sustainability or gender equality) that had emerged with the "new social movements." This explains the encounter, at least in some countries, between the theme of social justice typical of the "Old Left" and the defense of cultural differences, gender parity, or the natural environment more typical of the newer movements. Conflicts on wealth distribution thus do not—as proclaimed since the 1960s, at least for Western societies—appear to be pacified: Instead, wealth distribution is again becoming central in the political debate. In this sense, the movement on globalization presents the challenge to reopen the academic debate on the structural nature of conflicts, in a society that can no longer be simply defined as postindustrial. As Mary Kaldor (2000) observed, the traditional cleavage between neoliberalists and supporters of the welfare state interacts with the one between protectionists and cosmopolitans. How these new strains could be mobilized into new conflicts is a main issue on which our work has focused.

The movement not only builds upon old conflicts, but also faces new challenges. In the first place, the challenge of post-Fordist society has been seen as a weakening of traditional identities, with particular fragmentation of the social basis of the workers' movement. The deregulation of the labor market, with (especially in the 1990s) the spread of insecure and precarious jobs, further fragments the potential reference basis for social protest. From the cultural point of view, the movement must also face the challenge of an extremely individualized postmodern society. As Alain Touraine has noted (1997, 50), "The point is no longer, then, to recognize the universal value of a culture or a civilization, but quite differently, to recognize each individual's right to combine, to articulate in their own experience of personal or collective life, participation in the world of markets or technologies with a particular cultural identity." The processes of identification and recognition thereby acquire a new centrality for the analysis of the movement, where the construction of the feeling of belonging must adapt to the complexity and multiplicity of memberships. Values such as autonomy, creativity, spontaneity, and self-realization take on a central role (Ceri 2003; della Porta 2005a; Bennett 2005) and must be made compatible with collective action.

Summarizing, social movements are addressing some of the social and cultural challenges that have developed together with globalization processes at various levels. They primarily react to the effects of the liberalization of markets, framing them as consequences of political decisions dominated by the neoliberal agenda. At the cultural level, they support cosmopolitan values, suggesting alternative visions of globalization (globalization of rights, globalization from below, etc.). As we will see, in the different countries the global justice movement can be defined neither as a return of Old Left concerns that have been challenged by neoliberal policies, nor as yet another "new social movement." Although with cross-national differences, activists are in general not the traditionally understood "losers of globalization" (i.e., the less mobile and more protectionist): They are deep-rooted cosmopolitans, embedded in local networks but also often endowed with academic and linguistic skills (Tarrow 2005; della Porta 2005b; Fillieule et al. 2004). Although they share with the typical "new social movement" activists high levels of education, they are also (at least in some countries) heterogeneous in age and occupational base. With different shades in different countries, the movement blends old and new issues, reacting to the new challenges of the post-Fordist and "flexible" (or precarious) society and also to the opportunities arising from a trend toward individualization in the construction of new identities.

The Cross-National Comparison: Some Methodological Caveats and an Introduction to What Follows

We have now defined the main concepts used in our research and developed some hypotheses. The remaining chapters are original accounts of the characteristics of the global justice movement at the transnational level, in six European countries, and in the United States. In addition to building upon existing studies and research, all of the chapters—with the one exception of the chapter on the United States, which is more oriented toward building hypotheses for further studies—use empirical materials from systematic analysis of the networks of organizations involved in the main protests of the global justice movement as well as from surveys of activists.

This is the first outcome of the cross-national comparative research project Democracy in Europe and the Mobilization of the Society (Demos),[2] focusing on conceptions and practices of democracy in the Global Justice Movement in Italy, France, Germany, Great Britain, Spain, and Switzerland, as well as at the transnational level. The Demos project is composed of different parts, combining various methodologies.

First, based on secondary sources, we have collected information on the political opportunities and environmental resources available for the global justice movements in each country and at the transnational level, focusing on the specific national paths of mobilization through national and transnational protest campaigns and the weight of the different networks that compose the movement. In a second part, we looked at the Web sites of 266 social movement organizations in order to understand alternative communication strategies by movement actors, as well as their reciprocal linkages. Third, on the basis of the fundamental documents published online and offline by these organizations, we implemented an extensive discourse analysis of their visions of democracy. Fourth, we conducted interviews with social movement organizations to learn about the practical implementations of principles of horizontal participation and consensual decision making, as well as the extent and types of interactions with authorities. Fifth, we conducted a targeted, structured survey addressing the participatory visions and practices of participants in European demonstrations and events among the global activists participating in the fourth European Social Forum in Athens, which represents a main transnational meeting of the European global justice movement. Finally, we have developed a microanalysis of practices of deliberative democracy: Participant observation is oriented to understanding the activities of movement organizations, with particular attention paid to experiences of participatory decision making.

In this volume, we focus on the results of the first part of our research, but also integrate the secondary analysis of a growing number of existing studies with the firsthand knowledge acquired especially during our in-depth analysis of movement organizations' Web sites, their fundamental documents, and the activist surveys carried out at the national level during the preparation of our project. In this direction, we shall therefore rely upon some selected results of these parts of the Demos research, which will be used more systematically in further steps of our project. Some general remarks on the specific types of data used in the following chapters are in order.

As for the surveys of activists, referred to in all of the chapters on European countries, it must be recalled that the questionnaire is a method rarely used in research on social movements (but see Favre, Fillieule, and Mayer 1997; Van Aelst and Walgrave 2001). The rationale for this choice has been the long-standing skepticism for this specific research technique among both social movement scholars and social movement activists. In general, surveys—with their mainly closed questions—are indeed poor instruments for capturing the complex value system of activists, which requires more qualitative methods of analysis. Additionally, questionnaires have been recognized as more reliable on questions referring to behaviors than on those addressing attitudes. Besides the difficulties in assessing the influence of the interviewee's attempt to provide "socially desirable answers or rationalization," surveys tend to produce superficial or very standardized responses: "feelings and emotions, people's uncertainties, doubts, and fears, all the inconsistencies and the complexities of social interactions and belief systems are matters that are not easily tapped with survey questionnaires" (Klandermans and Smith 2002, 27). For all of these reasons, surveys are not the best way to analyze either concrete organizational praxis or organizational values (Dryzek 2004). Finally, specific difficulties in surveying activists have been noted, particularly the lack of a known population from which to build casual sampling.

While recognizing these limits, recent research on social movement activists has tried to use surveys as an additional source of information on more and more heterogeneous protest events and activists. In combination with other methods, the advantage of the survey is its ability to provide systematic information on a large number of individuals. In addition, methods of sampling moving marches or other protest events have been devised. With the above caveats in mind, surveys of global justice activists have been quite frequent—among others, at the anti-G8 protest in Genoa in 2001, the first European Social Forum in Florence in 2002, the second European Social Forum in Paris in 2003, and the protest against the G8 in Evian in 2004 (Andretta, della Porta, Mosca, and Reiter 2002 and 2003; della Porta, Andretta, Mosca, and Reiter 2006; Agrikoliansky and Sommier 2005; Fillieule et al. 2004). These studies offer important information about our global activists' associative experiences, forms of political participation, confidence in institutions, and identification with the movement.

Some chapters also refer to a specific result of our research on the Web sites of social movement organizations: the analysis of links between Web sites. Web site links represent an indicator of ties between organizations that has also been used in other research in order to describe "nets on the net" (see, for instance, Koopmans and Zimmerman 2003). As with other data referring to "virtual" activities, these must be handled with care. In fact, Web site links serve different purposes: In some cases, they link to Web sites of "sister" organizations, reflecting collaboration in "real" activities; in other cases, however, they simply lead to sites where information on selected issues can be found. Additionally, the selection of links does not always reflect the strategic alliances of an organization, being left to the more or less occasional preferences of a Web master or a few, more Internet-literate activists. With these caveats in mind, we have, however, used the data on the "virtual links" of our organizations as additional information to be combined with other indicators of the network structures of our national global justice movements.

A third type of data referred to in most chapters derives from the discourse analysis of the main documents of 244 social movement organizations. The analysis focused on 1) the constitution of the organization, 2) a document of fundamental values and/or intent, 3) any document specifically quoted in the constitution or the document of fundamental values and/or intent, 4) the "mission statement," 5) the "about us" and "frequently asked questions" sections of the Web site, 6) equivalent or similar material on the Web site expressing the "official" position of the organization as a whole.[3] For this part of the research, we developed a codebook on specific aspects of the movement discourse on democracy; that is, the organizational ideology of social movement organizations. This part is quite new from a methodological point of view. Documents describing the structure of social movement organizations have been analyzed in various research projects, but mostly within qualitative in-depth analyses of a few groups that had the advantage of providing a "thick" description but were difficult to compare with each other (for a review of the literature, see Clemens and Minkoff 2004; della Porta and Diani 2006). One of the rationales for enlarging the number of selected cases was indeed the heterogeneity of the global justice movement(s) in terms, among others, of organizational designs that made the selection of a large number of different groups particularly interesting. Although in devising our instruments for the quantitative research we could rely upon some previous experiences in other fields of research,[4] we were challenged by the presence of very different types of organizations: from political parties to unions, from large associations to small informal groupings, from transnational networks to local groups. The amount of written material varies by group, and we are of course more likely to find statements about democracy when the written production is larger. In particular, organizations having a formal constitution usually provide much richer information about the formal rules of decision making. A related problem is that, whereas more formal organizations often provide easy access to the selected documents, this is not always true for less formalized groups. On the basis of our qualitative knowledge we shall, in fact, account for these differences and their consequences in the interpretation of our results.

What emerges, together with the cross-country peculiarities, is an interesting picture of the similarities and diversities among the single movements within each country.

Some common cross-national paths are evident, first in the timing of the movements' evolution, with the radical 1970s, followed by the institutionalization of the 1980s, and then the reemergence of conflict in the 1990s. For all countries, the 1990s emerge as the decade in which some characteristics of the global justice movement developed more or less at the margins of the main movement families: 1) the return of direct action (e.g., in anti-road protests in the UK, or the *mouvement des sans* in France); 2) organizational networking in increasingly hybrid campaigns, platforms, coalitions (among them peace and antiwar); 3) the framing of "broker issues" on which different movements converged. In all countries, transnational campaigns such as the anti-MAI, anti-GATT (General Agreement on Tariffs and Trade), and Jubilee 2000, as well as the Intergalactic meetings organized by the Zapatistas (Olesen 2003) and some demonstrations on EU issues (such as the European marches of the unemployed) are significant milestones in this process. The relevance of the transnational networks is rightly stressed in the chapter referring to transnational mobilizations.

Offering a first attempt at summarizing the relevant characteristics of the global justice movement in six European countries, the United States, and at the transnational level, the remaining chapters describe the main characteristics of the movement(s) in their respective contexts, paying attention to their evolution in time. With different emphases, the various authors seem to agree on the presence of some common characteristics of the various groups, such as the demands of participatory democracy, skills in communication, emphasis on knowledge, preference for loose networking (all visible, for instance, in the functioning of the social forums). They also stress, however, some tensions in these mobilizations: ideological heterogeneity, but also deep differences in the conception of (internal) democracy and the repertoire of action. Indeed, the global justice movement does not seem split along the line of the previous movements that converged in it (women's, ecologist, labor, solidarity, and so on), but much more on other cleavages—for example, strategic differences, as with direct action versus lobbying (this is very clear in the UK); or organizational distinctions, as in the "disorganization" versus the NGO model (which emerges in Spain, but also in Italy and the UK).

Beyond these similarities, in singling out some strengths and weaknesses in/of the global justice movement, specific national images emerge.

Characteristic of the Italian movement seems to be its networking of the most diverse organizations and groupings, which converge in the critique not only of a right-wing government of a very special type, but also of the inconclusiveness of the center-left in opposition and especially its neoliberal twist when in government. The nodes constructed around the ecopacifist Rete Lilliput, the anti-neoliberal organizations, and the squatted social centers interact in a dense network. The development of alternative discourses and strategies within the Left, as well as opposition to the center-right government, seems to be particularly relevant in linking groups that are very different in terms of organizational structures and repertoires of action.

The chapter on the Spanish case emphasizes the internal cleavage between decentralized and locally oriented groups with radical claims organized around the Zapatistas network and the PGA, and more state-sponsored, moderate ones coordinated in an Attac-centered net. However, it also stresses a process of "Europeanization" within the Spanish movements, with increasing coordination and networking. Forms of action and organizations reproduce the split between an institutionalized part of previous movements (well integrated in state agencies etc.) such as the women's movement, and the survival of radical conceptions of struggles, nurtured by ecologists, squatters, and antimilitarists. A convergence in the GJM of old and new families of left-wing movements explains the high mobilization capacity of the movement, thanks to the support of the Partido Socialista Obrero Espanol ([PSOE] then in opposition), and the decline in mobilization as a consequence of the new (center) left government.

The struggle against social inequalities at the national level has emerged as central in France in the two different frames of the *mouvements de sans* and the unions' defense of the welfare state (Agrikoliansky, Fillieule, and Mayer 2005; Agrikoliansky and Sommier 2005). The traditional strength of "old" social movements (and the weakness of new ones) as well as the competition inside "la gauche plurielle" (Crettiez and Sommier 2002; Sommier 2003) are reflected in the French GJM.

The chapter on the global justice movement in the UK describes the intersection of (and tensions between) a network of formalized and well-established organizations and the survival (or even radicalization) of direct action groups (anti-road, but also, for example, the Liverpool dockers) who value grassroots organizational structures and disruptive repertoires. In the Jubilee 2000 campaigns, this tension is very visible, and it seems that—even if reduced—it is never resolved.

The chapter on Germany stresses the focus of the GJM in issues of development and solidarity with the South, represented by the Bundeskooperation Internationalismus (BUKO) as a central arena. However, the public image of the GJM is dominated by the German Attac branch, which has experienced an enormous rise. Forms of action and organizational structure seem to reflect the high degree of institutionalization of the German movement family/ies, with the dominance of well-structured and resource-rich Third World associations as well as ecological groups, although with tensions with some more radical, anarchist groups.

Similarly, the Swiss movement appears to be characterized by a strong role of well-established Third World and ecological associations, although with strong divisions with a more radical (and less structured) component. At the same time, however, it points to the visibility of more radical critiques of neoliberal capitalism, especially in the initial development of the protest. Unions are present—and this is a novelty for the Swiss social movements—but occupy a less central role than in the Southern countries. However, the Swiss chapter also stresses the emergence of new networks on global and multi-issue frames, with a first convergence of squatters, unionists, and activists from the associations of solidarity with the South of the world as early as 1998, in the anti-G8 protest in Geneva.

Finally, the chapter on the United States presents, in a more speculative way since systematic research is still missing, some hypotheses on the apparent difficulties of the global justice movement in sustaining the level of mobilization that had emerged at the protest against the WTO millennium round in Seattle. Although noting the growing participation of U.S. social movement organizations in the protest events organized by the global justice movement, as well as the interest of national public opinion in globalization processes, Jennifer Hadden and Sidney Tarrow describe a process of internalization, with a transfer from transnational into domestic activism, in particular on the war in Iraq.

Still an open question is the extent to which the European and the U.S. movements will continue to develop along different lines. Alternatively, the Europeans could follow the U.S. path toward a return to domestic protest, or the concern with global justice could move the latter toward transnational activism.

Notes

1. On transnational campaigns, cf. among others, Clark 2003a; Cohen and Rai 2000; Edwards and Gaventa 2001; Khagram, Riker, and Sikkink 2002.

2. The Demos project (http://demos.iue.it) is financed by the European Commission, 6th FP Priority 7, Citizens and Governance in a Knowledge Based Society, and (for the Swiss case) the Federal Office for Education and Science, Switzerland. The project is coordinated by Donatella della Porta (European University Institute). Partners are University of Kent at Canterbury, UK, Christopher C. Rootes; Wissenschaftszentrum Berlin fuer Sozialforschung, Germany, Dieter Rucht; Università di Urbino, Italy, Mario Pianta; Centre de recherches politiques de la Sorbonne (CRPS), Universitè Panthéon-Sorbonne, France, Isabelle Sommier; Instituto de Estudios Sociales de Andalucía, Centro Superior de Investigaciones Científicas (IESA-CSIC), Spain, Manuel Jiménez; and Laboratoire de recherches sociales et politiques appliquées (resop), Université de Genève, Switzerland, Marco Giugni.

3. Many, but not all of these materials were available on Web sites. In fact, after an analysis of the Web sites, we contacted the social movement organizations to ask for missing documents.

4. In particular, in research on political parties, party constitutions have been studied in research on organizational models, and party electoral manifestos have been analyzed as important sources of information on party ideology (see Klingeman, Hoffenbert, and Budge 1994).

Chapter Two

The Global Justice Movements

The Transnational Dimension

Mario Pianta and Raffaele Marchetti

The Transnational Dimension: Concepts and Context

This chapter examines the trajectory of the social movements that in the last two decades have addressed global issues with cross-border mobilizations. The global dimension of transnational social movements is analyzed with a focus on their transnational activities, on the history of their emergence, on their model of organization and political action, on their shared identities and common strategies. The key characteristics of the global justice movements (GJMs) at the global level shed light on the wider context in which their national developments take place. Whereas the other chapters of this book concentrate on the national level, we focus on the global dimension, analyzing the specificity of transnational networks, as distinct from domestic mobilizations, in terms of political environment, strategies, and actors' characteristics. Transnational networks and social organizations are characterized as *global* in relation to the issues they address, the political centers of power they challenge, and the way they are constituted and operate. Each of these elements sets them apart from traditional national social movements.

In order to understand their historical trajectory, it is necessary to tackle a number of conceptual issues regarding the theory, definition, and context of the GJMs. Many studies of political mobilizations, economic conflicts, and social movements developed around global issues have tried to understand them by extending in various directions the model of *national* social movements to a context of (limited) transnational actions. Although there is no shortage of empirical cases that fall into the pattern of a limited transnationalization of domestic activism, we believe that this approach is unable to capture the fundamental novelty of the global mobilizations on global issues that have occurred since the 1990s and more significantly after 2000, a novelty that has turned previous scattered and domestic mobilizations into global justice movements.

The starting point we propose is in the evolving relationships among politics, economy, and society in an age of global transformation and increasing international integration (Pianta and Silva 2003). At the global level, the sphere of *politics* is structured by the interstate system, where national states and international and supranational institutions exercise their power. Whereas at the national level the political relationships between state and citizens have been defined by constitutions, law, and democratic processes, at the global level, no universally coercive power of law has yet emerged, and, more importantly, no democratic processes of participation, deliberation, and voting have developed for the world's citizens. Existing political institutions have tried to elaborate new rules for economic and social activities appropriate for the new context of globalization, but have for the most part failed to properly address the global democratic deficit.

At the global level, the sphere of the *economy* is still predominantly structured by the operation of firms and markets, dominated by the search for profits and by a drive to turn into market commodities an increasingly wide array of activities previously provided and regulated by states and society, from knowledge to education and health, from public services to global public goods such as water and environmental protection. The resulting privatization, deregulation, and liberalization have since the 1980s characterized the model of neoliberal globalization that has asserted the power of markets and large industrial and financial firms over decisions made in the political sphere and over social behaviors. This has generated a profound sense of vulnerability and external imposition that has fostered political opposition and social activism.

Within this political and economic context, the emerging *global civil society* can be defined as the sphere of cross-border relationships and activities carried out by collective actors—social movements, networks, and civil society organizations—that are independent from governments and private firms and operate outside the international reach of states and markets.[1] Within such a sphere, many different and contrasting identities, interests, visions, and demands for change by collective actors can emerge, be expressed, and assert themselves. A major development has been the growing networking, activism, and social mobilization on global issues that has defended fundamental rights and advocated change in a transnational perspective. The demands and activities of civil society have moved beyond their interaction with the national political and economic spheres and challenged political and economic power across and above national borders. By creating a contested terrain where hegemonic projects are challenged, global civil society has called into question some fundamental aspects of the nature of the interstate system and of the global economy. In particular, it has advanced three sets of political demands: 1) demands to the state system for global democracy, human rights, and peace; 2) demands to the economic system for global economic justice; and 3) demands to both systems for global social justice and environmental sustainability. Conversely, both the state and the economic systems have put pressure on global civil society to adhere to their own values and norms.

In the emerging global civil society as a sphere of relationships among highly heterogeneous actors, different types of mobilizations can be singled out. Among them, *global social movements* can be defined as cross-border, sustained, and collective social mobilizations on global issues, based on permanent and/or occasional groups, networks, and campaigns with a transnational organizational dimension moving from shared values and identities that challenge and protest economic or political power and campaign for change in global issues. They share a global frame of the problems to be addressed, have a global scope of action, and might target supranational or national targets.[2] The focus of the analysis in the rest of this chapter is on the global social movements that have challenged the dominant model of relationships among global politics, economy, and society that can be defined as neoliberal globalization. Although a great variety of different mobilizations can be identified in this area, we will refer to them with the general term of *global justice movements,* for at least three reasons: first, all of them share values and identities opposed to neoliberal globalization; second, they have woven together an increasingly tight network of coalitions and campaigns; and finally, they have regularly met and planned initiatives at major global events. In particular, the emergence of global justice movements can be traced in three processes: first, the move of activism from the national to the global scale; second, its broadening from the single-issue mobilizations of individual organizations to a more comprehensive view and understanding of the challenges raised by neoliberal globalization; and third, the growing autonomy and self-organization of global movements from the spheres of politics and the economy.

According to this perspective, this chapter first provides a brief history of global justice movements since the 1970s, mainly based on the sequence of major events that have marked their slow emergence and high visibility on the global scene of the new century. Second, data on global civil society events are provided in order to examine the transnational repertoire of actions of the GJMs. Third, a profile of GJMs is proposed through the identification of their organizational structure and characteristics. Finally, a discussion of their identities, visions, and strategies leads to our conclusions on the transnational dimension of global justice movements.

The Emergence of Transnational Movements, 1970–1999

The origins of transnational social movements and networks of organizations active on international issues lie in the "new social movements" that originated in the 1970s around the themes of peace, human rights, solidarity, development, ecology, and women's issues.[3] National experiences differ widely in terms of the social relevance and political impact of such new social movements, and in their relationship with previous movements such as the workers' movement and trade unions. Still, at the transnational level there is little doubt that they have progressively developed an ability to address and mobilize around problems of a global nature. The *global nature,* by definition, of many of the issues at the core of new social movements, and their lack of interest in the pursuit of *state power*—a major difference from previous mobilizations—are two major factors in their ability to shift from a national to a transnational perspective within their typical "single issue" approach. Starting with their own specific issue, they have built networks for information and organizing, created the space for an emerging global civil society, organized protests and actions, broadened their agenda, argued for solutions across national borders, and interacted in original ways with the sites of supranational power.[4]

This process, however, is not without historical antecedents. Steve Charnovitz has traced them back to the late nineteenth century (Charnovitz 1997), showing that in a previous wave of strong international integration from the late nineteenth century to the 1920s, the establishment of supranational bodies such as the League of Nations and of scores of intergovernmental organizations was accompanied by equally flourishing international nongovernmental organizations (NGOs), social mobilizations, and civil society meetings. At several government conferences and in the operation of the League of Nations, civil society groups were often able to articulate proposals on a wide range of themes, including peace, national liberation, and economic, social, and women's rights; in some cases they were involved in official activities, opening the way for the formal recognition of NGOs in the Charter of the United Nations in 1945.

With the start of the Cold War, however, the space for international civil society activities became constrained and shaped by state power and policies. The international mobilization of civil society mainly took the form of trying to influence national government policies on decolonization, national self-determination, peace, human rights, development, and the environment. The social movements of the 1960s and 1970s challenged the political and economic order at the national and the international levels with a transformative perspective still focused on state power. A major exception was the women's movement, which opened the way for new forms of politics, social practices, and culture based on identity (Arrighi et al. 1989). An additional novelty came with the emergence of the first environmental mobilizations.

Within international institutions, NGOs had found since the 1970s a substantial opening in the UN system, in ECOSOC (United Nations Economic and Social Council), and in other agencies, although this official recognition has led, with few exceptions, to very modest results in terms of visibility, relevance, and impact on the operation of the international system (Gordenker and Weiss 1995, and the special issue of *Third World Quarterly*; Lotti and Giandomenico 1996; Otto 1996). The far-reaching political changes of the 1970s—East-West détente, the completion of decolonization, and a new attention to human rights and the parallel economic developments—as well as the end of the Bretton Woods international monetary system, the oil shocks, and the emergence of the North-South divide—raised new problems of global governance and opened the way to new centers of supranational decision making. Existing intergovernmental organizations, starting with the UN, played a renewed and broader role, and other forums were established; the first G5 summit was held in 1975. As global issues and supranational power became increasingly important, attention and action by civil society also increased. Moving on from traditional efforts to put pressure on nation-states, attention started to focus on global problems and on the failure of states to address them. Symbolic actions, at first small in scale and poorly organized, were followed by more systematic international work by civil society organizations, the creation of networks and cross-border mobilizations challenging international powers.

The 1970s and 1980s: Cross-Border Activism of "New Social Movements"

From the 1970s, the slow emergence of global movements can be best traced in the sequence of major international events that have provided opportunities for meetings, exchanges, and cross-border initiatives, creating a space for transnational civil society actions. Several streams of activism have monitored and flanked UN meetings on the environment, development, women, and human rights. In 1972, the UN Conference on the Human Environment held in Stockholm saw the participation of a few hundred NGOs active both inside and outside the official meeting (Conca 1995), and in 1974, the World Food Conference in Rome also included an active presence of NGOs (Van

Rooy 1997). Large NGO forums were also held in 1975, when the First World Conference on Women held in Mexico City launched the UN Decade for Women, as well as in succeeding conferences in 1980 in Copenhagen and in 1985 in Nairobi (Chen 1995). Global summits of this type, with the UN system and states allowing some room for civil society's voices, were possible because of the urgency of the issues, and because these themes did not challenge the Cold War ideologies of the time.

On more controversial political and economic issues, however, civil society had to organize its international activities independent of the operation of states, the UN, and other international institutions. In 1981, the peace movement began responding to this need with the European Nuclear Disarmament Conventions (Kaldor 2003). Following Bertrand Russell's initial International War Crimes Tribunal on Vietnam organized in 1967, public opinion tribunals were regularly held on peace, human, economic, and social rights. In parallel, a renewed wave of solidaristic activism developed on the issues of decolonization and Third World liberation struggle, generating intense cross-border mobilization between the North and the South such as those against the military regimes in Latin America (Chile, Argentina, etc.) and in support of Nelson Mandela's antiapartheid struggle in South Africa.

Another innovative event was the first gathering of The Other Economic Summit (TOES) in coincidence with a G7 meeting, organized in 1984 by the New Economics Foundation of London in association with the Right Livelihood Awards (an "alternative Nobel Prize" that has been awarded since 1980) (Ekins 1992). Initially taking the form of small conferences and media events with a strong alternative development and environmental focus, TOES have been regularly organized in cooperation with different international networks and civil society coalitions of the country hosting the G7 summit. In contrast to these early cross-border dynamics of new social movements, more traditional social actors, such as the labor movement, have remained largely focused on the domestic dimension, relying on friendly political forces and national governments for introducing social reforms and improving workers' conditions (Waterman and Timms 2005).

The rising cross-border activism of this period can be understood as a projection of the "new social movements" into a transnational scene, driven by the nature of the core issues of their mobilization. The limited development of institutions of global governance and of supranational political processes with the power to make decisions on such issues has reduced access by civil society organizations and constrained the space for such cross-border activism. Limited political opportunities, little internal resources, and fragmentation on a wide range of "single issues" explain why in the 1970s and 1980s transnational social movements did develop in the fields of peace, environment, women rights, human rights, and international solidarity, but remained separate and without mass participation. It is only in the following decade that these scattered movements gained awareness of their political potential, together with the capacity for a strengthened self-organization.

The 1990s: Global Social Movements on Separate Campaigns

The 1990s, after the end of the Cold War and the weakening of traditional ideologies centered on the search for state power, offered major opportunities for the growth of transnational social movements toward truly global ones. The first of these opportunities was the new role of the United Nations and of other institutions of global governance, which provided a political context in which global issues could be addressed by both the interstate system and the emerging global civil society. A key role was played by the large UN thematic conferences of the early 1990s, designed to chart the agenda for the twenty-first century on global issues, that were open to large participation by civil society organizations (UNRISD 2003). The second opportunity was the construction and consolidation of stable networks among civil society organizations, making possible permanent cross-border mobilizations even with limited resources.

The 1992 Rio Conference on the Environment and Development saw the presence of 2,400 NGO representatives; the parallel NGO Forum saw 17,000 participants. This was an unprecedented event in terms of size, media resonance, long-term impact on ideas and policies, and for the emergence of a global civil society involved in building networks, developing joint strategies, and confronting states and international institutions (Conca 1995; Van Rooy 1997). In 1993, the UN conference on human rights in Vienna saw the participation of thousands of civil society activists and addressed a key issue long neglected by states in the Cold War (Smith et al. 1998). In 1994, the Cairo conference on population led 1,500 civil society groups from 113 countries to forge new links around concerns regarding the conditions of women, families, and societies in the North and South.

In 1995, the Copenhagen World Summit on Social Development and the Beijing World Conference on Women led to a new visibility, relevance, and mobilization for global civil society. In Copenhagen, 2,300 representatives from 800 NGOs attended the official conference, and thousands attended the parallel events; in Beijing, 5,000 participants from 2,100 NGOs were at the summit, and 30,000 at the independent NGO Forum.[5] A large participation by NGOs (8,000 people from 2,400 organizations) also marked the NGO Forum parallel to the UN conference on human settlements held in Istanbul in 1996. In the same year, the FAO World Food summit was held in Rome, with a major involvement of NGOs in the official activities, in the NGO Forum, and in other parallel events. Again in Rome, in 1998, civil society organizations played a major role at the conference establishing the International Criminal Court.

A major global civil society event *without* an official UN summit was the Hague Appeal for Peace conference of 1999, held during NATO intervention in Kosovo, which gathered 10,000 participants from all over the world and involved several governments. A series of global civil society meetings held independently of UN summits, but with an explicit reference to the need for a more active and democratic UN, are the Assemblies of the Peoples of the United Nations organized every other year since 1995 in Perugia, Italy, by a coalition of Italian and international civil society organizations. They have regularly brought together representatives of civil society organizations from more than 100 different countries to discuss issues such as the reform of the United Nations, economic justice, and a stronger role for global civil society; each event included a 15-mile peace march to Assisi with participation ranging from 50,000 to 200,000 people. The theme of the 1999 Assembly was "Another world is possible" (Pianta 1998, 2001a, and 2001b).

Along the complex road of transforming cross-border activism on specific issues into global social movements centered on more global political challenges, a major development with a pervasive influence occurred with the Zapatista insurgency in Chiapas, Mexico, in January 1994. This insurgency, in fact, turned what could have been a typical, locally focused Latin American guerrilla action into a much broader challenge to the injustice of neoliberal globalization. Launched by the Ejército Zapatista de Liberación Nacional (EZLN) in coincidence with the start of the North American Free Trade Agreement (NAFTA), the rebellion aimed at protecting indigenous peoples and peasants from the repression of the Mexican state and the ravages of neoliberal economic policies. The Zapatistas declared no interest in achieving state power and aimed at exposing the profound link between local deprivation, the corrupt role of the national ruling classes, the burden imposed by international institutions, and the inhumanity of global capitalism. With their rebellion, and by calling on the solidarity of social movements from all over the world, the Zapatistas succeeded in protecting the Chiapas Indians from repression and forced the Mexican government to reconsider its policies on indigenous peoples. Their skilled use of political communication and the global media managed to link in an unprecedented way the local destruction of communities to global processes, politicizing traditional solidarity activism in a new way (Schulz 1998; Olesen 2004). Moreover, the extensive networks of support to the Zapatistas in several countries also became vehicles for furthering awareness of the challenge of neoliberal capitalism and of the need for international political action for global justice, with a pervasive and lasting influence on global social movements and their strategies.

A wide variety of experiences—the participation and challenge to UN World Summits, cross-border activism by "new social movements," the mobilizations around the Zapatista insurgency—gave strength to the emerging social movements and to their ability to oppose economic and political powers. In the late 1990s, this led to a growing number of parallel summits challenging G7-G8 meetings, IMF–World Bank meetings, European Union summits, conferences of North American and Pacific organizations, World Economic Forum meetings in Davos, and other interstate summits (Pettifor 1998; Houtart and Polet 1999; Pianta 2001b).[6] Parallel summits started from the need to confront the decisions of global powers on themes such as debt, international investment rules, trade, and development that increasingly concerned economic issues and moved on to challenge the consequences of the dominant model of neoliberal globalization. The protests at such events, often more confrontational than the parallel actions at UN summits, helped to broaden the vision and actions of transnational networks involved in global issues and to set in motion waves of global social movements.

This global spread became evident in Seattle in December 1999, when a broad coalition of (mainly U.S.) organizations and trade unions, together with a variety of transnational networks, challenged the WTO summit and the Millennium Round of trade liberalization talks. Seattle was the culmination of a long process, not a sudden outburst of antiglobalization sentiment. It captured the attention of the media, the imagination of people, and—at last—the attention of policy makers, because it had both the arguments and the strength to disrupt the official summit. Media coverage and innovative coalitions across countries and issues constitute two central factors in the success of the Seattle mobilization. Although the failure of the WTO conference was equally because of the divisions between the United States, Europe, and countries of the South, in the perception of social activists, public opinion, and trade officials themselves, this was the first time global civil society had a major, direct impact on the conduct and outcome of an official summit.

Forms of mobilization that were carried out in the late 1990s also significantly included major global campaigns that mobilized vast parts of civil society around the world, achieving important results. Particularly relevant among them are the campaign for the establishment of the International Criminal Court (ICC) (1995), the Jubilee campaign on Third World debt (1996), the campaign against the Multilateral Agreement on Investment (MAI) (1998), the International Campaign to Ban Landmines (1992), and the Treatment Action Campaign on HIV and AIDS (1998). The campaign for the establishment of the ICC was characterized by a strong action of technical lobbying on the various delegations to the preparatory conferences and ultimately to the Rome conference, where the statute was approved (Glasius 2005). The Jubilee 2000 campaign was directed at canceling the foreign debt of the poorest countries by the year 2000 and, through large-scale public opinion pressure, induced the creditor governments and the IMF to take the first steps toward debt relief of "highly indebted poor countries" (Pettifor 1998). The anti-MAI campaign aimed at stopping the Multilateral

Agreement on Investment proposed within the OECD; it succeeded through a strategy based on education and information, in which social pressure and convergence with the position of sympathetic governments (the French in particular) was crucial. The International Campaign to Ban Landmines mounted extensive pressure from public opinion and managed to secure support from governments at the interstate conference in Ottawa, where the Mine Ban Treaty (also known as the Ottawa Convention) was signed in 1997. This was the first civil society campaign to receive the Nobel Peace Prize (1997). Finally, the Treatment Action Campaign aimed at opening access to treatment and affordable medicines for people with HIV and AIDS; in this effort, public pressure was accompanied by legal strategies and support from governments from the South, leading to the WTO declaration on the priority of public health over intellectual property rights.

In the 1990s, the rise of global social movements was dramatic in all respects. Cross-border mobilizations have involved an ever-growing number of organizations, increasingly including countries of the South, linking them in stable networks and sharing information, resources, and strategies that were the backbone for the launch of several campaigns on global issues. The focus on specific "single issues" remained, but with a broader conceptualization of the challenges concerning human rights and economic issues and with a more direct political challenge to global powers. Such powers were identified either in supranational institutions (the OECD, the IMF, the WTO, the G7), or in the interstate system (the intergovernmental conferences on the ICC and Landmines). Especially in the first half of the 1990s, with the space offered by the large UN conferences, many transnational mobilizations adopted a perspective of "globalization of rights and responsibilities," opposed to the dominant neoliberal globalization.[7] Such a model was supported by some progressive national governments and found openings in the activities of a few international institutions. It envisaged a reformulation of rights and responsibilities on a global scale in the context of new arrangements for a more democratic and effective global governance (Commission on Global Governance 1995). Great expectations were generated and later turned sour, as few of the proposals for reform and policy innovations found their way through national governments and international institutions.

This evolution of transnational social movements from the 1970s to the 1990s has led to a greater focus on global problems and global political environment. The first wave of poorly organized transnational actions was soon followed by a long series of cross-border networks, international campaigns, counter-summits, and independent meetings with mass participation. These modes of actions allowed for scattered movements to gain increasing awareness of their political potential against global and national powers. Despite failures, the presence of a well-defined political context made possible the emergence of specific terms of contention and conflict along which global social movements developed, taking advantage of favorable political opportunities and growing support from an increasingly aware public opinion. All of these developments amount to the emergence of truly global social movements; the persistence of well-defined, distinct identities and of different, specific issues, however, suggest that the 1990s were still marked by mobilizations on separate issues, rather than by a more unified mobilization.

The Global Justice Movements in the New Millennium

At the turn of the millennium, a structural scale shift occurred in the nature, identities, repertoires of actions, and strategies of global social movements. The example of Seattle led to a dramatic proliferation of actions combining street protests against international decision makers and alternative proposals on global problems, which together developed into a radical challenge to the project of neoliberal globalization. The latter emerged as a powerful unifying symbol for the struggles of resistance and in the search for political, economic, and social alternatives. The focus on the challenge to neoliberal globalization, in fact, slowly but increasingly facilitated the recognition of common identities, visions, and policy agendas among the networks, organizations, and individuals mobilized in global movements. This has led to the emergence of what can be defined as *global justice movements*.[8]

Repertoire of Action and Transnational Events

A key element in the emergence of the global justice movements has been the rapid spread of transnational events and the evolution in their repertoire. Some of them followed the pattern of parallel summits established in the previous decade: The first major event after Seattle was a rather institutional one, the UN Millennium forum of NGOs held in New York in May 2000, with 1,350 representatives of more than 1,000 NGOs. This gathering did not achieve great social mobilization, but it produced an important and comprehensive document that inspired part of the movements in the following years (NGO Millennium Forum 2000). This helped broaden the vision of transnational networks that had entered the global arena from initiatives on individual issues and had previously been reluctant to engage in a comprehensive perspective on world challenges. Themes such as peace, disarmament, globalization, justice, equity, and democracy that had not been included in the previous UN summits or in the agendas of major global civil society events were put at the center of the final document. In parallel, the UN Millennium Summit of world governments adopted in 2000 the Millennium

Declaration, from which the Millennium Development Goals have been developed, a policy agenda that in recent years has opened new space for interaction and conflict among UN institutions, national governments, and campaigns by global social movements (UNDP 2003). [9]

Within this context, global movements stepped up their activism and developed an autonomous agenda for change. After Seattle, international meetings of transnational networks multiplied in a variety of forms. The first steps of these transnational mobilizations were the Prague protest against the IMF-World Bank meeting in October 2000, the Gothenburg protest at the EU summit in May 2001, and the large Genoa protest at the G8 summit in July 2001. From then on, global civil society meetings, convened by ever-growing coalitions of transnational networks and social movements, have proliferated in all countries and continents (see the other chapters of this book for pictures of the major European countries).

These events have taken place on a monthly basis in every part of the world. They have been characterized by mass participation in street demonstrations, ranging from the tens to the hundreds of thousands, with peaks of more than one million in the events in several European cities in the 2003 and 2004 global days of action against the U.S. war in Iraq. They have attracted very high media attention as well as growing police repression. Transnational networks active on global issues have multiplied, built alliances, and radical-ized their views and actions.

Together with the scale of mobilizations, however, key developments in the new century are also found in the focus and vision of global movements, in their identities and autonomy, in their forms of organization and aggregation, and in their challenge to global economic and political power. The turning point in all of these respects was the creation of the World Social Forum as a space for the meeting of all organizations, social movements, and indi-viduals that have challenged neoliberal globalization. In January–February 2001, the first World Social Forum was held in Porto Alegre, Brazil, followed every year by ever-larger events. It moved in January 2004 to Mumbai, India, returned to Porto Alegre in January 2005, decentralized to three continents in 2006, and will move to Nairobi, Kenya, in 2007. Dozens of regional and national social forums have been held on all continents, with thousands of organizations from all continents attending each one; the total number involved in these initiatives could be on the order of a few million people (Seoane and Taddei 2001; Teivainen 2002; de Sousa Santos 2003; Sen et al. 2004; Smith 2004).

Together with the establishment of the World Social Forum, the other most important novelty of recent years has been the organization of *global days of action,* with millions of participants in demonstrations and events in hundreds of cities all over the world. Such events took place against the U.S.

war and occupation of Iraq on February 15, 2003, March 20, 2004, March 19, 2005, and March 18, 2006. The *New York Times* identified the first of these dates as the birth date of global public opinion and civil society as a "second superpower." The values and politics of global justice movements were deeply challenged by the U.S. government policy of unilateral, unrestrained global power engaged in systematic preparations for war. Opposition to war and the search for peaceful forms of conflict resolution moved to the center of global activism, and in 2003 and 2004 the first two global days of actions were an unprecedented, enormous success, bringing together people and civil society groups on all continents with an extremely wide range of cultures, political orientations, and class and ethnic backgrounds. The success of such global actions can be associated with their ability to give voice and mobilize to the consensus of a large majority of world public opinion, reflected also in public opinion polls, thereby putting pressure for a change of course on national and global decision makers.

The rise of the global justice movements described so far can be empirically documented by the growth of international events of civil society organizations and movements.[10] Figure 2.1 reports the number of global events from 1990 to 2005. A pattern of sustained growth is evident, with key turning points at the end of 1999, with the Seattle protest against the WTO conference,

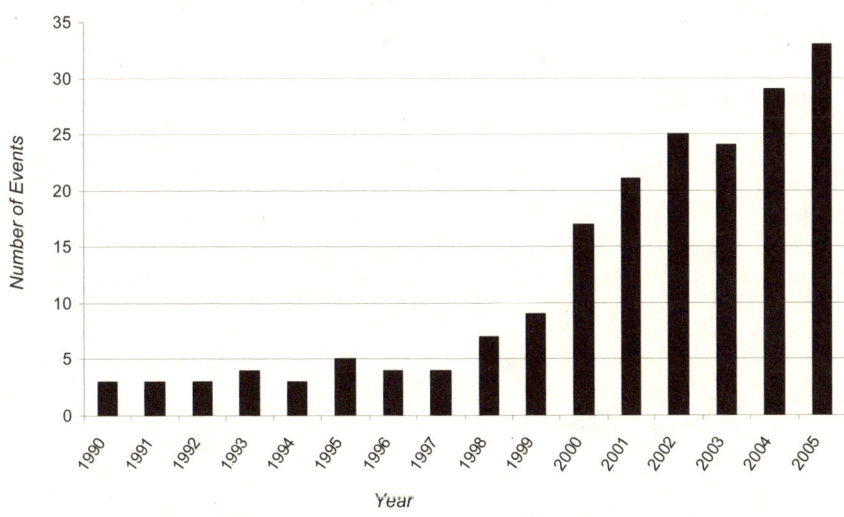

Figure 2.1 Growth of Global Civil Society Events, 1990–2005
Source: Data from Pianta and Zola 2005.

and in 2002 when the experience of world social forums became general-ized in all continents. Both points are marked by jumps in the number and nature of events. Events always include an international conference and, in most cases, a street demonstration, in addition to grassroots meetings and occasional media-oriented initiatives.

The evolution of the types of events from 1990 to 2005 is shown in figure 2.2. Before 1999, the limited number of civil society events—mainly parallel summits—is distributed in a rather stable way among confrontations with G7 or IMF meetings, UN summits, and the first independent civil society events. In the period 2000–2002, there is a proliferation of protests at other global and regional summits (in the EU and the Americas in particular), with extension of the Seattle model of protest to other arenas. These actions fall in the last period as they are replaced by (and probably converge into) the rapid growth of social forums and other independent civil society events. In recent years, these two types of mobilizations account for the highest (and fastest-growing) number of civil society events, showing the high degree of autonomy, self-organization, and activism reached by global movements. G8, IMF, or WTO parallel summits continue to grow slowly, and the relevance of UN summits peaked in 2000–2002 (when a series of conferences were held in order to assess progress achieved five years after the large UN world

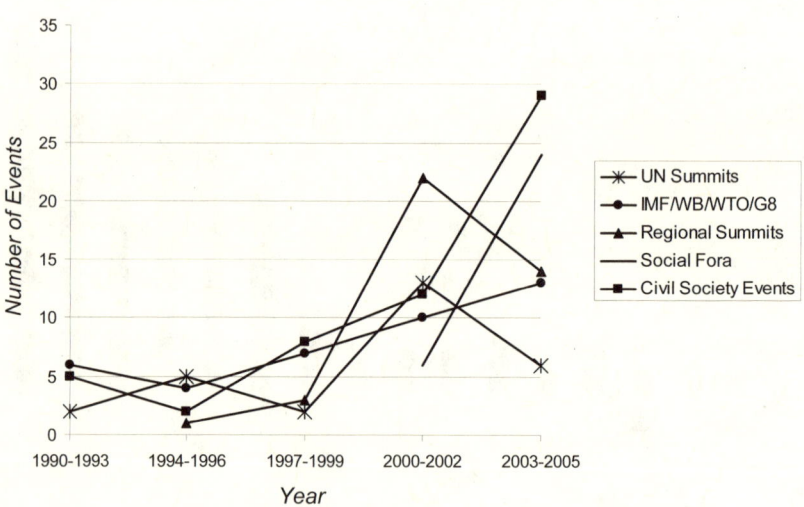

Figure 2.2 The Rise of Global Civil Society Events, 1990–2005

Source: Data from Pianta and Zola 2005.

summits) and later fell, owing to the reduced global role of the UN in a wide range of issues.

Since 2003, important developments are evident. The growth of global activities of civil society continues, with twenty-four events in 2003, twenty-nine in 2004, and thirty-three in 2005, widely spread across all continents. Latin America and Europe concentrate about 30 percent of all events, Asia and Oceania 16 percent, and North America and Africa about 8 percent. The remainder comprises events associated with actions taking place at the same time on all continents. The spread of events in the South is a major change compared with a decade ago; the importance of Latin American and Asian meetings is related to the world social forums, which now account for 26 percent of all global civil society events. Other meetings organized independently from official summits represent 37 percent of events. The rest is constituted by 5 percent of parallel events to UN conferences, 7 percent each to IMF, World Bank or WTO meetings, and to G8 summits, and 18 percent of parallel summits dealing with regional conferences (European Union, American, or Asian government meetings).

Organizational Structure and Transnational Networks

Central to the organization of global activism are transnational networks.[11] Their empirical relevance has been documented by a growing literature (Keck and Sikkink 1998; Katz and Anheier 2005). According to a survey on global civil society organizations active on global issues (Pianta and Silva 2003), more than two-thirds of the 147 responding organizations belong to an international network or coalition, and most organizations participate in one or more international campaigns. Networking emerges as a crucial aspect in their global activities and as the main form of organization linking nation-based groups to the cross-border activism of global justice movements. Beyond the formal ties of membership in a network or campaign, organizations have become interlinked in a variety of ways, relying on other groups for information, strategy, or international contacts. Some of these connections are made explicit in the links included in the Web sites of organizations. An exploratory analysis of the Web-linkages among thirty transnational organizations included in the Demos project (Marchetti and Zola 2005) has shown a very low degree of centralization and some degree of segmentation with reference to the issues addressed and the ideological perspective of organizations and groups.[12]

The crucial role played by transnational networks in the organization of the global justice movements requires specific consideration. They are forms of organization characterized by voluntary and horizontal patterns of coordination that are reciprocal and asymmetrical (McCarthy and Zald 1977; Tarrow 1996; Keck and Sikkink 1998; Anheier and Themudo 2002).

Flexibility and fluidity are two major features of the network organizational form. A flexible organizational structure enhances the capacity to adapt effectively to changing social circumstances and political situations, and a fluid structure, conversely, allows for porous organizational boundaries without enrollment ratified by formal membership.

Within the GJMs, in particular, a *transnational network* can be defined as a permanent coordination among different civil society organizations (and sometimes individuals such as experts), located in several countries, based on a shared frame on at least one specific global issue, and developing joint campaigns and social mobilizations against common targets at the national or supranational level. Transnational networks are key actors with a major role in terms of aggregation of social forces, development of common identities and visions, formulation of campaign strategies, and implementation of political struggles. In the last decades, transnational networks have been major advocates in the promotion of normative change in society, though they have also carried out alternative practices (such as fair trade or solidarity work) that are largely separate from the spheres of global politics and the global economy (Risse-Kappen 1995; Keck and Sikkink 1998). Hence, transnational networks can be considered the backbone of social movements engaged in the political struggle for global justice.[13]

Transnational networks are structurally different from national coalitions and traditional domestic networks. In particular, there are a number of distinctions in their emergence that set them apart from the widely studied national networks.

1. At the global level, the lack of common language, culture, and experience makes the rise of collective action more difficult. Missing a common frame, political culture, and repertoire of action, global networks have to be slowly built through deliberate, long-term efforts at linking a number of shared values, identities, mutual trust, common visions, and strategies among organizations of different countries. This complex process of *coalition and network building* is a key aspect of transnational networks and has been crucial for overcoming the problems of national differences and allowing a broader participation in global campaigns. Evidence of this process can be found in the wide heterogeneity of participation in world social forums, WTO-related struggles, or the Food Sovereignty Campaigns, where alliances are formed among actors as diverse as indigenous movements and unions of European farmers.
2. At the global level, the institutional system is less rigidly structured than it is within states, favoring the emergence within global civil society of forms of organization and coordination that are flexible and specific to the relevant issue. Networks are the most effective models for such

purposes. Examples include the mobilization in favor of the ICC, the anti-mines and debt relief campaigns, and the actions on women's issues.

3. At the global level, a plurality of institutional actors coexists (including different states), and often no single or final authority can be identified for a given issue. This creates opportunities for "vertical coalitions," where civil society networks can develop converging demands or tactical alliances with particular state actors (such as sympathetic governments) or supranational institutions (such as some UN agencies). The anti-MAI campaign, the International Commission on Dams, and the mixed alliances within the WTO context serve as examples.

4. Membership in transnational networks is also different in that it often excludes the participation of individuals. A number of costly barriers—including education, knowledge of foreign languages, travel costs, competence on complex global issues—prevent most individuals from taking part in the prolonged actions of the networks, with the exception of sporadic participation in global events of protest or pressure actions such as "mail bombing" or "net strikes."

5. A further characteristic of transnational networks is the frequent lack, even more than at the national level, of single, charismatic leaders. This is the result of three main factors: First, the horizontal structure of networks reduces the emergence of hierarchies and leaders. Second, the focus of transnational networks' work on "proximate" social movements means that leaders might be well known to activists, but have little exposure to the wider public. Third, there is a lack of symmetry between the cross-border width of a network and the nation-based media system and public opinion that produce the "demand" for movement leaders. Examples are provided by recent Nobel Peace Prize winners, such as Wandari Maathai (2004) and Shirin Ebadi (2003), who were unknown to the general public.

Identities and Opportunities

The frequent gathering of very large numbers of activists at international events has favored systematic discussions and exchanges of experiences, views, and proposals. The format of the events has generally offered wide opportunities for learning the complexities of global issues, for a critique of official policies, and for the search for alternatives. This process has led not just to a deepening of the understanding of individual issues, but to a broadening of the perspective of individuals and groups, linking together different issues into a bigger picture of global challenges. Over the years, this has helped to build common values and identities among activists from different countries, backgrounds, and fields of engagement. A widely shared critique of neoliberal globalization has emerged, with an alternative project of *globalization from below* (Brecher, Costello, and Smith 2000; Pianta 2001a and 2001b), emphasizing bottom-up, cross-border links, common demands and practices on participatory democracy, and economic and social justice.

The pluralistic project of a *globalization from below*[14] emerges as a widely shared perspective and as a crucial meta-frame that underpins different streams of mobilizations of the cross-border social movements demanding global democracy and economic and social justice. As argued elsewhere (Pianta 2001a, 2001b, and 2003), globalization from below can be defined as an alternative to the dominant model of neoliberal globalization, a project based on the core values of peace, justice, democracy, and protection of rights that is advanced in the activities of civil society organizations and social movements advocating change, opposing current policies, and proposing alternative solutions to global issues.[15] In particular, a recent study of major transnational networks within the global justice movements has shown that their main themes of action include social justice (with the associated issues of poverty, welfare protection, and social inclusion), human rights, and democracy, all embedded in a new form of globalism that we here call globalization from below (Marchetti and Zola 2005). The predominance of economic and democracy issues is also confirmed by other studies on globally active organizations and on global civil society events (Pianta and Silva 2003; Pianta and Zola 2005). Such a combination of vision, identity, and practical economic and political challenges is at the root of the mobilizations of GJMs and their ability to challenge global and national political and economic power.

Global justice movements have developed through coalitions and campaigns on global issues. In this context, the specific actions carried out, organized, coordinated, or encouraged by transnational networks have developed at several levels, including truly global actions, transnational or regional actions, and national/local actions by national/local network members for advancing global goals. Each type of action could have a differentiated impact on the "internal," "proximate," and "external" constituencies of a global network and could respond to specific needs, challenges, and opportunities emerging in different contexts (Tarrow 2001; Kolb 2003; Yanacopulos 2005).

Although the issues that motivate mobilizations can ultimately be global (though often mediated by the local dimension), the possibility for social movements to take off is entrenched in a net of political opportunities that combines both the national and the transnational domains of political action. In the link between globalization and the rise of global social movements, there is always an important role played by national conditions (McAdam et al. 1996a).

Within the general frame of a globalization from below, the interaction between the set of values shared by social movements and the global political and economic realities leads to the emergence of different projects of political change, rooted in particular opportunity structures. In national contexts, social movements are rooted in a thick web of social relations and common identities, have access to important resources (human, financial, and so on), but operate in highly formalized political systems that both allow and constrain their mobilization and impact. Conversely, at the global level, social movements and transnational networks face major obstacles and costs in building up cross-border relationships among civil society organizations with different cultures and languages; they have access to highly limited resources and face a political system characterized by the lack of democracy. Such a deprived institutional framework and the innumerable failures to address global problems generate a twofold effect: On the one hand, they offer opportunities for mobilization, as the lack of a political voice creates conditions for political protest; on the other, they constrain mobilization into the limited avenues offered by the opportunities associated with the unstructured international political system (della Porta and Diani 1999, 201–206). The lack of legitimate responses to the democratic deficit, together with the limited constraining capacity of the international system, thus offer a complex set of both motivational and political opportunities to mobilize.

In practice, the lack of a rigid, well-defined institutional setting similar to the national one can widen the options for political action. When there is a low degree of conflict and some institutional alliances are possible, "vertical coalitions" on selected global issues might emerge, with civil society organizations that might cooperate, or at least establish a dialogue, with particular supranational organizations (usually of the UN system) and with some "progressive" governments or regional bodies such as the European Union. When conflict is intense, on the other hand, it can be easily directed to the highest level, with a highly visible and effective challenge to the core of global decision making (as in the case of the G8 protests). In both cases, the results are greater opportunities for transnational networks to emerge as a legitimate and authoritative voice for global interests, extending their impact on public opinion and on civil society organizations prepared to join transnational networks and mobilizations.

The rapid growth of global justice movements documented in this chapter, and the diversity of their manifestations, are clearly associated with this "richness" of political opportunities at the global level and with the variety of forms of contestation that have become feasible for transnational networks and cross-border activism. Different opportunities are likely to be pursued by different organizations and networks within global movements. The combination of specific characteristics of social movements (such as values, identities, and political visions) and of external political opportunities on global issues has led to the identification of a variety of streams within global social movements. On the basis of their attitude toward globalization, the following typology has been proposed (Pianta 2001a and 2001b): 1) *reformists* with the aim to "civilize" globalization; 2) *radical critics* with a different project for global issues; 3) *alternatives* who self-organize activities outside the mainstream of the state and market systems; and 4) *resisters* of neoliberal globalization, who strive for a return to local and national spheres of action.

This range of perspectives can be found within global justice movements, sometimes with a degree of overlap. Such a typology is centered on the identity and political characterization of social movements and is based on their interaction with the political sphere and political forces. It might be useful for understanding the interaction of values and opportunities in a comparative perspective in a given conjuncture, but it is less relevant in charting the evolving identities within civil societies over time, which are bound to change their relationship to global and national politics.

Conclusion

This chapter has investigated the evolution in the last decades of social movements on international and global issues. It began with the examination of the first international mobilizations in the 1970s and 1980s and moved to the more global, though still scattered single-issue campaigns and international actions of the 1990s. With the turn of the millennium, a scale shift has been noted toward a more unified perspective that led to the emergence of global justice movements. The key elements of these mobilizations include a network structure, a more systematic development of cross-border mobilizations, and a stronger autonomy from political power. These global social movements profoundly changed their values, repertoires of action, identities, interactions with power, and strategies during these decades.

In spite of the different perspectives, ideologies, issues of concern, and strategies, the GJMs have emerged as a self-organized, autonomous actor on the global scene, with converging identities and visions and their own policy priorities and agenda for political change. They are able to articulate a vision for global political and economic relations that is alternative to the model of neoliberal, militarized globalization. Such mobilizations are clearly *global* in their values, in their policy demands, and in the reach of their activism. They converge in protesting the *injustice* of neoliberal globalization—its lack of political democracy, of peace, of economic fairness, of social rights, of environmental protection—and in the search for international democracy and economic and social justice. But they are composed of several streams of evolving *movements*, whose plurality is accepted as a strength and not a weakness in global mobilizations. Within them, different visions and strategies for change coexist and evolve.

The most effective way of conceptualizing such an unusual combination of coalitions and diversities, of convergence and pluralism, of global campaigns and local struggles, is the model of *globalization from below*. This perspective challenges the power of markets and states and represents a project aimed at restraining the rule of the market and the sovereignty of states, in the name of universal rights—human, political, social, and economic. Globalization from below aims to empower global justice movements and provides spaces for the self-organization of civil society. In doing so, it outlines an ambitious reconfiguration of the relationships among the spheres of the economy, politics, and civil society at the global level, and it suggests, at the same time, a practical roadmap for the specific mobilizations of the new type of cross-border activism embodied by the global justice movements.

Notes

We thank Martin Koehler and Duccio Zola for extensive discussion and Massimiliano Andretta, Donatella della Porta, and Lorenzo Mosca for useful comments.

1. A growing literature has addressed the definition of civil society, from its origins in Ferguson, Hegel, Tocqueville, to the critique of Marx, and the modern meaning emerging with Gramsci (Gramsci 1971; Bobbio 1976). See Cohen and Arato 1992; Lipschutz 1992; Falk 1999; Anheier et al. 2001b; Pianta 2001a, 171; Anheier et al. 2002 and 2003; Chandhoke 2003; Kaldor 2003. According to the United Nations Research Institute for Social Development (UNRISD) definition, "Civil Society is a complex social arena, with individuals and groups organized in various forms of associations and networks in order to express their views and fulfill their interests. They could constitute anything from a global advocacy movement down to a village self-help group" (UNRISD 2003, 1).

2. See introductory chapter for a definition of transnational social movements.

3. This section draws upon and expands previous work (Pianta 2001b and 2003). The evolution of "new social movements" has been addressed by a large literature (Melucci 1996; della Porta et al. 1999; McAdam et al. 2001; della Porta and Tarrow 2005).

4. The involvement of global civil society and global movements in campaigns challenging global powers has been studied by a wide range of approaches (Arrighi et al. 1989; Lipschutz 1992; Keck and Sikkink 1998; Waterman 1998; della Porta et al. 1999; Houtart and Polet 1999; Cohen and Rai 2000; Florini 2000; Grzybowski 2000; Klein 2000; O'Brien et al. 2000; Pianta 2001a, 2001b, 2002, 2003, and 2005; Seoane and Taddei 2001; Amin and Houtart 2002; Andretta et al. 2002; Teivainen 2002; Broad and Heckscher 2003; de Sousa Santos 2003; Pianta and Silva 2003; Sen et al. 2004; della Porta and Tarrow 2005).

5. On environmental, social, and women's issues, see the case studies in Chen 1995; Uvin 1995; Keck and Sikkink 1998; Cohen and Rai 2000; Florini 2000; O'Brien et al. 2000; Petchesky 2000; Rajagopal 2003.

6. As an example, in 1994, the parallel summit to the G7 meeting in Naples was organized by a coalition of dozens of Italian civil society groups called "The peoples' circle," with an alternative conference, a street demonstration, and media events set up in cooperation with TOES.

7. The development of transnational social movements addressing global issues has been interpreted with reference to three main models of globalization: neoliberal globalization, globalization of rights and responsibilities, and globalization from below (Pianta 2001b and 2001a; Pianta and Silva 2003).

8. For a bibliographical reference, see the introductory chapter.

9. Three other UN summits took place in the following years. The World Conference on racism and xenophobia held in Durban, South Africa, in 2001 showed that the well-tested process of UN summits involving civil society could fail to produce a consensus on highly divisive global issues. The UN-World Bank conference on Finance for Development held in Monterrey, Mexico, in 2002 showed the failure of the efforts to reform the policies of neoliberal globalization, even after the stock market crash of early 2001. The World Summit on sustainable development held in Johannesburg, South Africa, in 2002, documented the failure to reach most environmental goals set a decade before and the scaling down of several environmental objectives. The failures of these UN summits showed the boundaries that a perspective of globalization of rights and responsibilities could not trespass. Such an outcome was made starker—but not determined—by the arrival in January 2001 of the new U.S. administration of George W. Bush, with its unilateral pursuit of national interests that after the terrorist attacks of September 11, 2001, was turned into a strategy of global preventive war, leading to the U.S. wars in Afghanistan and Iraq.

10. The figures presented here are drawn from the study (Pianta and Zola 2005) that extends the first analysis of parallel summits (Pianta 2001b), where a rigorous definition of such events is provided.

11. Some would even argue that social movements in themselves are networks (Diani 1992b and 2003c).

12. On the basis of current categorizations (Diani 1992a and 2003c; Olesen 2004), this appears to be a polycephalous network in which direct and indirect ties form relatively distant connections, with the effect of broadening the links across countries, issues of concern, and types of organization.

13. This is not to say, however, that all global movements need transnational networks, or that networks are a sufficient condition for the emergence of global social movements. Cross-border mobilizations may develop on "backbones" different from organization-based networks, assuming different forms, models, and duration (an example might be Internet-based global campaigns). The experience of civil society organizations is also full of international coordinations that have never led to broad cross-border social mobilization (an example might be the international trade union movement). Moreover, not all networks are movements, for an additional component of political identity, protest, and mobilization is needed to constitute a social movement.

14. According to Falk, who introduced the concept, *globalization from below* has the potential to "conceptualise widely shared world order values: minimising violence, maximising economic well-being, realising social and political justice, and upholding environmental quality" (Falk 1999, 130). See also Brecher et al. 2000; Pianta 2001a and 2001b; Pianta and Silva 2003. A similar perspective, although with different concepts, is in de Sousa Santos 2003 and Sen et al. 2004. A comparative perspective is in Held and McGrew 2002 and Archibugi 2003.

15. In the survey of global civil society organizations (Pianta and Silva 2003, 17), when asked about the vision inspiring their actions, organizations answered *globalization from below* in 33 percent of cases and *humanized globalization* in 28 percent of cases; in all, 60 percent of respondents have a vision of globalization putting at the center civil society and human beings. In contrast, only 11 percent emphasize the need for a *governance of globalization,* and just 4 percent declare themselves *antiglobalization.* At the same time, however, one-sixth of respondents declare that their focus is on the *national/local dimension,* playing down the importance of globalization in their own identity and pressing for a turn toward localization.

Chapter Three

The Global Justice Movement in Italy

Herbert Reiter
(with Massimiliano Andretta, Donatella della Porta,
and Lorenzo Mosca)

A main characteristic of the Italian global justice movement (GJM) is its heterogeneity. Along with active involvement of organizations originating in the labor movement and an impressive presence of groups with a Catholic background, the movement includes activists from the social centers of the 1990s (autonomous youth centers in occupied buildings) as well as the "new" social movements of the 1970s and 1980s. In the first part of our contribution, we will underline the characteristics of the social movement sector and of the political opportunity structure in Italy that have facilitated cross-fertilization and networking among groups with such diverse backgrounds. In the second part, we will present the main organizational networks of the movement and their models of internal democracy.

Notwithstanding its heterogeneity, the Italian GJM features dense networks, with converging demands for social justice and democracy from below expressed by all of its sectors. We will argue in part three, in fact, based on the patterns of organizational networking and of past and present participation of activists in movement organizations, that the mobilizations against neoliberal globalization are sustained not by a mere coalition of organizations, but by a social movement in the strict sense. The transcendence of a coalition character is confirmed by the movement's success in constructing a master frame resonating with the system of meanings shared by most of its activists and supporters. In the fourth section, we will discuss the political opportunities for the Italian GJM and the reaction of the state and the political parties to its sudden rise. At least initially, this reaction was restricted to defining the movement as a public order problem, a characterization contradicted by an analysis of the movement's action repertoires: Although they show a strong propensity toward mass protest campaigns—including direct action—the GJM's tactics are overwhelmingly nonviolent.[1]

The Evolution of the Italian GJM: Origins and Turning Points

The emergence and rapid development of the GJM surprised not only politicians and journalists, but also social scientists. Research into the social movements of the 1980s and 1990s, in Italy and in other Western democracies, had singled out a trend toward the "normalization" and moderation of protest, with many social movement organizations (SMOs) shifting toward more conventional forms of action (such as lobbying), commercialization, and involvement in voluntary work. Movement organizations seemed to share a pragmatic, "concrete" language, an emphasis on specialization with a prevalence of "experts" over "ideologues," and a stress on the nonpartisan nature of their claims. Another common feature was a tendency toward organizational institutionalization, or at least structuration.

In its emerging phase, however, the Italian GJM could refer to another set of elements also common to the movements of the 1980s and 1990s. First, there was an emphasis on differential rights and continuing demands for participation from below, challenging the corruption of representative politics. In addition, notwithstanding a tendency toward organizational institutionalization, social movement organizations continued to rely mainly on activism. The social movements of the 1990s also continued to use protest, with radical forms of action surviving at the margins. Finally, criticisms of institutionalization, professionalization, and moderation of social movement organizations were increasingly voiced by radical grassroots groups toward the end of the last century, and some movement organizations acknowledged these criticisms.

The fact that in the 1980s and 1990s movement organizations became more and more involved not only in the formation but also in the implementation of public policies brought them into increasing contact with traditional third-sector organizations. Voluntarism in Italy had developed within the communist and the Catholic subcultures, with close ties to the Italian Communist Party (PCI) and the Christian Democratic Party. The collapse of the Italian party system[2] in the beginning of the 1990s largely liberated these associations from strictly political allegiances and opened them to new kinds of alliances, preparing the field for collaboration and cross-fertilization among social movement organizations, solidarity and voluntary associations, and radical grassroots groups (Marcon 2004; Rosi 2003).

Additional changes in the political environment contributed to successful networking: Throughout the 1980s and 1990s we saw a weakening of the Old Left, the main institutional ally of the movements, with the main successor party of the PCI, the Democrats of the Left (DS), moving toward an openly reformist position in the social democratic tradition. The relationship between the movements and the institutional Left, which in the 1980s and early 1990s was characterized above all by temporary alliances on specific issues (like peace), became increasingly conflictual in the mid-1990s with the return to government of the center-left coalition and its austerity policies. This shift contributed to the development of grassroots trade unions, but also to increasing opposition from within the institutional unions, bringing these sectors of the workers' movement into closer contact with social movement organizations and voluntary associations. Additionally, the government decision to participate in military interventions, among others in former Yugoslavia, strained the relationships between center-left parties and the peace movement.

Networking around issues of (social, political, ecological) global justice was favored by international developments as well. Especially in an early period, the Zapatista insurrection in Mexico provided an important point of reference, in particular for the social centers. The collaboration and mutual influences among groups from diverse cultural and political traditions gradually developed during the organization of a series of counter-summits (Pianta 2001a) and international campaigns like Jubilee 2000 or the protest against wars.

The G7 counter-summit in Naples in July 1994 constitutes an Italian example of these developments. Among the organizing groups, we find many of the organizations that were to play an important role in the Italian GJM, from Catholic (Beati i costruttori di pace, Pax Christi, Mani Tese), to ecological groups (Legambiente), from grassroots unions (Comitati Unitari di Base [CUB], Cobas), to associations connected with the institutional Left (Associazione Ricreativa Culturale Italiana [ARCI]). On the cover of a movement publication, we already find a slightly different version of a slogan that was to become prominent in Genoa in 2001: "Another way is possible, another world is possible [E' possible un altro modo, è possible un altro mondo]" (Onde Lunghe, July 1994). The organizers of the counter-summit were, however, conscious of the fact that the "summit of the movements" counterbalancing the economic and political forces of globalization still had to be organized, notwithstanding the first nascent nongovernmental transnational networks

(Meloni and Schettini 1994). Especially in retrospect, an attitude and a mood quite different from the one characteristic of the GJM mobilizations prevailed. For instance, Un ponte per, specializing in solidarity activities in the world's South and co-organizer of the 1994 counter-summit, underlined at its 2005 assembly that during the 1990s it had been a self-sufficient organization with few contacts with other social movement organizations, characterizing its 2002 decision to actively join the GJM as "the end of the crossing of the desert" (Un ponte per 2005).

The success of the November 1999 protests against the third conference of the World Trade Organization (WTO) in Seattle accelerated the processes of cross-fertilization and aggregation in Italy. The broad coalition realized on that occasion increasingly led Italian SMOs with quite different backgrounds to concentrate, for the sake of common campaigns, more on their commonalities than on their differences. In 2000, various successful coordination efforts brought together social centers, solidarity and voluntary organizations (both secular and Catholic), and a movement sector closer to the traditional Left in protests against, among others, the North Atlantic Treaty Organization (NATO), the Organization for Economic Cooperation and Development (OECD), and a fair on biotechnology in Genoa.

These experiences formed the basis for the organization of the protests against the G8 in Genoa in July 2001, launched at the first World Social Forum (WSF) in January 2001. More than 800 groups came together in the Genoa Social Forum (GSF), characterized by a very thin structure and an inclusive approach that relied largely on the resources put at its disposal by the member organizations. The GSF managed to attract organizations that had previously refused to join similar coordination efforts—all the more remarkable since adherence required the signing of a "work agreement" specifying the types of protest initiatives that were accepted and banned under its umbrella. Earlier versions of the "work agreement" excluding any kind of violence had previously been agreed upon at several of the coordinated protests in 2000.

The GSF (as later the European Social Forum [ESF]) functioned as a structure linking a galaxy of small groups, typical for new social movements whose organizational structure has been described as segmented, multicephalic, and networked (Gerlach 1976 and 2001). Compared with its precursors, however, the "movement of movements" is characterized far more by the presence of weak ties among groups maintaining differentiated organizational models. It is, in fact, the co-presence of different traditions that makes more structured models of coordination obsolete: The condition for an effective collaboration of groups with different social, cultural, and political backgrounds in a global mobilization seems to be the capacity to coordinate and cooperate while preserving one's own specificity. From the very beginning, the GSF considered this plurality a positive factor and one of its strengths. In fact, it was successful in putting together groups and organizations from different generations and various political and cultural backgrounds, remobilizing old activists and mobilizing new ones.

The Organizational Networks of the Italian "Movement for a Globalization from Below"

The emergence of transnational movements is facilitated by the adoption of a network structure, which in the case of the Italian GJM, characterizes not only the movement as a whole, but also its various sectors. A "network of networks" structure of the movement is in fact evident if one looks at the mobilization against the G8 in Genoa in 2001. The various "souls" of the movement aggregated into thematic sectors: the solidarity and voluntary associations, both Catholic and secular, around the Lilliput network in the ecopacifist sector; Attac and the organizations of the more institutional Left in the anti-neoliberal sector; and the social centers, in particular the White Overalls and the Network for Global Rights, in the anticapitalist sector. As can be seen in figure 3.1, however, the GSF did not represent the whole spectrum of groups challenging the G8. Some more radical groups chose to remain autonomous, sharply criticizing the GSF's attempt to present itself

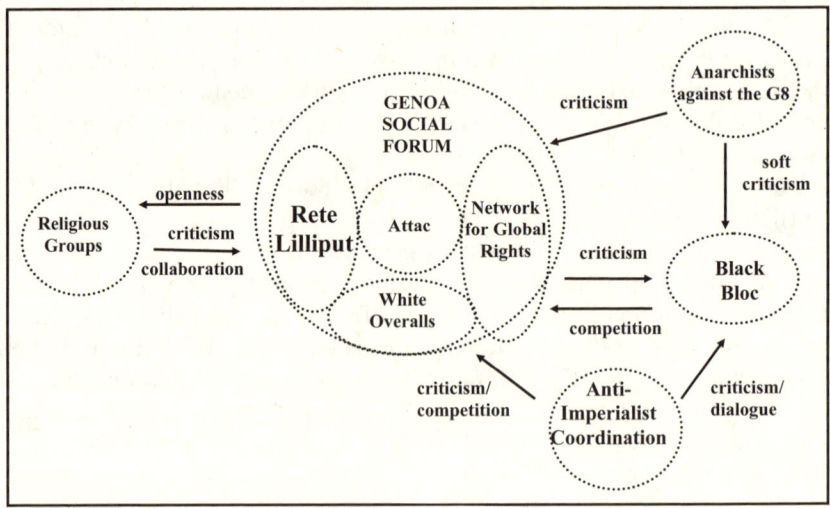

Figure 3.1 Key Genoa Protest Networks

as the representative body of the movement and to dictate the acceptable forms of action. These networks of anarchist and anti-imperialist inspiration (among them the Black Bloc) also criticized the WSF charter of principles as too moderate and reformist. The more moderate religious groups also remained outside of the GSF, marking their differences with an initiative that, according to them, did not exclude methods of a violent character.

As we shall see, the competitive and cooperative dynamics at work within and between existing SMO networks led to the configuration (and reconfiguration) of the GJM. Rather than a weakness, this organizational flexibility seems to represent a strength for a movement based on different identities that are valued rather than stifled.

Anti-neoliberalism: Controlling the Market through Politics

One of the organizations created *ex novo* for the anti-neoliberal mobilization, and undoubtedly the most influential at the transnational level, is Attac: Set up in France in 1998 with the aim of exercising democratic control over the supranational institutions guiding the process of economic globalization, Attac spread to dozens of countries, with national sections enjoying a high degree of autonomy. Attac-Italy began forming in 2001, as a national network incorporated in the wider international one (Finelli 2003a; 2003b). It is supported by the left-wing daily *Il Manifesto* and by a broad section of associations traditionally close to the Left, even if they are not affiliated members—for instance by the ARCI, the historic recreational and cultural association of the PCI, "refounded" in 1994 as an autonomous "new association."

In Italy, as in other European countries, trade unions and currents of social-democratic and communist (or postcommunist) parties, especially *Rifondazione Comunista* (RC), also congregated around Attac. In this context, the importance of the development of grassroots unionism during the 1990s and growing criticism of neoliberal politics inside the established unions has to be underlined. Critical unions had developed, in competition with the traditional ones, during protest against reform of the labor market implemented by center-left governments. Especially at the end of the decades, frames of opposition to deregulation of the labor market and cuts in the welfare state spread also among rank-and-file members of the traditional unions who (re)appropriated their organizations as vehicles of mobilization.[3] In July 2001, the confederated unions (Confederazione Generale Italiana del Lavoro [CGIL], Confederazione Italiana Sindcati Lavoatori [CISL], and Unione Italiana del Lavoro [UIL])[4] decided not to take part in the days of mobilization in Genoa. The FIOM (metalworkers of the CGIL) participated fully in the initiatives, however, and many demonstrators in Genoa carried the CGIL flag. Subsequently, not only FIOM but also the internal current "Cambiare Rotta" (Change Course) convinced the CGIL of the importance of a global movement for workers' rights. The CGIL participated in antiwar demonstrations, and the new global movement took part in various strikes called by the confederated unions. Relations between the movement and the CGIL intensified on the occasion of the general strike called in spring 2002 against the reform of the workers' charter proposed by the center-right Berlusconi government, culminating in full CGIL adherence to the Florence ESF.

Between Ethical Commitment and Nonviolence: Ecopacifism

In the last few months of 1997, some of the Italian organizations that had promoted campaigns for peace and against economic globalization since the late 1980s decided to participate in periodic meetings. The setting up of an "inter-campaign table"—as a place for coordinating organizations engaged in campaigns focusing on different issues but with the same general objectives—enabled representatives of the various Italian organizations to meet, get to know each other, and compare and define work methods based on a process of consensual decision making and common pathways. The project to create a network called Lilliput was officially launched in July 1999, and from then on began to define an organizational structure (a network of local nodes) that was to prove particularly serviceable to the objectives of mobilization (Veltri 2003b). Lilliput thus took its first steps before the Seattle protests, although active involvement of local groups in the project started only after the drafting of a manifesto in the first months of 2000. The network's name derives from Jonathan Swift: The image of the Lilliputians immobilizing Gulliver symbolizes the strategy of uniting the strength of many small groups to block the giants of neoliberal globalization.

The Lilliput network consists of dozens of local "nodes," in which activists and organizations from different backgrounds participate. Among the environmentalist organizations active in the network we find well-established ones such as the Italian section of the World Wildlife Fund (WWF). The participation of these organizations seems to invert the tendency to institutionalization that typified the environmentalist movement in the 1980s and 1990s in Italy, as in other European countries (Rootes 2003a; della Porta and Diani 2004a). The tension between the institutionalized environmental associations and more radical groups that emerged especially toward the end of the 1990s has certainly not diminished today; but the GJM sees more moderate, but well-organized, environmentalist organizations coming together, cooperating and talking with grassroots radical ecologist groups.

Alongside the "Green" component of the network we find the area of Catholic-inspired associations like Pax Christi. The Italian section of Pax Christi, founded in 1954, changed radically in the late 1970s, becoming involved in annual peace marches. Often critical of the ecclesiastical hierarchies, according to Fabio Giunti, a representative of its Genoa chapter, it defines itself as "a leaven within the church" and regards the G8 as a "structure of sin" (Marradi and Ratto 2001, 31). Other Catholic-inspired organizations are active in development cooperation or promotion of critical consumerism, organizing boycotts of transnational corporations that violate workers' rights and environmental protection standards. Many nongovernmental organizations (NGOs) operating in the world's South are also part of the Lilliput network.

In recent years, religious-based organizations have been more involved in international as well as national politics, cooperating with different sectors of local and global civil society. The importance and extent of the involvement of religious-based organizations in the GJM emerges, for instance, from the participation of Caritas Europe in the promotion of the ESF in Florence. This involvement has been connected with general trends: Many religions responded to declining membership with increasing engagement in issues of morality and society beyond narrow questions of faith (Clark 2003b, 12f.; see also Livezy 1989; Keck and Sikkink 1998; Gadner 2002). More specifically, in Italy this development can be attributed in part to the continuing influence of Catholic grassroots currents involved in the movements of the 1960s and 1970s. Also important are the consequences of the collapse of the Christian Democratic Party, whose position in the party system was taken over by Berlusconi's "Forza Italia," which was culturally alien to large sectors of the Catholic voluntary associations. Within the religious world, in fact, mechanisms of organizational appropriation were particularly visible.

Against Capitalism: The Area of "Antagonism"

A third sector that joined the GSF is that of the social centers, characterized by a low level of internal coordination. The Italian social centers are numerous (some 200 were counted at the end of the last decade), but also very heterogeneous in cultural background, objectives, and forms of action (Dines 1999). A pioneering study in the early 1980s in the Milan area had already identified the social centers' relationship with institutions (negotiation, or confrontation/refusal/distance) as a particularly problematic point, observing in some cases processes of institutionalization and professionalization, with resources granted by institutions in exchange for carrying out sociocultural activities (Grazioli and Lodi 1984). In the last decade, a sizable proportion of the Italian social centers has undergone a process of "commercialization," with growing emphasis on offering services paid for by member-users (della Porta and Diani 1999). This process, though not implying renunciation of activities of a political and social nature (Berzano,

Gallini, and Genova 2002), is marked by the abandonment of a classical revolutionary vision, increasing interaction with the political system, and moderation in action repertoires.

An evolution of this type characterizes the social centers from which the White Overalls (tute bianche) developed. Some of these squatted social centers gradually became "legalized," establishing and maintaining good relations with parties such as the Greens, and especially RC. In their action repertoires, they privilege civil disobedience actions that they define as non-violent but protected, collective, and self-organized. These actions consist, for instance, in reaching police lines and attempting to move into the out-of-bounds "red zones" by "pushing and shoving." The activists wear protective materials for their physical safety, but objects of aggression are banned. At Genoa, the Giovani Comunisti, the youth organization of RC, assembled at the Carlini stadium together with the White Overalls.

Other social centers have dissociated themselves from a process of legalization and institutionalization they stigmatize as a "reformist drift" (Berzano and Gallini 2000). Starting in March 2001 with the Naples mobilization against the UN-Global Forum on e-government, the Network for Global Rights began to form—a coordination between the Cobas (grassroots unions) and social centers mobilized on labor, the environment, and immigration. In contrast with previous mobilizations, when the radical social centers had not joined forces with the more moderate groups, the Network for Global Rights participated in the GSF, although with some internal dissent. At Genoa, the White Overalls and part of the Network joined in the Disobedients.

In conclusion, their internal evolution has led many social centers to join the movement's coordination structures even if they sometimes feel the need to underline their own identity: In particular, at the ESF in Florence, the Disobedients opted for a "looser" presence, taking part in the official forum events but also organizing parallel discussion groups that took place separately and distinct from the forum. Other groups have chosen to remain "autonomous," severely criticizing the institutionalization of the movement. The latter groups, in fact, started to organize meetings alternative to the official European social forums.

Local Social Forums

At the local level, activists from the three networks we have just described, as well as from other organizations, often meet in social forums. Many local social forums developed a few months before the protest against the G8 in Genoa in order to coordinate the mobilization. In most cases, they survived, and many more were formed in that year and in 2002. In the spring of 2003, 170 social forums were catalogued in Italy, not only in cities, but also in rural areas (della Porta 2005a and 2005b).

The Italian local social forums usually define themselves as open, public arenas for permanent discussion; a forum is, in this interpretation, "a platform for the local civil society" (Fruci 2003, 174). The charter of the Florence Social Forum states: "We are individual citizens, unions and associations, movements and self-organized groups, Florentine political and social actors that assemble in the Social Forum of Florence. We feel part of an international movement that aims at challenging the oligarchies and their anti-democratic procedures, represented by the big global economic and military organizations" (http://firenzesocialforum.net/cartafsf.html; accessed September 2005). The regulations define the role of the forum as "a network structure composed by individual and collective actors that share the principles and the analyses contained in the charter. It is an instrument to act at various levels. It is first of all a table for confrontation, not a monolithic political actor. Its subjectivity is expressed in movement forms and it refuses dogmatic positions" (http://firenzesocialforum.net/regolamentofsf.html; accessed September 2005). Similarly, the Catania Social Forum states that the movement is composed of "a kaleidoscope of colors and experiences" (Piazza and Barbagallo 2003, 6). In the various areas, the local social forums have taken different forms, often involving individuals and organizations of the institutional Left.

Internal Democracy

The question of internal democracy is highly salient for a movement with the objectives of democratic participation and the democratization of the institutions of globalization. The three main organizational networks of the Italian movement all make explicit reference to the themes of participatory and deliberative democracy (Finelli 2003a; Veltri 2003a; Becucci 2003). The principles of participation and dialogue, infrequent recourse to voting, time-limited delegation on specific questions, control of delegates, and the consensus method can be found also in the local social forums, often marked by the absence of leadership, presence of thematic groups, horizontality, and so on (Fruci 2003).[5]

The dilemma of how to reconcile efficacy in decision making with participation and deliberation has, however, been addressed in various ways (see table 3.1). The degree of formalization and specialization is highly differentiated: Attac-Italy has a constitution, fee-paying membership, individual membership cards, and an organizational structure with a clear division of labor and high degree of specialization. The Lilliput network does not have a constitution, but rules and procedures have been clearly defined in a manifesto and a formally approved document of fundamental values. Membership is not formalized, but considerable specialization developed inside the network. The degree of formalization of the Disobedients is extremely

Table 3.1 Organizational Characteristics by Networks

	NETWORKS		
ORGANIZATIONAL STRUCTURE	*Attac-Italy*	*Rete Lilliput*	*Disobedients*
Formalization	High (defined in a constitution)	Medium (defined in a manifesto and a document of values)	Weak (not defined official documents)
Specialization	High (national working commissions)	High (thematic working groups)	Low (no groups or commissions)
Main Decision-making Body (Other Than Assembly)	National council	Sub-node	Council
Composition of Decision-making Body	Defined by common agreement between local and national levels	Expression of thematic groups, intercampaign table, local nodes	Local spokespersons and delegates of associated parties and unions
Center-Periphery Relationship	Local level contributes to selection of members of National Council	Local level represented within decision-making body by macro-regional spokespersons	Local level represented within decision-making body by local spokespersons
MODEL OF DECISION MAKING			
Type of Leadership	Concentrated (but not individual)	Diffuse (with rotation according to different issues)	Concentrated (charismatic and individual)
Decisional Method	Majority rule	Consensus method	Unanimity

low: There is no official document defining the organizational structure of the network, and the functions of the various organizational bodies are not clear.

In all three organizational networks (and in the local social forums), the assembly is formally the main decision making body, but various forms of executive or coordinating committees have evolved—often (especially in the case of Lilliput) after intense discussion—with different degrees of (formal and informal) power. Attac-Italy follows a more "associational" model, bent, however, on assuring a high level of participation by guaranteeing the involvement of the local level in the selection of the National Council. The Disobedients are an example of an "assemblary" model, with a national assembly meeting every two or three months; however, they have never publicized how members of the national council are selected, nor have they indicated when or where it meets or what decisions it takes. In addition, they do not seem to pursue efforts to improve internal democracy similar to those of the other two networks. Lilliput can be described as "deliberative-participative," leaving decisions to the national assembly and the assemblies of the thematic groups. The sub-node (its coordinating committee) remains restricted to a service function, but has considerable autonomy in emergency situations.

Leadership is of a diffuse type in the case of Lilliput (and of local social forums) but more concentrated in Attac and the Disobedients—in the latter case also more often individual and charismatic. Various levels of attention to deliberation emerge if we look at the modes of decision making adopted by the three organizational networks. According to its constitution, Attac applies the majority criterion in its executive committee and a mix of majority rule and consensus in its assembly. Rete Lilliput practices the consensus method (typical also for the local social forums), whereas the Disobedients seek to reach unanimity. It is important to stress that the Disobedients' unanimity does not coincide with Lilliput's consensus. The consensus method is above all an often time-consuming process for reaching a decision acceptable to all. It is neither unanimity (because the outcome might not be everybody's first choice) nor a majority vote.

In the cases of both Lilliput and Attac, tension remains between the horizontal (local nodes, territorial committees) and the vertical (sub-node, national council) bodies, tied up with the trade-off between participation and efficiency: In both cases, the organizations operating at the local level ask for full sovereignty and are critical of the arbitrariness of the bodies operating at the national level and of the concentration of power at the top. In the case of the Disobedients, by contrast, no such tension seems to have emerged, probably also because of the more limited degree of coordination among the various autonomous social centers.

The Building of a Movement Identity

Organizational Networking

The plurality of organizational models and of social, political, and cultural backgrounds within the movement can be interpreted as evidence that this is not a GJM, but rather distinct SMOs forming temporary and shifting alliances on global justice issues and for specific protest events. The organizations participating in the movement in fact continue to play an important part in the mobilization of activists and sympathizers. About a quarter of the activists interviewed in Genoa stated that they learned about the movement through the organization to which they belong, and one-third stated that the organizations had a significant role in informing them about the anti-G8 demonstrations. However, not only the organizations as such but also the cooperation among them, the networks they form, and the dialogue they set in motion all encourage individual participation.

The results of our research on documents produced by Italian GJM organizations can give us an indication of such relationships.[6] A first observation refers to the relatively high number of Italian organizations allowing for both individual and collective membership. This feature indicates a highly reticular, networked organizational structure and is characteristic of the most recent generation of Italian organizations: Of the seventeen organizations (of a sample of forty-one) that allowed for both individual and collective membership, thirteen were founded after 1990. This reticularity seems confirmed by the importance that their formal documents (such as constitutions, platforms, or programs) attribute to collaboration with other movement organizations, not only in general or with those working in the same thematic area, but also with those sharing similar values but working on different themes: Only eight of our forty-one organizations make no mention of collaboration/networking with national SMOs, and only fourteen do not mention collaboration/networking with transnational SMOs.

Additional indications on the networking of the Italian GJM organizations emerge from an analysis of hyperlinks on these same organizations' Web sites.[7] Important in this context are the different functions in a social movement network, in particular centrality and brokerage. As Mario Diani (2003b) states, centrality is related to visibility and the capacity to access media and institutions, whereas brokerage refers to the capacity of mediating between otherwise secluded movement sectors by allowing communication and information exchange.

According to our link analysis, four organizations have a central position (showing the highest number of links): Rete Lilliput (presented previously in detail), Peacelink (a pacifist online portal founded in 1991), Legambiente (a national environmental organization founded in 1980 with close links to the Italian Communist Party, which became autonomous in 1986), and Indymedia-Italy. The importance of the new media for the movement is revealed by the fact that two of the organizations (Peacelink and Indymedia) specialize in information and communication through the Web. The characteristics of one of these organizations (Indymedia-Italy, the national branch of an international network of the GJM) underline the transnational aspects of the movement and its networking. Since three of the four most central Web sites belong to the ecopacifist sector, we can assume that this sector plays a pivotal role for the GJM in the online environment. Finally, alongside two organizations whose foundation is directly connected with the GJM (Rete Lilliput and Indymedia-Italy), we find two organizations surviving from previous movement generations, one of them (Legambiente) at least originally connected with the institutional Left.

A look at the brokerage function confirms the importance of continuity with previous protest waves and of the connection with those sectors of the traditional Left sympathetic and attentive toward emerging movement demands: Among the three Web sites favoring communication between different movement sectors, we find the ARCI, the historic cultural and recreational organization of the PCI mentioned previously, which had been a founding member of both the Tavola della Pace (an important network of the peace movement) in 1996 and of the Italian branch of Attac in 2002. A brokerage function is also fulfilled by the online version of *Il Manifesto* (the most important Italian New Left daily newspaper, promoted in 1971 by a group expelled from the Communist Party in 1966), and by the Web site of the weekly *Carta*, which was created in 1998 as a periodical magazine distributed with *Il Manifesto* but subsequently independent. *Carta* has had ties to the GJM from the start.

Activists and Networks: From Bloc Recruitment to the "Movement for a Globalization from Below"

Even if SMOs continue to play a significant role, their importance seems diminished when compared with previous protest cycles. In the GJM, participation by individuals outside the organizations calling for the mobilization is particularly marked: Among Italian participants, only 44.6 percent at Genoa and 41.6 percent at Florence reported belonging to any of the organizations that had organized or endorsed those two events. The spread of individual participation indicates the movement's capacity to attract sympathizers from outside the "bloc recruitment" of members of networked organizations, also reflecting the stress on a new type of militancy seeking to combine subjective creativity with the development of collective identity. The presence of this form of activism appears particularly significant in the GJM.

Considering only those demonstrators belonging to organizations formally adhering to the GSF and the ESF, and focusing on the most visible and important networks, according to our activist surveys demonstrators affiliated with the anti-neoliberal area represented 39.5 percent at the Genoa anti-G8 mobilization and 38.8 percent at the Florence ESF; 29.9 and 27.2 percent, respectively, were members of ecopacifist organizations; whereas 24.5 percent at Genoa and 24.1 percent at Florence belonged to the more radical area of the autonomous anticapitalist Left.[8] A growing number of activists claimed

Table 3.2 Activists' Participation (Past and Present) in Associations

	Percentage of Activists	
	Genoa (2001)	ESF (2002) (only Italians)
Student Groups	52.0	55.6
Charity/Voluntary Associations	41.4	49.2
Autonomous Social Centers	35.0	36.9
Recreational Associations	34.4	51.7
Parties	32.2	30.3
Nongovernmental Organizations	32.0	32.1
Environmental Associations	24.2	42.8
Unions	19.0	26.3
Religious Movements	17.6	20.2
Antiracist Associations		27.0
Local Citizens' Committees		20.7
Women's Rights Associations		16.2

participation in the activities of a local social forum rather than a particular sector (3.8 percent at Genoa and 9.9 percent at Florence).

Activists have very variegated past and present organizational experiences, ranging from new social movement organizations and student collectives to social voluntary associations and ecological groups, from religious movements to trade unions, political parties, and social centers (see table 3.2). A similar pattern emerges for the participants in the Florence ESF who were not actually members of any movement organization. Of the thirteen types of political, social, or religious groups listed, the "nonorganized" declared they were or had been members, on average, of 4.5 types of organizations, and the "organized" of 4.6. As it is largely documented, multiple participation in various organizations favors interorganizational exchanges, facilitating relations among the different groups (Diani 1995).

If we take a closer look at the patterns of individual organizational affiliation in the ESF database, we note that individuals join not only different organizations in the same sector of the movement, but also organizations forming part of movement sectors with quite evident cultural differences. In fact, 28.2 percent of the activists have shared experiences in both anti-neoliberal/traditional Left and autonomous/anticapitalist organizations; 27 percent have been in both anti-neoliberal/traditional Left and ethical/ecopacifist organizations; and 52.3 percent have been associated with both autonomous/anticapitalist organizations and ethical/ecopacifist associations. Whereas 35.2 percent of activists have been or are in organizations of a single movement sector, 36.5 percent participate, or have participated, in the activities of organizations in two sectors, and 14.4 percent have been or are members of groups belonging to all three sectors.[9]

The widespread experience of multiple affiliation points to the prevalence of activists characterized by a complex identity and open to diversity, which reflects the movement organizations' discourse on tolerance for differences. At the same time, the existence of a network of activists with experience of participation in organizations of various sectors has certainly facilitated interorganizational relations. We can accordingly conclude that the movement of movements is interwoven in networks at both meso (group) and micro (individual) levels.

The Construction of a Master Frame

The basis of a "common view" of the GJM has been built by way of what David Snow and Robert Benford have called "meaning work" (1992, 136). Through "meaning work," social movements symbolically construct a collective subject (the working class, the people, the nation, environmentalists, women, and so on); mobilize supporters; persuade sympathizers to become involved in a collective action; and convince broader public opinion that the movement's claims are "fair" and the status quo "unjust" (Gamson 1992). Although the meaning work is important in every social movement, it has a particular importance for the "movement of movements" because of its heterogeneity—not only of the social constituency addressed by the movement and the constituency that actually mobilizes, but also of the set of potential mobilizing structures (NGOs, SMOs, political parties, trade unions, voluntary associations, and so on).

The master frame of the GJM. Our analysis of the formal documents of a sample of forty-one Italian GJM organizations shows that they are multi-issue organizations: In these documents, ten organizations explicitly declared support for one to five issues, fifteen for six to ten, and sixteen for ten to sixteen. Although located in different movement sectors, to a considerable extent these organizations also share the same concerns: Of our sample, 82.9 percent explicitly declared support for peace/antimilitarism, 73.2 percent for social justice and defense of the welfare state, 65.9 percent for immigrants' rights and antiracism, 58.5 percent for ecology, 58.5 percent for human rights, 51.2 percent for solidarity with Third World countries (another 39.0 percent for global distributive justice), 48.8 percent for another globalization, 43.9 percent for democracy, and 43.9 percent for anti-neoliberalism.

The presence of multi-issue organizations sharing many of the same concerns facilitated frame-bridging. In movement documents like "Our aims"—the GSF's call for the anti-G8 mobilization in 2001 (www.arci.it/

gsf/doc-eng.htm, accessed October 2005)—or the "Call of the European Social Movements" by the ESF in 2002 (www.movsoc.org/htm/tex_art_euromovsoc_engl.htm, accessed October 2005), symbolic and positive value is attributed to the heterogeneity of the movement. Especially the Florence call, with a significant focus on the process of coming together in successive mobilizations, reveals a clear memory of the evolution of the movement's identity.

If various actors want to mobilize together, they must reach an understanding about the identification of a problem and the attribution of blame and causality. In the case of the GJM, this imputation of common causality has been socially built through what Sidney Tarrow (2005) defined as "frame condensation," by which different targets, perceived as the causes of problems, are "condensed" in one "meta target." Condensing the target on neoliberal globalization allowed a logical connection between the various sectorial problems by attributing them to the same macro-cause: The ESF call attributes, among other issues, social injustice, environmental degradation, and oppression of women and ethnic minorities to "a European order based on corporate power and neoliberalism."

Another essential function of the master frame is to find shared solutions for the problems "represented." The movement documents focus especially on democracy from below and on social justice—the Genoa call for action called for "democratic processes and new horizons of social and economic justice"—linked to the principle of solidarity, to environmental justice, and to peace. The self-definition as "a movement for a globalization from below" emphasizes first and foremost the stigmatization of a "top-down" representative democracy. The movement is critical of both national institutions, thought to be powerless or at best inadequate to guide globalization, and of supranational ones, because of the specific policies they adopt and their deficits in democratic accountability.

These cognitive connections reinforce the relations between different organizations and sectors: Social justice is directly linked with the frames of the "old" social movements (unions, left-wing parties, and radical anticapitalist movements); environmental justice bridges the frames that emerged with new social movements; the solidarity frame is widespread among religion-based movements. The master frame provided the symbolic basis for unifying various types of movements: the old with the new, the religious with the secular, the workers with the peasants, the antiauthoritarian women and student groups with the more established and bureaucratic unions and leftist parties, the "polite" and professionalized NGOs with the "impolite" and very loosely connected radical grassroots movements, and so on.

Having defined causes and effects, and having stated that "a different world," "another Europe," is possible, people are called to mobilize in collective action. The call for struggle, mobilization, meetings, and communication both inside and outside the movement expresses de facto demands for democracy. In this context, explicit reference is made in the Genoa call to the right to protest, "not to be subjected to groundless restrictions."

Activists' schemata. If a collective identity process is really at work, the frames developed by the organizations of the GJM should resonate with those of activists and supporters. In order to analyze individual schemata of the mobilization, we asked ESF participants an open question about what was, in their view, the main goal of the movement. The answers were then classified according to the "dimensions" laid out by respondents.

The Italian ESF participants referred mostly to the diagnostic (what's wrong) and prognostic (what should be done) elements of the master frame structure: Only 1.0 percent of respondents referred to a simple "antiglobalization" schema. As many as 45.3 percent of participants expressed the need for a "democratization from below" that included the intergovernmental organizations (IGOs) and existing democratic systems; 33.4 percent pointed to the social dimension of the problem and interpreted the movement as a struggle for social rights, workers' rights, and social justice. Participants also often (19.7 percent) stressed the need for a moral change, of values consistent with human relations based on solidarity, and the ecopacifist schema resonated with 17.4 percent of participants. Anti-neoliberalism as such was mentioned by 17.4 percent of participants; other respondents (13 percent) referred instead to a classic anticapitalist schema.

The activists in Genoa in 2001 (before September 11) referred to very similar dimensions: As many as 40.8 percent referred to democracy from below, 37.2 percent to social justice, and 29.8 percent either underlined ecopacifist schemata or stressed ethics and solidarity as the main goals of the movement; 16.2 percent referred to anti-neoliberalism, 11.1 percent to anticapitalism, and only 4.1 percent to a generalized antiglobalization schema (Andretta et al. 2002, 99). This relative continuity from Genoa to Florence indicates that a collective identity with shared ideas is developing. Such a pattern is confirmed by the fact that the individual schemas adopted are relevant in the structure of the master frame: Neoliberal globalization is identified as the problem, with its solution in more democracy, social and environmental justice, and solidarity.

Moreover, our data (see table 3.3) show that ESF participants do not adopt only sectoral frames. All schemata are present in each sector, and, in particular, social justice and democratic participation are the most central in each sector. In addition, the individual schemata of participants with no organizational affiliation are similar to those who are affiliated, except for the scant presence of anticapitalism.

Table 3.3 Schemata of Italian ESF Participants by Sector Affiliation (Dummy Variables)

Types of Schemas	Sector Affiliation (in %)							
	Ecopacifist	Anti-Neoliberalist	Anti-Capitalist	Local Social Forums	Total (%)	Cramer's V^a	Unorganized	Cramer's V^b
Anti-Neoliberalism	12.5	18.2	19.1	24.2	17.4	n.s.	14.8	n.s.
Social Justice	29.5	43.6	25.0	27.3	33.4	.17*	38.9	n.s.
Anticapitalism	1.1	15.5	23.5	15.2	13.0	.25***	7.4	.11**
Ethics	30.7	17.3	13.2	12.1	19.7	.18*	25.6	.07*
Ecopacifism	24.1	13.4	14.9	18.8	17.4	n.s.	16.3	n.s.
Democracy from Below	55.2	41.1	40.3	43.8	45.3	n.s.	42.1	n.s.
(N)	87–88	110–112	67–68	32–33	298–299		406–405	

Key: *** = significant at the 0.001 level; ** = significant at the 0.01 level; * = significant at the 0.001 level; n.s. = not significant.

[a] Cramer's V of cross-tabulation between organized participants. (Cramer's V is a correlation coefficient used for nominal variables. It varies between −1 and 1, 1 indicating a perfect positive correlation, −1 a perfect negative correlation, and 0 no correlation.)

[b] Cramer's V of cross-tabulation between unorganized participants.

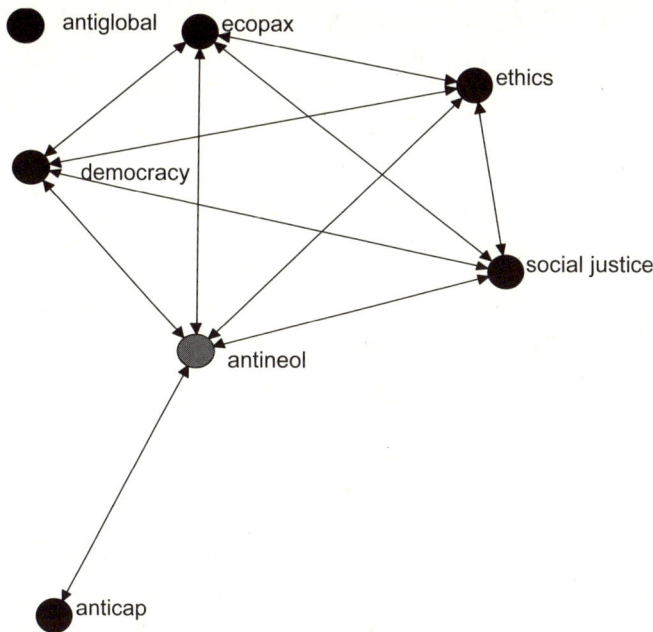

Figure 3.2 The Network of Activists' Schemas

Note: A link between two frames is established when at least 10 percent of activists share both at the same time.

In their answers, ESF participants often referred to more than one dimension, bridging different schemas. Except for antiglobalization, all schemas are connected, with anti-neoliberalism, social justice, ethics, ecopacifism, and democratization from below forming a very cohesive semantic connection. Although all the schemas mentioned are central, anti-neoliberalism emerges as the most central, serving in fact as a broker with regard to anticapitalism (figure 3.2).

Our analysis confirms that the master frame integrates the organizational actors of the transnational movement. What is more, it resonates with the system of meanings shared by most of the activists and supporters, as the schema analysis of participants in the Genoa protest and the Florence ESF demonstrated. Our findings suggest that the master frame, condensing on the meta-target "neoliberal globalization," facilitated the bridging of social justice, democracy from below, ethics, and environmental justice. This provided the symbolic umbrella under which "old" and "new" social movements, issues, and organizations could be linked. The result is not a uniform collective identity, which is in any case opposed by the movement, but a strong identification with a collective *process*. In fact, activists identify more with the movement than with the single, well-structured organizational bodies that take part in it.[10]

The Global Justice Movement and the Italian Political System

The Movement as a Public Order Problem

In the history of the GJM, clashes between police and demonstrators have been frequent, the incidents around the Genoa G8 in 2001 being a particularly vivid example.[11] State authorities, in Italy as elsewhere, mainly blamed the movement for these incidents, which they saw as being caused by the violent action repertoires of some of its sectors and exacerbated by a generally ambiguous attitude toward the problem of violence. The dominant reaction of Italian institutional politics toward the emerging movement was in fact to present it as first and foremost a public order problem.

Our analysis of the formal documents of movement organizations, however, has shown that most of the organizational functions mentioned indicate moderation: If 82.9 percent of our organizations mentioned protest and mobilization as part of their repertoire, thus confirming the bottom-up and participative drive of the movement, 76.6 percent referred to information and awareness raising, 51.5 percent to lobbying, the same percentage to the supply of services to their constituency, and 29.3 percent to advocacy.

The results of our activist survey at the ESF in Florence confirm these trends and demonstrate that the movement is characterized by a overwhelmingly nonviolent repertoire of action, although rich and varied and not excluding direct action. The repertoires can in part be traced back to previous waves of mobilization: 97.3 percent of the activists declared having participated in public meetings, 95.3 percent in strikes, 91.2 percent in the signing of petitions, 82.9 percent in sit-ins, 74.8 percent in the occupation of schools or universities, 73.2 percent in leafleting, and 69.9 percent in boycotts. In addition, 54.4 percent had tried to convince someone to vote for a party, 35.1 percent had been party activists, and 26.9 percent had occupied abandoned buildings.[12]

To the existing action repertoire, the movement has added forms of protest such as transnational counter-summits and campaigns. The latter encouraged the emergence of cross-national links, but also of links among groups on the national level, as the development of the Rete Lilliput shows. Present as early as the 1980s in the repertoire of protest, counter-summits have changed over time, with greater emphasis on street demonstrations, which became the terrain of direct interaction with police forces. Our data, however, indicate that in comparison with the Italian movements of the 1970s, the GJM takes a far clearer position of nonviolence. Only a small minority of the respondents at the Florence ESF included violence against property in their action repertoire (6.1 percent). Our preceding survey at Genoa—where the "work agreement" of the GSF bound the signatories to respect all forms of direct, peaceful, nonviolent expression and action declared publicly and transparently—had shown a similar picture: As many as 90 percent of the demonstrators interviewed in Genoa (95.7 percent for the ecopacifist sector, 92.7 percent for the neoliberal sector, but also as many as 78.9 percent for the anticapitalist social centers) declared never having resorted to violent tactics.

Nonetheless, at Genoa and at numerous other protest events organized by the GJM, the police did not apply in a coherent way the "negotiated management" or "de-escalation" strategies, developed in the 1970s in the face of increasingly heterogeneous movements with violent fringes (della Porta and Reiter 1998a; della Porta and Fillieule 2004). Among other explanations (e.g., the plurality and horizontality of the movement that made dialogue with the police more complicated and the incomplete democratic reform of the Italian security forces), a main cause for the violent escalation lies in the political marginalization of the GJM.[13] Not only did the Italian center-right government respond by refusing to acknowledge the movement as a partner to be talked with, seeing and presenting it instead mainly as a problem of public order; the center-left institutional actors, during and after Genoa, also expressed mistrust toward the movement.

The Political Parties and the Movement

In terms of national political opportunities, the Italian center-right government in power from 2001 to 2006 could count on a rock-solid parliamentary majority in the functional carve-up of power, curtailing legislative-executive dialectic. In addition, since high-profile personalities are the subject of judicial inquiries, the executive has passed laws oriented at extending its control over the judiciary. A center-right government whose main coalition partner had strong neoliberal leanings and whose next strongest partner has a long-standing law-and-order electoral platform was faced by a center-left alliance, weak in organizational and until very recently electoral terms, whose two largest components—DS and Margherita—competed for the centrist electorate.

The recognition of the movement as a legitimate political actor has in fact long been uncertain on the part of the Italian center-left. The debate on the preparatory phases of the G8 demonstrations—to a large extent conducted while the center-left was still in government—evolved without any interaction between the movement and the main center-left parties who, except for RC and some Greens, seemed indifferent to or ignorant of the growing mobilization on the issue of globalization. The skepticism and uncertainty that the Ulivo (center-left coalition) had shown vis-à-vis the movement while in government continued when it went into opposition. After Genoa, the Ulivo was not to line up as decisively in defending protest rights as the Italian Left parties had traditionally done; many DS figures criticized the GSF and the movement's strategies, which in the parliamentary enquiry commission were defended only by the representative of RC. Some considerable time after the Genoa events, a spokesperson of the GSF publicly denounced an attempt staged by the center-left to split the movement into "good guys and bad guys" and of the "illusion that they have of being able to build their own fortunes by allowing the right wing to defeat the movement" (Agnoletto 2003, 157).

The traditional tendency of the PCI of disowning any autonomous opposition movement to its left, as well as uneasiness with the GJM critiques of policies of privatization of public utilities and deregulation of the labor market that the DS had actively supported, might explain this closure. To the institutional Left—even to those who were sympathetic to its aims—the movement remained a phenomenon that stimulated politics, "being a marker" for the problems to be addressed. At the same time, the institutional Left continued to insist on its political monopoly, considering the movement incapable of developing answers to the world's problems. The reawakening of interest in more participatory forms of politics is, therefore, viewed by social democratic parties as a danger. Although part of the electoral reservoir of the institutional Left, activists also challenge a party model built around elected representatives and relating to the electorate through mass media, communication experts, and opinion pollsters (della Porta 2001).

Politics and Antipolitics

The lack of institutional allies was balanced at least partially by the significant consensus that the movement seems to have in society, confirmed specifically in the debate on the violence at Genoa. The police conduct was in fact denounced by a broad range of associations forming a strong, if fluid, coalition supporting civil rights, and surveys confirmed similar concerns on the part of public opinion.[14] Even before the G8, the movement had enjoyed some support from within the DS—in particular from its youth section (Sinistra Giovanile) and the thematic area Altrimondi (Otherworlds), actually members of the GSF. After the events of Genoa, criticism of the party's vacillations became more acute in areas close to the DS. Although part of the institutional Left established connections with the movements, in particular through the organizational process of the ESF in November 2002, their mistrust continued to be high. The two main parties of the center-left coalition were not present at the ESF closing demonstration. Closer proximity to the movement was shown only by the smaller parties of the Italian Left such as the Greens and especially RC.

The timid openings on the part of the Italian center-left parties mirror the more consistent criticism leveled at neoliberal globalization by trade unions, and, on a more general level, by public opinion. Indeed, protests against globalization seem to have been successful in awakening public opinion. In June 2001, a short time before the G8 summit at Genoa, an opinion poll revealed that 45 percent of Italians felt sympathetic with the movement's arguments, 28 percent did not, and 27 percent had no opinion (*La Repubblica* June 17, 2001). A later survey by Simulation Intelligence Research showed that between 70 and 80 percent of the respondents were in favor of canceling Third World debt, "equality of economic and working conditions for workers worldwide," doing away with tax havens, and were against genetically modified food as well as wars; more than half supported the Tobin Tax and freedom of movement for migrants. Overall, 19 percent of those surveyed replied that the "noglobal" movement was "very positive," and 50.9 percent said it was "quite positive" (only 16.1 percent felt it was quite or very negative). Again, a 2003 survey conducted by the Demos and PI agency showed that 52 percent of the population had taken part in political and protest demonstrations over the previous year, with an especially high percentage among the young. This same survey revealed that 33 percent of Italians had taken part in peace marches during 2003, 15.5 percent had participated in boycotts against certain brand names, and 65 percent were concerned about the possible effects of globalization. Although unemployment was the most serious problem signaled by the interviewees, private institutions (the stock exchange, banks, industrialist associations, and privatized health care) saw public faith in them drop sharply (74 percent of those interviewed replied that "the state should not 'make room' for the private sector in health care and education"; in *Venerdì de La Repubblica* December 19, 2003, 27 ff.). In 2004, the position of rigorous pacifism ("*No to the war with no ifs or buts*") was supported, according to a Demos survey, by two-thirds of the Italian population, with about one-third of the sample having taken part in protest against the Iraq war (*La Repubblica* May 23, 2004). Dissent concerning neoliberal strategies is also emerging within the political and nonpolitical elite.

Conclusion

Some of the characteristics of the Italian GJM can be traced back to developments within the left-wing social movement families during the 1990s: a diminishing importance of (New) Left ideology; an increasing pragmatism with concentration on concrete projects, accompanied by the development of specific skills and expertise; the willingness to forge alliances with groups of different political and cultural backgrounds, but involved in projects with similar objectives. Also important were phenomena emerging more at the margins of the dominant social movement organizations: the growing importance of grassroots union organizations; the rise of a new generation of activists; a return to direct action.

For the Italian case, the importance of the collapse of the traditional party system—to be attributed to the fall of the Berlin wall on the one hand and to the political corruption scandals on the other—has to be particularly stressed. This breakdown "liberated" large sectors of communist- and Catholic-inspired voluntary organizations from their traditional party allegiance. At the same time, with the increasingly moderate course of the DS (the largest successor party of the PCI), the role of the Old Left as an ally, a patron, or a broker for social movements diminished. It was during the period of the center-left governments in the second half of the 1990s that third-sector associations and social movement organizations formed alliances against austerity measures.

As a peculiarity of the Italian GJM, above all its great heterogeneity—in cultural, political, and ideological terms, and also in action repertoire—has to be stressed. The networking necessary for the emergence of such a movement was certainly facilitated by the fact that two big international movement events, the Genoa G8 counter-summit and the first ESF, were organized in Italy. The particular characteristics of the center-right government that came to power in 2001 and public reaction to the repression witnessed in Genoa also contributed to the success of subsequent mass mobilizations.

Notwithstanding its heterogeneity, the Italian GJM seems to have developed a common master frame, rotating around the claims for participatory democracy and social justice that were dominant in all the movement sectors we have analyzed. In this context, the experiments in internal democracy should also be considered, bent at strengthening, in varying degrees, participation and deliberation conducted by organizations from all movement sectors. Although we have witnessed a recent decline in mass participation, the networking among different sectors of the Italian GJM did continue beyond the ESF in specific protest campaigns and various initiatives at the local level—despite occasional tension developing especially around incidents of radical direct action.

Notes

1. For empirical evidence, we will rely on our past research (Andretta et al. 2002 and 2003; della Porta et al. 2006), in particular on the activist surveys we conducted

at the Genoa anti-G8 mobilization in 2001 and at the European Social Forum in Florence in 2002. Additional data were collected as part of the Demos (Democracy in Europe and the Mobilization of the Society) project (http://demos.iue.it).

2. The fall of the Berlin wall led to the decision to reform and rename the PCI, opposed by a minority in the party that later founded Rifondazione Comunista. The corruption scandals of the early 1990s virtually wiped out the Christian Democratic and the socialist parties.

3. On the "reappropriation" of more structured organizations by their base, especially during periods of high mobilization, see McAdam, Tarrow, and Tilly 2001, 44.

4. The Italian trade union rebuilt itself on a unitary basis around the CGIL in 1944, before the end of World War II. The tensions of the Cold War led to the division of the unitary union in 1948 and the formation of three major trade union confederations: the CGIL (of socialist and communist inspiration), the CISL (Catholic), and the UIL (secular). Toward the end of the 1960s, these three organizations got closer again, forming a confederation that became increasingly conflictual during the 1980s.

5. The local social forums usually define themselves as arenas for discussion, collaboration, and cross-fertilization, not as organizations. They are structured on the basis of informal "work agreements," often foreseeing quite autonomous working groups focusing on specific issues (Del Giorgio 2004; Fruci 2003).

6. These data were collected as part of the Demos project (see note 1, as well as chapter 1).

7. It must be noted (e.g., in the interpretation of the result that some groups, among them the Disobedients, appear quite isolated) that our analysis refers only to the link section of the Web sites of a limited sample of Italian GJM organizations.

8. At the ESF in Florence (2002), the Gruppo di Ricerca sull'Azione Collettiva in Europa (GRACE) interviewed 2,384 activists, randomly selected, using a semistructured questionnaire (1,668 Italians, 124 French, 77 Germans, 88 Spanish, 118 British, and 309 from other countries) (see della Porta, Andretta, Mosca, and Reiter 2006 for more details). The ESF data presented in this chapter refer only to the Italian activists. At the Genoa anti-G8 protests (2001), GRACE had interviewed 763 Italian activists, using the same methods (see Andretta, della Porta, Mosca, and Reiter 2002 for more details).

9. The remaining 13 percent belong to none of these sectors but to leisure associations, or to no organization at all.

10. In Genoa, 75 percent of our interviewees responded that they identified (enough or much) with the movement as a whole, a finding reflected by the participants in the ESF in Florence, 77.2 percent of whom share strong identification with the movement as a whole. Such a high identification with the movement as a whole, coherently with a multiple and layered identity, does not exclude identifying with both a specific sector (about 57 percent in Genoa and as much as 75 percent in Florence), and a specific organization (44 percent and 67 percent, respectively).

11. For a detailed account of the Genoa days, see Gubitosa 2003.

12. The degree of similarity of the protest experience acquired by activists among the various organizations and networks seems to be high; however, some types of experience are more widespread in some sectors (more squatting among social centers, more party-based activity in the anti-neoliberalist sector, and so on).

13. For a detailed discussion of the policing of transnational protest, see della Porta and Reiter 2004; della Porta, Peterson, and Reiter 2006.

14. According to a PeopleSWG survey, for instance, 57 percent of those interviewed held that "the violence and beatings suffered by the demonstrators on the streets and in the jails were really serious," as against 28 percent regarding them as largely media exaggerations.

Chapter Four

The Global Justice Movements
in Spain

Manuel Jiménez and Ángel Calle

Origins, Opportunities, and Main Features

It was only in 2000, after the protests in Seattle, that the global justice movements (GJMs) started to capture public attention in Spain.[1] During the Seattle World Trade Organization (WTO) meetings, the (limited) protest events taking place in Spain received little coverage (usually in the local media) and were not labeled, in any case, as part of the new global movement.[2] The leading newspaper *El País*, for instance, began to refer to the "*movimiento antiglobalización*" and the involvement of Spanish activists in the course of the year 2000 as a consequence of the protests in Millau, France (June), Nice (December), and, above all, Prague (September). The numerous Spaniards in Prague and, especially, their high presence among the protesters arrested, marked the entrance of the Spanish GJMs into the public eye (quite often because of the spread of images covering the symbolic violence practiced at counter-summits). Nevertheless, protests taking place in Spain remained small and almost neglected by the media until 2001, when they began to be noticed as a consequence of the campaigns against the World Bank in Barcelona, and, most of all, the Spanish European Union (EU) presidency during the first semester of 2002.

However, as we will show in this chapter, the origins of the Spanish GJMs can be traced back to the mid-1990s. As in other contexts, the Spanish global movements encompass a heterogeneous set of groups and networks, but with relatively high participation of organizations linked to the leftist social movements that emerged during the transition to democracy (ecologist, radical feminist, antimilitarist, squatters, etc.) and a limited presence of trade unions (with the exception of minor trade unions such as the Confederación General del Trabajo [CGT]) and political parties. Christian activists have also played an important role in the mobilization, especially through the solidarity NGOs' networks.

This chapter highlights the distinctive features of the GJMs in Spain, as explained by the political context and the organizational features of leftist social movements. However, we will also point out the similarities between the Spanish GJMs and the experiences of other countries. To a great extent these similarities are connected to new patterns in the Spanish contention scene: increasing coordination and extension of patterns of alliances in global campaigns, incorporation of new discourses focusing on criticism of current processes of globalization and decision making in representative democracy, and new protest repertoires. In this sense, it can be argued that the Spanish GJMs are (local) expressions of a new cycle of mobilization with a global scope, which could be considered as entailing a sort of assimilation of the Spanish contention to the rest of the representative democracies.

Organizational Origins and the Political Opportunity Structure

In order to understand the specificities of the GJMs in Spain, we must consider the features of the leftist social movements and their particular evolution in the Spanish political context.

Spanish new social movements are distinctively marked by their late emergence within a cycle of mobilization of opposition to a dictatorial regime and the transition to democracy in the late 1970s (Jiménez 2005, 57). In this sense, their organizational roots are well differentiated, by at least three features, from the new social movements that came into being in other European countries during the 1960s and 1970s. First, links among different movements have been traditionally weaker, as they did not experience a common countercultural wave as in other countries (Álvarez 1995; Rucht 1988). This initial absence of strong overlapping memberships among different movements, as well as the scarce experiences of collaboration, reduced patterns of mutual (interorganizational) identification and intermovement cooperation. Second, violence did not figure in the protest repertoire of these movements, reflecting the moderate nature of the Spanish protest culture configured during the transition (Jiménez 2005). Furthermore, both the libertarian roots of some of these networks (particularly in some pacifist and ecologist groups) and peripheral nationalisms favored decentralized organizational models and localism, making it difficult to advocate for stable coordination on a statewide basis.

In terms of the political opportunities available to social movements, the model of "*transición pactada*" involved a tacit agreement among elites on the need to demobilize civil society in order to ensure a successful political transition. After the transition, the state grew notably, increasing the areas of public intervention but also adopting a commanding (closed) policy style (Subirats and Gomà 1998, 18). The demobilization strategy had a decisive impact on the new rules and practices of the new political system as well as on the reduction of potential allies among established elites (Jiménez 2005).[3] After an initial period of institutional flexibility, a closed political structure was consolidated (Subirats and Gomà 1998). The measures to guarantee a successful transition implied institutional restrictions such as strengthening the executive over the parliament,[4] the design of an electoral system favoring large parliamentary majorities (i.e., low levels of electoral competition), very narrow mechanisms for direct democracy, and so on. The main pluralist feature of the political system came from the territorial decentralization achieved in the course of the 1980s and 1990s (Colomer 1997). However, as far as leftist social movements are concerned, the receptivity of the new territorial administrations has been also limited. In this political context, access of new demands and the visibility of leftist social movements have been highly contingent on the political configuration of power, with more favorable contexts in periods of greater electoral competition (i.e., critical elections) with the socialists in the opposition (early 1980s and early 2000).[5]

From the 1980s onward, the state's twofold strategy of demobilization characterized movement-state interactions, influencing the process of consolidation of the new social movements. On the one hand, a co-optation strategy aimed at the institutionalization of social movements orienting their activities toward the provision of social services, with limited access to the decision-making process and reduced political autonomy. Those social movements with organizational origins closer to the leftist political parties followed this pattern of consolidation. As in the cases of the international cooperation and women's movements, this trend would imply rapid organizational growth with the establishment of a great number of NGOs, many of them state based, but with a relative low political profile. These organizations would get a great deal of the growing number of (young) volunteers experienced in Spain during the 1990s (Calle 2000; Rodríguez 2003). Although there are obvious differences among them, in general they are characterized by a high degree of professionalization, a weak (not very cohesive) collective identity, and a low profile in terms of contention (Jiménez 2005). In other cases, as in the neighbors' or, to a lesser degree, the peace movement, co-optation would entail the demobilization of the movements.

On the other hand, a second set of movements did not tend toward institutionalization, at least not in a consistent way. This more radical sector, along with some alternative trade unions and minor groups within the institutionalized social movement sector nongovernmental organizations (NGOs), provided the preexisting organizational infrastructure upon which the GJMs crystallized from the late 1990s onward. This more radical sector has in common the limited patronage role played by political parties in their emergence phase and the articulation of demands that implied radical policy change, in particular on environmental or antimilitary issues. The various administrations (state, regional, local) rejected their demands, adopting a strategy of repression. Owing in part to this situation, their access to decision making has been highly dependent on the political configuration of power[6] within a logic of interaction with authorities mainly based on conflict, as has been the case for the ecologists (Jiménez 2005), the peace-antimilitarists (Ajangiz 2000; Sampedro 1997), and the squatters (Martínez 2002; Calle 2004). In the radical sector, organizational consolidation has taken longer. These groups are often characterized by decentralized structures[7] and low levels of professionalization along the lines of typical social movement organizational models, although each case has its own peculiarities. Scant material resources have been counterweighted by a gradual increase in activism and relational resources (intergroup cooperation).

The results of a survey administrated by Benjamín Tejerina et al. (2005) among 166 GJMs activists seems to confirm the central role played within the Spanish GJMs by the new social movement organizations (ecologist, human rights, women, etc.) and the weaker involvement of labor movement and political parties.[8] More specifically, 77 percent of the activists declared that they identified themselves with new social movements, whereas only 35 percent identified with the labor movement and 12 percent with other movements like the students or neighbors. Along the same line, 53 percent declared membership in social movement organizations, with only 12 percent and 17 percent in trade unions or political parties, respectively (Tejerina et al. 2005).

The evolution of the Spanish social movement is, however, marked by a gradual configuration of cohesive identities and increasing interorganizational coordination capacity, paving the way to intermovement cooperation in global campaigns. The large participation of a new generation of activists, many with experience in the voluntary sector and in multimovement campaigns, has supported this trend.[9] In fact, increasing intermovement cooperation has facilitated the configuration of a meta-identity under the GJMs or "alter-globalization" networks that permits and fosters the convergence of different social actors under a shared self-perception of belonging to a "movement of movements." This confluence was evidenced in the campaigns during the Spanish presidency of the EU or the antiwar demonstrations of 2003.

In general, their demands (or meaning frames) have gradually tended to merge and radicalize. For instance, those NGOs with a higher political profile have taken on antimilitaristic or feminist demands, and new collectives talk about debt relief and democracy along with ecological debts (Citizens Network for the Abolition of the Foreign Debt [RCADE]); antimilitarists have expanded their claims from antimilitarism to global justice demands under the banner of a fight against "social violence"; and so on (Calle 2005a). We could talk, then, of the construction of a networked discourse (different conflicts that are linked but autonomous), fed from, and feeding into, the previously mentioned meta-identity shared by activists.

In the late 1990s, in a political conjuncture characterized by the right-wing policies of the conservative party in power, movement and group convergence was favored by what can be denominated a radical democracy meta-frame, boosting a new cycle of mobilization.[10] Radical democracy includes demands for the strengthening of democracy through innovative practices (toward deliberative, direct, inclusive, and horizontal experiences of action, coordination, and participation), as well as a shared diagnosis that stigmatizes the deficits of the Spanish democracy and the advance of a neoliberal agenda supported by agents that are considered quite undemocratic (International Monetary Fund [IMF], WTO, EU, and so on).

In relation to this last point, the traditionally moderate protest repertoire has been gradually modified, giving way to civil disobedience repertoires and nonviolent direct actions. New resources and spaces of confluence are now available for radical and alternative mobilization. The Internet can be also considered as playing a major role, both in promoting new structures of participation (forums or sites linked to organizations or campaigns), convergences, or information sharing (www.nodo50.org), and as a virtual space for socialization and exploration of the free use of new technologies (www.sindominio.net). Furthermore, the spread of the Internet has helped in the interlinking and spread of new audiovisual experiments to provide channels of expression for democratic radical viewpoints (participation is open to different collective groups) in line with the wide range of positions endorsed by the GJMs.[11]

The GJMs in Spain: Campaigning and Networking

From 1992 onward, we found protest events and campaigns organized by groups that play a significant role in the promotion of the GJM networks in Spain. We could regard those events of contention as real "learning laboratories" in which new patterns of collaboration, action, and discourses are increasingly explored. Most of these previous experiences had an international scope, in terms of both networking and the issues at stake. Most of their promoting groups were directly linked to the previously mentioned radical new social movement sectors (antimilitarist, ecologist, etc.), as well as to alternative trade unions, with more sporadic participation by political parties or institutionalized NGOs (acting more as recurrent allies than as promoters).

In 1994, the international campaign of "50 Years Is Enough!" against the fiftieth anniversary of the IMF and the World Bank, traveled to Spain by means of ecologist groups such as Aedenat (now in Ecologistas en Acción).[12] An international counter-summit was held during the official summit of the World Bank in Madrid. Notwithstanding its limited public impact, it can be considered a milestone in the evolution of radical contestation in Spain. A great variety of organizations, ranging from pacifists to minor political groups and international solidarity networks, participated in the protests, including a symbolic blockade of an official event.

This first experience of antiglobalization protest helped the consolidation of the GJM networks. In 1996, the Movimiento Anti-Maastricht (MAM) was founded, an informal network composed of diverse anticapitalist activists linked to the ecologists (Aedenat/Ecologistas en Acción), the squatters movements (social centres of Madrid and Barcelona), leftist parties (as Izquierda Unida), minority trade unions (such as the libertarian CGT), extra-parliamentary political groups (Centro de Asesoría y Estudios Sociales [CAES]), and locally oriented networks working on social issues (for example Baladre, some neighborhood groups). Although the MAM progressively lost momentum after 2000, it did serve to foster an anti–European Union discourse and to coordinate new campaigns after the Seattle protests. It was particularly relevant in the organization of the Euromarches (1997–2000), a European campaign that helped to introduce the discourse of the GJMs into labor organizations and vice versa (bringing labor issues into the new global movements). The MAM also contributed to forging alliances with autonomous sectors linked to the social centers.[13]

Coming into existence in 1993, a network called Plataforma 0.7 (a state-wide platform linked to grassroots Christian organizations)[14] entered the scene of the international solidarity networks, breaking the proinstitution-alization tendency of the NGO sector. The participation of institutionalized actors (most of them linked to the Catholic Church) was reflected in its mass mobilization capacity. Its most remarkable actions were the establishment of a protest camp, occupying the central avenue Paseo de la Castellana in Madrid for several weeks, and a demonstration of 100,000 people, both in 1994.

In the late 1990s, new forms of international solidarity were introduced into Spain. This would greatly contribute to the II Encuentro Galáctico held by the Zapatistas in 1997 in various Spanish cities. Two networks of pro-

Zapatista and pro-Movimiento de los Sem Terra (the Brazilian movement of the landless) groups, established at the local level, started consolidating. These groups supported not only solidarity with poor countries, but also intervention in the dynamics of mobilization at home. Thus their work went beyond the traditional role of NGOs in terms of awareness raising or institutional pressure. Organizational structures were quite horizontal, helping to create new structures of participation by tackling, in terms of discourse, the neoliberal agenda.[15]

In the late 1990s, the anti-neoliberal discourse progressively gained room in the Spanish contention landscape. In parallel, participation in international actions (from the Euromarches gathering in Amsterdam in 1997 or Köln in 1999, to the global days of action promoted by the Peoples' Global Action [PGA] from 1998 onward against the international summits of intergovernmental organizations such as the G8, the WTO, and the IMF) paved the way for, although yet weak, intermovement relationships and strengthened their international ties, favoring the incorporation of new contention performances into the traditionally moderate Spanish protest culture. In fact, Spanish activists recognized changes in the patterns of alliances, discourses, and repertoires as the three main contributions of the emergent global movements.[16]

These trends of change crystallized in the main campaigns that marked the evolution of the Spanish GJMs in the early 2000s: the social consultation on debt cancellation (2000), the IMF and World Bank meeting in Prague (2000), the (failed) World Bank meeting in Barcelona (2001), the Spanish presidency of the EU (January–June 2002), and opposition to the war in Iraq (2003).

In 1999, a new protest campaign was coordinated by the RCADE,[17] with the aim of organizing a *consulta popular* (nonofficial referendum) on debt abolition to coincide with the March 2000 general elections in which over a million voters took part. The preparation of this unofficial referendum brought together wide sectors from various social movements in Spain: Almost 23,000 activists participated in 458 municipalities. The *consulta* and the RCADE itself were run in a highly decentralized manner. The "nodes" (groups located in towns or city neighborhoods) were free to decide how to organize themselves and the events and campaigns in which they chose to take part.

Despite the high level of participation, the campaign was given scant media coverage. According to the press analysis conducted by Jerez and Sampedro (2001), the diffusion of a protest action that criticized the institutional political parties was considered to be of little "interest to their political ally" (see also RCADE 2001, 175). Later, the RCADE continued to function as an informal network,[18] although its membership dropped to some 1,000 activists, thus confirming the weakness of the ties between local groups and the ebb and flow of mobilizations as participants' involvement shifted between the campaigns and their organizations of origin (particularly in the case of the NGOs). Its discourse has taken on an increasingly wider scope to endorse a critique of globalization in general and strengthening democracy. In fact, several members of the RCADE would collaborate in forming many of the local groups of the Movimiento de Resistencia Global (MRG).[19]

The "Prague 2000" campaign on the occasion of the World Bank and IMF summit gave a decisive boost to the organization of the GJMs in Spain. The preparation of this campaign, with the creation and later consolidation of the MRG, led to the construction of a common working space for collective groups that had already denounced the consequences of globalization and capitalism. MRGs and other alterglobalization groups managed to mobilize more than one thousand travelers to the anti–World Bank protests in Prague, whereas between twenty and thirty thousand protestors took part in parallel actions in various Spanish cities.

As Gomà et al. (2004, 9) point out in the case of Catalonia (although this argument can be extended also to the rest of Spain):

> participation in the Prague 2000 campaign brought with it a series of innovations that affected the ranks of the GJMs: new ideas were adopted regarding the repertoire of collective action which would be tested in Spain (i.e. the emphasis on non-violent direct action, creative actions, blockades, media guerrillas, etc.). New ways of taking the protest to the streets were discussed in order to rework the classic protest model and make it more effective. Special notice was taken of the counter-summit model as a space for debate, critique and alternative proposals. Actions were more thoroughly prepared and a qualified legal and anti-repression committee was set up. Importance was placed on counter-information and press releases in the alternative media (with Indymedia at the centre of activity). Finally, connections were made with important organisations and movements that were active on the European scenario (i.e. the Italian *Ya Basta,* the English Reclaim the Streets), groups with whom Spanish activists (especially from the social centres) forged international contacts and exchanged ideas.[20]

The experience of the Prague counter-summit had an immediate impact on the Spanish context, especially in the Campaign against the World Bank summit on development held in Barcelona in June 2001.[21] As Gomà et al. (2004, 10) have concluded from interviews, the activists themselves stated, "this campaign constituted one of the most plural and unitary spaces for people and groups to come together and participate in recent years in Catalonia and Barcelona, so much so for the social movements as for the participating organizations."

During the semester of the Spanish presidency of the EU, the GJMs prepared a statewide Campaña contra la Europa del Capital y de la Guerra (Campaign against the Europe of Capital and War). The meetings of the European Councils in Barcelona (March 15–16, 2001), and Seville (June 21–22, 2001), were the two events upon which the mobilization efforts were concentrated. The campaign was organized in a decentralized manner in each of the cities that were to host the various meetings of the Spanish EU presidency (coordination was episodic and informal) in much the same way as the Campaign against the World Bank: Assemblies were held to make key decisions, while work was carried out in independent committees and through the Internet.

In Barcelona, the antiglobalization front was articulated around four different sectors. The Campanya contra l'Europa del Capital i la Guerra was the principal initiative behind the counter-summit, including the mass demonstration held on March 16 in which other already existing platforms took part. One of them, the Foro Social de Barcelona (FSB),[22] consisted of traditional leftist parties such as the PSC (the Catalonian branch of the PSOE, holding office in the city council) and global networks politically akin to them (such as Attac[23] or NGOs such as Intermon-Oxfam) and the most important trade unions (Comisiones Obreras [CCOO] and Unión General de Trabajadores [UGT]). Groupings ideologically rooted in the Italian autonomous movement and articulated around social centers developed common initiatives under the name of Barcelona-Tremola and the Març-Attack collective. Finally, the Plataforma Catalana contra l'Europa del Capital included groups from Catalonia and the Basque Batasuna as well as other nationalist political forces. These groups' participation actually allowed the Spanish right-wing government, and the media under its control, to articulate a discourse associating the entire GJM and its protesters to violence and terrorism.

In Seville, the GJM campaigned around a single platform called the Foro Social de Sevilla (FSS), made up of ecologists, antimilitarists, students, feminists, neighborhood associations, minority trade unions (such as the CGT-Confederación General de Trabajadores, or SOC-Sindicato de Obreros del Campo), and left-wing parties like the communists of Izquierda Unida or the ecologists of Los Verdes. Neither the PSOE nor the key trade unions formed part of the protest alliance.

The main actions of the GJMs during the Spanish presidency were characterized by a hitherto unknown level of participation, as well as by the absence of any (remarkable) violent episodes.[24] These circumstances reinforced the positive image of the GJMs in Spanish public opinion, despite the delegitimizing strategy pursued by the Spanish Government of the Partido Popular (PP) (Jiménez 2003). In spite of the campaign's success in terms of mobilization capacity, critical global networks expressed their doubts as to the sustainability of the movement. Some sectors defended the need for a sounder organizational basis in order to create stable statewide structures of coordination, whereas others viewed this proposal as a threat to the network's flexibility, choosing instead to continue to coordinate only for specific mobilizations. The later dissolution of the MRG in Catalonia can be explained by the prevalence of the latter position.[25]

In the course of these campaigns, internal debate regarding the relationship between the movement (particularly its more radical sectors) and more institutional sectors (specifically political parties) gained relevance. In Barcelona, for example, the creation of the Foro Social de Barcelona (FSB), headed by political parties and trade unions, was regarded with a fair amount of distrust by key sectors of the Campanya, who viewed this event as an opportunistic electoral ploy in an attempt to attract more electors by referring to the antiglobalization movement's discourse.

The mobilizations in 2002 helped the articulation of a strong opposition against the occupation of Iraq in 2003, as well as other initiatives such as the European Social Consultation. For example, on February 15, the global day of protest against the imminent invasion of Iraq saw massive demonstrations in more than fifty-five Spanish cities with the participation, according to more conservative estimates, of three million people (Jiménez 2006).

However, the antiwar campaign also marked the initial phase of a period that could be classified as "ebbing" (González 2003; Calle 2005b; Echart et al. 2005), in which the intensity of the protests diminished and the movement's mobilization capacity markedly decreased, as shown during events such as the World Bank meeting held in Madrid in 2004 and subsequent antiwar rallies (even more, after Zapatero's withdrawal of the Spanish troops from Iraq) or the Referendum on the European Constitution. Several factors contributed to the decline of mass mobilization: 1) activists themselves were discouraged by the lack of visible progress on the global issues endorsed by the GJMs, 2) difficulties were encountered in coordinating the different networks at the national level during the Spanish EU presidency and antiwar demonstrations in 2003, 3) activities took place increasingly at the local level, and 4) many of the channels of access to the institutions and the media once open also to the more radical sectors of the GJMs were shut down following the PSOE's victory in the 2004 general elections.

From the organizational perspective, the declining levels of protest confirmed the traditional inability of the radical sector of social movements to consolidate stable statewide structures. With the exception of the local social forums and common spaces on the Internet (the different Indymedia servers in Spain—in particular in Madrid, Barcelona, Euskalherria, and Galiza—as well as Nodo50 or Rebelion), the new structures of participation have shown themselves to be too weak to sustain their protests (Attac, RCADE) or have almost disappeared altogether (most of the local MRGs, some forums like the Social Forum of Barcelona).

The Movement Identity: The Construction of a Meta-Frame around Radical Democracy

As already mentioned, the Spanish GJMs inherited from the leftist social movements some of their distinctive organizational characteristics such as the prevalence of decentralization and low levels of formalization. In fact, these features seem to distinguish the global movement in Spain from other cases analyzed in this book. The comparative analysis carried out in the framework of the Demos project on the basic documents of 244 groups in 6 European countries and at the transnational level, 37 of them rooted in Spain, indicates that the Spanish groups present the highest levels of "informality" and "localism": 84 percent of the organizations have a local level presence (against, for instance, 69 percent in France and 76 percent in Italy) and only 13 percent have formal statements about the goals of their organizations (whereas British, German, Italian, and Swiss organizations are more than 40 percent).

The same analysis also indicates the relative importance of what we have called the radical democracy meta-frame. In the discourse analysis of the organizational ideology expressed through basic documents of the mentioned European groups,[26] terms like *participatory democracy* are mentioned by 35 percent of the Spanish organizations, a figure above the average of the European sample (28 percent).

These facts are reflected in terms of discourses and patterns of coordination and repertoires of action exhibited by the (previously described) structures of mobilization developed, mostly, after the protest in Seattle. In all of them, we find coordination patterns that emphasize horizontality, decision-making processes based on consensus reached through local assemblies, and frames that stress democracy as a common basic value: citizen control of financial markets (Attac), citizen participation (RCADE), local autonomous spaces for action, challenges to the representative and capitalist systems (MRG), and so on.[27]

It can be argued that radical democracy provides for a common meta-frame, or a basic set of principles, underlining and connecting a series of networked claims (distribution of wealth, environmental sustainability, gender equality, etc.) that usually are referred to, in the mass media and in some academic works, as a general demand for global justice. This frame has facilitated the confluence of very diverse and atomized movements and groups. Similarly, heterogeneity is also reflected in terms of the individual profiles of participants in the new structures of mobilization, characterized by different ideological tendencies as well as generational belongings (although young people are more present in radical actions and groupings).

The radical democracy frame has been symbolically boosted by the Zapatistas, who advocate reinventing democracy without making appeals to closed narratives of social change, inviting instead experimentations and innovations—as expressed in their (well known in GJM circles) slogan: "*preguntando, caminamos*" ("asking, we walk"). This proposal is consistent with the spread of a critique of neoliberal globalization, perceived as an economic way of thinking that reduces the sovereignty of citizens and states in favor of supranational architectures such as international institutions and transnational corporations.

The radical democracy frame was strengthened in the course of the 1990s, not only because of the Zapatista influence and the new contention discourses coming from Latin American countries in general (Movimento dos Sem Terra, MST), but mainly owing to characteristics of the domestic political context at the end of the decade. First, activists realized the need to unite their efforts in order to overcome the wide atomization of social movement organizations.[28] Second, movement demands converged against the conservative turn of the PP policies and the increasing level of repression of protest. To a certain extent, social movements' confluence to oppose the judged undemocratic style of the government resembled the experiences of the coordination of movement organizations during the transition period that supported the protest for democracy.[29]

Third and last, new technologies such as the Internet, although not creating a "horizontal" culture, definitively amplify the possibilities to expand frames oriented to radical democracy by promoting exchanges between different ideologies and cultures of mobilization "from below." Practices such as the promotion of copyleft or free software are regarded as not only a mere technological tool to challenge big corporations' controls, but also as important political strategies oriented to build up horizontal relationships among citizens (see http://www.sindominio.net/faq.php3).

The emergence of the radical democracy frame acts as a pole of reference for the diverse sectors of political contention, introducing new practices and discourses: new social movements, labor movements, and, above all, new networks of participation established after the Seattle protests.[30] However, the radical master frame does not "force" traditional groups to renounce to their "old references."[31] In general, the labor movements still maintain the "class struggle" as an identitarian reference, no matter whether they are found on libertarian roots (CGT) or Marxist ones (Corriente Roja, a communist trend that left Izquierda Unida in 2004). Development NGOs instead tend not to make use of the radical democracy frame in order to sustain their demands; they prefer to adhere to "thematic" values like international solidarity, which has partially contributed to situating these groups, in the local field, at the borders of the GJM protests.

Furthermore, radical contention in Spain is also deeply rooted in traditional cultures of mobilization such as nationalism and libertarianism. These two cultures resonate with basic GJM characteristics such as horizontality and decentralization in terms of coordination and action. Nationalism has, however, two (contradictory) implications concerning social mobilization. On the one hand, nationalism (but also regionalism) represents a cultural opportunity to promote collective identities, helping the constitution of an "us" and the sharing of common worldviews. In the case of Spain, along with the process of political decentralization, nationalism has contributed to the establishment and the strengthening of protest campaigns in Catalonia and the Basque country. On the other hand, nationalism can also act as an ideological cleavage that keeps social actors from exploring new discourses and alliances (Kriesi et al. 1995).[32]

Libertarian roots are present in the Spanish GJMs: not so much in the form of historical references to anarchist revolutionary ideology (such as those represented by the Confederación Nacional del Trabajo [CNT]), but more as a hypersensitivity toward undemocratic power structures—as reflected in the active presence of libertarian activists in local struggles against urban development projects or in the defense of the labor rights of the most deprived citizens (as immigrants)—that connects and enhances anti-neoliberal discourses (Calle 2005a, 216). Specific practices of radical ecologism/pacifism or local autonomous groups (such as those present in the social centers) and most prominent libertarian organizations such as CGT have played a bridging function between libertarian and radical democracy paradigms.

Is it possible to identify diverse frames coexisting within the GJMs and structuring their networks? A way to address this question is to examine interorganizational linkages, of which Internet links to Web pages are a public expression. Also, Internet links can be displayed in order to orient visitors to Web sites where they can gather information (news sites, institutional references such as the United Nations Development Programme [UNDP], World Bank, United Nations, etc.). On this basis, we can depict two basic poles of reference. On the one hand, there are those organizations that predominantly orient their Internet links toward other networks involved in the GJMs (movement-oriented links). In most cases, these are either organizations linked to the radical sector of new social movements (ecologist, antimilitarist, etc.) or new (post-Seattle) organizational structures.[33] On the other hand, we identify in our sample a set of organizations that, rather than linking to other protest groups, prefer to redirect visitors to institutional sites (public administration, parties, and multilateral institutions). Here we find, mainly, institutionalized actors such as political parties (Izquierda Unida) as well as NGOs (national branch of Oxfam, Amnesty International, or national umbrella organizations such as Red Acoge, Coordinadora Estatal de Comercio Justo, etc.).[34]

The distinction between more movement-oriented and more institutionally oriented sectors tend to overlap with the one suggested by other authors between the "PGA environment" and "Attac environment." The first would be closer to international initiatives coming from networks such as PGA, Zapatismo, and Euromarches. The second would instead be more connected with the World Social Forum.[35]

In analytical terms, the differences between these two sectors are also reflected in their discourses and attitudes toward alliances with established political actors, and in terms of movement coordination. For instance, sectors allied with left-wing parties, such as the peak trade unions or networks such as Attac, aim at promoting a reform in world structures in order to "govern" capitalism in line with the most social-democratic stances seen in the World Social Forum. Groups that intervene locally (generally linked in horizontal networks) maintain that change must occur through the radical modification of everyday conditions considered as precarious or even devastating. They ask for the end of the current neoliberal labor policies (CGT and autonomous sectors), the rejection of patriarchy (feminists), or sustainable local models of production and consumption (ecologists), to name but a few. Yet, as we have said before, there are numerous groups that fall between these two organizational forms. For instance, networks such as RCADE alternate their work on global issues (abolishing foreign debt) with mobilization at the local level (some groups are active in neighborhood networks or in processes to demand direct democracy).

In terms of coordination, the more reformist sector stresses the need for a more stable structure, whereas the more radical groups share the opinion that the fundamental objective of the "network of networks" is to multiply and spread protests in a (more spontaneous) dynamic of resistance. Illustrative of this tendency, the MRG Catalonia's decision to dissolve came about from a reluctance to establish formal organizational structures:

> The MRG of Catalonia was founded as a network, a space for communication between collectives and initiatives. However, it began to turn into an identity, a static structure. We felt that it needed to be destroyed! […] We want to take steps forward, experiment, take risks. If there is one thing we have learned in these years of struggle it is that the time of hollow structures has ended. They form part of a past which is overcome by the rich reality of movements and the participation of civil society in Catalonia. The wealth of this widespread network cannot be reduced within the borders of any umbrella organization, even if certain objectives of the spaces of coordination have been useful at times. […] The movement is just that: something that moves. No static idea of forum, structure, organisation could speak in its name, nor can it serve as a substitute. (MRG public report, January 2003)

Tied to this discussion is the debate on whether to implement decision-making practices consistent with the radical democracy discourse or to adopt organizational models closer to the representative logic in order to achieve greater political pressure, introduce movement demands into the political agendas, and establish "symbolic alliances" with political parties. In general, hybrid models, whose most significant example can be found in local social forums, seem to be gaining ground.

A New Repertoire of Contention: The Modification of the Spanish Moderate Protest Culture

The cycle of protest associated with the emergence of the GJMs is, among other features, characterized by the generalization of civil disobedience initiatives and the search for alternative forms of public communication and debate. These emerging types of actions have been reproduced in several Spanish GJM initiatives, such as mass consultations and informal referendums (on foreign debt in 2000, war in Iraq in 2003, EU Constitution in 2004), reclaim-the-streets demonstrations, as well as the promotion of open and participatory spaces on the Internet (virtual assemblies, copyleft, etc.).

As for the reclaim-the-streets-like demonstrations, we could consider the counter-summit in Prague as the boost for this kind of initiative.[36] Back in Spain, the activists that had experienced the June 2001 protests against the World Bank emulated the "white overall" style of the Italian Disobbedienti there by organizing a demonstration against Barcelona's bourse. Nonauthorized demonstrations performed by nonviolent but civilly disobedient activists were held again in 2002, during the protest campaigns against the European Union in Barcelona (around one thousand people) and Seville (about one hundred). Joining similar initiatives in other European cities, more radical and colorful Maydays took place in Barcelona (more than one thousand people in 2004 and 2005) and Seville (a few hundred in 2005).

Above all, among the new networks, calls emerged for the development of a strategy of "social disobedience" (Iglesias 2002; Calle 2005a) that would crystallize in the amplification of old initiatives inside the GJMs (e.g., the questioning of taxes that could sustain military expenses, such as the one promoted by the Alternativa Antimilitarista-MOC), in the promotion of alternative technologies (e.g., the democratization of software and Internet access, see www.sindominio.net), or in anticonsumerism campaigns (see, e.g., www.yomango.org, www.boicotpreventiu.org).

The diffusion in Spain of new repertoires of civil disobedience experienced abroad contrasts with the limited attention paid to other types of movements' activities present in the political repertoires of GJMs in other contexts. According to the mentioned analysis of organizations' Web sites, although protest and mobilization are the most frequent functions/objectives explicitly mentioned (65 percent), organizations seem to invest fewer resources in other strategies such as spreading information/influencing the mass media/raising awareness (38 percent) or political education (30 percent).

The inclination of new global movements in Spain, as compared with other European organizations, to emphasize protest over the search for stable structures for collective action, could be explained by the influence of libertarian traditions favoring action over the elaboration of ideological constructions or the establishment of organizational infrastructures (Álvarez 1975, 272), as well as by the limited material resources and lack of potential (stable) allies among institutionalized actors. Consequently, platforms devoted to specific campaigns (the antiwar Aturem la Guerra or the Consulta Social Europea against the European Constitution) play a prominent role in the Spanish GJMs. They contribute mainly to maintaining a protest agenda in the short term. And, although campaigns are also oriented toward sensitizing citizens, they do not result in stable organizations capable of or willing to sustain educational or reflection tasks in the long term.

The modifications in the political repertoire introduced by the GJMs can be observed in table 4.1 that compares the resorting to various forms of collective mobilization among activists and the general population. Forms of protest have been ordered according to the differences in terms of use between activists and the general population (third column).

The results show not only that, as one could expect, activists resort to the selected forms of protest more frequently, but also that their repertoire is particularly different from the one of the general population in those forms

Table 4.1 The Protest Repertoire among GJM Activists

	% of Population*	% of GJMs Activists**	Differences*** (% Activists/ % Population)
Violence against Property	0.3	8.4	28.0
Occupation of Public Building	1.5	32.5	21.7
Protest through Internet/Mobile Phone	3.6	41.0	11.4
Boycott Products	6.0	47.0	7.8
Attend Demonstration	12.9	95.2	7.4
Take Part in a Strike	8.2	46.2	5.6
Sign a Petition	23.3	64.5	2.8

*Source: CIS: Estudio 2450, *Ciudadanía, participación y democracia* (2002). Figures indicate the percentages of those interviewed (Spaniards over the age of eighteen) who declared having carried out these forms of protest in the previous twelve months.

**Source: Tejerina et al. 2005. Figures indicate the percentage of activists interviewed who declared having resorted to these forms of protest.

***Figures indicate the ratio of the realization of the various forms of participation between activists and the general population.

that involve either a greater level of disruption, higher technical skills (such as the use of information communication technologies for expressing dissent), or the new political consumerism.

The use of symbolic violence is debated within the GJM. However, far from promoting the creation of "black blocks" at the EU counter-summits (2002), the bulk of activists involved in civil disobedience performed actions in the line of those invented by the Italian "white overalls" or British "reclaim the streets." Social disobedience seems to be more attractive in Spain, partially owing to the extended recognition and legitimacy gained by the peace movement against compulsory military service during the 1980s and 1990s.

Nevertheless, and not surprisingly, the recent history of police interventions with GJM protests in Spain presents similarity with the Italian case. In both cases, the model of "King's police" seems to prevail over the "citizens' police," a feature reinforced in Spain by an "incomplete political transition"—that is, the maintenance even after Franco's death of some features of the former regime, such as the use of police repression following governmental preferences on the specific protest demands.[37] In particular, police intervention at the demonstrations against the World Bank (Barcelona 2001) was severely criticized by all political groups except the conservative party PP, then in power. They were blamed for either being very harsh or even for provoking incidents in order to spread an image of "violence" on the part of GJM activists. Along the same lines, surveillance strategies were used—among others, in the control of GJM activists' Web sites. Both conservative and social-democratic governments have closed frontiers when an international summit was to be held. Repression of initiatives has been a consistent response when mobilization has developed around immigrant demands (Seville 2002, Barcelona 2004) or when elections have been selected as scenarios for actions such as citizens' consultations (against foreign debt in 2000, or about the EU project in 2004).

Based on a manipulated debate about "movement violence," the image of GJMs depicted by mass media and the political institutions themselves can be considered part of a state strategy oriented to discourage protests and claims by the GJMs that would challenge the programs or agendas of parties in power (see Calle 2005a, 155ff.). This political use of the media is facilitated by a high level of partisanship in the media and the absence of mass media sensitive to the demands of social movements. Indeed, the activities and demands of social movements conflicting with the sphere of interest of the main political parties have been given scarce media attention. For example, as we mentioned previously, in 2000 the self-managed referendum on the foreign debt of poor countries went unnoticed by the principal means of mass communication.

However, since the protest at Seattle, the Spanish press has paid increasingly greater attention to the mobilizations led by the GJMs. The moment of maximum coverage occurred during the Spanish presidency of the EU, during the first quarter of 2002. As in other countries, media attention had been principally focused on the issue of violence, and in spite of the strategy of criminalization by authorities, as shown by the high number of news stories about the security measures during the European Councils as well as in the repeated references to the GJMs.[38] Media interest was also increased by the police response to the movement. Nonetheless, the debate about the consequences of the current pattern of economic globalization has reached the media and political agendas. In addition, the Spanish public views the GJM in a favorable light[39]—undoubtedly owing in large part to the PSOE's openness to the social movements during the party's final period in opposition (2000–2004).

From this general perspective, the GJMs' success was undeniable. To a different degree, traditional leftist parties in Spain have incorporated the movement's critiques into their discourse.

In turn, these two different institutional responses to the GJM, the "repressive one" based on the security discourse and the "assimilative one" that, at the discourse level, incorporates the movement critique into the party competition dynamic, has intensified the process of construction of the public identity of the movement. In this context, during the Spanish presidency of the EU, the movement managed to find an equilibrium between a wide set of varied actors, from established political actors (such as the PSOE) to radical groups. These circumstances permitted the movement to counteract the criminalization strategy pursued by the right-wing government. Eventually, the absence of violence seemed to consolidate a positive public image. However, media coverage of the movement's demands and proposals did not correspond to the organizational efforts invested by the protest's organizers. The communication and press committees of both La Campanya and the FSS underlined this fact:

> The media were more interested in the events (data about the number of persons in the campsite, participation in the protest events) than in the alternative ideas debated in conferences and workshops. This situation is illustrated by the attitude of journalist during the press conference on the 22nd during which, while prestigious personalities like Eric Toussaint or Paul Nicholson were speaking, journalists preferred to leave the conference room to interview one of the Foro's spokesperson[s] about the details of the demonstration that was to take place [a] few hours later. (Comisión de Comunicación y Prensa, FSS, Report July 10, 2002)
>
> After the massive demonstration of March 16th we have the impression that media treatment has been correct, although the message has lost force. It has been hard to balance the resources of the FSB, which has tried to present the success as "its own achievement." We made an enormous effort to counteract the criminalisation's strategy, as a consequence we have been portrayed as the most civic movement, but at the price of losing the substantive message (against

the Europe of Capital). (Campanya contra l'Europa del Capital, Assembly's minutes, March 2002)

In both cases, the GJMs' perception about its capacity to get its message into the media discourse reflects the dilemmas and challenges that the media logic imposes on social movements. In this sense, both assessments confirm and complement previous findings about the nature of movement-media interaction. Concerning the media preference for institutional sources of information, La Campanya's considerations clearly reflect how the presence of the PSOE and other institutionalized actors in the FSB diminished the media coverage of core organizations of the GJMs.

In this sense, the success of the GJMs' efforts to countervail the criminalization strategy deployed by the national government not only diverted resources from the attempt to communicate the movement's demands, but also, to the extent that the GJMs in Barcelona put forward a peaceful image, the attention of the (national) media dropped off. The more peaceful the GJMs appear before public opinion, the greater the incentive of institutionalized actors to come close to the movement and act as "interlocutors" of the growing number of sympathizers. But despite the inclusion of the globalization problem into the media and political agendas, the GJMs find it difficult to get access to the public debate.

Conclusion

Shared experiences have boosted the confluence in the evolution of European leftist social movements from the 1990s onward: Prague 2000 (against the World Bank and IMF) acted as a European burst of Seattle-like protests. European Social Forums, the alternative summits surrounding it, PGA meetings, and less "mediatic" encounters (like the camps without borders) have facilitated contacts and promoted common protests (the marches against the Iraq invasion on February 15 were agreed on at the first European Social Forum in Florence). Networks such as Euromarches, Attac, or the campaign for foreign debt cancellation (Jubilee 2000, CADTM, RCADE, Rete Lilliput) strengthen the European ties. The Zapatista influence is especially strong in the Italian Tute Bianche, the British Wombles, and the supporting committees in Spain. Reclaim the Streets has become a protest repertoire of more autonomous and radical protests used, beyond Great Britain, in Spain, Italy, and other countries, under this name or during demonstrations such as the Maydays against precarious labor. In this sense, the GJMs in Spain have brought about the integration of Spanish political contention into the broader protest cycle experienced in other representative democracies.

Participation in global campaigns has acted as laboratories of actions producing a reconfiguration and expansion of interorganization and inter-movement alliances as well as the bridging of discourses on local and global problems, on issues of a different nature (i.e., labor and environmental), or between the North and the South, and so on, and the modification of the protest repertoire. This increasing interconnection has supported the emergence in Spain of the radical democracy meta-frame that is visible in personal attitudes (increase of multimilitancy, heterogeneity of groups), new organizational structures (from the end of the 1990s onward), and new and in some cases more radical repertoires of action that tend to facilitate organizational coordination and citizen participation.[40]

New technologies such as the Internet play a major role in promoting the extension of alliances, apart from being a powerful instrument of horizontal communication and struggle. The Internet is mainly used among grassroots and radical networks as a tool for action (offering the GJMs' calendar) and for the interchange of information (through open forums), particularly for post-Seattle organizations. In contrast, more formal organizations use it as a tool for education, funding, and gaining public visibility.[41]

Nevertheless, many of the characteristics that define this "movement of movements" in Spain are conditioned by the legacy of preexisting cultural and political patterns. From a cultural point of view, peripheral nationalisms and libertarian roots are two mobilization cultures that favor the decentraliza-tion of protests and the networking approach (in terms of coordination and discourses), above all when dealing with statewide campaigns or groups. In terms of political structures and alliances, we can note the absence of large organizations that give stability to the GJMs, as in other countries: Attac, SUD, and Confédération Paysanne in France, Attac in Germany; Attac, Arci, Rete Lilliput, or Disobbedienti in Italy. In particular, in comparison with other European countries, we notice the minor role played by large NGOs as well as more difficulties in establishing stable alliances with left-wing (parliamen-tary) groups, unlike in Italy (i.e., Rifondazione Comunista) or France (Liga Comunista Revolucionaria [LCR]).

Both cultural and political particularities, along with the existence of peripheral nationalisms, reinforce two features of GJMs in Spain. First, the greater atomization of groups compared with other countries: The local nodes of Attac that developed in several Spanish cities are not coordinated at the national level, and the same is true for the Indymedia servers. The high degree of horizontality makes it difficult to distinguish between more stable networks and more ad hoc coalitions (even for state organizations like Ecologistas en Acción).

With respect to the mass media, none of the Spanish dailies seems particu-larly sensitive to the demands of the GJMs. Thus their visibility in the public eye is dependent on the varying degree of support by institutional actors (principally the PSOE) or the media coverage of their violent actions. The PSOE's rise to power in 2004—which led to the closure of media opportunities—and its withdrawal from social forums and platforms against the occupation of Iraq have revived the traditional cleavage between members of the "alter-globalization" movement and "social democratic" sectors in Spain.

Notes

We thank Donatella della Porta for her valuable comments and editing suggestions.

1. We understand GJMs as a wide and varied set of protest networks that take part in (and identify with) the international cycle of contention and take regular part in major international events such as counter-summits and social forums.

2. *El País,* for instance, described as squatters a group of activists taking part in a protest event in Barcelona during the Seattle protests against the WTO meeting (*50 okupas irrumpen en la Bolsa de Barcelona* [50 squatters rushed into Barcelona's stock market]. *El País,* Cataluña edition, January 12, 1999).

3. The Spanish democratic transition not only established a closed political opportunity structure for excluded interests (such as many of those represented by new social movements), but also, as the literature on transitions has underlined, those decisions on institutional design that were taken as temporary measures remained unaltered as time passed, determining the functioning of democracy once the new regime consolidated (Karl 1990).

4. The executive has the capacity to influence the autonomy of other institutions such as the judiciary, the public mass media, the police, and so on.

5. Also, the crystallization of potential political opportunities linked to the process of political decentralization and the increasing multilevel nature of many decision-making processes has depended on the changing configuration of power.

6. Basically, these movements have found allies among established elites, either in the context of critical elections with the socialists in the opposition, or in those decision-making processes where different political parties were in power in the various territorial administrations involved.

7. The territorial configuration of the state in autonomies (or autonomous regions) has favored the organizational decentralization of both sectors of social movements, but in particular has reinforced the principle of local autonomy of radical groups in regions characterized by strong nationalist movements. Even groups that came into being under a statewide territorial scope (such as the Alternativa Antimilitarista-MOC and some NGOs) have experienced a trend toward decentralization.

8. We thank Benjamín Tejerina and his collaborators for providing us with this information.

9. As many as 67 percent of the activists interviewed in the mentioned survey were thirty years of age or younger (Tejerina et al. 2005).

10. Radical democracy can be presented as a new political paradigm that aims at promoting participation and deliberation (from social forums to new structures of

participation) and opposes the process of globalization "from above" as well as the political logic of representation and the orientation toward the provision of services by the more moderate NGOs.

11. As, for instance, free radios (Red con Voz), information agencies (ANIA), local television stations (Assemblea per la Comunicació Social), or journals (*Diagonal*).

12. Still earlier was the campaign against official celebrations of the discovery of America: Desenmascaremos el 92 (Let's unmask the 92).

13. Carrying out, from 1998 onward, decentralized campaigns in the cities of Madrid, Valencia, Córdoba, or Barcelona, under the name of Rompamos el Silencio (Break the Silence). These campaigns met once a year for a week at a time. The protests were organized in much the same way as the marches against unemployment (Euromarches): Each day the events revolved around a particular issue (unemployment, immigration, women's rights, economy and development, and so on).

14. Christian groups have been very active in grassroots movements (international solidarity, communist) as well as in leftist parties (IU, PSOE); see Díaz-Salazar (1996 and 1998).

15. See, respectively, www.pangea.org/ellokal/chiapas and www.mstmadrid.org.

16. According to the results obtained by Tejerina et al. (2005) in their survey of Spanish activists, 64 percent considered changes in patterns of alliances with other organizations as the main organizational change experienced as a consequence of participation in "antiglobalization" initiatives. New forms of action and mobilization (50 percent) and new discourses and targets (49 percent) are also highlighted as most remarkable changes. Also mentioned (by 27 percent of interviewees) are changes in the sociological profile of members (27 percent), although little change is perceived in the leadership or organizational structure.

17. The RCADE originated from several preexisting groups and mobilization experiences: mainly Plataforma 0.7 Percent, but also the individuals and groups supporting the Zapatista movement, Ecologistas en Acción, NGOs, Christian grassroots networks, and so on (see Calle 2002, RCADE 2001, www.rcade.org).

18. To launch decentralized initiatives such as the Popular Legislative Initiative in favor of international solidarity, the European Social Consultation, or, in 2005, on the problem of foreign debt, "Who owes who?"

19. The MRG, named Hemen eta Munduan in Euskadi and Navarra ("here and in the world"), developed from within preexisting informal networks such as the MAM, the autonomous sectors behind the "7 days of social protest" campaigns, and RCADE, successfully attracting many young people (Herreros 2001; Calle 2004). They emerged "from below," with widespread use of the Internet as a means of interaction, first in Barcelona and later all over Spain.

20. In fact, it soon became a reference for the PGA at the international level. However, given the lack of any structured statewide coordination, activities at the international level were limited to those undertaken by the groups themselves.

21. After the counter-summit in Prague, many of the groups took part in protests against the EU summit in Nice (groups from Cadiz and Catalonia), the World Economic Forum in Davos (groups from Catalonia and Madrid), Bové's trial in Montpellier (groups from the Basque Country and Saragossa), as well as in domestic contention related to the accident of the *Prestige* oil tanker near the Spanish coast, the National Hydrological Plan, and the immigration law.

22. From 2002 onward, many local social forums have emerged as initiatives promoted by a wide variety of groups attempting to implement at the local level the key principles and objectives of the World Social Forum at Porto Alegre. These new structures of participation also share the common goal (achieved to varying degrees) of bringing together groups with a variety of views, as well as organizing discussions and debates.

23. Attac groups in Spain were founded starting in 2000 as a consequence of an appeal made in 1998 by Le Monde Diplomatique. Compared with Attac France, Italy, or Germany, it is a more loosely organized coordination of local and autonomous groups (see www.attacmadrid.org and www.attac-catalunya.pangea.org). Their members, in the most classic style of traditional NGOs, support the group but do not take part in the decision-making processes. Their political strategies are mostly media oriented. Attac has more success in bringing together social-democratic sectors, including many intellectuals and liberal professionals, than more radical activists.

24. In Barcelona, 300,000 people participated in the main march, during which ninety-four people were arrested. In Seville, the number of participants was also very high (100,000), with only three arrests. In Madrid, another 100,000 participated in the demonstration organized during the EU-Latin America summit in May.

25. By 2003, reluctant to become a formal (static) organization, most of the MRG groups had dissolved. In Catalonia, some of the MRG's activists reorganized around the Xarxa de Mobilització Global (Global Mobilization Network) that mainly attracted communist and Trotskyist local groups.

26. These are documents referring to organizational ideology, including constitutions, documents of fundamental value or intent, a formally adopted program, a mission statement, the "about us" section of the Web sites, as well as their FAQs.

27. Similarly, in the activist survey conducted by Tejerina et al. (2005), participation was mentioned as a main priority of their organizations. More specifically, 49 percent and 32 percent of interviewed activists mentioned social participation and the promotion of spaces for citizens' participation, respectively, as the main goal of their organizations. Other issues regarded as important were gender equality (50 percent), human rights (45 percent), and environment and sustainable development (42 percent).

28. In this sense, early 1990s campaigns such as "Let's unmask the 92" or "50 Years Is Enough" can be considered as key learning experiences for subsequent attempts at coordination.

29. It is also manifested through slogans that became popular during the large mobilizations against the PP and which are central to understanding the massive protests on March 13, 2004, two days after the bombings in the Madrid railway station and one day before the general elections unexpectedly won by the PSOE: "*lo llaman democracia y no lo es*" (they call it democracy, but it isn't). See Sampedro (2005) for an analysis of the bridges between the frames and the physical networks of these protests and those of the GJMs. Even political parties supporting the GJMs, like IU, have stressed the demand for a "democracy from below" in their political programs.

30. For instance, Ecologistas en Acción emerged in 1998 as a network of ecologist groups (and networks) adopting participatory internal practices and prone to encouraging protests and process of coordination within the GJM (members were

very active in the *consultas sociales* of 2000 and 2004 about foreign debt, the antiwar campaign in 2003, the opposition to the EU constitution, and so on).

31. As after the 1970s, when political parties embraced gender or environmental discourses without renouncing their workers' roots.

32. For instance, in the Basque country, different views about the "national issue" kept the Foro Social de Euskal Herria from going beyond one meeting.

33. In our sample we find groups such as RCADE, Alternativa Antimilitarista-MOC, Ecologistas en Acción, Xarza Mobilizacio Global, Indymedia, Nodo 50, Foro Social de Sevilla, Foro Social de Palencia, Red de Apoyo Zapatista, Plataforma Rural, and so on. Even within this sector we can distinguish between those groups with preferences for thematic Web links and those that link instead with transnational GJM actors (social forums, alternative encounters organized by PGA sectors) or events (global days of action, women's world march, etc.).

34. However, we also have organizations, like Attac-Madrid, Jóvenes-Izquierda Unida, and STE, which make use of both strategies.

35. Despite the analytical value of this distinction, in practice it is difficult to establish clear-cut divisions: Internal debates within the GJMs usually involve multiple poles and sectors rather than a clear "confrontation" of these two sectors (González 2003; Echart, López, and Orozco 2005, 60).

36. These forms of demonstration were, somehow, already practiced by activists in the squatters' milieus, with distinctive features such as no demand for authorization, party-style march (with music etc.), and the reclaiming of public spaces as a most prominent message (Adell 2004).

37. On this, see della Porta and Reiter (1998b); Jaime-Jiménez and Reinares (1998); Jiménez (2005, 168).

38. This section reports on a study of the construction of the GJM's public identity during the Spanish presidency of the EU (2002), based on news items appearing in *El País* newspaper (see Jiménez 2003; Jiménez and Alcalde 2002).

39. Different surveys converged in indicating that the Spanish citizens feel that "antiglobalization" protests have aroused their awareness about injustices caused by the advance of the so-called globalization. See CIS Study n. 2606 at www.cis.es and Flash EB (2003); "Globalisation Report," Flash Eurobarometer, http://europa. eu.int/comm/public_opinion/flash/FL151bGlobalisationREPORT.pdf, n.151b.

40. This meta-frame would be more present in southern Europe as a consequence of the existence of more contacts with Latin American networks (such as the Zapatistas or Movimiento de los Sem Terra), as well as the most prominent critics of the national democratic systems.

41. Even if the analysis of movement organization Web sites conducted within the Demos Project indicated that the relative weakness in resources of the Spanish organizations is reflected in reduced use (e-mail, search engines, online education, news sites).

Chapter Five

The Global Justice Movement in France

Isabelle Sommier and Hélène Combes

Seattle is presented as the birth date of the global justice movement (GJM).[1] But, as many authors have emphasized, the GJM has taken very specific national trajectories and developed at a different pace, in a different way, and with different actors, depending on the particular context in each country. In France, its dynamic was made possible by the reorganization of the protest movement, which had begun by the end of the 1980s (Sommier 2003). It expanded with the 1995 strikes against the retirement reform plan; new organizations and new activist characteristics emerged at that time. These circumstances gave the French GJM several specific features, especially its social aspect and its particular relation to politics.

Above all, one must keep in mind the impact on France of François Mitterrand's election to the presidency in 1981, which brought the Left back into power after twenty-three years in the opposition and put on the governmental agenda a number of demands voiced by the social movements of the 1970s, especially those of homosexuals and women (coverage of abortion costs, improvement in the condition of independent women, professional equality, and so on). This change resulted in declining mobilization of the new social movements, as their actions were oriented toward lobbying and direct collaboration with the Socialist government. Feminism, for example, receded as a social movement and was redirected toward interest-group actions. The subordination of the struggle to the electoral outcome (and thus to partisan strategies), as well as internal conflict over the issue of "reformism," helped to create and reinforce divisions already present within each family of the movement, such as the ecologists.

At the same time, traditional mass organization entered a period of crisis. First of all, it should be noted that political parties and unions have always been structurally fragile in France. Furthermore, as in most Western countries, they faced significant erosion during the 1980s, together with a major crisis of confidence. Membership in political parties dropped from 875,500 in 1982 to 628,000 ten years later. This decline, which indeed was not as spectacular as in other countries, because of the structural weakness of mass organizations in France, clearly had a greater impact on left-wing parties, whereas traditional and radical right-wing parties began to grow, partly filling the gap. The penetration rate of political parties (number of party members in proportion to the number of registered voters) in French society is the lowest in Europe (2.6), compared, for instance, with the United Kingdom (3.3), Italy (9.7), Belgium (9.2), or Austria (21.8) (Ysmal 1994, 50). The trend was particularly obvious where trade unions were concerned: According to estimates, unions lost half their membership between the mid-1970s and mid-1980s. With union membership rate estimated at approximately 9 percent of the active population today, hiding a definite cleavage between the private and public sectors (8 percent in the private sector versus 26 percent in the public and semipublic sector), France is, here again, in the worst position among the Western countries. The yearly number of labor-management conflicts in the private sector dropped, for example, from an average of more than four thousand in the early 1970s to three thousand in 1982; since 1992, it has reached the lowest level since the post–World War II period, with an average of fifteen hundred. Similarly, the number of strikers has declined, with an average of about two million in 1970 and two hundred thousand in 1990.

Under these circumstances, France's mobilization capacities look peculiar and ambivalent in comparison with those of its European partners. In France, the crisis of traditional activism seems stronger and deeper than elsewhere. In spite of—or perhaps because of—the weakness of traditional interest groups, France is periodically shaken by massive social conflicts, which keep surprising its neighbors and even nourish the stereotype of a permanent "French fever."

While traditional organizations (trade unions and political parties) were facing a substantial decline in membership during the 1980s and 1990s, the number of associations governed by the Law of 1901 increased twofold. These associations vary in form and type. They are viewed positively for their local community involvement, pragmatic projects, flexibility, active membership, and provision of services. The majority of these organizations are involved in environmental issues. Between 1980 and 1995, forty thousand associations specializing in these areas were created. Humanitarian associations focused on Third World countries and human rights issues also grew in number, and in the 1980s, social solidarity associations were set up, such as the "Restos du coeur" founded by the humorist Coluche. This period was also characterized by the rise of antiracism groups such as SOS-racisme (founded in 1983) and the Mouvement immigration banlieues (1995), which uphold immigrants' rights in a context of growing racism and radical right-wing parties. These new organizations focus on "rebuilding social ties around specific concrete goals rather than rebuilding political meaning" (Barthélémy 2000, 121). They are the *single-issue groups*. Many of them have become highly institutionalized, providing social services that were formerly the responsibility of the welfare state.

New forms of collective action (in particular, new styles of unions and "movements of the dispossessed") emerged quite successfully in terms of visibility as well as mobilization. In 1988, the movement of the unemployed started occupying unemployment insurance office buildings; in 1990, homeless people began setting up camps in Paris streets and public squares and organized squats of empty buildings. Five years later (1995), the largest strike since 1968 took place; in 1997, the new movement of civil disobedience of immigration laws expanded; and so on. A new cycle of protest seemed to arise, with the intensified development of broader, more widespread social conflicts, greater efficiency, and new structuration of social movement organizations (SMOs). New issues and analyses appeared, circulated, and evolved. Since 1995, the term *the social movement* has become an identifying label for activists and helped to create a homogeneous area of contention.

This dynamic at once revealed and produced a transformation of the Left: The context of political change between the Right and the Left transformed the image of the Socialist Party (PS) and provoked deep disappointment regarding the possibilities of political change—whereas the French Communist Party (FCP) drastically declined and the other parties on the left were excluded from Parliament. The "policy of rigor" implemented by socialist governments, and their inability to control rising unemployment and poverty, were a source of great disappointment and adversely affected the Socialist Party's image. On the other hand, the social context seemed to favor a different Left, critical toward the institutional Left. Increasingly, this associative or "movementist" Left (*gauche mouvementiste*) challenged the governmental Left and presented itself as the "real Left." The gap between them was interpreted as the expression of a process whereby activism gained political autonomy (Péchu 2001; Mathieu 2004).

The Multiple Origins of the GJM

The Prerequisites for the GJM

The renewal of protest was not just a factor in the emergence and development of the French GJM, it was a necessary factor. After the apathy of the early 1980s, the reorganization of some families of the social movement can be symbolized by two dates. The first is the 1989 Bicentenary of the French Revolution (Agrikoliansky 2005). Alongside the official celebrations and the G7 meeting in Paris that took place at the same time, two initiatives that can be viewed as prefiguring the GJM, rallied unions, humanitarian associations, human rights associations, and left-wing political parties around the issues of debt, solidarity with the South, the policies of international institutions, and the environment. A demonstration followed by a concert on July 8 and then an "alternative summit" on July 15 focused on the issue of canceling Third World debt. Both events also marked a transformation within the sphere of activism and solidarity that gave rise to the initiatives. The name change from Centre d'études anti-impérialistes, founded in 1966 by the "Pieds rouges" (Left and extreme Left government employees performing alternative military service while also engaged in the anticolonial struggle), to Centre d'études et d'initiatives de solidarité internationale (CEDETIM), reveals a rapprochement with Christian Third World organizations and the emergence of a reconfiguration of humanitarian-based international solidarity.

The year 1995 was definitely the key moment in the reorganization of the spectrum of the protest movement and was seen by some as the "first revolt against economic globalization." First of all, because it appeared as an exception in the context of the significant decline in strikes, given the very strong mobilization of state and public service employees against the Juppé[2] plan of special retirement programs, with 3.7 million person-days on strike in the public sector and two million in the private sector. It publicly formalized the shift within traditional unionism, symbolized by the struggle for petitions concerning retirement system reform: On one side, the CFDT[3] against the strikers; and on the other side their supporters, mainly traditional unions, that is the CGT and FO[4] as well as radical or radicalized unions such as the FSU[5] and new unions federated in the Group of 10.[6] It also tended to establish a connection between the unions and the "*sans*" (dispossessed) movement that emerged in the second half of the 1980s (Sommier 2003, 104–107; Mouchard 2002). The shift increased in 2003 with the mobilization against the Fillon[7] project to reform the retirement system for state employees, and against the reform of unemployment benefits for *intermittents du spectacle* (temporary workers in the cultural and artistic sector), in June 2003: 68 percent of the French activists who participated in the European Social Forum (ESF) in November 2003 had taken part in the strike movement during spring 2003, and 36 percent had been active in the *intermittents* movement.

The experience of 1995 created a dynamic of selective alliances: CGT involvement with undocumented immigrants in 1996; squats of unemployment insurances office buildings by unemployed people with the support of unions (CGT, SUD, CNT);[8] mobilization against the unemployment benefit reform that brought together the CGT, FSU, Group of 10, DAL, and Agir ensemble contre le chomage! (AC!) in May 2000; sporadic strikes since the autumn of 2001 of the temporary workers in the fast food sector (McDonald's and Pizza Hut), including Dd!,[9] the CNT, SUD, and CGT. In any case, the 1995 strikes represented a break in the recent history of collective action by remobilizing activists and building bridges between the trade unions and new associations. This dynamic enabled the organization of European marches against unemployment, associating various groups in the European Union during the spring of 1997. Starting from Sarajevo, Tangiers, Lapland, and Ireland, the cortèges went through French, Spanish, Italian, German, British, and Swiss towns and ended up bringing together fifty thousand participants in Amsterdam on June 14, 1997. The experiment was repeated two years later, with thirty thousand people converging to demonstrate "against unemployment, precariousness, and exclusion" in Cologne, where a summit of the European Union and the G8 was being held.

The year 1995 was also important for the renewal of feminist struggles with a demonstration, organized at the initiative of the CADAC,[10] mobilizing around one hundred associations representing about forty thousand people on November 25 to denounce the "return of a moral order" favored by the policies of the right-wing government. Afterward, the Collectif national des droits des femmes (National Collective of Women's Rights) was set up, holding a national meeting in favor of women's rights in March 1997 that employed demonstrations and lobbying (participation in discussions on abortion and the thirty-five-hour workweek). For other families of the social movement or groups like the Confédération paysanne (Farmers' Confederation), 1995 signaled a change that encouraged more proactive mobilizations and collaboration with other organizations involved in "the social movement."

The Stages of the GJM

Before the first label of the movement (*antimondialisation*) emerged in 1999, several events can be considered as structuring the GJM. Two of them revealed the symbolic domination of two organizations: Attac and the Confédération paysanne. Another appeared to be a trailblazing event. Before Seattle, the French organizations were indeed a driving force in causing the breakdown of the international negotiation of the MAI (Multilateral Agreement on

Investment), conducted under the aegis of the Organization for Economic Cooperation and Development (OECD) during the winter of 1997–1998. The mobilization began after the agreement documents were revealed on the Internet, uniting various organizations, trade unions (e.g., SUD and the CGT finance branch), associations (e.g., DAL and AC!), think tanks (Global Citizens, Observatoire de la mondialisation, etc.), as well as individuals, notably filmmakers, who circulated a number of petitions. As mobilization and public debate increased, the French government broke off the negotiations, and no agreement could be reached.

The GJM is obviously largely associated with one organization: Attac. The Association for the Taxation of Financial Transactions for the Benefit of Citizens was created in June 1998 by Bernard Cassen, a professor at the University of Paris VIII (formerly the University of Vincennes and well-known locus of post-1968 critical thinking) and director of *Le Monde Diplomatique,* following an editorial by Ignacio Ramonet, entitled "Disarm Financial Markets." Its success was immediate. The association had 35,000 members and 150 local committees (Denis 2005).[11] Several well-known personalities from a variety of backgrounds as well as organizational entities engaged in reconfiguring the sphere of protest (Confédération paysanne, the Group of 10, SUD-PTT, AC!, DAL, Dd!, and so on) are members of Attac. It is managed in a very original way. In addition to a conventional board of directors and a national office, Attac is supervised by a scientific council made up of researchers, university professors, and trade union activists. The monthly journal (*Lignes d'Attac*) and a collection of publications aim at providing arguments for expertise and promoting a "Movement of Popular Education oriented toward Action" that eloquently expresses the GJM's search for alternative knowledge. Based on its platform, its founding members, and its project it is indeed the French organization most massively oriented toward the production of counter-analyses. France was lagging behind many other countries in building up activist expertise, particularly the North American continent and its "file activism," which included organizing conferences, producing counter-reports challenging official reports, decoding texts, and so on. Attac is also the French organization with the broadest international ramifications (about forty national groups). Originally, it was aimed at fighting for the implementation of the Tobin tax (the name was taken from the Nobel Prize winner in economics in 1981) on financial transactions, corresponding to a deduction of 0.05 percent. But like other organizations, Attac's strength is due in large part to its key position at the crossroads of several struggles and, consequently, to its readiness to "globalize the struggles" not only into the economic and financial but also the social and environmental fields. It should be noted that the range of issues it deals with has been considerably enlarged from the time of its creation to the present day.

On August 12, 1999, between two and three hundred sheep breeders gathered around José Bové, the spokesman for the Confédération paysanne (Farmers' Confederation) and started dismantling a McDonald's restaurant in Millau to protest the heavy taxation of Roquefort cheese by the United States.[12] A few days later, four activists, one of them José Bové, who has become a symbol of the struggle against "*la malbouffe*" ("bad food," i.e., fast food sold by large corporations), were arrested. During their trial in 2002, at the beginning of the following summer, more than forty thousand activists met for two days to "put globalization on trial." The verdict was dissuasive: a ten-month jail sentence, with nine months suspended. At the same time, José Bové was sued for having dismantled the research on genetically modified organisms (GMO) at the National Institute of Agronomic Research (INRA, Institut National de Recherches Agronomiques) in Montpellier and sentenced to three months in jail. A huge solidarity movement was organized to demand his release, with a petition to obtain a pardon from the president of the republic.

Bové's sentence led to a widespread outcry for several reasons. The criminalization of activist actions was becoming more and more frequent in France. Furthermore, the difference in the government's attitude toward the diverse organization of farmers was patently obvious: Attac's competitor, the FNSEA,[13] was not penalized for its actions, whereas Confédération paysanne actions not only drew a sizable police presence but also resulted in criminal proceedings. Court action merely served to attract further media coverage of the anti-GMO movement and, more generally, of the movement against "*la malbouffe*." Starting in 2003, José Bové distanced himself from the Confédération paysanne and became involved with a new group, the Collective of Voluntary Reapers. This collective, mostly active in southwest France, aims at destroying the testing of transgenic plants in open fields and advocates civil disobedience. Elected officials, especially from the Green Party, take part in the group's actions wearing their tricolor scarves.

Since 2000, the label *antimondialisation* has commanded attention from the media. For example, there were forty-four references to the movement in the daily newspaper *Le Monde* in 2000, rising to 211 in 2001 and 188 in 2002—with references in the latter year marked by the gradual substitution of "alter" in place of "anti" (Contamin 2005). After the gathering at Millau, the most important GJM event in France was the protest held during the European summit in Nice in December 2000, where unions and movements of the "dispossessed" were still predominant.

Attac and the Confédération paysanne were to be instrumental in promoting the new cause. The idea of holding the first counter-summit in Porto Alegre, parallel to the one in Davos, was a joint initiative of the Brazilians and the French, led by Attac with Bernard Cassen and the Peasant International Via Campesina, with the Confédération paysanne playing a leading role.

The French delegation, with five hundred activists, was the largest European delegation in 2001. During the second counter-summit, held in January 2002, it was decided, largely at the behest of the Italians and the French, to import the forum format to the European continent.

The organization of the ESF in Paris in November 2003 was another important step for the French GJM. Several months earlier, from May 30 to June 6, 2003, on the occasion of the G8 summit in Evian, a series of demonstrations aimed at denouncing neoliberal globalization took place on both sides of the Franco-Swiss border in Annemasse, Geneva, and Lausanne, and an alternative summit (*Sommet pour un autre monde*) was organized. Among the French groups participating in the mobilization (38 percent of the participants were French), trade unions (SUD, and G10, as well as FSU and CGT) still played a central role (Fillieule et al., 2004). The mobilization was characterized by clearer involvement on the part of NGOs working on development issues (such as CEDETIM), some of them marked by a Christian heritage, as well as associations specializing in popular education or immigration issues.

During the ESF, 51,000 participants attended 55 plenary conferences, 271 seminars, and 280 workshops. According to ESF figures, 80,000 people attended the closing session. The organization of the ESF gave widely varying organizations that did not traditionally work together a chance to meet, fostering ties between competing organizations (Agrikoliansky and Sommier (with Hajji) 2005, 292). However, the differences were also clear. Some groups, such as the young people of "Intergalactics" (Réseau intergalactique 2003), criticized the institutionalization of the ESF; media activists and anarchists decided to organize simultaneously independent forums (MetallosMedialab and the libertarian social forum, respectively) to differentiate themselves from "reformists" while joining them in the demonstrations. This "antagonist area" was more palpable during large-scale gatherings such as the alternative village organized for four days at the anti-G8 protest, or at the major meeting organized under the slogan "The World Is Not for Sale" in July 2003 on the thirtieth anniversary of the struggle of the Larzac farmers against a military camp and in view of the WTO summit in Cancún, Mexico. More than 150,000 people attended. Twenty-three percent of the French participants in the ESF (November 2003) had taken part in the Larzac meeting four months earlier.

The Multiorganizational Field of the French GJM

The multiple affiliations of activists are essential to understanding the French networks. They allow people to claim allegiance to a specific organization, while at the same time giving them the feeling of being a part of a

Table 5.1 French Activists Involved in the Anti-G8 and 2003 ESF

	Anti-G8 Evian (N = 841)	Second ESF (N = 1,413)
Alter or No-Global	30.8	40.9
Union	14.5	34.6
Humanitarian Organization	15.4	25.8
Environmentalist Organization	16.4	19.2
Political Party	17.4	17.0
Pacifist Organization	7.9	18.0
Human Rights Organization	12.2	18.6
Organization against Racism	13.0	16.0
Feminist Organization	5.3	10.0
Solidarity Organization	11.7	16.0
Gay and Lesbian Organization	2.7	4.5
Antagonist Area	5.3	3.6
Neighborhood	6.7	12.5
Youth Organization, Popular Education	10.5	17.9
Student Union	14.1	12.9
Religious Organization	6.1	9.2
Consumer Organization	4.0	6.7
Independent Media Network	–	7.2
Farmers' Organization	1.9	3.3
Movements of the "Dispossessed"	8.9	8.3
Other Organization	15.7	12.5

Source: Centre de recherches politiques de la Sorbonne surveys

homogeneous whole.[14] According to the ESF survey, activists declare they are affiliated with an average of 2.4 organizations, including 1.5 in an active way (the average is 2.7 for the anti-G8 activists).[15] Of course, the largest organizations in the ESF, such as Attac, are specifically related to global justice. Forty percent of the activists are affiliated to one of these organizations but always combined with membership in another. Thirty-five percent are affiliated with trade unions, reflecting their predominant position within the French GJM. Humanitarian organizations come next in line (26 percent), followed by environmentalist associations (19 percent), political parties (17 percent), pacifist (18 percent) and human rights organizations (19 percent), organizations against racism (16 percent), feminist organizations (10 percent), solidarity organizations (16 percent), and so on (see table 5.1). Two-thirds of the members of these organizations claim to have an active role.

For young participants, the hierarchy of the organizations changes drastically: Trade unions, which come in second place for the overall total of participants, drop to fifteenth place. Logically, the youth and student movements tend to be predominant among the young population of our sample, together with the pacifists and "autonomous" groups. As Fillieule and Blanchard (2005, 161–162) note, in contrast, young people are less involved in political parties and organizations against racism, solidarity, neighborhood, and religious associations.

Although the primary pool of activists comes from organizations specializing in the denunciation of neoliberalism and hence recently created (mainly Attac), they are in the minority among the organizations that participate and even organize GJM events. For instance, the Comité d'initiatives français that organized the second ESF was made up of three hundred groups, including seventy-six trade unions,[16] twenty-four humanitarian or solidarity associations, twenty-one journals or think tanks, fourteen environmental groups, and so on (Agrikoliansky and Sommier [with Hajji] 2005, 291). The founding dates of the main organizations involved in the GJM in each family (32) can be viewed in relation to the national timeline. Of the total, 15.6 percent were set up before 1968, 25 percent between 1969 and 1989, 37.5 percent between 1990 and 1999, and 15.6 percent after 2000. Thus, 65.6 percent were created after 1981, the year in which the Left came to power, and half were created after 1995, the year of the movement against the social security reform plan, which also marked the "renewal" of protest in France. As many as 21.8 percent of the organizations in the sample came into existence after 1998, the year in which Attac was founded, and correspond to the GJM generation in the strict sense.

The GJM can be seen as a cooperative sphere associating, in varying degrees and ways depending on the stakes and events (demonstrations, campaigns, forums, counter-summits, and alternative spaces), with several movement families that have undergone, over a number of years, a revival of activities and/or symbolic radicalization marked by a refounding event.

New unions of employees and farmers have played a central role in GJM development. Among farmers, the Confédération paysanne was founded in 1987 with the unification of two associations influenced by Marxism in the 1970s and also opened up to New Social Movements (NSMs) such as ecological and antimilitary movements. It contests the dominant farmers' union, FNSEA (Fédération Nationale des Syndicats d'exploitants agricoles), which is well integrated in the state apparatus and refuses high-yield farming practices. The Confédération paysanne focuses on finding an alternative method for agricultural production that meets environmental requirements (biological agriculture, favorable to rural development), with human-sized farms and a sense of solidarity with farmers in Third World countries (Purseigle 2005). Its opening to the international level was facilitated by international ties forged during the Larzac struggle against the expansion of a military camp (1970–1981). The Confédération paysanne also inherited its "direct action" approach from the 1970s (destruction of the GMO fields). With José Bové, it shows a special talent for capturing media attention. Its spokesman is highly skilled at articulating the problems of society today (see for instance *la malbouffe*) and cultivates in his speech and physical appearance the image of the farmer who is the master of his traditions. However, both the excessive media coverage of José Bové and his strategic choices of action have led to internal tensions.

The employee unionism has undergone deep changes with the new unions SUD (Solidaires, Unitaires, Démocratiques). The first SUDs were created in the 1980s by unionists that had been thrown out from CFDT. Today, there are about thirty SUDs; most of them have joined the Group of 10 federation (Groupe des 10, now Union syndicale Solidaires). In 1998, a protest agenda denounced the injustices of the market economy and underlined the importance of environmental issues and the preservation of public services. Their members are characterized by a commitment to a wide range of social and civil rights issues. They also belong to many networks, such as Agir ensemble contre le chômage! (AC!, Acting Together against Unemployment) and Attac. This is a typical feature of the new organizations: They increase the number of their areas of action, thereby modifying the traditional typology of collective action. Furthermore, this new type of unionism became involved in societal issues and in building links among all types of social conflicts for three reasons: the influence of radical leftist thinking, the determination to fight corporatism, and the call to widen the struggle (in continuity with 1968). The goal is to achieve a synthesis between unions and NSMs. SUD has become a central actor in national and transnational mobilizations and is in the forefront of the GJM in France. As a result of its involvement and the success of GJM issues, traditional unions are showing interest in it (Béroud and Ubbiali 2005). The Confédération paysanne and the SUD have many points in common: They share the aim of developing unionism for social change and continuing to support causes such as rights for the unemployed and undocumented immigrants. They are often members of organizations such as Attac and are major actors in the global justice movement.

New unionism, especially SUD, is historically linked to the *sans* (dispossessed) organizations, especially the jobless, which succeeded in bringing the issues of exclusion and precariousness into the center of public debate during the second half of the 1980s. This has also shaken up traditional unionism, which has been blamed for insufficiently representing the most vulnerable members of society. These new associations are obviously challenging the unions in terms of social questions, as events organized by the GJM, such as the FSF, demonstrate. The associations were to help push the union confederations to join in the transformations under way, most notably that of the nascent antiglobalization movement. Two of them are predominantly involved in it: AC!, created in 1993, was behind the Euromarches against precariousness and unemployment in 1997 and 1999; the DAL (Droit au logement, Right to Housing, founded in 1990) aims at connecting the struggles of the homeless with the transnational network No Vox.

A second center is made up of humanitarian organizations and movements for the defense of human rights. The older humanitarian organizations have a denominational origin, such as Secours catholique and the CCFD (Comité catholique contre la faim et pour le développement, Catholic Committee against Hunger and for Development, 1961), or an anticolonial mission such as Terre des hommes (1963), the CEDETIM (1966), or Ritimo, which, since 1985, has associated with forty-five documentation centers in the Third World that were established since the 1970s. Others are more recent, such as umbrella organizations of local associations: Artisans du monde (1974) and Max Havelaar (1988), dedicated to fair trade; Peuples solidaires (1984) and 4D (Dossiers et débats pour le développement durable, 1993), dedicated to sustainable development; Survie against hunger (1984); *Agir ici* (1988); and so on. These associations have federated around the CRID (Centre de recherche et d'information pour le développement, Research and Information Center for Development, created in 1976), which now brings together forty-seven international solidarity associations (like the Cimade, the CCFD, Frères des Hommes or, Solagral). The CRID is oriented toward expertise and lobbying and is involved in forums and counter-summits, such as the Summit for Another World (Sommet pour un autre monde, SPAM), organized with the CEDETIM during the mobilization against the G8 summit in Evian in 2003.

The movements for the defense of human rights are now associated in the GJM (essentially in forums), above all as groups with high expertise to provide to the GJM, for instance on the issues of immigrants' and demonstrators' rights. They are of two types: movements on a transnational scale such as the Human Rights League (Ligue Française pour la défense des droits de l'homme et du citoyen, founded in 1898 in the context of the Dreyfus Affair) and Amnesty International (whose French branch was founded in 1971, ten years after the founding of AI), or on a strictly French scale, such as the Cimade (a Protestant association created in 1939) or the GISTI (Group for Information and Support of Immigrants, set up in 1972). Today, they have in common the struggle against racism and violations of the rights of foreigners, particularly police violence. It is for this reason that they formed legal teams during GJM demonstrations.

The NSMs have always been weak in France, and they faded away during the 1980s. Their new visibility, after this period of latency, confirms Verta Taylor's thesis about abeyance structures (Taylor 1989). Among them, environmental protection movements such as the antinuclear movement and anti-GMO movement are the most visible. Feminists remobilized on the occasion of the preparation for a national demonstration in 1995 and then for the "World March of Women against Violence and Poverty," which took place at the headquarters of the UN on October 17, 2000. The pacifist movement is rather weak in France and is linked to political parties, particularly the French Communist Party, which started the Peace Movement, Mouvement de la Paix, in 1948. One might also add the small Mouvement pour une alternative non violente (MAN; or Movement for a Nonviolent Alternative), founded in 1974 by Jean-Marie Muller, and Agir contre la guerre (ACG; Act against War), created in January 2002. Thus, in spite of the appeal signed by about a hundred organizations, the worldwide demonstration for peace on February 15, 2003, was weaker in France than elsewhere (around 250,000 people in Paris).

The parties on the left are still present, but they work discreetly, for example through the intermediary of a journal or youth organization, either because their presence is officially prohibited (during social forums) or problematic (in particular for the Socialist Party). The Trotskyite LCR (Ligue communiste révolutionnaire, created at the end of the 1960s) plays a central role because of the staunch commitment of its activists in several families of the movement and because of its strategy of building a "Left-Left pole," mostly based on movement activism. The Communist Party became involved later on, especially after the organization of ESF, because it controls three municipalities where the ESF took place. The Green Party is also present through environmental associations and in anti-GMO campaigns developed since 1999, above all in 2003. The ties between the GJM and political parties grew stronger during the campaign against the European Constitution and, more broadly, in the political context of a rightist government and the crises of the Left, particularly since April 2002 when the socialist candidate Lionel Jospin failed to reach the second round of the presidential elections. Libertarian parties occupy a special place. The Anarchist federation, Alternative libertaire and No Pasaran, which grew out of antifascist movement renewal in the 1980s (the SCALP, Section carrément anti-Le Pen, against the National Front leader) operate in the antagonist area of the GJM that organizes separate initiatives alongside the "official" ones.

The last important center is made up of intellectual (in the widest sense) initiatives. Movements have often sought "people resources" to support their causes—either personalities with good media coverage or experts. They seek support from individuals with professional skills useful in defending their cause, such as lawyers, economists, and others. This recourse has given intellectuals a new position, first theorized in the 1970s by Michel Foucault with the notion of the "Specific Intellectual." From this point of view, the strike movement of November–December 1995 was a turning point: Pierre Bourdieu became the intellectual figure of critical thinking, and France began to overcome the disadvantage of lagging behind in expertise.

What is known as the "intellectual awakening" started with the "petition battle" within the intellectual milieu on the issue of the retirement system reform plan in 1995: a petition in favor of it revolving around the journal *Esprit* and a petition "in support of the strikers" revolving around Bourdieu.

It should be noted that the petition form of action continued in 1997 with the call for civil disobedience against the Debré law on the status of immigrants.[17] In this context, a series of new groups came into existence: Appel des économistes pour sortir de la pensée unique (Call from Economists to escape from single-minded thinking), Acrimed (Action critique medias—Media Critique Action), and Raisons d'agir (Reasons for Action) with Bourdieu in 1996. In the following years, new intellectual journals such as *Multitudes, Vacarme* (initiated by Act-Up Paris), *Mouvement,* and the Trotskyite *Contretemps* came out to try and articulate knowledge and political activism. These journals echo and sometimes criticize GJM events and attempt to give an impetus to debates on movements. Most of them came together in the *Archipel des revues* during the second ESF. The think tanks most involved in the GJM are Espaces Marx (before 1995, Institut de recherches marxistes, close to the French Communist Party) and the Copernic Foundation, created in 1998, which regularly publishes reports describing employer projects and had some influence when the Left returned to power in 1997 (for instance, in preparing the 1998 Law on Exclusion). Two of them were even members of the ESF organization secretariat.

The Social Imprint of the Movement

In the context of ideological decline, the multimembership has expanded, marking a break with former traditional political activism. In fact, up until the 1970s, groups were characterized by exclusive political activism,[18] in contrast to today's idea of networking for several causes at a time (Sommier 2003). As we have seen, the movement "for globalization from below" brings together, under this federating slogan, people sympathetic to a wide variety of causes. However, the ties between organizations and multimembership are variable: The indicator of a close relationship—based upon the multi-belonging network of 1,744 activists—is highest for GJM organizations and environmental groups (Fillieule et al. 2004, 33). We can suggest that, with the growing success of the GJM, the specialization of claims by the various organizations is decreasing. In other words, the movement has resulted in unifying issues; organizations often import—sometimes even formally—the issues of other groups (for instance, environmental issues are now integrated into trade union and Attac statements). As Nadège Fréour sees it, under these conditions, the choice of an organization may be related more to the offerings in the repertoire of collective action than to its core issues (Fréour 2005). Such a dynamic and the multiple positions taken by activists favor an inclusive identity.

The great majority of French participants in the ESF declare they identify very much (39 percent) or quite a bit (38 percent) with the GJM as a whole or with one specific component. This might seem surprising, considering the extreme heterogeneity of the organizations and the issues. Their variety and even their fragmentation are obvious when one reads the ESF program. The five main issues of the plenary sessions were extremely broad, even a hodgepodge: "for a Europe of peace and justice," "for a social and democratic Europe of rights," "for a society of social justice, environmentally sustainability and food sovereignty," "for a democratic Europe of information, culture and education," "for a Europe that welcomes migrants."

Activists have several characteristics in common: Socially, they belong for the most part to the middle and upper classes, with a high level of education and some preparation for transnational activism, such as linguistic abilities and the experience of living abroad (Gobille and Uysal 2005). Politically, they are clearly and massively oriented toward the left. They are suspicious of institutions: 70 percent of the ESF participants do not trust regional authorities, 82 percent national authorities, 72 percent political parties, 76 percent European authorities, and 62 percent the UN. But 54.5 percent do trust trade unions, 77 percent NGOs, and 90 percent citizen associations.

Whatever their organizational membership, they share common representations of the world. Their main goals and motivations to participate in GJM events are identical: North-South disparities and environmental issues are most frequently mentioned both by anti-G8 and ESF participants, followed by the "power of multinational corporations" for the former and the "threat to public services" for the latter (see table 5.2). They agree with proposals to "really change society": "promote participatory democracy," "strengthen international law," and "make a radical break from current patterns of economic development," and the proposals are seen as the principal solutions for the two groups (but not in the same order), followed by "reform international financial and economic organizations" (for the ESF participants) and "get rid of capitalism" (for the anti-G8 activists). One can see the reformist orientation of the majority of the activists. A special place can be given to the propositions "favoring economic change and anti-productivism," which seem to fit more with a logic of breaking with the social and economic order. This more radical orientation can be analyzed in relation with the high intellectual and cultural background of this population. In our view, this sensibility is related to what Luc Boltanski and Eve Chiapello call the artist critic, increasingly denouncing the alienation induced by the capitalist system, the merchandizing of life, and social control. If this hypothesis proves to be valid, it would be the first time since 1968 that social criticism (and its thematic exploitation) and the artist critic (and its alienation theme) have joined together in a social movement.[19]

Waiting for further research, one can put forward two hypotheses to explain the slight difference between the anti-G8 and ESF samples. As far

Table 5.2 Main Issues and Motivation for Participating in GJM Events

Political Stakes	Anti-G8 (N = 841)	ESF (N =1,413)
North-South Disparities	19.2	14.7
Threat to Public Services	8.0	13.5
Environmental Issues	12.0	12.0
Fight against Capitalism	12.7	10.0
Power of Multinational Corporations	12.6	9.4
Fight against War	5.3	5.8
Unemployment and Precariousness	2.0	6.9
Illegitimacy of International Organizations	8.5	6.8
Ethnic/Racial/Sexual Discrimination	2.4	4.6
Gender Inequalities	2.1	4.4
Financial Speculation	4.8	3.0
Others	2.1	2.0

Source: Centre de recherches politiques de la Sorbonne surveys

as the ESF is concerned, it is necessary to underscore the result of a two-fold context of political sensibility and of mobilization, which makes the participants in the ESF more sensitive to the issue of public services, and, in a wider sense, to the French social model. This latter issue is becoming steadily more heated in France because of the rightist government's policy. The political prominence of this issue has probably been reinforced by the decision to hold the forum in municipalities run by the Left (one socialist and three communist dominated). This explains the particular attention given to social challenges such as unemployment, precarious employment, and discrimination. On the other hand, we can presume that the participants in the anti-G8 mobilization, which included a demonstration, alternative villages, and a counter-summit, are more radical than those participating in an event less costly in terms of time and activist involvement like a Paris forum. In any case, the population of the anti-G8 is younger (71 percent of the sample is under 35 years old, versus 50 percent at the ESF), less educated (50.4 percent hold a college/university degree, versus 69 percent at the ESF), and the antagonist area is more present within it.

To use Jean Cohen's categories, we are looking at a self-limiting radicalism (Cohen 1985), as already pointed out by the studies on the new protest forms (Sommier 2003). Their goals can be summarized as the defense or the extension of rights and democracy: the right to housing, the right to have a job, social democracy, and so on. The *Sans* movements are good examples of the extension of this framework. They rapidly expanded their claims by interconnecting their various social misfortunes; for instance, poor housing is responsible for poor health and problems in school. Therefore, decent housing might be viewed as the key to obtaining rights in general. This dynamic has led the DAL to create a new association, Dd!, which aims at fighting all forms of exclusion. Even when groups use direct action such as squats, they do so in reference to a constitutional right or a right considered to be superior to the one that was violated (for instance, here, the right to have a home versus the right to private property). Such references to the law (and belief in it) also exist within the GJM, for instance, in the organization of the "debt tribunal" or the "G8 trial."

An overarching framework enabling the unification of demands was first developed within certain movement families. An example of this is the creation of the *sans* label, which has federated the struggles of the homeless, the unemployed, and undocumented immigrants since 1996. The overall framework of "fighting against neoliberal globalization" gradually emerged with the growing success of mobilizations. This success has facilitated the construction of a common identity and binding the social movement families together. Within this overall framework, everyone can find the cause of his or her own social misfortune: environmental damage, poverty in the South, social disparities, patriarchal domination, unemployment, and so on. One or another of these topics will serve more or less as the core issue for mobilization, depending on the type of protest, and consequently one family of the social movement will be more involved in preparing the mobilization (for example, trade unions in the mobilization against a European summit on social issues as in December 2000, humanitarians in the protest against an FMI meeting, and so on). The "dominant" issue ("social" or "environmental," for instance) will depend on the core group. In France, the social aspect is clearly dominant (this is no doubt directly related to the sociological composition of the activists, dominated by the public sector). The diversity of demands and multi-issues foster the aggregation of a maximum number of organizations that can easily find a common theme with which they can identify. The slogan "another world is possible" expresses the belief of the activists in the possibility of change and the necessity to act in this direction. However, it provides no indication as to how the change is to be implemented. Nevertheless, one cannot imagine consensus on any proposal. Thus, the GJM enables anticapitalist and anti-imperialist topics to reemerge in the post–Cold War era, topics that are more socially acceptable because they are formulated in a new, euphemistic rhetoric.

Another recurring issue in the GJM was already quite central to the new associations: the search for radical democracy (precisely the goal of the organization Démocratiser radicalement la démocratie). In a collective book, the Association pour l'emploi, l'information et la solidarité des chômeurs et précaires (APEIS), SUD, and the Confédération paysanne explain the sense of their action by the concept of "democratic subversion" to point out two issues: first, the lack of democracy in their previous organizations (which led them to create new ones); second, their desire to extend the scope of democracy (Dubourg et al. 2001). Participatory democracy is perceived by the activists to be the best solution to fulfill this aspiration: This proposal ranks first as the way to "really change society," and it achieves consensus among half of the ESF participants (although one wonders whether they truly understand the meaning of the expression, which seems to function as a "magic word," along with "civil disobedience").[20]

This issue has had an impact on the internal functioning of associations. The most recent associations operate—or at least claim to operate—on the principle of direct democracy, a method promoted since the 1970s. For example, in AC!, the members make decisions by reaching a consensus as opposed to voting for a majority rule; this method is used to organize GJM events, especially the ESF.[21] Horizontal and nonhierarchical structures are preferred, such as federalism in Solidaires, unitaires et démocratiques–Postes et télécommunications (SUD-PTT), so that their local unions have full autonomy to make their own decisions, including publicly expressing their disagreement with the position held by the national direction. These groups also seek to drastically limit the number of permanent staff—as in Attac, which has 6 staff members for 35,000 members—because they are critical of political professionalization. Paradoxically, their activism, which is mostly expertise and lobbying, would favor professionalization because it requires highly qualified and specialized skills.

The issues of injustice and democratic deficit are common to activists at both the national and the transnational levels. They express a general sociocultural process: the moral argumentation used in political discourse, the use of emotional resources, and the emphasis on pain have been particularly evident in humanitarian associations since the end of the 1970s. Their success has transformed the sphere of protest and provoked "a clear shift away from a political-offensive level to a humanitarian-defensive level" (Sommier 2003, 230). The demands for extending the scope of democracy are linked to the considerable expansion of education and a sense of political skill (Gaxie 1978). In a conference on participatory democracy, Pierre Rosanvallon argued that the conception of democracy prevalent in the movements could be summed up in the traditional notion of citizenship: A citizen is both actor and supervisor, because trust and suspicion toward institutions cannot be separated. New movements use caution and denunciation in opposition to "those who are asleep" (Rosanvallon 2005).[22]

This double framework is visible when one looks at the values put forward by our sample of about thirty organizations of the GJM. The general reference to another form of globalization is followed by solidarity with Third World countries, democracy, global distributive justice, and a whole series of rights (in descending order of priority: human rights, workers' rights, women's rights, gay/lesbian rights, immigrant rights). Nevertheless, it should be emphasized that social issues clearly come first: social justice, defense of the welfare state, fighting poverty, social inclusion. Once again, this shows the imprint of social issues on the French movement.

A Large Repertoire of Collective Action

The GJM repertoire of collective action carried out by the new associations includes squatting buildings, breaking into pharmaceutical laboratories (Act-Up), and sabotaging sites (McDonald's and the destruction of the MGO fields). It aims at generating an outcry and denouncing what activists consider an injustice. The purpose is to attract public opinion through the choice of memorable actions and targets that are symbolic of the denounced wrong-doing. Cécile Péchu qualifies this illegal action as sector based, because it is directly related to the demand put forth by the mobilization (Péchu 1996, 123–124). The current repertoire of collective action has been influenced by three forms of action:

1. Direct action is the legacy of the actions of certain leftist groups during the 1970s. From a scientific point of view, the term must be understood in the restricted sense of its first promoters—the anarchists of the beginning of the twentieth century—even though activists use it to describe spectacular and generally symbolic actions (the famous "nonviolent direct actions" celebrated in the GJM). The specific feature of direct actions such as squats consists in the fact that the aim of the action is directly achieved without any intermediary or recourse to the State, the owner, or the manager. As Cécile Péchu has shown, it might respond to the famous paradox of the collective action by providing individual retributions in order to encourage participation.

2. Civil disobedience was rediscovered to protest against the conditions of the *sans-papiers* (undocumented immigrants) in 1997. It was used by GJM activists and some Green Party–elected representatives in the context of the struggle against GMOs during the summer of 2004. It is no doubt the main disruptive instrument because it opposes legitimacy to legality; participants present themselves as the guardians of democracy.

3. The festive style of the NSMs, which marks a break from conventional actions, especially those of trade unions, is reinforced by the GJM. A kind of aesthetics of revolt has sometimes been developed by specialized groups (for instance the ephemeral Apprentis agitateurs pour un réseau de résistance globale [Aarrg; Apprentice agitators for a network of worldwide resistance]—and now the Brigade des clowns [Clown brigade]). The importance of protest art surrounding a mobilization facilitates transnational circulation and reciprocal influences.

If we refer to the second ESF survey, we note that French participants seem to stage larger protest actions than the average of other European activists.

They are very active and experienced in terms of protest action, and they always give evidence of more experience than the sample as a whole (including the French): 97 percent have signed a petition (92 percent in the whole sample), 96 percent have taken part in a demonstration (90 percent in the whole sample), 72 percent have gone on strike (63 percent in the whole sample), and 75 percent have distributed leaflets (66 percent in the whole sample). We are looking at a highly experienced group, at least in terms of nonviolent activism. No doubt, this helps create the feeling of belonging to a coherent movement.

Referring to the classification of repertoires of action proposed by Hans-Martin Uehlinger (1988) and Dieter Fuchs (1991), Tangui Coulouarn and Ariane Jossin (2005, 140) have broken down the actions into three categories:

1. Demonstrative repertoire of action (legal and nonviolent): petitions, participating in groups of reflection and discussions, demonstrations, symbolic actions, leafleting, boycotting products or stores or countries, strikes, hunger strikes, fasts, and prayers.
2. Civil disobedience (illegal and nonviolent): occupying buildings (factories, schools, etc.), resistance to the police and blocking traffic (sit-ins, etc.).
3. Political violence (illegal and violent): damaging property and physical pressure (constraints) on people.

There is disagreement within the GJM about whether or not to use violence. Some activists include as part of their strategy the aim of breaking the law—in other words, civil disobedience—and using violence (for example, crossing the red zone of supranational summits, occupying buildings, blocking traffic in Annemasse and Geneva at the Evian counter-summit in 2003, and so on), but they face a lot of criticism within the organizations. "The cleavage over violence is not simple: it is also an important challenge, because it enables subtle tactics of positioning and differentiation within the movement" (Coulouarn and Jossin 2005, 142). It is therefore important to study the attitude of the activists toward this issue. Only one-third of the sample would agree to use violence, but the acceptance of a particular type of action is more a matter of effectiveness than of ethics. The types of action included in the demonstrative repertoire are thus considered "quite" or "rather" effective by more than 60 percent of the participants, those in the confrontational repertoire by 38 percent to 62 percent of the participants, depending on the type of action and those in the repertoire of political violence by less than 16 percent of the people in the sample (Coulouarn and Jossin 2005, 142). More than half of the participants consider them ineffective, probably because violence brings negative media coverage to the protest movement, which might cause a loss of support of part of the population.

The great majority of participants have used legal and nonviolent actions (demonstrative repertoire); more than one-third have used illegal and non-violent actions (confrontational repertoire) and almost half declare themselves ready to do so; more than two-thirds of the activists refuse political violence (Coulouarn and Jossin 2005, 149–155). The choice of one type of action over another often depends on the context, the activist's experience, and the sociological characteristics of the individual. Thus, the members of the three groups just described can be classified in terms of level of education and occupation. Those who favor political violence have a somewhat lower level of education: 50 percent hold a degree equal to or above a bachelor's degree (versus 55.5 percent for the two other groups), and 8.5 percent did not finish high school (versus about 6 percent for the two other groups). Similarly, there are more workers (3.6 percent) and employees (11 percent) than among those using the demonstrative repertoire (7 percent employees, and no workers) and activists in favor of civil disobedience. There is also a difference according to professional situation: The unemployed are over-represented in the political violence group, whereas retired people and university/high school students are overrepresented among the demonstrative group (Coulouarn and Jossin 2005, 146–147).

Recourse to illegal action is not the only method used. Other, more traditional forms of action are used as well, such as petitions, demonstrations, and direct contact with political parties represented in the Parliament. There is even a forty-member Attac committee in the National Assembly and Senate in France. Lobbying and legal battles have taken on considerable importance. Organizations thus combine both styles of action: protest and lobbying.

The availability of recourse to the whole spectrum of methods of action, from the most conventional to the most unorthodox, depends partly on the variety of GJM actors who, as we saw earlier, have simultaneous connections with interest groups and social movement organizations. The borderline between various kinds of organizations becomes more blurred as times goes by, no doubt because they cooperate with each other within the GJM. Yet their methods of action remain quite eclectic. For instance, DAL has always used illegal actions (squats of buildings) to denounce poor housing and find lodging solutions, and, at the same time, lobbied in favor of better housing, insisting on the application of the law of requisition of vacant buildings in favor of the homeless or those living in poor housing conditions. It also has recourse to legal action to protest against expulsion from houses. The same is true of Greenpeace, whose repertoire combines spectacular actions and opinion campaigns with lobbying authorities and scientific personalities. Wide-spectrum activism is conducive to a certain professionalization and specialization of activists because it favors those who have special competence and expertise (in law, economics, agronomy, etc.) to contest a decision legally and/or intellectually. This scientific dimension of activism or "case activism" (*militantisme de dossier*) (Ollitrault 1996), in which the Green movement has been a forerunner, developed significantly after 1995 and subsequently with the GJM in journals and think tanks.

The *extension du domaine de la lutte*—extension of the scope of the struggle—also provides a wide range of activist methods for ordinary activists (*militantisme à la carte*): 1) traditional methods such as demonstrations, 2) radical methods through participation in direct actions or civil disobedience (squats, uprooting GMO plants), 3) scientific methods as expertise, for example in social forums, and 4) half-festive half-activist methods at large meetings and alternative villages. The GJM therefore draws on the three levels of action brought to light by Michel Offerlé: the level of the number ("counting" one's forces by demonstrations and petitions), the level of virtue (denouncing a scandal through spectacular actions or organizing debt or G8 tribunal, and so on), and the level of science to further a legal guerrilla or lobbying action.

Conclusion

The French GJM is clearly positioned on the left and is divided on the subject of its relationships with the political sphere. Two main tendencies emerge: The first is in favor of institutionalization, or at least bringing the movement into the political field, whereas the second seeks to remain *politique autrement* (politically different) and stay away from the realm of politics.

The question of the relationship of these organizations with political parties is quite complex. This is particularly true of the Revolutionary Communist League, LCR (Ligue Communiste Révolutionnaire). Many of its members are involved in a number of groups: CADAC, SUD, AC!, Dd!, Attac, and others. With its central position, the LCR would like to build a radical left-wing party, "*gauche radicale*," and become its leader. In 2004, it chose an electoral alliance with another Trotskyite party, Lutte Ouvrière, and combined both strategies of mobilization and electoral participation (Sommier 2003, 295).

On the other hand, at the beginning of the legislative campaign of 1997, a petition entitled "We Are the Left" (*Nous sommes la gauche*) urged the institutional Left not to forget the Left rooted in social movements. In 1998, the petition "For the Autonomy of the Social Movement" (*Pour l'autonomie du mouvement social*), signed by "social movements activists, union members, intellectuals, citizens" was perceived as a warning to the PCF and the LCR, which were suspected of wanting to co-opt leaders of the "Social Movement" to be candidates on the list for the European elections.

Public disenchantment with political parties has no doubt contributed to the often-successful creation of "civil society candidates" for local (*municipal*) elections. These candidates were supported by local organizations. In March

2001, civil society lists *(listes citoyennes* headed by the organization motivé-e-s) accounted for 10 percent of the candidates in seven large cities in France, particularly in Toulouse with the music group Zebda.

From the standpoint of the radical Left movement, when Lionel Jospin was eliminated from the first round of presidential elections on March 21, 2002, it became even more urgent to rebuild the Left. Since then, there has been one petition after another. In late 2004, journals and newspapers of varying tendencies (*Politis, Témoignage Chrétien, Mouvements, Ecorev, Inrockuptibles,* and others), joined with associations to launch an initiative aimed at organizing "social forums for elections" in preparation for the 2007 elections, for the purpose of building "electoral campaigns as social and cultural movements." Some of them hope that José Bové will become the candidate of the "antiliberal Left," extending from the extreme Left to the Greens.[23] This new experience, following upon previous calls to "rebuild the Left" based on "actors in the social and cultural movement," is another illustration of the gap between the parties and movements of the Left, and of the "growing autonomy" of the associative realm (Péchu 2001; Mathieu 2004) in relation to the partisan field of the Left observed in France over the past fifteen years. There is no doubt that for most activists, these movements and the GJM have to "regenerate" the Left.

Notes

Translated by Francine Simon-Ekovich and Susan Taponier.

1. The term *GJM* is not really adapted to the French case. It is never used by activists, and the authors consider it too general. Nevertheless we will use it in order to respect the homogeneity of the entire book. The most neutral term would be *antiglobalization movement* in order to signify the opposition to financial and economic globalization. The term *antimondialisation* was imposed in 1999 by observers like journalists and led activists to find in 2002 another one: *Altermondialisation* had to signify the opposition to a certain kind of *mondialisation* (globalization) and the project to promote alternatives.

2. Alain Juppé was prime minister of the Right government; he was considered the heir apparent of President Jacques Chirac.

3. The Confédération Française Démocratique du Travail was founded in 1964 through a decision taken by the majority to secularize the CFTC (Confédération Française des Travailleurs Chrétiens).

4. The Confédération générale du travail (CGT), created in 1895, is the oldest French union. The domination of the Parti communiste français (PCF) within the organization led to the scission of Force ouvrière (FO).

5. The FSU (Unitary Union Federation) is the first state employee organization, born in 1993 from a majority scission of the FEN (Federation of National Education).

6. The Group of 10 (now "Union syndicale Solidaires") was created in 1981 by ten unions, which were not affiliated with a confederation. It developed itself on a clearly antiliberal line when the unions SUD (Solidaires, Unitaires et démocratiques—Solidary, Unitary and Democratic) joined it. The SUD unions were born starting at the end of the 1980s, after different movements of exclusion from the CFDT. This group of unions is the most involved in the GJM.

7. Minister of social affairs in the Raffarin government (under the presidency of Chirac). His reform plan brings the number of years of contributions required in order to get full retirement benefits in the public sector to the same number required in the private sector.

8. The Confédération nationale du travail is an anarcho-syndicalist union founded in 1946.

9. Droits devant! is an association for the rights created by DAL (Droit au logement) in 1994.

10. The Coordination des associations pour le droit à l'avortement et à la contraception, created in 1987, is an umbrella organization encompassing twenty-eight groups (associations, unions, and parties) in favor of abortion rights and contraception.

11. The membership has dropped to 25,000, probably as a consequence of the very violent conflict that currently affects its direction.

12. Actually, this interpretation of the action was made afterward by the national direction of the CP and had a large success and impact, as we know. But this action had actually been decided by a local group without keeping the national level informed, and without any global reference. See Bruneau 2004.

13. The Fédération nationale des syndicats d'exploitants agricoles, created after World War II, is the largest farmers' union. Historically, it is invested in farming policy and a productivist vision of agriculture.

14. The Centre de recherches politiques de la Sorbonne (CRPS) has conducted two surveys, combining quantitative and qualitative methods on the Global Justice movement, during the anti-G8 mobilization in Evian (June 1–3, 2003), and during the second European Social Forum (November 12–15, 2003), which took place in Paris and its surroundings. The questionnaire (translated into Spanish, Italian, English, and German) consisted of around forty questions and had several goals: the reconstitution of the activist's trajectory (former and current course, conditions of information and coming to the forum, global justice movement experiences, types of sociability); the understanding of their motivations and visions of the world (their relation to the modes of action, their assessment of the efficiency of these mobilizations, their priorities of struggles, their degree of trust into the institutions, and their degree of identification with the movement …); the precise drawing of their sociographic profile, especially through an assessment of their relation with the international dimension (practice of foreign languages, experiences in foreign countries, etc.). Two thousand questionnaires were gathered at the anti-G8 mobilization and 2,600 at the ESF. It is very interesting to compare these two events, because they show two very different GJM's types of involvement; the first one is probably more costly in terms of time (because of the necessity to take the trip during a period of strikes) and of risks (alternative villages, demonstrations, and blockade) than the second.

15. The data presented in this paper come from the survey realized by the CRPS

team during the European Social Forum in November 2003 (Paris-Saint-Denis), and have been analyzed in the collective book *Radiographie du mouvement altermondialist français* (Agrikoliansky and Sommier 2005) and in particular in chapters 4 (Gobille and Uysal 2005), 5 (Coulouarn and Jossin 2005), and 6 (Fillieule and Blanchard 2005). In order to analyze the French global justice movement, the activists living in France have been put together in a separate data bank.

16. The number of unions is overrepresented, because many local unions and professional branches signed the appeal even though their national confederation did it as well. Nevertheless, unions are dominant in the French GJM.

17. The Debré laws, from the name of the interior minister in the Juppé government, intend to fight against illegal immigration and work. Article 1 of the law plans that anybody lodging a foreigner must inform the municipality, and foresees a further creation of a national file of the hosts. This provoked an unprecedented movement of petitions (120,000 signatures) and a series of demonstrations in the context of future legislative elections in 1997.

18. We mean here a stable belonging to one main organization or several belongings to satellite organizations connected to the main one, for instance the Communist Party and its satellite groups, the union CGT, the feminine organization UFF, the student union UEC.

19. On the distinction between the two forms of critique, see Boltanski and Chiapello 1999.

20. About twelve items were proposed to the militants: They had to choose three of them.

21. For an analysis of this functioning and a confrontation between principles and reality, see I. Sommier in Agrikoliansky and Sommier 2005, 19–43.

22. Pierre Rosanvallon calls participatory democracy a "kind of indirect democracy" and considers it *impolitique* (nonpolitical). Active democracy would be a better expression than indirect democracy.

23. Such a strategy is currently being discussed within the Greens, PCF, and LCR, probably without any result.

Chapter Six

The Global Justice Movement in Great Britain

Christopher Rootes and Clare Saunders

On July 2, 2005, some 225,000 people marched through the streets of Edinburgh in the largest demonstration the Scottish capital had ever seen. The occasion was the imminent G8 summit meeting at nearby Gleneagles at which the UK prime minister had pledged to highlight the economic plight of the world's poorest countries. The march was the culmination of the "Make Poverty History" campaign, a campaign that the Roman Catholic Primate, Archbishop Cormac Murphy O'Connor, has called "the greatest moral upheaval since the campaign against the slave trade." Despite competition from the simultaneous Live8 concert in London, the march drew more than half its participants from beyond Scotland and, despite a large and vigilant police presence, was wholly peaceful and overwhelmingly nonconfrontational. No doubt reflecting the very large participation from the churches, it seemed more a procession of witness than a protest.

During the following week, however, as the G8 leaders assembled and deliberated, numerous protests were staged in Edinburgh, in the immediate vicinity of the conference site, and at other locations in southern Scotland. These latter protests were organized by activists affiliated to the recently formed Dissent! network, who, in contrast to the organizers of the Make Poverty History (MPH) march, declined to negotiate routes and protocols with the police in advance. The resulting uncertainty was cited to justify the biggest policing operation in Scottish history as police, often in full riot gear and drawn from forces from all parts of the UK, confronted protesters. Yet, despite a few skirmishes and isolated instances of property damage, these protests were overwhelmingly nonviolent.

These events illustrate the diversity of the complex phenomenon that we identify as the "global justice movement" (GJM) in Britain. Its identity as a movement is uncertain, since it embraces two principal but largely noncommunicating strands, one consisting of a uniquely rich and long-established constellation of aid, trade, and development, human rights and environmental organizations, and the other of a variety of radical groupings, mostly of the anarchist Left; a third, socialist strand is uneasily related to both.

The divisions within the movement that are represented and subsumed by these strands present a considerable obstacle to an account of the GJM in Britain that aspires to be more than merely a catalogue of events. Because the proponents of direct action and the anarchists have been the noisiest strand of the GJM and have been responsible for most of the most spectacular and confrontational events associated with it, the GJM has sometimes—mistakenly—been identified wholly or mainly with them (Saunders and Rootes 2005). The extent of that mistake was apparent in Scotland in July 2005. Because the G8 meeting was the focus for mobilization of all strands of the GJM, it provided a unique opportunity to assess the relative strengths of the various strands of the movement. By contrast with the massive numbers mobilized by MPH, the various direct action protests during the following week attracted probably no more than 5,000 people in total. The fact that the latter protests were on weekdays, whereas MPH was on a Saturday, might somewhat flatter MPH, but the disparity is nonetheless huge. Even if one takes all the 50,000 subscribers to the direct action newsletter *Schnews* to be members or supporters of the GJM, they are still massively outnumbered by the tactical moderates who form the great bulk of the supporters of MPH. For that reason, our account of the GJM in Britain embraces both the events that have marked the development of the movement and the networks and coalitions that have become its most characteristic organizational form and in which aid, trade, and development organizations (ATDOs) have played the leading roles.

Although many of the themes of the GJM were prefigured by the anarcho-punk, anticapitalist, and radical environmentalist protests of the 1980s and 1990s (see Rootes 2003d; Rootes and Saunders 2005; Saunders and Rootes 2005), the event that marks the symbolic birth of the GJM in Britain was the Jubilee 2000 action to encircle Birmingham on the occasion of the G8 meeting in 1998. But, before we consider that action and the events that followed, it might be helpful to describe some of the strands that have contributed most directly to the development of the GJM in Britain.

In the next section, we discuss the development of the aid, trade, and development lobby toward social movement politics and the role in this process of environmental movement organizations, before focusing on the series of days of action that have become the most public manifestations of the GJM. Then, having introduced the principal actors, including the autonomous direct action networks associated with the most controversial GJM protests, we turn to an examination of the campaign coalitions so characteristic of the movement and the variety of forms of networking that exist among organizations active in the GJM. After briefly considering the ideological diversity of the movement and the ways in which its activists frame the issues, we then consider the repertoires of action employed by GJM organizations and activists, and the alliances between them and other recent popular mobilizations, notably the antiwar movement. Finally, we address the place of the GJM in the long sequence of social movement mobilizations in Britain and the implications of the divisions within the GJM for its identity as a social movement.

The Origins of the GJM in Great Britain: Lobbies, Movements, and Campaigns

The GJM in Britain has grown out of the confluence of three quite distinct streams: a large and well-established assemblage of mainly charitable organizations that have historically been focused on the giving of aid to and the promotion of economic development and human rights in what used to be called "the Third World" and is now, misleadingly, more often called the "global South"; an environmental movement, some of whose leading organizations have become increasingly concerned with the implications of global social inequality; and a more amorphous succession of direct action groups and autonomous protest networks most visible through the days of action they have staged. We shall consider each in turn.

Aid, Trade, and Development NGOs, and Campaigns

Aid, trade, and development organizations (ATDOs) began to develop in Britain in the aftermath of World War I. Save the Children was among the first, followed after World War II by others such as Oxfam. Beginning with relief for refugees and support for others adversely affected by war, from the 1950s British ATDOs undertook development projects designed to tackle the root causes of poverty, and from the 1960s supported local self-help. By the 1970s, the fundamentally political causes of poverty became apparent.

Nevertheless, as charities, most ATDOs were wary of crossing the line into political advocacy, especially in the wake of the 1980s Charity Commission investigation of Oxfam (Black 1992, 269–271; Clark 1991, 34–37; Commins 1997, 147). Their roots in Christian philanthropy and their heavy dependence on government funding also constrained them to moderation. At least until very recently, it was probably more accurate to refer to ATDOs collectively as a "lobby," rather than a "movement" (Edwards 1999, 167). During the 1990s, however, ATDOs became increasingly vocal critics of the neoliberal agenda.

An early exception to the charitable norm was the World Development Movement (WDM). Founded in 1970, WDM describes itself as "a democratic movement of individual campaigners and local group members from diverse backgrounds" and "Britain's leading campaigning organisation for changes that benefit the world's poor" (www.realworld.org.uk/wdm.html; accessed 9/23/05). WDM believes that the fundamental causes of world poverty cannot be overcome without changes to the policies and practices of governments and business interests in wealthy industrialized countries, and, free from the constraints of charity law, undertakes campaigns designed to change policies of governments and companies that marginalize the poor.[1] WDM's choice of the label *movement*—as well as its decision not to seek charitable status—reflects the climate of the 1970s when social movements were confidently proposed as successors to parties and direct action was a more plausible strategy than lobbying in the struggle to change the world.

WDM's example did not immediately transform the aid, trade, and development lobby, but it did signal changes in civil society that would later make it possible for ATDOs to begin to conceive of themselves as part of a movement and to expand their repertoire of action beyond lobbying. Since the 1960s, Britain has become a much more participatory society, steadily increasing numbers of people having participated in protest or having come to accept it as legitimate.[2] It is against this background of increasingly widespread tolerance of and disposition to protest that the aid, trade, and development lobby has developed into the major strand of the GJM. Links with previous waves of protest mobilization are mostly indirect. It is the environmental movement that provides the most direct link. Emboldened by the rise of campaigning organizations such as Friends of the Earth (FoE) and Greenpeace from the 1970s onward, the tactical repertoire of the environmental movement was expanded in the 1990s by alliances forged in the course of anti-roads protests, and direct action was legitimated by their apparent success (Rootes 2003b and 2003d).

British organizations, including Christian Aid, Oxfam, Action Aid, the Catholic Institute for International Relations, and WDM were active in the international campaign against the 1986–1994 Uruguay Round of multilateral trade negotiations (Wilkinson 1996, 254), but the campaigns against the Multilateral Agreement on Investment (MAI) and the General Agreement on Trade in Services (GATS), and the Jubilee 2000 coalition, are more direct antecedents of the GJM in Britain (Raghu and Skanthakumar 2001, 16).

The MAI aimed to create uniform rules on market access and legal security, remove barriers to investment flows, increase employment, and improve living standards, and it would have given corporations the right to sue states in international courts for limiting investments or capital flows without good reason. In 1997, British nongovernmental organizations (NGOs) became concerned that the MAI would give disproportionate power to transnational corporations (Bray 1998) and that protection of local markets, health, and environments would not be considered sufficient reasons to restrict trade (Farnsworth 2004, 60). The campaign brought together a broad range of religious and environmental organizations, trade unions, and ATDOs, including WDM, Oxfam, WWF-UK (formerly World Wide Fund for Nature), Northeast England Greens, FoE, Corporate Watch,[3] UNISON (the major public-sector trade union), and Christian Aid. Mirroring the range of interests that have become characteristic of the GJM, this campaign was the springboard from which wider and deeper critiques of the workings of the global economy were launched. Tactics included conventional lobbying, with WDM kick-starting an extensive letter-writing campaign, through direct action by Corporate Watch, which occupied the London offices of the International Chamber of Commerce. The organizations involved moved on, as part of a transnational network of NGOs, to critique the World Trade Organization (WTO) and GATS.

Jubilee 2000 grew out of the British Debt Crisis Network that was led by the New Economics Foundation (NEF), Christian Aid, and WDM. By lobbying, these organizations secured improvements in World Bank and International Monetary Fund (IMF) debt policies through Heavily Indebted Poor Country Initiatives (1996). But the resultant trickles of aid hardly touched the debt burdens of the poorest countries, and resistance by creditor countries made them difficult to implement. This lack of progress persuaded NGOs concerned with trade that the issues needed a higher public profile. In April 1996, the Trade Crisis Network began taking the coalition forward, with tentative support from the Catholic Agency for Overseas Development (CAFOD) and Tearfund (aid organizations linked to the Catholic and evangelical churches, respectively). In October 1997, the formal coalition was launched with more than seventy supporting organizations, including trade unions, international aid and women's organizations, and the Green Party, chief among them Christian Aid, CAFOD, the Methodist Church Division of Social Responsibility, the United Society for the Propagation of the Gospel, the Church Missionary Society, Oxfam, WDM, Save the Children, the International Labour Organisation, and NEF (Peters 2000).

Guided by religious principles and human rights concerns, the initial priority of Jubilee 2000 was to ensure that unpayable debts were written off by December 31, 1999, and that all other debts were reduced to levels that would allow sustainable human, environmental, and economic development (Pettifor 1998 and 2001). Jubilee's critique of the G8, IMF, and World Bank assimilates the anti-debt movement to a broader movement critical of international financial institutions, the agenda of neoliberalism, and the lack of democracy within international financial institutions.

Environmental Movement Organizations

We have already suggested that the environmental movement was an important exemplar in the transformation of the tactically conventional ATD lobby into a social movement, but the interest of environmental movement organizations (EMOs) in the issues central to the GJM itself requires explanation. British EMOs have come to see themselves as part of a global movement dealing with global issues as their understanding of the complex and interrelated issues entailed by effective action on environmental issues has become increasingly sophisticated and as national governments have yielded sovereignty on environmental issues to transnational organizations such as the European Union (EU) and multinational corporations (Rootes 2004).

Since the early 1990s, the coordination of EMOs in transnational networks of various kinds has increased (Rootes 2005). EMOs played important roles in the preparatory conferences for the 1992 Earth Summit, and, within the limits of their resources, they have been increasingly active in transnational campaigns and alliances.

Most major British EMOs recognize that transnational capital and markets contribute significantly to environmental degradation, but FoE in particular has made a significant shift toward embracing issues of social inequity and global trade. FoE's main campaign themes for 2003–2008 are environmental justice, sustainable economies, environmental limits, and accountability/participation. The environmental justice theme aims to make considerations of social equity central to the way the public and decision makers view environmental issues. It incorporates a campaign for "climate justice," seeking an equitable climate change treaty, and "action for justice," working with community groups suffering injustices. The sustainable economies theme anticipates a sustainable economic agenda that, inter alia, challenges the legitimacy of the WTO. The "corporate accountability" theme highlights socially and environmentally damaging corporate practices and seeks to introduce a new regulatory framework, and "reduce resource use" (FoE 2002a; Saunders 2004).

For FoE, global trade abuses democracy, threatens human rights, disregards the environment, and widens the gap between the rich and the poor. Concerned that GATS would override nation-states' abilities to enforce their own environmental legislation, FoE campaigned alongside ATDOs, asked its members to write to their members of Parliament (MPs) to complain about the lack of democracy in GATS negotiations, and petitioned Members of the European Parliament (FoE 2002b). FoE was centrally involved in the coordination of a "trade justice march" timed to coincide with the Geneva WTO meeting in June 2002, which attracted 5,000 people, most of them supporters of NGOs such as FoE and Oxfam. In September 2003, FoE, accusing Prime Minister Blair of being "in the pocket" of big business, called on him to resist the expansion of the WTO's remit at its meeting in Cancún (FoE 2003).

FoE and Greenpeace UK have for some time participated in the "summit hopping" characteristic of the direct action strand of the GJM. However, although impressed by the scale of the Seattle demonstration against the WTO and the broad range of interests it mobilized, FoE leaders are, like those of Jubilee, careful to avoid involvement in the ruckus that is often the outcome of large-scale international demonstrations (Sheila Freeman, post and volunteers coordinator at FoE England, Wales, and Northern Ireland, interview with Clare Saunders, February 2004).

Days of Action, Direct Action, and Autonomous Networks

Protests at international summits and "days of action" have become increasingly frequent. British activists have been involved principally in those closest to home and in local solidarity actions. We focus here on those that mark the most important milestones in the development of the GJM in Britain: the Birmingham G8 protests of May 1998; the J18 "Carnival of Resistance" (June 18,1999); solidarity actions in London on November 30, 1999; S26 in Prague (September 26, 2000); and the May Day protests from 2000.

In May 1998, seventy thousand people, including bishops, middle-class professionals, and radical environmental protesters, formed a human chain around Birmingham in an action called by Jubilee 2000 to raise the profile of debt in the G8 discussions (Glasius 2001, 331). In preceding weeks, NEF organized meetings and workshops to spread awareness of debt issues and the role of the G8. Christian Aid brought activists to represent the Poor Eight nations. Speakers at the Jubilee rally included UNISON's general secretary, keynotes from organizations, including the African Liberation Support Campaign, Tearfund, Christian Aid, WDM, NEF, and politicians, including the then-secretary of state for International Development, Clare Short (Pettifor 1998, 116). A street party followed, organized, with help from London Reclaim the Streets (RTS), by a small group of radical activists, mostly from Manchester and Nottingham. Despite efforts by street party organizers to choose a time and location that would not disrupt the Jubilee 2000 action, and to encourage people to attend it before going to the party (Trapese 2005), some organizers of Jubilee's human chain regarded the street party organizers as direct competitors, and, believing police warnings that the party would be a public safety crisis intended to sabotage the Jubilee action, obstructed attempts to publicize the street party. In the event, to the embarrassment of the street party organizers, several partygoers took fruit and vegetables from a market stall and threw them at the police, who promptly terminated the party (Trapese 2005).[4]

If the encirclement of Birmingham was an overwhelmingly moderate and peaceful action, the next major event took a more radical turn. On June 18, 1999, 10,000 people converged in the heart of the City of London to participate in the "global" J18 "Carnival of Resistance and International Day of Action." Most involved in the protest, and in spreading the message globally via Internet networks, were RTS, Earth First!, and the anarchist group, London Greenpeace (Notes from Nowhere 2003, 184). The day began with a blockade of London Bridge, a critical mass demonstration, pickets by animal rights activists at McDonalds, and a "die-in" staged by anti-arms trade activists covered in fake blood (Lancaster J18 Collective 1999; Tyler 2003, 191). The main action involved a march, followed by a convergence in the financial center of the city. The march split into four "blocs" all headed for the London International Financial Futures Exchange (LIFFE) building. While most in the crowd were enjoying the impromptu street party and dancing to the samba band, sound systems, and punk bands, a minority of protesters attempted to occupy the LIFFE building. Windows were smashed, the lower entrance was bricked up, and the ground floor was flooded when protesters sabotaged a fire hydrant (Tyler 2003, 193). LIFFE stopped trading after a "sustained physical and cyber attack" (Chesters 1999). Policing was less than restrained; seventy-six people were arrested and forty-six injured.

No less confrontational were the protests on November 30, 1999, the date of the "battle of Seattle," when activists called for a global day of action, resistance, and carnival "in recognition that the *capitalist system*, based on exploitation of people, societies and the environment for the profit of a few, is the prime cause of present social and ecological troubles" (VER 2000a). In Britain, activists occupied Lloyds Bank and a Nestlé factory, and organized a rally and street party against the privatization of public transport outside London's Euston station. Approximately two thousand protesters were met with what activist sources describe as heavy-handed policing.[5]

The action in Prague against the IMF and the World Bank (September 26–28, 2000) has been described as "the biggest self-generated mobilization of British people to a political situation in another country since the Spanish War" (*Schnews* 2004, 197). The action was planned by INPEG (Initiative against Globalization), a coalition of American, British, and some Czech activists (Voices from Ecological Resistance [VER] 2000b). Three marches were planned, taking different routes to the conference center. British activists, mostly from Earth First! and RTS, devised a fourth route. Socialists and Trotskyites dressed in pink, Ya Basta in yellow, the anarchist/autonomist/black bloc in blue, and the five hundred British activists wore pink and silver.

The British bloc, calling itself "Tactical Frivolity," proposed not a passive blockade, but "active nonviolence." Wearing clothing that provided no protection, their actions included polishing policemen's boots with luminous pink feather dusters, symbolizing resistance to "machismo and violence" as much as to neoliberalism (Chesters and Welsh 2004, 331). The march was organized by consensus; when marchers were unsure of the route, a flag with a picture of a confused fish was hoisted, and affinity group delegates had to discover what decision needed to be made, return to their groups, discuss it, and then reach a decision (VER 2000c).

The playful strategies of Tactical Frivolity are part of a general trend toward greater use of harmlessly mischievous and comical tactics in direct action networks (Chesters 2000). Members of the Clandestine Insurgent Rebel Clown Army (CIRCA) rebel against state surveillance, believe in improvised forms of action, seek to transform the lives of participants, dress as clowns, and fight for life and the environment in the "war against capital" (CIRCA 2004). This has included playfully disruptive actions at army recruitment centers, where clowns have polished soldiers' boots, and in Scotland during the G8 summit. The Space Hijackers organized Circle Line Parties on the London Underground and, during the European Social Forum (ESF) (October 2004), the Corporate Games. These included musical chairs in Starbucks, Bingo (based on what customers ordered) in McDonalds, hide-and-seek in the GAP, and British Bulldog in a Nike store. Participants were disqualified if they purchased anything from the stores in which the games were taking place (Space Hijackers 2004).

Some British activists were inspired after their participation in the Yellow Bloc in Prague to emulate the Italian Tute Bianche. Thus the Wombles emerged in 2001, attending demonstrations wearing helmets and padded overalls for self-defense, and directly challenging police cordons, allowing demonstrators to escape (Donson et al. 2004, 19).

May Day 2000 coincided with the launch of Indymedia UK.[6] "Impressive actions" took place in several towns and cities, including Manchester, Sheffield, and Glasgow, but it was the London protest that attracted most controversy. There, anarchist veterans of the 1980s tried to insinuate their politics into the organization and practice of the protest and to use the developing anticapitalist movement as a vehicle (VER 2000d). Activists from Anarchist Black Cross and London Greenpeace were part of the "action faction" that produced leaflets advertising four days of action, but it fell to RTS to organize mass action at short notice, and in the aftermath of the J18 and N30 "riots." The action began with a critical mass bicycle ride around central London and, in an attempt to discourage violence, "guerrilla gardening" in Parliament Square. For days preceding the protest, the tabloid press carried rumors of police intelligence, predicting that guerrilla gardeners would use gardening tools as weapons in a full-scale riot (Tempest 2002). To avoid that, organizers provided only plastic trowels. Although the protest was chaotic, it was mostly peaceful, but there was limited property damage, and the statue of Winston Churchill was decorated with a turf punk-style Mohawk and graffiti. Later, RTS attempted to draw protesters away from possible confrontation with police, but large numbers filled Whitehall in a march to Trafalgar Square. Police observed the guerrilla gardening, the march, and even the painting of graffiti on the national war memorial, without intervening, until a small group ransacked a McDonald's restaurant full of customers. The day resulted in ninety-five arrests and nine injured police officers. Whereas protesters viewed the police as heavy-handed, the press and many observers criticized them for excessive leniency. Even the guerrilla gardening was represented in the press as disorder tantamount to riot (Donson et al. 2004).

In the days preceding May Day 2001, the media again carried lurid predictions of violence. This, together with expectations of harsh policing, probably reduced numbers. Organizers called on affinity groups to undertake autonomous actions, with a critical mass in the morning and a convergence in the afternoon. After the debacle of 2000, police responded to "anticapitalist" protests with precautionary, firm, or heavy-handed tactics. On May 1, 2001, police penned protesters into Oxford Street for up to eight hours, allowing neither peaceful protesters nor innocent bystanders to leave unless they gave their names and addresses and consented to being photographed.[7]

In subsequent years, May Day demonstrations have had a lower profile, and the police response has been considerably more relaxed. Action in 2002 was focused around Mayfair, with embassies as targets for self-organized affinity groups; a mass "village football" game, jesters, and jugglers lightened the tone. Protests in 2003 were directed against presumed beneficiaries of the Iraq war—oil companies and arms traders (Morland and Carter 2004, 90–91). In 2004, following poor turnout at coordination meetings, the London May Day Collective decided not to coordinate a day of action, but instead to hold a picnic at which the future of the movement could be discussed (Some Members of the London May Day Collective 2004).

Confrontational direct action has declined in the wake of public opprobrium and firm policing. Radicals hoped that J18 would attract large numbers of the hitherto moderate or inactive to their version of the cause. In the event, the violence came as an unpleasant surprise to most who participated in the protests and, far from generalizing the mobilization, had the effect of restricting subsequent "anticapitalist" protests to activists less averse to confrontation. The May Day 2000 debacle served only to confirm the isolation and tactical bankruptcy of the "disorganized" radicals and led ultimately to the dissolution of RTS, which had until then been regarded as one of the more inspiring and exportable of the innovations of the previous decade. Certainly, the developments of direct action and confrontational protest in the years since the founding of Jubilee 2000 have had almost nothing to do with the development of that wing of the movement organized around ATDOs.

Organizations and Networks

The broad campaigning coalitions—Jubilee,[8] the trade justice movement (TJM), and MPH—are the most characteristic organizational forms of the GJM in Britain. The TJM and MPH mark a symbolic shift for the aid, trade, and development sector because, like WDM, FoE, and Greenpeace before them, in order to avoid any constraints upon their political activity, they have not sought charitable status.

Campaigning Coalitions

The TJM was established in 2001 by a small steering group drawn from some forty British aid NGOs to campaign "for fundamental change to unjust rules and institutions governing international trade, so that trade is made to work for all" (www.tjm.org.uk; accessed November 11, 2006). Consciously emulating the form of the Jubilee 2000 campaign, TJM resulted from interorganizational discussions about how best to influence the UK government's stance during and after the Doha round of trade negotiations and campaigned to persuade the government not to sign the free trade agreement on foreign investment proposed at the WTO meeting in Cancún. It again came to prominence when 25,000 people participated in its all-night vigil outside Parliament on April 15, 2005, in the lead-up to World Poverty Action Day. Describing itself as "fast growing," in April 2005, it was a coalition of sixty-six organizations, including ATD charities, churches, trade unions, student organizations, and EMOs.

The Make Poverty History coalition was more prominent and more inclusive. Bringing together, at its peak, more than five hundred British NGOs, including JDC, TJM, and many charities, campaigns, trade unions, faith groups, student unions, and local groups, and enjoying prominent celebrity endorsements, MPH campaigned for "in nine words: trade justice, drop the debt, more and better aid."[9] Like TJM, which includes a prominent link to MPH on its Web site, the organizers of MPH believed that, with the UK hosting the G8 summit (at which poverty in Africa was a key theme) and holding the EU presidency, 2005 provided an unprecedented opportunity to tackle trade, aid, and debt issues.TJM and MPH are "virtual" organizations that scarcely exist beyond their Web sites and the campaign events they organize. Beyond them—and often embraced by them—is a wide variety of types of organizations, some formally organized, others networks, and some merely temporary projects that last only the lifetime of a single protest. Local networks of activists usually coalesce around a particular protest, as they did with J18 action groups that formed across the country and, more recently, with the Dissent! network developed from December 2003 in preparation for the July 2005 G8 meeting.

Radicals considered MPH too reformist and its rally too distant from the G8 meeting to have any real impact. The Socialist Workers' Party (SWP) and the Campaign for Nuclear Disarmament (CND) proposed a conference /alternative festival closer to Gleneagles, but this, allegedly funded through the official security budget of the G8, was regarded by activists aligned with Dissent! as a sellout.[10] Dissent! was nonhierarchical, participatory, made decisions by consensus, and had no office, spokespeople, members, or staff. It was instead a loose, self-educating network open to anyone, organized through bimonthly small-scale meetings, occasional gatherings, and an e-mail discussion list. Dissent! was supported by the Trapese (Take Radical Action through Popular Education and Sustainable Everything) educational road show, which toured social centers and towns encouraging formation of local Dissent! groups. In spring 2005 a major gathering of Dissent! activists formulated proposals for action. In the event, both the scale and the impact of its actions in Scotland were modest. Such cross-issue and biodegradable networks (Doherty 2004) contrast with the hierarchically structured, formal organizations that constitute the great bulk of the GJM and have provided the core of its three great campaign coalitions.

The main characteristics of JDC, TJM, and MPH are summarized in table 6.1. Aside from their slightly different foci—JDC's is debt, TJM's is trade justice, and MPH's was debt, trade justice, *and* improved aid—and longevity, the coalitions differ in their organizational structures. MPH formally existed only during 2005, although its e-mail supporter network still uses the name to alert subscribers to opportunities for action. JDC and TJM are much more formal; as registered companies, they have articles and memoranda of association, which MPH lacked. TJM has, and MPH had, specialized divisions of labor, with working groups of experts carrying out delegated roles. JDC works much less formally, member organizations bringing resources to the campaign as they see fit. All three networks are/were controlled by central committees, which, in the case of JDC and TJM, make decisions by majority vote. MPH made decisions by consensus. For JDC and TJM, the committee broadly represents the membership structures. MPH, a much larger coalition, was controlled by representatives of the four key organizations responsible for founding it, along with ten representatives elected from the remaining membership. Only JDC has its own local-groups network. Local groups can only join TJM if they have no national counterpart. MPH allowed local groups to join as collective members. In practice, only MPH had local groups

Table 6.1 Key Networks of the GJM in Great Britain

	NETWORKS		
ORGANIZATIONAL STRUCTURE	*Jubilee Debt Campaign*	*Trade Justice Movement*	*Make Poverty History*
Formalization	High (expressed in Articles and Memoranda of Association)	High (expressed in Articles and Memoranda of Association, and Standing Orders and Regulations)	Low (expressed in a manifesto and founding document)
Specialization	Not specialized (members merely have to provide resources to the campaign)	Specialized (contains working groups that consist of experts)	Specialized (contains working groups)
Main Decisional Organism (Other Than Assembly)	Board of directors that delegates to committees as it sees fit.	Board of directors that delegates to the planning group as appropriate.*	Coordination team that delegates to a support center.
Composition of Decisional Organism	Directors consist of representatives of all collective members and local branch representatives.	Directorship broadly reflects the composition of the TJM.	Consists of representatives of four core networks—JDC, TJM, BOND and the Stop Aids Campaign, plus ten others elected by the assembly and three co-opted members.
Center-Periphery Relationship	Representatives of local branches sit on the board of directors.	Open only to national organizations. A local organization may join and will be treated as an equal member if it is a local group that does not have a national counterpart.	Does not have local groups, although local groups may affiliate to the campaign whether or not they have a national counterpart.
MODEL OF DECISION MAKING			
Type of Leadership	Concentrated directorship. Re-elected annually, maximum three-year term.	Concentrated directorship. Re-elected annually, maximum three-year term.	Concentrated directorship. Four key networks remain constant in the directorship.
Decisional Method	Majority rule	Majority rule	Consensus

Note: *The planning group develops campaign strategies, decides campaign demands, plans activities, and creates and supports working groups.

Source: JDC 2001a, JDC 2001b, TJM 2004, TJM 2005, MPH 2005.

affiliated as collective members, and it contained relatively more regional groups. TJM and MPH counted few international organizations as members, whereas they comprise 12.5 percent of JDC's membership.

In all three coalitions, ATDOs predominate, but religious or missionary organizations are (proportionally) twice as common in JDC as in MPH. Education and awareness-raising ventures were significant only in MPH. Religious ATDOs formed a much smaller proportion of MPH than of JDC and TJM. Trade unions and workers' rights organizations are considerably more prominent in JDC than in TJM or MPH. Organizations concerned with health issues were more common in MPH than in other networks, whereas human rights organizations are relatively more prominent in TJM. Peace groups were less well represented in MPH than in JDC or TJM (see table 6.2).

JDC, TJM, and MPH are broad networks, but beyond the co-occurrence of names on lists of supporting organizations, how much networking is there among them? We have two takes on this. First, we present analysis of the cross-referencing among a cross section of GJM organizations (GJMOs) on their Web sites. Second, we present evidence from our interviews with and survey of participants in the July 2005 MPH march in Edinburgh.

Table 6.2 Types of Member Organizations of Key British GJM Networks (Percentages)

Type of Organization	JDC n=65	TJM n=58	MPH n=487
Aid Trade and Development (Not Religious)	21.5	20.7	19.4
Religious or Missionary	21.5	15.5	10.6
Environmental	6.2	8.6	3.1
Education/Awareness Raising	1.5	1.7	11.9
Workers' Rights/Trade Unions	12.3	5.2	6.2
Religious Aid Trade or Development	18.5	17.2	7.8
Health	1.5	1.7	8.5
Children's Rights	1.5	3.4	4.7
Human Rights	1.5	5.2	4.1
NGO Support or Networking	0.0	0.0	4.1
Peace (Not Religious)	6.2	6.9	3.1
Voluntary Work Overseas	0.0	1.7	2.3
Race/Immigrants Rights (Not Religious)	1.9	0.0	2.1
Alternative Economics	3.1	0.0	1.0
Religious Peace	0.0	3.4	1.6
Disabled Support	1.5	1.7	1.6
Religious Race/Immigrant Rights	1.5	0.0	1.3
Other or Unknown	7.1	6.9	6.7

Networks in Cyberspace: Internet Links among Key GJMOs

Thirty-seven key GJMOs were selected as representatives of key strands of what we consider to be the GJM (Rootes and Saunders 2005). The selected Web sites cover debt relief, antiwar, religious inspiration, youth, the environment, trade unions, anarchist, antagonist, international solidarity, lesbian/gay groups, antiracism/immigrants rights, political parties, human rights, fair trade, movement communication, and social forums. The most important organization from each sector was chosen on the basis of the extent of its participation in GJM events since 1998 and our estimation of its importance within the movement. A matrix of Internet links among these organizations was constructed. Of the thirty-seven organizations, twenty-four had an autonomous Internet links page, which was analyzed. A further nine are included in the matrix because they were listed on the links page of at least one of those twenty-four organizations, even though they did not have links pages themselves.

The resultant network diagram (figure 6.1) shows that organizations from the various strands that make up the GJM are networked—in cyberspace at least. The trade union Transport and General Workers' Union (TGWU), for example, is listed on the Web sites of the Tobin Tax Network, *Red Pepper* magazine, and Globalise Resistance. Stop the War (STWC), chosen to represent the peace sector, has links with the Muslim Association of Britain, SWP, Globalise Resistance, Green Party, and others. FoE, linked to radical direct activist Web sites, peace, ATDOs, and trade unions, appears relatively central. Most central are Indymedia, *Schnews,* and WDM. Each has an in-degree above ten, which means that ten or more other GJMOs in the network list them on their links pages. It is hardly surprising that online activist newsletters/newswires are among the most commonly linked sites. More surprising is the fact that WDM is linked to the rest of the sample considerably more extensively than the broad interorganizational networks, TJM (in-degree = 2), JDC (in-degree = 5), STWC (in-degree = 5), or MPH (not linked at all). However, this network diagram cannot fully illustrate the complexity of Internet links among GJMOs. The case of MPH illustrates one particular weakness. Fourteen GJMOs in the sample are members of the MPH coalition, and half of them, at the time of analysis, displayed the MPH logo on their Web site, yet none included MPH on its links pages, perhaps because MPH was founded in November 2004, and the Web sites were analyzed in March 2005, or perhaps because MPH was regarded only as a virtual organization. Furthermore, each organization was chosen as representative of a movement or specialist organization, each of which has its own complex web of Internet links. A thirty-two-node network cannot demonstrate the full complexity of each organization's links. The *Schnews* Web site, for instance, has 913 links, but because only autonomous links pages were analyzed, Indymedia, which lacks an independent links page but has many links embedded in its Internet postings, scores an "out-degree" of zero (that is, with no links from ego to others). At the other end of the spectrum, Globalise Resistance, the SWP's anticapitalist "front" group, has the highest out-degree (18 links from ego to others) as it seeks to identify with the broader movement, but an in-degree of only three (only Stop the War, *Red Pepper,* and the SWP mention it on their links pages).

Networks in the Street: Participants in the
Make Poverty History March, July 2005

The high point of the MPH campaign was its attempt to replicate the encirclement of Birmingham with a massive rally and march in Edinburgh on July 2, 2005, on the weekend preceding the opening of the G8 meeting at Gleneagles. This highly publicized event became the focal point for the mobilizing efforts of an unprecedentedly broad spectrum of GJM groups. Although some direct action groups regarded MPH as impossibly reformist and concentrated their efforts on organizing protests closer to Gleneagles, they did not entirely dismiss MPH, and individual activists were not discouraged from marching. Moreover, Globalise Resistance actively encouraged supporters to participate in the MPH march and laid on transport to enable them to do so. For these reasons, the MPH march can be considered the largest manifestation of the broadest range of the GJM in Britain to date.

Our account of the GJM thus far has been focused on protest events and the organizations affiliated to campaigns. What, however, is not apparent from an organization-focused account is how centrally their members and supporters have been involved in GJM actions and the overlaps among them. The participation of activists in multiple organizations helps to foster collaboration among organizations and has been shown to serve as a fairly reliable predictor of actual interorganizational linkages (Diani 1995; 2003a). In order to capture this hitherto elusive but critically important dimension of the GJM in Britain, we surveyed the participants in the MPH march. We did this by means of an eight-page, mail-back, self-completion questionnaire, and by conducting face-to-face interviews based on a one-page schedule, with a random cross section of participants. In the event, we distributed 2,000 questionnaires and conducted 493 interviews.[11]

Of those we interviewed, 52.7 percent claimed membership of one or more campaigning organizations, associations, or NGOs. When asked with which of these they most closely identified, 255 respondents named a total of 92 different organizations, fully reflecting the extraordinary diversity of

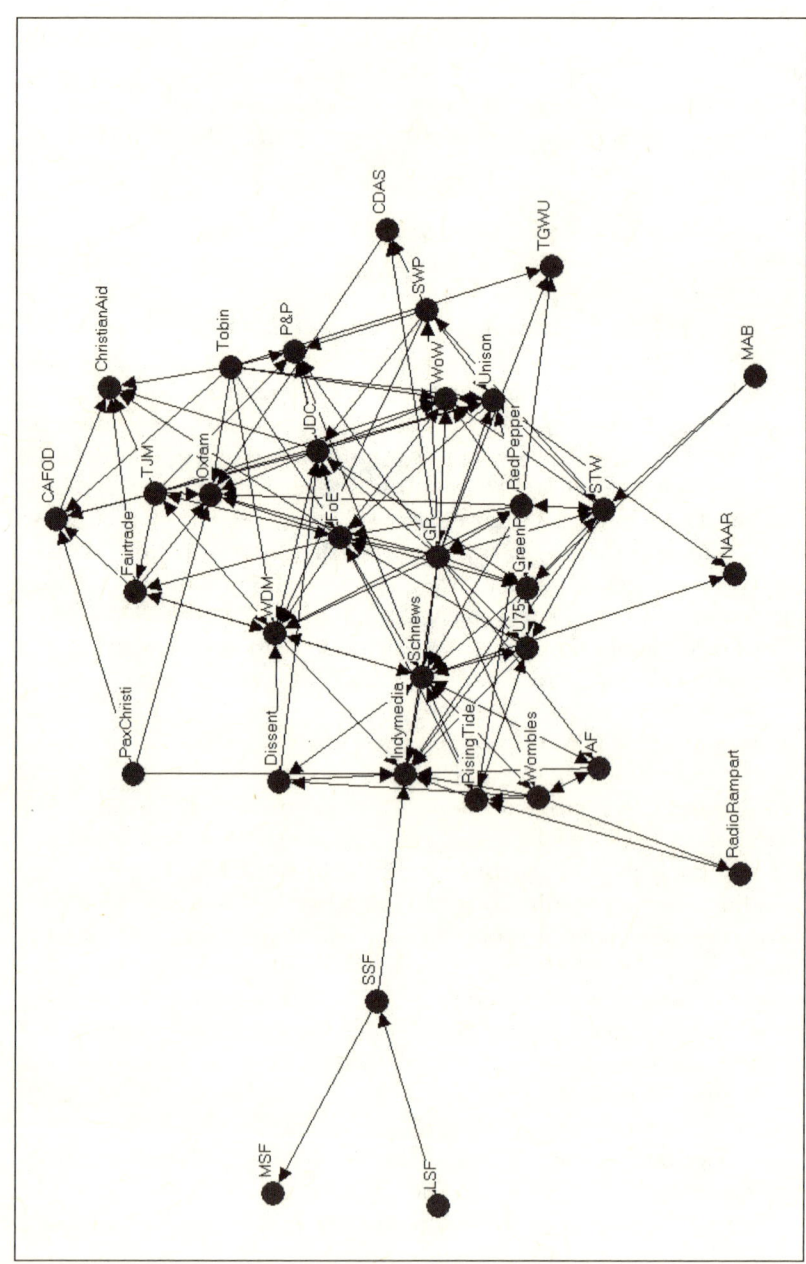

Figure 6.1 Internet Links between Key GJM Organizations

Key for Figure 6-1

AF	Anarchist Federation
CAFOD	Catholic Agency for Overseas Development
CDAS	Committee to Defend Asylum Seekers
Dissent	Dissent!
Fairtrade	Fairtrade Foundation
FoE	Friends of the Earth
GR	Globalise Resistance
GreenP	Green Party
Indymedia	Indymedia United Kollectives
JDC	Jubilee Debt Campaign
LSF	London Social Forum
MAB	Muslim Association of Britain
MSF	Manchester Social Forum
NAAR	National Assembly Against Racism
Oxfam	Oxfam UK
P&P	People and Planet
PaxChristi	Pax Christi UK
Radio Rampart	Radio Rampart
RedPepper	*Red Pepper*
Rising Tide	Rising Tide UK
Schnews	Schnews
SSF	Sheffield Social Forum
STW	Stop the War Coalition
SWP	Socialist Workers' Party
TGWU	Transport and General Workers' Union
TJM	Trade Justice Movement
Tobin	Tobin Tax Network (now called Stamp Out Poverty)
U75	Urban 75
Unison	Unison
WDM	World Development Movement
Wombles	White Overalls Movement Building Libertarian Egalitarian Struggles
WoW	War on Want

the GJM. The organization most often named—Amnesty International—accounted for just 9 percent, followed by Christian Aid (7.5 percent), Oxfam (5.1 percent), CAFOD (4.7 percent), and WDM (4.3 percent). Environmental groups (including the Green Party and Women's Environmental Network) together accounted for 10.6 percent, with FoE and Greenpeace accounting for 4.3 percent and 3.9 percent, respectively. Socialist groups (including Respect and Globalise Resistance) accounted for 9.4 percent, with the SWP most often named (3.2 percent). Both were far outnumbered by those who identified with ATDOs (33 percent). Churches or religious groups accounted for 9.4 percent (or 22.7 percent including faith-affiliated ATDOs such as Christian Aid and CAFOD). Peace and antiwar groups accounted for another 10.6 percent, but trade unions for only 4.7 percent and antiracist or ethnic solidarity groups for only 2.4 percent.

Our survey of MPH marchers revealed extensive overlapping memberships. Of marchers claiming membership of or close identification with FoE, 42 percent were members of or identified with Amnesty, 36.8 percent with Greenpeace, and 33 percent with Oxfam. Of respondents claiming membership of or close identification with Amnesty, 18 percent were members of or identified with FoE, 29 percent with Greenpeace, and 30 percent with Oxfam.[12]

With so many organizations involved in the GJM and interlinked in such various ways, representing interorganizational linkages is no simple task (but see Saunders 2005). However, the broad picture of linkages among different social movement sectors is perhaps more important for our purposes. Figure 6.2 portrays the pattern of marchers' organizational memberships/identifications grouped by movement sectors.

Unsurprisingly, the sector with which most marchers claimed an organizational affiliation or close identity was aid/trade. Of the 255 respondents who claimed membership or close identification with an aid/trade organization, many were also members of at least one organization from each of the religious (99), human rights (102), environmental (84), and peace (22) sectors. It appears that the core of the movement consists of organizations concerned with trade/aid, religion, human rights, and the environment. Peace, workers' rights/trade unions, antiracism, socialist, women's rights, and prodemocracy sectors are connected to core organizations via multiple memberships, but counted many fewer marchers as members/close identifiers. Anticapitalist organizations were barely mentioned. The race/ethnic solidarity sector is least well connected via interpersonal linkages to the rest of the movement, and race was the most marginal of the movement concerns analyzed. The prodemocracy sector—the smallest sector represented here—lacks connections with organizations working on antiracism/ethnic solidarity, socialism, and women's rights. Apart from the antiracism and

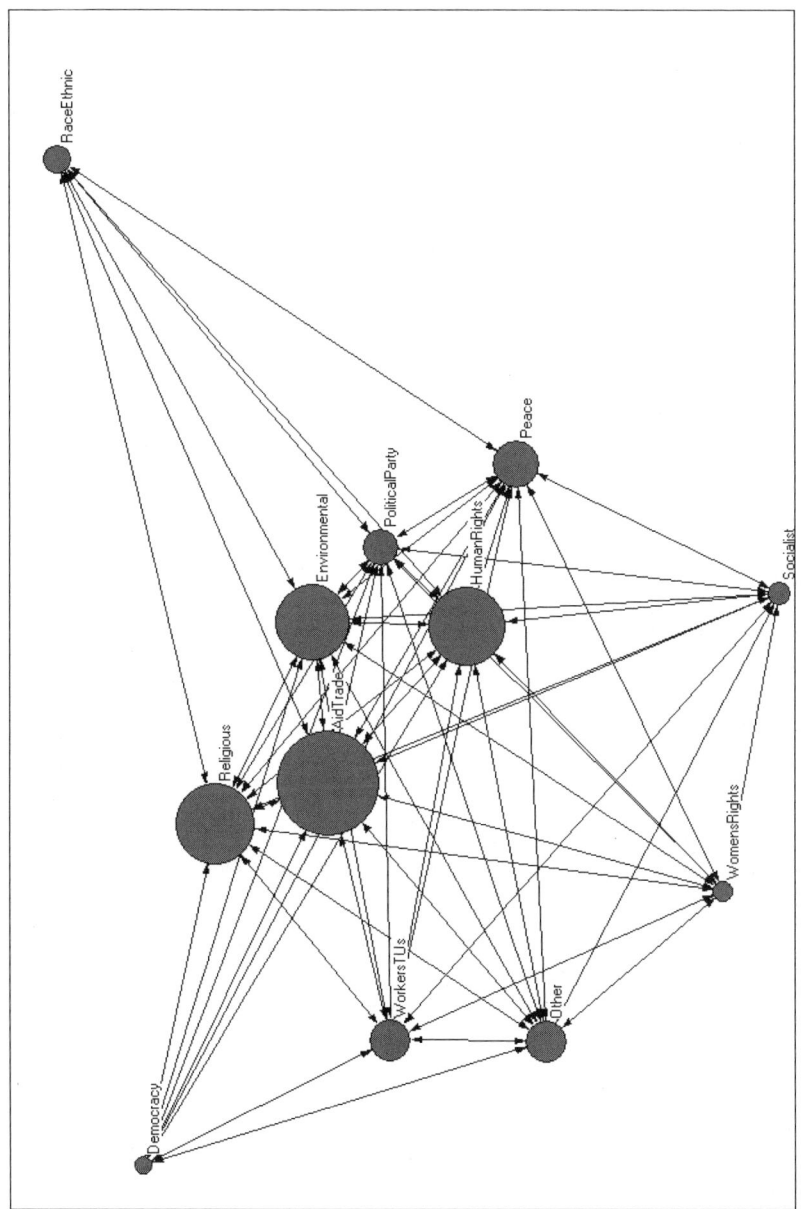

Figure 6.2 Interorganizational Membership/Identification Coincidence Network by Sector

147

Table 6.3 Activists' Participation (Past and Present) in Campaigning Organizations

Type of Campaigning/ Voluntary Organization	Past or Present Membership/Active Involvement (N=538) %
Social Justice/Antipoverty	58.4
Environmental	54.2
Aid/Trade/Development	52.8
Human Rights	52.0
Religious Groups	48.7
Workers' Rights/Trade Unions	43.2
Peace/Antiwar	42.6
Immigrant/Race	30.4
Women's Rights	25.4
Socialist	21.1
Prodemocracy	20.8
Animal Rights	17.4
Local Social Forums	16.3
Gay and Lesbian Rights	14.0
Antiglobalization	13.9
Anticapitalism	10.3
Social Centers/Squats	3.4
Communist	2.7
Anarchist	2.0

prodemocracy sectors, the network is "complete," that is, there are links between all movement sectors.

Overall, a remarkable 89.9 percent of MPH marchers claimed previous involvement in at least one voluntary, advocacy, or campaigning organization (see Table 6.3). The MPH march brought together activists from a broad range of movement sectors, but only a minority (43.2 percent) of marchers acknowledged any involvement with trade unions.

Framing the Issues

The ideological diversity of the movement is clear. Although its components are all, more or less, critics of the neoliberalism of the "Washington consensus," some focus on one issue or group of issues. Others embrace a range of issues. Radicals are dismissive of the reformism of environmental groups such as FoE and Greenpeace and of human rights and ATDOs, but even though both the direct action groups and the SWP are broadly "anticapitalist," they have very different conceptions of an alternative society and the means appropriate to getting there. For direct action activists, the common themes of the movement are anarchy (rejection of hierarchies, authority, the state, and party politics), communitarianism, and ecologism (VER 2000a). The SWP, on the other hand, is formally organized and committed to building revolutionary socialism and tends to regard the environment as a marginal or, at best, secondary issue.

To explore the extent to which MPH marchers shared concerns, we asked them to list, in their own words, what they thought should be the priorities of the GJM. Of the 412 who answered this question, 376 mentioned at least one of trade/aid/development, climate change, corruption, democracy, the environment, health, human rights, peace, race/immigration, and workers' rights. Unsurprisingly, the great majority (84.3 percent) considered that trade/aid/development should be a priority of the GJM (Figure 6.3), but 78 percent listed at least one other issue; of the 328 activists listing aid as a priority issue, 18 also listed climate, 32 mentioned corruption, 26 democracy, 53 the environment, 28 health, 36 human rights, 40 peace, 10 race/immigrants' rights, and 13 workers' rights. This suggests that marchers regard "global justice" as multifaceted, requiring concerted action on a number of issues.

Figure 6.3 shows activists' issue priorities schematically, with links drawn between campaign themes in cases in which at least 10 percent of activists mentioning one theme also mentioned another. Of those who listed aid as an issue, at least 10 percent also mentioned the environment, human rights, and peace, but fewer than 10 percent mentioned any other key issue (democracy, health, corruption, climate, workers' rights, and race/immigrants' rights). Of those mentioning workers' rights, at least 10 percent mentioned every one of the key issues listed above. This dense network of overlapping concerns is consistent with characterizations of GJM identity as "*tolerant*" or "*flexible*" (della Porta 2005a, 186). If "the great strength [of the movement] is that there are big issues around which there is strong convergence" (della Porta 2005a, 201), MPH, at the individual as well as at the organizational level, provided a "big issue" that allowed just such convergence.

Action Repertoires and Movements Alliances

Despite the prominence of formal NGOs in the GJM, it has usually been radical or autonomous organizations/networks that have been most prominent in the summits and days of action that have provided its most public face. Environmental and ATDOs have generally been more restrained, formally participating in summits and/or mounting separate actions. For example,

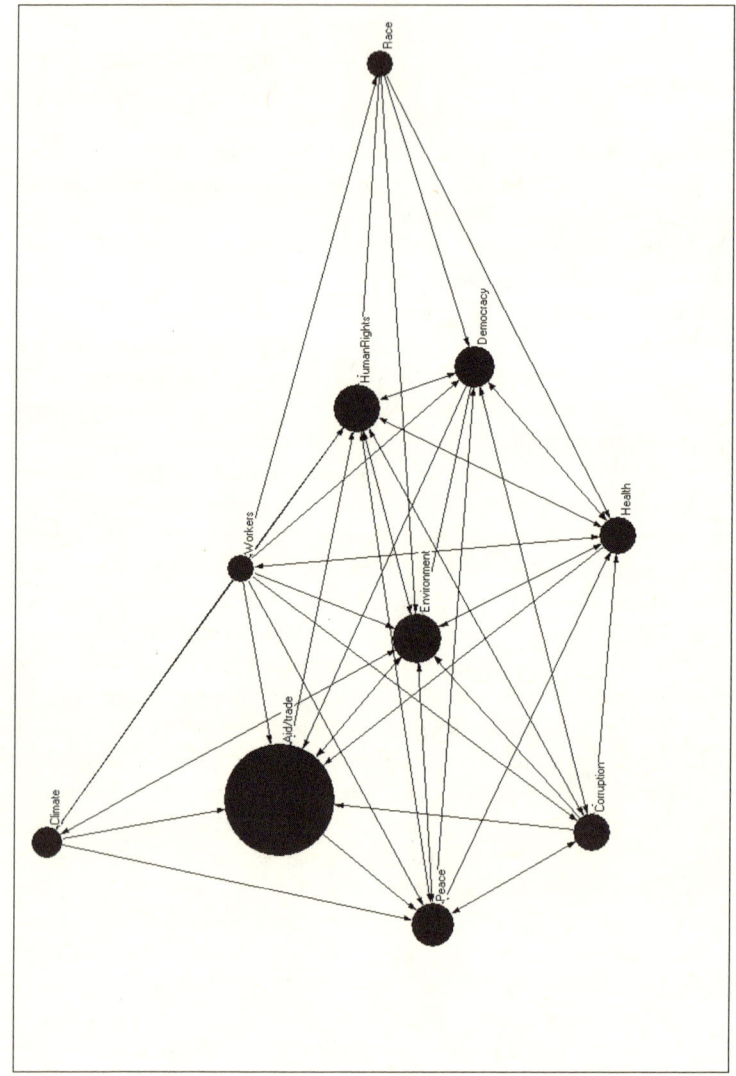

Figure 6.3 The Network of Issue Priorities among Make Poverty History Marchers

Note: The size of the nodes is scaled to represent the total number of individuals who mentioned each issue; therefore the aid/trade node is the largest and the race node is the smallest.

although Jubilee 2000 took part in the protests against the IMF and World Bank in Prague in 2000, concerned about violence, it was careful to remove its supporters before the main demonstration began (Ford and Poolos 2000, 215). Fear of being tarnished with the brush of violence or disorder has, especially since Genoa, J18, and May Day 2000, deterred most ATDOs and EMOs from prominent involvement in days of action at which confrontation was anticipated. The more confrontational protests have been only loosely organized by radical activists, coordinated largely through e-mail lists, Web postings and meetings, Internet sites like Indymedia and Urban75 assisting the activist community to come together in virtual space to discuss propositions, coordinate actions, and share experiences (Atton 2003). Convergence centers near the protest site are designed to allow protesters to meet and to hone their ideas for action.

The action repertoire of the movement ranges from the conventional, insider strategies of some of the most well-respected ATDOs to the window-smashing of tiny minorities of anarchists at anticapitalist demonstrations. Actions have included nonviolent direct action (commonly blockades and occasionally sabotage), mobilizing public opinion through the press (using mediagenic stunts), petitioning, and letter writing. Overwhelmingly, however, the repertoire of those who identify with the movement and act in its name is nonviolent and nonconfrontational. Only about one in four (26.8 percent) of the MPH marchers interviewed had never participated in a march or rally before, and almost a third were veterans of more than five marches or rallies. Not surprisingly, the great majority (75.3 percent) had never participated in direct action, especially as, from their comments, many associated it with violent or anarchic protest. What was surprising, however, was that more than one in six (18.2 percent) said that they had participated in direct action at least twice, the great majority of them more than five times. This is further evidence of the inclusiveness of the MPH march. The various movement families that have come together in the GJM are linked to one another by interorganizational and interpersonal networks at elite and local levels (Rootes and Saunders 2005). Especially at the local level, radical ecologists often have links with those engaging in direct action against the war, campaigning for animal rights, and supporting refugees. Sometimes the same activist is active on all of these issues. Trade unionists have made links with RTS activists. EMOs have forged links with campaigning groups and have joined in short-term alliances with radical activists; FoE, for example, is part of the No New Oil coalition that includes the direct action group Rising Tide, which consists mostly of former RTS activists. Antiwar protests have involved broad alliances incorporating the old and new Lefts, antiracists, environmentalists, pacifists, feminists, and Third World activists.

Since 2001, a network of groups has collaborated to organize days of direct action aiming to close down the biennial Defence Systems and Equipment

International (DSEI) arms fair. In 2001, this included a march and vigil, with speakers from the peace movement, including CND, and a "Fiesta for Life against Death" direct action protest, supported by RTS and the Wombles, which drew on the pink and silver theme and included a street party, samba band, and cycle-powered sound system. The larger 2003 action, deliberately multiheaded to make it more difficult to police, included direct action by Greenpeace, while representatives of Globalise Resistance, Amnesty International, and others addressed pre-march rallies.

Direct actions against the imminent Iraq war were well under way by the beginning of January 2003. Among many instances of direct action, the Greenpeace flagship, *Rainbow Warrior*, blocked the departure of military supply vessels for Iraq. On February 15, 2003, the Stop the War Coalition, CND, and the Muslim Association of Britain coordinated a march that attracted some two million people and has been credited with forging links between religious and peace movement activists (Stop the War Coalition 2005).[13]

Protests proliferated in Britain under the Thatcher and Major Conservative governments (1979–1997) (Rootes 2003d), but the Labour government elected in 1997 offered few provocations to social movement activists until it embraced the Bush administration's "war on terror" and the invasion of Iraq, and so provoked the biggest demonstration ever seen in London. Although the British government has not resisted the global justice agenda—indeed, it has been a leader in debt relief and poverty alleviation measures—the circumstances and consequences of the "war on terror" have made it possible for global justice to be employed as the "master frame" of social movement activism in the present decade.

Widespread protests against the Iraq war provided the more radical elements of the direct action movement with unprecedented opportunities to broaden their base. Direct activists, EMOs (including Greenpeace and FoE), the Green Party, Muslim, ethnic minority, and human rights groups, socialists, and no borders activists all rallied to the cause. But if the "antiwar movement" can be framed as part of the broader movement for global justice, it is a mistake simply to assimilate the antiwar movement to the GJM. The antiwar movement had many of the characteristics of a classic peace movement, mobilizing vast numbers of people in the buildup to the conflict but rapidly losing momentum thereafter. The mobilization was overwhelmingly one of moral protest, and it overlaps considerably with the later mobilization of MPH. Given that the 2003 antiwar protests mobilized so many people, it is scarcely surprising that almost half the participants in the MPH march had previously participated in an antiwar demonstration, and it is perhaps just as noteworthy that more than half had not. It is revealing, however, that a well-advertised antiwar demonstration in Edinburgh the day after the great MPH march attracted only some 1,500 people. Moreover, although the antiwar coalition was broader than previous iterations of peace and antiwar protests in Britain, it did not include most of the ATDOs so prominent in the GJM. The mobilizations overlap, but they are nevertheless quite distinct.

Although there are links, albeit generally indirect links, beyond the large coalitions of JDC, TJM, and MPH to more radical campaigners, such links are neither frequent nor strong. If this is a single movement, it is a segmented one.

Conclusion

The development of social movements in Britain has sometimes been told as the history of an unfolding sequence of interlinked mobilizations and campaigns (see, e.g., Lent 2001), a long wave of protest, which is both conditional upon and has contributed to the development of a less deferential and more participatory form of society in which the boundaries of legitimate political expression have been progressively pushed beyond the strictly conventional (Rootes 2003d).

Viewed thus, the GJM is simply the culmination or the latest iteration of a well-established process (see Rootes and Saunders 2005; Saunders and Rootes 2005). That, however, is to overlook the novelty of the GJM and the contribution to it of people and of an NGO sector—religious groups and ATDOs—that were little if at all involved in earlier waves of social movement action. Only the peace movement involved any substantial number of the religious, and even it attracted only peripheral interest or support from ATDOs. Thus the GJM, far from being simply a continuation and outgrowth of earlier social movement mobilizations, is a significant innovation. To view it otherwise is to privilege the role of actors and events that, however considerable their contribution to argument and debate, are numerically quite marginal to the movement.

There is, however, clearly shared concern among groups and organizations that differ in their tactical repertoires, expressed by a recognition that global financial institutions are at the root of many of the single-issue problems. Networking and alliance building are increasing among different types of organizations, and there is a shared sense of participation in collective action.

Christopher Brooks (2004, 562) suggests that "the master frame [of the movement] is a democratic one designed to increase ... accountability and input into the decision-making processes of organizations perceived to be promulgating the negative effects of globalisation." This is broad enough to allow a variety of SMOs and activists to participate, from anarchists, socialists, and communists, to those concerned with environmental, peace, religious, feminist, homeless, indigenous rights, migration, race and social justice issues, the labor movement, urban squatters, and others.

But if some strands of the movement appear to be focused on building democracy from below in order to counter the increasing power of international financial institutions, others—notably most of the ATDOs that mobilize the big battalions of demonstrators and petition-signers—are more pragmatically focused on policy reforms than on radical institutional change.

The sheer diversity and complexity of the movement is striking. MPH alone was an extraordinary coalition, but it was by no means simply an umbrella organization of the whole movement, for it did not include the more radical groups, even though many radical activists marched in Edinburgh. The state of the movement in mid-2005 was well illustrated by the front page of the Globalise Resistance Web site; as well as detailing its own activities, it displayed links to G8 Alternative, a network of Scottish groups organizing protests against the G8 meeting, and to the Dissent! network, on the one hand, and to MPH on the other. Globalise Resistance, which makes no secret of the fact that almost half its steering committee are SWP members, was, however, held at arm's length by both.

The GJM in Britain differs from its continental counterparts in several respects. Attac, so important in France and, latterly, in Germany, is negligible in Britain, whereas the aid and development charities and NGOs and religious groups are prominent and highly mobilized and have a well-developed globalist agenda. Local social forums, so characteristic of the movement in Italy and elsewhere, are few and weakly developed in Britain. Issues such as "precarity," which resonate loudly in countries where mass unemployment is rife, have so far found only a faint echo in Britain, where unemployment has remained low for more than a decade. It is probably this that explains the relatively low profile of trade unions in the GJM in Britain.

Another peculiarity of the GJM in Britain is the presence of the SWP. However, although the SWP has been energetic and, as ever, enterprising in the formation of "united front" organizations, it has not been able to hegemonize the movement. Its many initiatives, local as well as national, have undoubtedly contributed to the dynamism of the movement, as it has sought, by involving itself in campaigns, locally as well as nationally, to encourage popular mobilization and, by injecting a revolutionary socialist critique of capitalism, to move those campaigns toward the left.[14] But suspicion of the SWP's motives as well as aversion to its brand of socialist politics has led radicals and reformists alike to keep a wary distance even when campaigning against a common enemy. However, if the SWP has been unable to hegemonize the movement, it also appears that its presence has not divided the movement or poisoned the water. The movement *is* divided, but it is divided according to the prior histories, commitments, and preferred values and action repertoires of its diverse constituents, and to these the SWP is little more than a sideshow.

Purists might object that there is a difference between a campaign and a movement, and that while coalitions are characteristic of the former, identity is required before we can be confident of the existence of the latter (della Porta and Diani 1999, 20). However, identity appears to us to be overestimated as a necessary condition of social movements, and it would seriously underestimate the GJM in Britain to represent it as a mere campaign coalition of national organizations. The preparations for the protests against the G8 made visible an extremely broad and diffuse movement that, perhaps especially in its many local manifestations, transcends the divisions between and among the campaign coalitions and other campaigning organizations. As with the environmental movement of the 1990s, the nonidentity of groups and organizations campaigning for a broadly conceived common purpose is a strength rather than a weakness of the GJM in Britain.

Notes

We wish to thank Brian Doherty for his helpful comments on earlier drafts of this chapter.

1. In fact, WDM was created as a direct response to the Charity Commission's restrictions on the activities of aid charities. When in 1969 aid charities, including Oxfam, Christian Aid, and War on Want, joined forces to launch a new campaign coalition, Action for World Development, to work to achieve an increase in national aid budgets and political action on aid and trade, the Charity Commission pointed out that Action for World Development infringed on charity laws and warned that if charities engaged in political activity, those responsible could be required to reimburse to the charity any of its funds that were spent on activities outside the limits of its charitable purposes (Black 1992, 154). In response, the founder members agreed that a separate organization should be established to carry out the political work they deemed important (Macdonald 1972). Thus the WDM was born, but the constraints of the Charity Commission prevented other organizations from working openly in partnership with it, thus precluding its development as a full-fledged movement, even though it was sometimes able to act as a coordinating body for them.

2. The proportion saying they would go on a demonstration in response to an unjust law rose from 8 percent in 1983 to 17 percent in 1994 and 20.5 percent in 1998 (Jowell et al. 1999, 320). Indeed, in 1994, 8.9 percent said they had gone on a demonstration in such circumstances (Curtice and Jowell 1995, 154), and by 2000 this had risen to 10 percent (Bromley, Curtice, and Seyd 2001, 202). In response to a differently worded question in 1996, 31 percent said they "definitely" or "probably" would go on a protest march or demonstration, and 5.5 percent said they had actually done so in the previous five years (Jowell et al. 1997, 320).

3. Corporate Watch keeps a watchful eye on the workings of corporations, especially where they have vested interests or negative effects (Plows 2004, 99).

4. We are indebted to Brian Doherty for additional information on this event.

5. As in most of these cases, what activists describe as heavy-handed policing, others have described as firm but restrained policing proportionate to the challenge or threat as assessed from intelligence reports. Since there are no neutral sources, it is impossible to judge, but it does seem very likely that at least some activists went to such protests prepared to offer violence or provocation to the police. In the N30 protests, for example, a police van was incinerated.

6. Indymedia was not without precedent in Britain. Similar provision for the uploading of reports onto the Web was developed for the J18 protests in 1999.

7. Police increasingly photograph protesters at demonstrations and make use of powers to stop and search. The filming or photographing of protesters is often preliminary to later arrest, as it is often considered tactically better to avoid immediate intervention that might provoke wider reaction.

8. Jubilee 2000 reformed in 2001 as the Jubilee Debt Campaign (JDC).

9. Its Web site (www.makepovertyhistory.org) listed 521 member organizations on September 28, 2005.

10. In the event, the G8 Alternatives summit was held in central Edinburgh.

11. The response rate to our survey (28.2 percent) is broadly in line with that to recent similarly administered surveys in Britain. The interviews served as a check on the reliability of the survey. The most substantial differences between survey respondents and interviewees were that the former were rather more female and older and even more highly educated than the interviewees, of whom 70 percent were university or college graduates.

12. Despite the fact that participants could list only the *five* organizations with which they were mostly involved or most closely identified, overlaps appear considerably more common than those found by a 1993 survey of members of FoE and Amnesty International. Grant Jordan and William Maloney (1997, 119–120) found 12.8 percent of FoE members were also members of Amnesty, 5.7 percent of Oxfam, and 31.9 percent of Greenpeace, whereas 12 percent of Amnesty members were members of Oxfam, 16.9 percent of FoE, and 33.7 percent of Greenpeace. The apparently increased frequency of multiple memberships among MPH marchers might reflect the development of multiple and "tolerant identities" among activists, but it might simply be that marchers are more likely to have multiple memberships than more passive (or committed) members.

13. For more on the anti-Iraq war protests and the peace movement, see Rootes and Saunders 2005.

14. The SWP did, however, actively discourage the formation of autonomous local social forums, arguing that they were premature in view of the state of development of working-class consciousness in Britain and fearing that they would distract from the more important mobilization for the European Social Forum in London in October 2004 (Gillan 2006a and 2006b). It is, however, unlikely that this suffices to explain the relative underdevelopment of local social forums in Britain.

Chapter Seven

The Global Justice Movements
in Germany

Dieter Rucht, Simon Teune, and Mundo Yang

In the summer of 2001, a new political actor called Attac entered the public stage in Germany. Mainstream media began to cover the group, and Attac's membership soared to one thousand within one month. How did such a small and thus far unknown group manage to attract so much attention, and how did it come to be perceived, later on, as the central player in the global justice movements (GJMs) in Germany? Several facilitating factors came into play. First, Attac was connected to a major and spectacular event: the mass demonstrations and partly violent clashes between police and political activists on the occasion of the G8 summit in Genoa in July 2001. Though few German Attac members actually participated, the protesters from Germany became publicly associated with Attac.

A second factor was related to Attac's ingenious media strategy. The group offered a kind of "embedded journalism," that is, an opportunity for journalists to travel with activists to Genoa by bus, to interview the participants, to keep in contact with the press speakers during the event, to make use of an e-mail and SMS-pager service, and eventually to become more deeply involved in the network of activists (Kolb 2005).

Third, *Der Spiegel,* a widely read weekly political magazine, referred to Attac in a twelve-page article on the Genoa events, the GJMs, and the underlying issues (*Der Spiegel,* July 23, 2001). This article was consequential because this magazine is an important, if not the most important, inter-media agenda setter in Germany.[1] Moreover, there was a need for orientation on the part of the media with regard to what they dubbed the "antiglobalization movement"—a complex field of diverse actors that even insiders have difficulty grasping in its entirety.[2] Until this point, this field was not associated with one particular and clearly recognizable group. By highlighting Attac, the media and in particular *Der Spiegel* gave a "face" to a diffuse and fragmented body of groups.

Fourth, the very term *Attac*, although originally an acronym for the odd and complicated name of the original French group (*Association pour la Taxation des Transactions pour l'Aide aux Citoyens*), was a media-savvy label that was likely chosen for precisely this reason. *Attac* sounds like "attack" (German: *Attacke*, French: *attaque*), evoking images of conflict, aggression, and probably violence—hence news values from a journalist's perspective. In fact, in its early phase of public appearance in Germany, Attac was mistaken by some politicians and parts of the public as an extremist group prone to the use of violence. This misrepresentation was soon corrected, but the image of Attac as a powerful group at the center of an allegedly "new" and exciting social movement remained. For many journalists and large parts of their audience, Attac continues to epitomize the global justice movement. However, the reality is much more complex: One cannot speak of a "new movement," and Attac is not its one and only key player.

The story of Attac exemplifies that images constructed by the mass media are not to be taken at face value. Instead, we must take a closer look at the actual history and trajectory of the complex set of actors to whom we refer as the "GJMs" in Germany. The GJMs are rooted in and inspired by prior movements, most notably the new social movements of the 1970s and 1980s and the New Left of the 1960s, which, in turn, are linked to much earlier predecessor movements. Moreover, the rise of the GJMs in Germany has to be understood in the broader social and political context of postwar Germany. Accordingly, we will briefly lay out this context (1) before focusing on more specific aspects of these movements, namely, their emergence and development (2), structural and ideological configuration (3), identities (4), and action repertoires (5). We conclude with some more general statements on the status and prospects of the movements.

Observers from Germany and abroad have argued that postwar (West) Germany continued to be shaped by an authoritarian, nondemocratic political culture inherited from the past. Political conflict was generally met with suspicion, and in light of the experiences with the Nazi regime, social movements tended to be seen as a threat to democracy. This picture has changed in subsequent decades. West Germany, and eventually the unified new Germany, is widely recognized as a full-fledged democracy, not only in terms of its formal institutions, but also regarding its political culture. To a considerable extent, this change can be attributed to social movements.

Today, the prodemocratic movements that existed during the 1950s and the first half of the 1960s have been largely forgotten. However, the so-called extra-parliamentary opposition—including the student movement of the second half of the 1960s—plays an important role in the country's collective memory, particularly because these groups marked a qualitative breakthrough in Germany's history. Authoritarian values and behaviors, rigid bureaucratic structures, capitalist exploitation, warfare in Vietnam and other countries, and forms of imperialism of varying degrees of subtlety came under heavy attack. Though the student movement barely made an impact on formal political institutions, let alone the capitalist structure of the economy, it definitely influenced the political culture and, more specifically, inspired a subsequent wave of social movements.

In the wake of the student movement that quickly collapsed after 1969, a second generation of social movements emerged, labeled new social movements (NSMs), which flourished and continues to be active today. These waves of movements, although clearly exhibiting a left leaning, had few overlaps with the labor movement. Regarding energy and environmental policies, for example, trade unions and NSMs generally considered each other as opponents throughout the 1970s and the first half of the 1980s. By contrast, partial and temporal alliances on issues of peace and disarmament could be formed, for example, against the NATO double-track decision in the early 1980s. Regarding their organizational culture and political styles, however, trade unions and NSMs had little in common, with the former being much more hierarchical than the NSMs seeking "democracy from below" (Koopmans 1995; Roth 1994).

Since the late 1990s and clearly as an outgrowth of the NSMs, a new generation of movements, namely, the GJMs, has developed and gradually entered the public scene in Germany. Interestingly, this set of movements, despite emerging independently from the labor movement, was gradually able to build links with the trade unions based on the identification of neoliberalism as a common target.

Although the labor movement traditionally relies on a strong internationalist ideology, this orientation had few consequences for the German trade unions' protest activities from the 1950s through the 1990s. Even the gradual growth and deepening of the European Union did not derail the German unions from their domestic orientation. However, with the public debate and globalization's repercussions in many spheres of life, social movements—from the far Right to the trade unions to the far Left—began to view globalization, or certain aspects of it, as problematic. Whereas the Right extremists rejected globalization altogether and promoted a chauvinistic policy of renationalization (Greven and Grumke 2006; Leggewie 2003), the labor unions and emerging GJMs took a more diffuse or ambivalent stance. This position is also reflected in the widely used self-description of the movements as *Globalisierungskritiker* (critics of globalization) rather than *Anti-Globalisierer* (antiglobalists) or *Globalisierungsgegner* (opponents of globalization).

Regardless of the primary motive of their critique—be it saving domestic jobs and maintaining a given wage level or narrowing the increasing gap between rich and poor countries—the source of all these problems was perceived to be essentially the same: a brutal, unrestricted "turbocapitalism," driven mainly by multinational corporations and stock markets, and flanked by political elites who converged in praising the benefits of a globalizing neoliberal system. Although the fight against neoliberalism serves as a common negative dominator for otherwise very heterogeneous social movements (Rucht 2002b), the idea of global justice and its various derivations in the fields of labor, human rights, civic rights, ecology, peace, poverty, indigenous cultures, and so on denotes a positive master frame. This frame can bring these groups together not only on the basis of a diffuse leftist ideology, but also in specific campaigns, as exemplified by the mass demonstrations Germany experienced in 2003 and 2004.

Compared with the earlier generations of leftist movements in Germany, this bridging of issues and movements appears to be a very recent phenomenon. At a closer look, however, this seemingly new trait can be traced farther back, as can other features that, mainly based on journalist accounts and self-descriptions, seem to characterize a "new" type of social movement.

The Emergence and Development of the Global Justice Movements in Germany

Many different political traditions and ideologies, mainly stemming from the NSMs, have played a role in the GJMs' formation. One of its older traditions is that of socialist internationalism. Revived in Germany after World War II, this orientation was especially important for the student movement of the 1960s. This was also the period when German Third World initiatives with other ideological backgrounds put global inequality on the agenda and ran several campaigns to promote just world trade and human rights (Olejniczak 1999). Since then, quite different political currents and initiatives have been active in this field, for example in the support for militant liberation movements like the Sandinistas in Nicaragua and the fight against racism in Southern Africa.

Activists from Third World initiatives and from the domains of peace, ecology, world economy, human rights, and many other fields were engaged in joint activities very early. The mobilizations on peace issues in the 1980s might serve as an example for these broad coalitions (Holmes Cooper 1996). However, a profile comparable to the GJMs did not emerge until criticism of the world economic order and the structure of the world market were condensed in a shared framing of diverse global problems. This shared framing developed in the context of mobilizations that were similar to the GJMs' protests at the turn of the millennium. As early as May 1985, a counter-summit and street marches accompanied the world economic summit in Bonn (Holzapfel and König 2001, 25). Approximately twenty-five thousand protesters, including a large block of autonomist groups, took to the streets to challenge those responsible for "starvation, exploitation, and imperialism" (according to the manifesto). Joint mobilizations in the 1980s culminated in the mobilization against a meeting of the International Monetary Fund (IMF) and World Bank in Berlin in 1988, where some 150 ideologically diverse groups signed a declaration criticizing international institutions (Gerhards and Rucht 1992). As in earlier protests, the central frame uniting protesters was "imperialism," allegedly represented by the IMF and World Bank. At the end of a "week of action," eighty thousand protesters took to the streets to oppose the policy of free trade. Yet with the end of the Cold War and German unification, their hopes for a "new internationalism" soon dwindled.

The bankruptcy of authoritarian state socialism did not discredit the ideology of the NSMs because they had never supported such systems. However, especially the radical and militant parts of the internationalist movement became disillusioned with the once-admired Nicaraguan Sandinistas, who did not shy away from corrupt practices after having seized power. Owing to new political conditions on the international level, terms such as *Third World* or *anti-imperialism* no longer seemed adequate. An example of the difficulties of Left radical internationalism in these years is the Bundeskongress entwicklungspolitischer Gruppen (BUKO). Since its founding in 1977, BUKO's annual conferences—facilitated by the financial support of the Protestant Church—had been the most important stage for the internationalist and Third World spectrum to set agendas and initiate debates. Its membership and influence grew constantly during the 1980s, followed by a phase of ideological self-occupation and stalemate in the early 1990s. In this situation, two developments, one on the moderate end of the spectrum and the other on the radical end, shaped the early profile of the GJMs in Germany.

The first development was the reappropriation of protest by moderate organizations that were experiencing the limits of their mode of action in the late 1990s. After a process of institutionalization that had begun in preexisting groups as early as in the 1980s, many movement organizations concentrated on bargaining with authorities to reach their goals. Initiatives active on the international level, now labeled as NGOs, came to the fore as new windows of opportunity opened to collaborate with intergovernmental institutions in the early 1990s. Some of these groups were allowed to participate in official delegations at the UN World Conferences (most notably on climate issues in Rio de Janeiro in 1992), but their policy impacts were limited. For example, hopes for more development aid because of disarmament after the Cold War were not fulfilled. It became apparent in activist discourses from different policy domains that neither the international institutions nor the German government of Social Democrats and Greens, which came to power in 1998, would implement substantial changes (Eberlei 2002). This situation contributed to criticism of an alleged "NGOization" of social movements. The participation of movement actors in intergovernmental institutions was time consuming, and, moreover, fostered the establishment of a class of experts more or less detached from the grassroots groups. In response to these developments, protest regained importance even among the more moderate organizations.

Another part of these developments came from the lessons learned from transnational campaigns in which German organizations and networks were engaged. The German Initiative to Ban Landmines, especially the development assistance organization Medico International, played an important role in the International Campaign to Ban Landmines. As a result, in Germany and many other countries, weapons classified as antipersonnel landmines are now banned (Gebauer 1998). Similarly, the German Erlassjahr network for debt relief participated in the global Jubilee 2000 campaign that led to a partial cancellation of debts for Southern countries and an intensified dialogue between Northern and Southern activists (Yang 2005). In contrast to the common lobbying work of the NGOs, these campaigns relied on political pressure exerted in direct talks with decision makers as well as on mass protest and public education. Without institutionalized access to powerful international organizations, and largely independent from national governments, the two campaigns worked both with and against state institutions. In this regard, they reflected the rising importance of protest politics for moderate movement activists.

The second development shaping the emerging GJMs occurred in the radical spectrum. While moderate organizations had experienced their heydays in the context of UN conferences, the more radical grassroots groups responsible for major mobilizations in the 1980s lost importance (Hierlmeier 2002, 112). However, this situation was soon reversed. By the mid-1990s, the *indígena* uprising in Chiapas (Mexico) that was part of the resistance against the North American Free Trade Agreement (NAFTA) served as a guiding star for the post-socialist Left. It raised awareness about the negative consequences of free trade agreements and demonstrated the existence of viable autonomous structures and a political consciousness that strictly opposed the colonization of everyday life by capitalist principles (Brand 2002). As in other countries, the activities of the Peoples' Global Action (PGA), an offspring from the Zapatista ideas, played an important role in shaping how the German social movements perceived global problems. The Zapatista abstention from dogma and utopia, as expressed in the slogan *preguntando caminamos* (we advance by asking questions), as well as the call for direct democracy and the rejection of state-oriented politics, resonated among German groups with an autonomist tradition (see *The Antagonist Field* below). In these circles a "globalization from below" appeared as a positive reference point as early as the mid-1990s. In 1998, the campaign against the Multilateral Agreement on Investments (MAI)[3] contributed to strengthening the anti-neoliberal frame. In their "PGA manifesto," the Zapatista-inspired group specified the target of the campaign: "Today, capital is deploying a new strategy to assert its power and neutralise peoples' resistance. Its name is economic globalisation."[4]

Both the reorientation of moderate movement organizations toward direct action and the revival of radical initiatives built up the base for the GJMs' surge in the late 1990s. Earlier protests challenging the same targets had been less robust, for example in July 1992, when seventeen thousand demonstrators peacefully gathered in Munich to oppose a joint summit of the G7 and EU. Several hundred of them were encircled and finally detained by massive police force (Holzapfel and König 2001, 27).

Unlike in many other countries, the Seattle protests in late 1999 were not a decisive moment for the GJMs in Germany; rather, the realignment of movement actors and the transnational revival of protest became most apparent in the protests that took place in Cologne during that same year. A key actor was the temporary Alliance Cologne 99, comprising peace and development groups, youth organizations of political parties, student groups, NGOs, and radical leftist groups. This network organized street demonstrations and a counter-summit focused on decreasing wages, forced displacement, and power structures in the world market. Organized by a specifically transnational network, the European March against Unemployment, Job Insecurity, and Exclusion was held on May 29 with thirty thousand participants. This march, along with a counter-summit held by more moderate groups, was meant to send a critical signal to the subsequent EU summit in Cologne starting on June 3. During the summit, radical groups organized smaller protest events.

A second wave of protest two weeks later was directed against the G8 summit in Cologne, culminating in massive demonstrations. In addition, PGA organized a caravan bringing peasants to Europe from the global South (mainly from India). During these events actors not only exhibited a clear transnational profile but also presented a manifesto that, compared with the internationalism or anti-imperialism of the 1980s, included a new framing: "In the contemporary shape of neo-liberalism, the ruling world order continues to pose a threat to the people." Neoliberalism was introduced as a central concept to interpret the problems in the world and to unite the disparate struggles of thematically distinct movements. Even the very act of protesting was remodeled translocally.

To oppose the G8 summit, protesters took to the streets on "J18"—a global action day promoted by PGA on June 18, 1999—not only in Cologne, but also in dozens of other places around the globe. In London, the "Carnival against capital" ended in the devastation of some parts of the business district. The next day in Cologne, some thirty-five thousand demonstrators followed a call issued by the German Jubilee 2000 branch and encircled the site of the governmental meeting with a human chain to underline their claims for debt cancellation. These protests revealed the character of the rising GJMs in Germany: The actors involved came from various movements with different foci. They had begun to build networks in order to overcome national borders and narrow issue specialization, declaring their struggle as a joint effort in resisting neoliberal politics.

After the demonstrations in Genoa, which eventually triggered public interest in the GJMs, a rearrangement in the field of actors became visible. Groups that previously had a dominant status in the discussion about globalization lost visibility; others—mainly those associated with the political climber Attac—gained importance.

A crucial turn in the agenda of the GJMs was forced by the events of September 11, as attention shifted from global inequalities to terrorism and war. In 2002, the GJMs began participating in mobilizations surrounding the annual Conference on Security in Munich, using the slogan "from Genoa to Munich" to frame the conference as a matter of global justice. Peace protests and war in general also clearly dominated the agenda in 2003; apart from the peace groups, Attac played a significant role within the GJMs in mobilizing against the war on Iraq. Many activists of the GJMs joined the networks of the peace movement and vice versa, engaging in tactics such as civil disobedience by blocking U.S. military bases in Germany, as seen in the peace activities of the 1980s. A survey conducted at the peace demonstration on February 15 in Berlin, where around half a million participants protested against the upcoming war in Iraq, underscores this development: Three out of four respondents sympathized with the GJMs in Germany (Rucht 2003).

Later in 2003, the trend toward local or national social policy issues facilitated cooperation with trade unions, Left parties, and unemployed initiatives. The longstanding corporatist arrangements between Left parties, trade unions, and other interest groups were undermined by the accelerated retrenchment of the welfare state by a government composed of Social Democrats and Greens. Local social forums and more traditional action coalitions (*Aktionsbündnisse*) mushroomed in many cities. One year later, a wave of demonstrations against cutbacks in unemployment assistance brought together a broad coalition of unemployed, trade unionists, left-radical parties, and activists from the GJMs.

Overall, the composition of the GJMs continues to be in motion. On the one hand, their waning radicalism is reflected by the salient position of Attac and ongoing dissociation of antagonist groups who criticized the dominance of the traditional and bureaucratic Left. On the other hand, many new members have joined the GJMs, and new initiatives like the local social forums have emerged.

The Configuration of the German Global Justice Movements

As indicated, the events described previously have been organized and supported by political groups and organizations with diverse thematic and ideological backgrounds. In order to comprehend the complex configuration of the German GJMs, we locate the relevant actors in a political field, that is, defined by two dimensions: (1) the kind/type of criticism raised and (2) the preferred organizational model for the group or movement (see figure 7.1). The two dimensions are marked by two opposite poles. On the one hand, indicated by the vertical axis, criticism could be directed against specific features of the political and economic regime (this is labeled a reformist position) or against the liberal-representative and capitalist model as such (the radical position). On the other hand, different organizational logics mark the extremes, as indicated by the horizontal dimension. The "organized" pole stresses the advantages of a firm and clearly structured organization. Efficacy, rationality, and the priority of goal attainment suggest the building of large and formal organizational entities. Opposite this is the "spontaneous" pole that values the spontaneity and autonomy of group members. The ideal of spontaneity is more easily met in small organizations with a low degree of formalization and division of labor. Representation via delegates is either limited or entirely absent.

Thus, the position of the global justice movement organizations (GJMOs) in this field is defined by their distance vis-à-vis the political and economic system as well as their organizational preference. This position also mirrors their relationship to other groups.[5] Considering these relations, we can identify two subfields of fairly distinct actors—one moderate and the other antagonist.[6] Following a different approach, moderate grassroots groups and Trotskyite groups are part of the GJM field beyond the antagonist and moderate camps. In addition, other actors are forming intermediate networks. In Germany, two quite different types of networks—Attac and the Social Forums—were established. They are meant to provide a permanent basis for integrating diverse movement actors. Ideological and organizational differences that separate the radicals from the moderates are a constant cause of conflict and delineation. Yet intermediate networks have been successful to a certain degree in bridging both competing fields.[7] A link analysis of

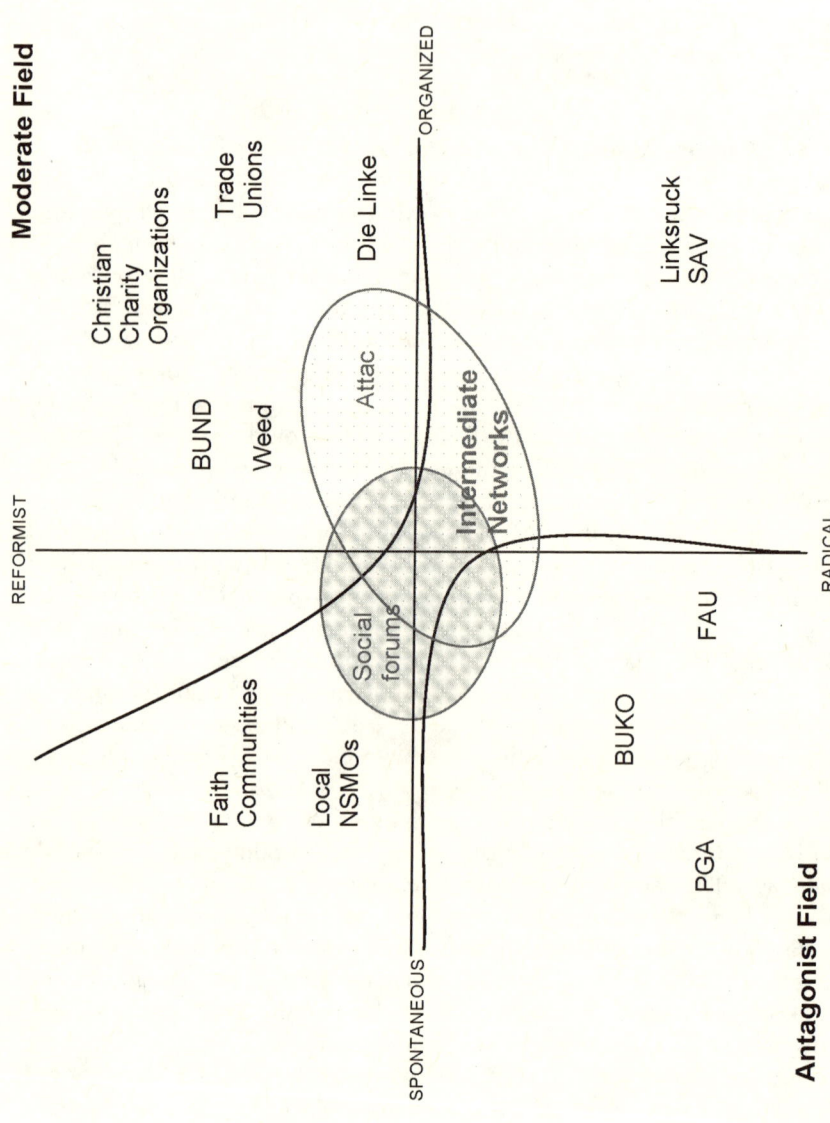

Figure 7.1 Fields of Actors of German GJMs

forty-three Web sites related to the GJMs shows that there are indeed groups that serve as a point of reference for moderate and radical activists alike. Those that are linked on part of the highest number of groups—Attac, Weed, and BUKO—constitute an informational core of the GJMs.

The Moderate Field

The first field of actors located in this tableau is composed mainly of interest groups that rely on considerable resources. Most of them have developed a high degree of formalization and professionalization. The membership can support the organization passively by donations and/or actively by local engagement, but it has little influence at the national level. Although their properties are similar, the background of these organizations is manifold.[8] On the one hand, parts of the moderate GJMOs are anchored in a tradition that favors a firm organization. This is true for Christian charity organizations committed to development aid such as Misereor, Evangelischer Entwicklungsdienst, and Brot für die Welt. The public-sector trade union ver.di and the metalworkers' IG Metall, which formed alliances with GJMOs, also belong to this category. On the other hand, organizations evolving from the NSMs are the result of a more recent process of institutionalization. They developed in single-issue fields such as human rights (Amnesty International), development (Terre des hommes), environmentalism (BUND as part of Friends of the Earth), and others. Most of the organizations that once emerged from the antagonist spectrum of the NSMs are also characterized by ideological moderation. With other moderate groups, they share an affirmative position toward the existing economic and political system.

Since the mid-1990s, GJMOs in the moderate field have intensified their collaboration and politicized their activities. BUND and Misereor, for instance, worked together to promote the concept of sustainable development in the aftermath of the Rio Conference (Misereor and BUND 1996). For the Christian sector, rank-and-file groups organizing fair trade pioneered a paradigm shift toward a global justice frame and challenged the notion of charity. Gradually, major organizations started to blame political institutions such as the IMF for their neoliberal policies. Likewise, single-issue organizations such as BUND broadened their thematic scope and collaborated with cross-issue and transnational campaigns. For instance, BUND twice joined Attac and Greenpeace to organize the congress "McPlanet," where issues of economic globalization and the environment were discussed. Attac has also become an important ally of the trade unions. Joint mobilizations on social and political issues as well as congresses like the 2004 "Perspektiven-Kongress" are proof of a mutual interest in collaboration.

Other actors intervening in the field of the GJMs include political parties and associated organizations. Important support comes from state-subsidized political foundations that are closely linked to center-left parties: the Friedrich-Ebert-Stiftung, the Heinrich-Böll-Stiftung, and the Rosa-Luxemburg-Stiftung. These foundations, associated, respectively, with Social Democrats, Greens, and Die Linke, have organized several discussions at World and European Social Forums; they continue to support social movement activities in Germany and abroad. Whereas these foundations prove to be important alliance partners for movement actors, the parties of the Social Democrats and Greens have largely lost this connection. In East Germany, where the post-communist PDS (Partei des Demokratischen Sozialismus) has its stronghold, there already existed an overlap between this party and some GJM groups. In the western part of the country, by contrast, the cultural lag between the PDS and the constituency of the GJMs inhibited collaboration. Since its foundation in 1990, the PDS has not typically attracted West German leftists. Instead, the dissatisfaction with governmental politics in the second term of the red-green government led to the foundation of a new party, the Wahlalternative Arbeit und soziale Gerechtigkeit (WASG—Electoral Alternative for Labor and Social Justice), in March 2004. Composed mainly of former social democrats and long-standing trade unionists, the majority within this party opted for an etatist renaissance. With the announcement of a future merge, WASG and the renamed PDS (now Die Linke) collaborated in the early federal elections in September 2005, receiving approximately 9 percent of the vote. The party's parliamentary group is trying to strengthen its links to extra-parliamentary forces with an office that establishes and maintains contacts with social movements. The party declares the GJMs a "central point of reference" for their work in parliament (Die Linke, press release, January 24, 2006).

The Antagonist Field

Contrary to the moderate approach, the common denominator of the antagonist field is a radical critique of capitalism. Antagonist groups also reject the effects of "strong" organization such as hierarchy and ideological moderation, instead sticking to the spontaneous ideals of autonomy. Accordingly, antagonist groups within the GJMs rarely rely on enduring cooperative structures. Instead, these groups are scattered and engage selectively in thematic campaigns or work with local networks.

Antagonist groups are an offspring of several radical traditions that developed within the NSMs, mainly in the areas of ecology, urban issues, and women's rights. Stressing unconditional self-determination, these groups have been a vibrant part of the German Left. One of the most important currents emerged in the late 1970s; calling themselves "autonomist," these groups criticized the collectivist approach of the student movement but adopted its anti-authoritarian and spontaneous traits. In the developing subculture of squatted houses and local plenary assemblies, radical democracy and militant resistance were closely linked (Schwarzmeier 2001). To a certain extent, autonomous and other radical groups experienced a thematic void in the 1990s, when the Zapatista insurrection created an important incentive to the spontaneous Left. The hallmarks of PGA were embraced by segments of this current and inspired the creation of new networks. A strictly anti-institutional network, PGA functions without speakers, representatives, or coordinators; joint meetings are organized by so-called convenors. These ad hoc characteristics are typical of groups sharing the antagonist understanding of political activism.

Anarchist groups, which have always been weak in Germany, round out the antagonist end of the spectrum. The most important organization is the Freie Arbeiterinnen und Arbeiter Union—Internationale Arbeiter Assoziation (FAU-IAA), which has several hundred members. Despite programmatic overlaps, there is little cooperation between anarchists and autonomist groups. One exception occurred when anarchists and autonomist groups joined unemployed and social initiative groups in protesting the reduction of welfare allocations in 2004.

Networks and campaigns within the antagonist field have mainly been created around thematic foci. The BUKO federation, for example, brings together internationalist groups. Most of the small local initiatives that engage in the BUKO combine tangible development projects with a radical critique of the status quo. At present, the network consists of more than 150 member organizations. Despite a certain degree of formalization, BUKO's organizational model embraces self-organization and bottom-up politics. Antiracist groups, which emerged predominantly in the 1990s, form another thematic cluster. Some of them collaborate in the Kein Mensch ist illegal (nobody is illegal) campaign, which opposes state repression against refugees and the readiness of airlines to deport "illegal" immigrants. In this framework, cooperation with moderate actors such as Christian parishes and human rights groups can be observed. More recently, initiatives from the antiracist and unemployed realms also focus on precarious working and living conditions. Among other activities, they organized the first Euromayday parade in Hamburg in 2005.

Grassroots and Trotskyite Groups

Not all groups active in the GJMs are wholly located in either of the fields previously described. In fact, there are several smaller groups and networks that are difficult to situate. Many groups that emerged in the framework of the NSMs continue to be skeptical of large organizations. Partly because of the federal structure of the German state, there is a strong tradition of locally scattered groups that focus on local engagement with an emphasis on democratic participation. However, most of these groups have undergone ideological moderation that does not necessarily imply unambiguous relations with authorities. Whereas some groups engage in service projects that are mainly or entirely funded by governments, others keep distant from state institutions. Although less visible in the political discourse, most of these groups engage in protest activities or consciousness raising. Peace groups, for example, coordinate via the umbrella Netzwerk Friedenskooperative, whose precursor networks organized mass protests in the 1980s. Today, peace networks have diminished in terms of numbers of activists but continue to play a significant role on the meso-mobilization level. On occasions such as the war in Iraq, peace groups have been able to pool activists from diverse backgrounds. However, these temporary mobilizations do not reconcile conflicts between differing currents.

Akin to NSM grassroots groups, rank-and-file Christian groups represent another important part of the German GJMs. The most salient forum for a broad discussion of the faith communities is the Protestant Kirchentag, a huge biannual convention. In this context, the political implications of environmental problems and poverty have long been discussed. Global justice issues have increasingly gained importance, peaking in a thematically focused assembly space at the Kirchentag 2005 in Hannover, where many international protagonists of the GJMs and the social forum process gathered. The grassroots character of religious engagement in the GJMs is also mirrored in the debt relief campaign Erlassjahr.de, which has involved more than a thousand groups, many of them local Christian initiatives.

Another special case that fits with neither the antagonists nor the moderate field is the Trotskyite current.[9] On the one hand, these groups cling to a strictly anticapitalist stance, suggesting proximity to the antagonist field. On the other hand, their orientation toward mass organization separates them from the spontaneous currents of the antagonist field. This emphasis on organizational rigor is mirrored in the groups' own structure; especially Linksruck—the German branch of International Socialist Tendency—has a reputation as a hierarchical and opaque organization. Trotskyite groups have consistently collaborated in networking initiatives of the GJMs in order to promote their cause within the Left community. In addition, the Trotskyite tactic of "entryism," that is, the infiltration of larger groups, has led to the participation of Linksruck and Sozialistische Alternative (SAV) in the formation of both Attac and WASG. In spite of their small numbers (SAV and Linksruck are reported to have several hundred members each), these groups are very active and can be seen at most demonstrations and network meetings of various leftist movements.[10]

Intermediate Networks

Attac. Attac, as a mixture of an organization and a network, combines attributes of both the organized and spontaneous poles, allowing for a variety of ideological positions. The network was founded in 1999 by some fifty social movement organizations, to provide a platform for actors critical of neoliberal globalization—with the notable exception of far-right and racist groups. Attac has both individual and collective members who take part in a council and elect a national coordination committee, which speaks for Attac vis-à-vis the public and organizes national campaigns. Its almost 16,000 individual members and 250 local groups (2005 figures) are proof of a fairly widespread network in Germany.

As mentioned in our introductory paragraph, Attac was initially ignored but experienced a media hype during and after the Genoa events. The Attac congress in October 2001 was enthusiastically attended by some three thousand visitors; shortly thereafter, the network underwent a "crisis of growth," according to Attac-spokesperson Sven Giegold (see Leggewie 2001, 19). The small group of activists was troubled with multiple organizational tasks, and some local groups feared infiltration by Trotskyite groups. However, with the exception of some temporary stagnation, the growth of Attac was remarkable during its first five years of existence. Attac's budget increased to 1.25 million Euros in 2005 and within a short period, the network underwent a process of professionalization. It now possesses an office, composed of both paid staff and volunteers, which deals with logistical problems and offers expertise to local groups and third parties. In the public perception, Attac continues to be *the* organization representing the plurality of GJMs. In this role, Attac is widely covered by the media but hardly ever heard about in institutional politics. Nevertheless, Attac has come to serve a brokering role in the mobilization of protest. With the exception of many antagonist groups, the network's attempt to integrate a broad scope of social and political actors has been successful. Groups and organizations of almost every social movement currently ally with Attac—even if only on a temporary basis. This is facilitated by Attac's thematic breadth, which now encompasses issues of social policy, ecology, and peace.

Social Forums. Apart from Attac, the GJMs developed another, specifically local organizational structure for linking people from diverse backgrounds. The charter of the World Social Forum in Porto Alegre—which codifies the common cause of anti-neoliberalism, the plurality of participants (excluding parties and guerrilla groups), and the refusal of binding decisions—serves as an important reference point for local social forums.[11] Though the founding process in Germany in 2003 was sluggish and attracted scarce attention in the mass media, by 2005 local social forums had been established in at least fifty cities, municipalities, or regions. Cuts in welfare provisions quickly became the main impetus for action and accelerated the spread of local social forums. Most social forums have difficulty balancing the two contradictory roles of providing a discursive space (in line with the Charta of Porto Alegre) on the one hand, and being a political actor seeking strategic intervention in local conflicts on the other (Haug et al. 2005). Still, most local social forums have managed to combine their critique of neoliberalism with a focus on local problems such as welfare cuts and the privatization of public services, thus making the movements' claims accessible and attractive to many citizens in their region.

The first national Social Forum was held in July 2005 in the Thuringian capital of Erfurt. Large groups like the trade unions and Attac dominated the organization. This dominance was challenged by some grassroots activists, who finally decided to organize an "open space" within the Social Forum to realize the ideal of nonhierarchical communication. The majority of the approximately two thousand participants proved to be experienced activists. A survey we conducted in Erfurt[12] showed that 80 percent of participants had experiences with demonstrations of the GJMs. One-third of respondents held a leadership role within their respective group. Obviously, this national Social Forum did not succeed in attracting many citizens beyond this activist core, and it failed to meet expectations in terms of participation and impact on the broader movement sector. Moreover, unlike global and continental forums, the Social Forum in Germany triggered neither emotion nor enthusiasm. However, activists who wanted to enhance their networks found the meeting helpful. The next national forum is planned for 2007.

With the survey data gathered in Erfurt, we are also able to draw a more detailed picture of the themes and traditions within the current GJMs. Thematic clusters and foci are visible in the group affiliations of activists. Only 16 percent of the respondents had not been actively involved in a political group within the last five years. The remaining respondents named multiple affiliations with different issue-specific groups or groups with multiple thematic orientations. Most frequently, activists declared themselves members of trade unions (27 percent of the participants), anti-neoliberal groups (23 percent), or peace groups (20 percent). Leaving aside the middle ground, the least frequent groups were farmers (1 percent), anarchists, and queer groups (both 2.5 percent).

By concentrating only on those 206 individuals (two-thirds of all respondents) who specified two or more group categories, we can draw a network structure. Links in the network represent information about multiple memberships of respondents. Peace groups, trade unions, and anti-neoliberal groups attracted the highest number of links, indicating the brokering role of these groups. Overall, the network reveals a highly decentralized, plural, and densely interconnected array of themes and groups within the GJMs. No category is isolated in the sense that links between certain nodes are absent, and even quite counterintuitive relations can be found. For example, three participants declared themselves to be actively involved in both a Trotskyite group and a church group. The network structure based on the original twenty-four categories was quite complex and did not reveal significant thematic centers or clusters, allowing us a meaningful data reduction. We reduced the variables to seven clusters based on theoretical considerations (see figure 7.2). As can be seen, some nodes, like trade unions and parties or NSM issues, are more important than others; but all nodes are relatively evenly related to their neighbors.

The network reflects the fact that most respondents were active within trade unions/parties, anti-neoliberal groups and Local Social Forums, and New Social Movements. These three clusters form a triangle. Each cluster within this triangle is more frequently associated with the two other poles than with other clusters. For socialist, Trotskyite, communist, religious, autonomous, and anarchist groups, this triangle is the most frequent reference point. Trade unions and political parties in particular are frequently linked with socialist, Trotskyite, and communist groups. Figure 7.2 shows a surprising structure of dense interconnection, with anarchists and autonomist groups relating to trade unions and parties as well as to socialist, Trotskyite, and communist groups.

Conflicting and Unifying Identities

As networks of different and often conflicting actors, social movements are diffuse phenomena (Rucht 2005); in fact, their unity may primarily be a matter of imagination. What keeps social movements together is a collective identity, a notion of commonality that is related to interests, values, and adversaries. The construction of a "we" distinct from the "others" is a process that evolves mainly in the course of contestation. In this vein, it is a self-attribution that is simultaneously acknowledged by the ascriptions of outsiders (Melucci 1996). The constructivist character of identity is particularly relevant in the case of the GJMs. The pluralist layout of the GJMs reminds us that an individual's belonging contains multiple identities, whereas it is "rare that a dominant identity is able to integrate all the others" (della Porta and Diani 1999, 100). To assess the weight of a common identity within the GJMs, two questions arise: What is the "we" that is referred to in the context of the GJMs? And which schisms contradict the notion of commonality?

Results from the survey at the first national social forum in Erfurt show that many of the participants identify with the GJMs. Around 71 percent of the respondents purported a strong identification with the *globalisierungskritische Bewegung*. But figures drawn from a single event of the GJMs might be a dubious indicator for the salience of this identity, especially without comparing it to other identities to which people relate. In fact, it is likely that other, more specific identities dominate the political engagement of movement activists.

The uniting factor that served to integrate many of the groups previously described is the struggle against neoliberalism. As a common frame, this notion is apparent in joint mobilizations and networking efforts beyond these

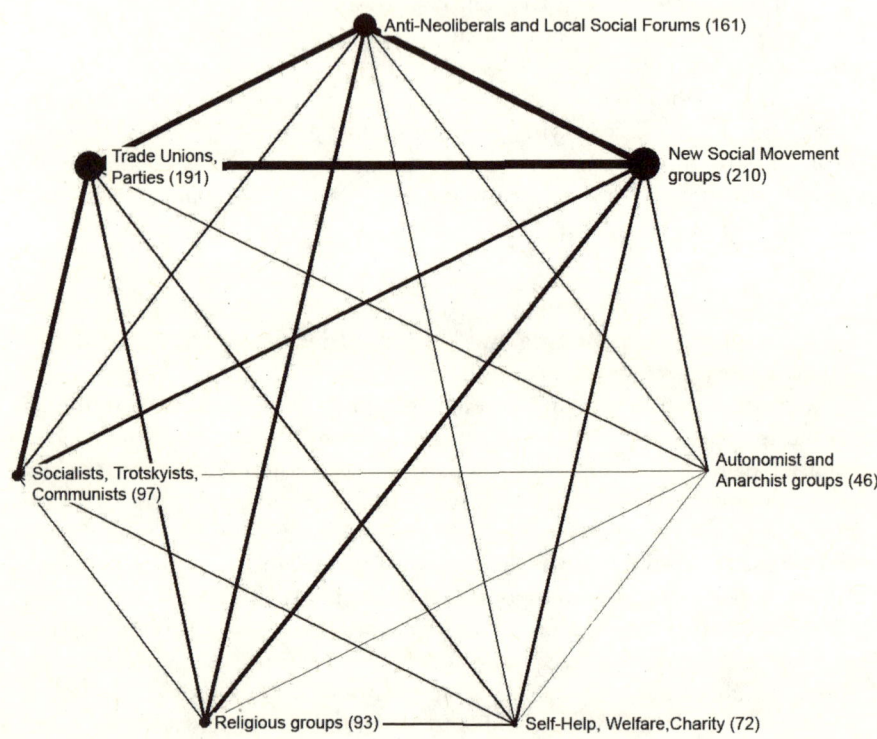

Figure 7.2 Network of Thematic and Organizational Clusters Based on Data Gathered at the First German Social Forum in Erfurt

Note: This reduced network represents the affiliations of those 164 respondents who were active within more than one of the 7 clusters. These clusters are based on a total of 870 links. The sizes of nodes and lines are correlated with the total number of links a node receives and a line contains. For the total number of links that a node comprises, see the parentheses following the labels.

episodes. Still, the actual content of this frame is not uncontested. On the contrary, cleavages continue to separate actors located in different political fields. Controversies about the aims, the organization, and the means of mobilization mirror different belongings that are probably more important than the commonalities. These cleavages can be observed particularly in those intermediate networks that are supposed to integrate all currents, as the case of Attac demonstrates.

During its foundation, Attac was criticized for its main policy proposals. People engaged in BUKO questioned the Keynesian approach of some Attac founding members who concentrated on financial transactions without referring to the underlying capitalist logics (Wissen 2002; Fritz 2002; Zwei Seelen in einer Brust 2004). Rejecting the implicit call for governmental reregulation, critics stressed the crucial role of state actors in promoting neoliberal politics. They referred particularly to the repressive police activity during the protests in Genoa (Brand and Wissen 2002). Obviously, the core disagreement was the question of "what is at stake: a fundamental critique of capitalism or merely a socially acceptable regulation of capitalism" (Stützle and Kanzleiter 2002, 26). The failed attempt to reconcile the anticapitalist and the moderate critique led to a moderation of Attac. Radical leftists who complained about signals to exclude their approach left the network. This process was intensified by a discussion about the anti-Semitic tendencies of an economic critique that concentrated on the financial sector.[13] As a consequence of these discussions, critics of Attac even called into question the very idea of anti-neoliberalism. Instead, they argued for a focus on capitalism as a determining structure. Beyond these discussions, the way political groups and networks should be organized is another area of conflict. Grassroots activists lamented that an oligarchic clique in the federal office and the coordination committee of Attac sacrificed the rank-and-file concept in favor of an "NGOization" that focused on power politics and campaigning "from above" (Bergstedt 2004).

As with Attac, ideological and organizational conflicts also arose in local social forums. The dominance of powerful organizations and the tendency to understand the forum as an organization in its own right was criticized by spontaneous groups and led to homogenization, as people with differing views simply left. Splits and counter-forums could be observed in several major cities. Obviously, some of the aspects that separate actors engaged in the struggle against neoliberalism are stronger than those uniting them. In particular, the two opposing fields of antagonist and moderate groups distance themselves from each other.

Similarly, the understanding of the territorial scope of anti-neoliberalism seems to vary between different actors. Whereas organizations predominantly addressing problems in the framework of the nation-state (e.g., trade unions) define their engagement against neoliberalism primarily as a national affair, those groups dealing with more obtrusive transnational issues (e.g., many environmentalist and solidarity groups) underline the global dimension of their struggle.

In the German case, the unity suggested by the singular of "one global justice movement" is openly challenged. The term *Globalisierungskritiker,* introduced by some activists as a positive point of reference for the German GJMs, was adopted by the media, though mostly with exclusive reference to Attac. Only a few groups use the label as a self-description, and surprisingly, a common label is absent in most internal discussions. The notion of anti-neoliberalism might have bridged cleavages in some major mobilizations (namely, those against international financial organizations and international summits), but this commonality *ex negativo* does not conceal differing understandings of what is at stake. Continuing conflicts about anticapitalism, hierarchies, and militant forms of action suggest that specific ideological and organizational identities are more relevant than a shared broad identity as members of one global justice movement.

Action Repertoires

Ideology, structure, and action of movement groups are linked, but their relationships to one another might be more complex than they first appear. For example, a radical ideology might be combined with a highly centralized or a highly decentralized group structure. In a similar vein, radical ideology is not always combined with radical action. Which actions a group or a movement as a whole actually performs depends not only on belief systems, but also on organizational structures and, probably more so, on external factors such as political opportunities, the strategies and actions of adversaries, and the role of third parties. Movement actors are rarely bound to one particular form of action. Rather, they can draw on a broader action repertoire, defined as "a limited set of routines that are learned, shared, and acted through a relatively deliberate process of choice" (Tilly 1995, 26). Given the diversity of ideological premises, structures, arenas, and experiences of global justice groups, it is no wonder that the diversity and cleavages among these groups are also mirrored in their repertoires of protest and their actual choice of actions. Broadly speaking, the general preference for either moderate or radical forms of action also applies to the GJMs, though some qualifications have to be made. Although it is true that the most ideologically radical groups tend to use the most radical forms of action—forms that ideologically moderate or pragmatist groups would never accept—it is clear that the radicals also participate in certain moderate actions (with the exception of lobbying). Moreover, groups that do not exactly belong to one or the other ideological camp also tend to be more flexible in their selection of actions and thus, depending on circumstances, could draw on either the more radical or the more moderate part of the repertoire. In addition, shifts can occur over time.

Key players that we attributed to the moderate field (for example, the church-bound charity organizations and the higher-level bodies of the trade unions) stay within the spectrum of moderate actions, ranging from lobbying to public education to nondisruptive street protest. In line with their moderate profile, direct action is not an option for these groups. Most of the protest events initiated by moderate GJMOs are flanked by highly professionalized public relations. Regarding the four elementary strategies toward mass media—adaptation, attack, alternative, or abstention (Rucht 2004)—these groups have chosen an adaptive attitude. Most have press spokespersons and consider the needs of journalists when organizing protests or spreading information. Owing to significant financial resources and their respected standing in terms of critical expertise, moderate groups are well represented in the media and are therefore able to promote their cause broadly.

Still, we can observe a shift of emphasis in the actions of some moderate groups. The focus on lobbying strategies that prevailed among those groups until the mid-1990s was challenged by two experiences. On the one hand, hopes for substantial policy changes were disappointed by established politics. On the other hand, a few campaigns were successful because of a combination of diverse means such as lobbying, street protest, and the raising of public awareness. These factors resulted in a "rehabilitation of protest" (Brand 2005). Resourceful actors readopted street protest as a key strategy to impose pressure on decision makers. Nevertheless, confrontational demonstrations are highly unlikely to be organized or attended by established interest groups or by unionists. Instead, lobbying and other forms of cooperation with authorities (and economic actors, respectively) continue to be their most relevant form of action. The bylaws of the BUND, for instance, define acting for environmental aims in the legislative process as one of the organization's objectives.[14] Owing to representation in official advisory councils and the use of legal instruments to intervene in the political process, some movement organizations have significant weight in institutional politics. Accordingly, moderate groups—particularly environmental and development GJMOs—have established close contacts with national and supranational authorities.

By contrast, most antagonist groups deploy confrontational forms of action. Though few actively promote the use of violence, most shy away from explicitly rejecting it. This ambivalent stance often leads to vague statements on violence or a general line of granting to each group the right to choose its own forms of action. If antagonist groups form blocks within demonstration marches, occasional confrontations of mostly young people with the police do occur. However, violent protests of German GJMs' groups are rare.[15]

Although most violent actions are by no means innovative, groups from the antagonist spectrum have applied some new forms of confrontational and/or theatrical actions. One aim of such interventions was to stop the privatization of what these groups perceive as public goods. In order to reappropriate the city, groups adopted some activities used in Anglo-Saxon countries such as Reclaim the Streets and Critical Mass. With street theater and happenings, the repertoire of earlier movements was also revived (Grothe 2005). Antiracist groups added "no border camps" to the radical action repertoire. These camps are designed to locally concentrate direct action against the politics of "fortress Europe" and to foster a dialogue between camp activists and citizens in the surrounding area.[16] Numerous police attacks against the "no border camps" are proof of authorities' discomfort with these bases for direct action. More recently, the idea of "appropriation" was revived by Spanish activists and subsequently by small German groups as well. Their approach of politically motivated shoplifting (*"Yomango"*) was applauded by parts of the antagonist camp. With the idea "to pose the right to a beautiful life here and now against the impertinence of daily capitalism" (AG Widerstand der Gruppe felS 2003, 13), several antagonist groups demanded free public transportation, education, and cultural events ("Berlin for free" or "Hamburg for free") in the summer of 2004. Thus, the call for appropriative forms of protest can be seen as a sign of revitalization and increased visibility of radical politics.

Not surprisingly, lobbying is perceived as neither an alternative nor a complement to street protest. Radical activists fear that this tactic ultimately fosters the co-optation of parts of the movement and facilitates their opponents' strategy of "divide and rule." In line with this position, the relation of antagonist groups to the mass media is largely characterized by abstention (for instance, even large groups have no press officer). From the radical groups' perspective, collaboration with the established media is senseless, given the media's support for the capitalist system and their focus on violent clashes with the police to the neglect of substantial information on the movements' point of view. Media strategies instead concentrate on alternative forms of information dissemination (cf. Rucht 2004), for example through direct forms of communication or the use or even the creation of independent media, newsgroups, and Web sites. Not surprisingly, in addition to broader information platforms such as Nadir.org and the Left unionists' Labournet.de, a German branch of Indymedia has been established for Web-based communication. Today, Indymedia plays an important role in the communication of leftist activists.

As already indicated, groups located in the intermediate ideological spectrum also tend to adopt a more flexible attitude regarding their choice of actions. For example, Attac, with its protests from the local to the transnational level, has applied a broad variety of forms of action. Apart from organizing and/or participating in mass demonstrations (including those in collaboration with trade unions), Attac groups have also performed small symbolic actions. One of the first of the network's campaigns, in 2001, was directed against tax havens. In this context, rowboats loaded with fake money were landed on an inflatable plastic island set up in Hamburg's Lake Alster, symbolizing the worldwide practice of money laundering. Owing to improved media strategies and a strict adaptation to the needs of mass media (see the introduction), Attac has consolidated its central role in the public perception of the GJMs in Germany (Kolb 2005), thereby also raising criticism on the part of radical groups. In a discussion at the twenty-fifth BUKO conference in 2002, leading Attac activist Peter Wahl defended Attac's media strategy: "We allow for the growing role of television. In the media-staged social drama of 'pro' and 'contra' Attac has chosen the 'contra' role" (*die tageszeitung*, May 13, 2002).

Considering the crucial role of the media, the tendency within the wider public to discriminate against more radical forms of action led Attac to firmly reject violent forms of protest after the Genoa incidents. Attac spokespersons committed themselves to nonviolent protest regardless of the actual amount of police repression. Notably, the centrally organized public relations approach does not exclude the use of independent media such as Indymedia or the production of videos. Regional groups are particularly active in spreading information concerning their actions via the Internet. Mailing lists and electronic forums are common tools for internal communication.[17] Compared with the Web sites of other organizations in the context of the GJMs, the Attac site has a distinctly interactive profile. Because the raising of awareness for the risks and consequences of international trade is a central aim, education represents another means of strengthening and broadening the movement. To this aim, a pool of lecturers has been established, various forms of online and offline information have been set up, and an annual summer school is held.

The position of the GJMs toward party politics and electoral engagement is not easy to summarize. Although in the late 1990s and early 2000s most movement activists kept all political parties at arm's length, the situation has changed more recently. With the rise of the WASG, involvement in parties has again become an option for a small segment of movement members, just as it was in the early phases of the Green Party's development. Even though most activists of the GJMs tend to vote for Die Linke and some became members of the WASG, identification with the new party tends to be low within the GJMs. In the survey we undertook at the Social Forum in Erfurt, more than 70 percent of the participants declared their intention to vote for Die Linke in the upcoming federal elections. Yet only 7 percent specified one of the parties (WASG and Die Linke) as the group they considered most important for their political identity. In general, older movement activists are more prone than their younger counterparts to engage in party politics.

In sum, the German GJMs rely on a very broad and variegated action repertoire. The moderate and radical ideological camps subscribe to different segments of this repertoire, with one part strictly excluding violence and the other rejecting lobbying. Groups located in the intermediate field typically are more flexible in their selection of action forms, though none of them explicitly endorses violence. Considering changes over time, it appears that the moderate spectrum has become more open toward confrontational strategies, but certainly not to violence.

Conclusion

As we have shown, the GJMs in Germany did not come as a bolt out of the blue. Rather, they are strongly rooted in diverse strands of earlier progressive movements. Accordingly, they have evolved more gradually and more slowly than is commonly assumed. Interestingly, the Seattle protests did not constitute an important facilitator for bringing these movements to the public fore in Germany. Rather, the belated reaction of the mass media led to the sudden "discovery" of these movements and, consequently, an exaggeration of their newness in the early years of this century.

The German GJMs, like most other movements, tend to emphasize their commonalities and often refer to themselves as an internally diverse but still unified movement, a "movement of movements." Indeed, a few aspects do support such a view. Most groups converge in what they define as the major problems in this world; most identify neoliberalism as a key evil and central target. Many groups also join in occasional mass demonstrations, congresses, and other kinds of gatherings of GJMs. Moreover, the movements are often portrayed by their external critics and opponents as entities of "antiglobalization," thereby strengthening the image of a single unified movement.

A closer look, however, reveals that, first, there are fundamental cleavages between various ideological currents of the GJMs, most notably between what we have termed the moderate and the antagonist camps. The existence of an intermediate sector of groups and networks allows these to speak to both other camps, but it does not make these camps compatible with each other.

Second, we maintain that occasional gatherings and common rhetoric is not enough to provide the basis for a robust common identity. Rather, we argue that more specific group identities along ideological, organizational, and/or thematic lines are prevalent. For example, feminist groups within the broader network of GJMs feel primarily bound to the feminist movement and not to the much more diffuse GJMs. The same applies to environmentalists, human right groups, trade unions, and so on. This is not to say that commonalities among different kinds of movements and ideological currents are purely fictional, but they are not as strong as many activists claim, and many observers take them for granted.

Third, when it comes to defining the underlying mechanism of the problems to be addressed, the strategies to be chosen, and the organizational forms that are needed, significant differences (if not open conflicts) become apparent. One might argue that this is a feature of many movements, past and present. However, we think that the GJMs are more heterogeneous in their thematic concerns, ideological stances, and strategic preferences than most prior social movements. They are a loosely connected set of more distinct movements and campaigns that promote the idea of an encompassing movement without being able to realize it. This view is supported by the way key organizers of the World Social Forums and other more geographically specific forums defend their concept of the forums as a mere platform. They argue that the whole structure would break down should the participants try to agree on a more specific ideology, set of priorities, or choice of strategies. Not accidentally, and to the regret of militant groups at the radical fringe, no attempts are made at the social forums to issue resolutions or to engage in joint actions beyond colorful marches.

To determine whether the German GJMs have distinct traits that clearly distinguish them from their counterparts in other countries would require a detailed and difficult analysis. From the available information, we would argue that German groups, on the whole 1) had a belated public appearance compared with those in France or Italy; 2) are more strongly rooted in the NSMs than in most other countries; 3) are less radical than, say, in Italy, but more so than in Scandinavian countries; 4) have fewer links to the trade union sector than in Italy and France; 5) have a greater mobilization potential than in Spain; 6) have more groups in the intermediate segment (between the antagonist and the reformist camp) than in Great Britain; and 7) are less connected to transnational campaigns and movements than in France, Great Britain, or Italy.

What have these movements in Germany achieved? And what are their prospects? After many years of hegemony of the neoliberal discourse within the public sphere, the GJMs were able to produce cracks in this picture (Brand 2005). They have challenged the idea that there is no alternative to neoliberalism and achieved a "reversal of the burden of proof" (Leggewie 2001, 18) when it comes to the market as the key mechanism for improving the state of the world.

On the other hand, several obstacles have limited the impact of the GJMs and led to a phase of stagnation. First, the configuration of movement groups is tilting toward the professionalized and national associations that, on the whole, tend to be less radical than the small and local groups. A significant proportion of the radical Left refuses to join coalitions with groups that do not share their basic criticism. Even more, they complain about attempts to pacify or even silence radical voices and about a lack of delineation vis-à-vis right-wing currents. Unlike in a number of other countries, potential allies such as charismatic intellectuals or farmers' associations are far from playing a role in Germany. Additionally, the social forums, which proved important for the development of the Italian movements, did not attract broader parts of the German GJMs. Nevertheless, in the medium term, we expect the continuation and perhaps even further growth of the GJMs in Germany. However, they are likely to face more internal and external problems, and they will encounter more difficulties in gaining further terrain. Even though their impact on specific policies might be limited, we think that these movements, like their forerunners, will contribute to a more democratic and less authoritarian political culture.

Notes

1. See also the detailed article on Attac in *Süddeutsche Zeitung,* July 19, 2001, p. 10.

2. As *Der Spiegel* put it, "It is precisely this diversity that makes it so difficult to understand this movement and confuses its critics" (July 23, 2001 p. 23).

3. The MAI envisaged a deregulation of Foreign Direct Investment.

4. See www.nadir.org/nadir/initiativ/agp/en/pgainfos/manifest.htm.

5. Unlike Pierre Bourdieu's notion of the political field, we do not refer to the composition of different forms of capital, even though these (economic, social, and symbolic) resources are obviously important in the configuration of the field. For an elaborated adaptation of Bourdieu for the analysis of social movements, see Crossley 2003 and Péchu 2005.

6. The label *antagonist* is defined by its opposition to the political and economic regime and not necessarily by its juxtaposition to the opposite moderate field.

7. The humanitarian Medico International, for instance, exhibits many structural attributes of the moderate field, but favors a radical approach to fighting grievances. Accordingly, the organization often engages in discussions with activists from the antagonist field.

8. For the sake of clarity, only some of the groups active in the GJMs are specified in figure 7.1.

9. This applies to a range of other communist and socialist groups as well. However, these circles are not as visible as the Trotskyites, although they significantly engage on the local level.

10. Linksruck posters and newspapers are present in great numbers in every significant demonstration march of the GJMs in Germany. Interestingly, most of the posters are carried by nonmembers who sometimes even purchase them because of their unconditional and straightforward messages (e.g., "George Bush—Terrorist No. 1").

11. For the English version of the Charter of Principles, see www.forumsocialmundial.org.br/main.php?id_menu=4&cd_language=2.

12. At the Social Forum, 785 questionnaires were distributed to participants in the registration area. With 317 copies returned to a box or sent back by mail, the return rate is about 40 percent. The survey included questions taken from earlier surveys at the European Social Forums in Florence 2002 and Paris 2003. In addition, we asked about ideals and practices of democracy in the group, the movement, and at the level of general politics in Germany.

13. Against the background of an irreconcilable conflict between Antideutsche and anti-imperialist currents regarding the prevalence of anti-Semitism in the radical Left, the debate about a supposedly anti-Semitic position in the Attac network had a profound impact on the image of Attac within the radical Left community. The phenomenon of Antideutsche visibly developed as a reaction to pro-Palestinian and partly anti-Semitic positions in the radical Left since the turn of the century. The members of this current insist on reminding the Left of an anti-Semitic tradition within the radical leftist current and denounce German guilt in general, symbolically stressing the legitimacy of the Israeli state (Hanloser 2004).

14. See www.bund.net/lab/reddot2/pdf/satzung_2004.pdf.

15. For instance, an arson attack in Berlin targeting a facility owned by the department of foreign affairs was attributed by the authorities to the GJMs. A claim of responsibility referred to the "colourful protests against capitalist globalisation" and pleaded for a "broad and also militant campaign" against the G8 summit in Heiligendamm in 2007 (*tagezeitung*, October 20, 2005).

16. A similar approach can be observed in the preparations for the G8 summit in Heiligendamm: Radical groups will follow the British example and organize an "info-tour" across Germany and neighboring countries to spread information about the G8 and economic globalization locally.

17. Following the example of the U.S.-based moveon.org, an Internet-based mobilization site, campact.de, was established in 2004 emanating from Attac circles.

Chapter Eight

The Global Justice Movement
in Switzerland

Nina Eggert and Marco Giugni

In this chapter, we depict the main characteristics of the Swiss global justice movement (GJM) as manifested since its emergence into the public domain in the late 1990s. Following the definition given in the introduction to this volume, we characterize the GJM as "the loose network of organizations (of varying degrees of formality, and including even political parties) and other actors, engaged in collective action of various kinds, on the basis of the shared concern to advance the cause of justice (economic, social, political, and environmental) among and between peoples across the globe."

Our discussion is based on the four main elements of what Doug McAdam et al. (2001) have called the "classic social movement agenda" for explaining contentious politics: political opportunities, mobilizing structures, collective action frames, and repertoires of contention. These four aspects are seen as mediating factors between social change (the ultimate origin of all contention) and contentious interaction (the "dependent variable"). *Political opportunities* include the signals that encourage social and political actors to form social movements (Tarrow 1996). More specifically, they refer to all those aspects of the political system that affect the ability of challenging groups to mobilize effectively. Here we focus in particular on the structure of national cleavages that are reflected in the Swiss GJM, the alliances of the movement with institutional actors such as political parties, and the state responses to the movement's mobilization. *Mobilizing structures* are the formal and informal vehicles through which people engage in collective action (McAdam et al. 1996b). We can distinguish between two basic types of mobilizing structures: formal organizations (for example, Attac) and informal networks (that is, the web of interpersonal contacts and exchanges among movement activists and participants); we analyze both types within the Swiss GJM. *Framing processes* define the symbolic and meaning construction by social movement activists and participants (but also other parties) relevant to the interests of social movements and their challenges (Snow 2004). Here we address in particular the main claims made by the Swiss GJM and the identification with the movement. Finally, *repertoires of contention* refer to the limited sets of claim-making routines available to social movements at a given historical moment (McAdam et al. 2001)—in other words, the array of available means of action through which social movements mobilize. Here we focus on the forms of action displayed by the Swiss GJM.

No less than other social movements, the structure and mobilization of the GJM is influenced by certain aspects of the political opportunity structure stemming from the national context in which it evolves. In other words, the national context plays a crucial role even for an eminently transnational movement such as the GJM. As two among the leading students of transnational contention and global activism put it, "[b]ecause we do not believe in a distinct transnational sphere, we think that these domestic factors are crucial determinants of the strategies of movements active transnationally" (Tarrow and della Porta 2005, 242).

Three aspects of the political opportunity structure are likely to exert an important influence on the mobilization of the GJM in Switzerland: 1) the national cleavages and conflict lines that are reflected in the movement's mobilization, 2) the alliances with institutional actors, and 3) the state responses to the movement's mobilization. Concerning the first aspect, two main features of the social and political context play an important role for the structure and mobilization of the Swiss GJM: the weak imprint of the class cleavage and traditional social conflict line carried by the union sector (although unions do participate in the movement) and the strong presence of the new social movements (NSMs). In particular, we must stress the strong presence of the ecology and solidarity movements (the two strongest and most resourceful NSMs in Switzerland during the 1980s and 1990s) within the GJM.[1] These two movements, and the NSMs in general, have represented the main extra-parliamentary force in Switzerland since the 1970s (Kriesi et al. 1995), as compared with countries such as France in which the class cleavage has remained more salient and in which the labor movements and other more traditional movements have been dominant. In this respect,

Switzerland resembles countries like Germany, in which the NSM sector has displayed a strong level of mobilization. As a result, the characteristics of the GJM reflect in part its inheritance of the actors and claims of these movements, as we shall see in more detail in what follows.

The main allies of the GJM within the institutional arena are obviously to be found on the Left. More specifically, the small parties of the Left and extreme Left (both old and new) actively support the movement's claims and activities and can often be considered as part of the movement in a broader sense. The same holds for the labor unions, especially the smaller and more radical ones as well as the public-sector unions. Although not opposed to it, the main leftist party, the Socialist Party, is less supportive of the movement, especially of its more radical wing and actions. This attitude resembles the one traditionally taken by the socialists toward the NSMs (Kriesi et al. 1995) and can be explained by the party's quite ambivalent position within the government (minority member of the governmental coalition). Given the federalist structure of the country, the movement might find more Socialist Party support in the cantons in which the party is not in government—although such a situation is rare.

The state's responses to the mobilization of the GJM have departed radically from the tradition of protest policing in Switzerland. Although the Swiss state, in cross-national comparison, has traditionally been characterized by a generally inclusive strategy and low levels of repression (Kriesi et al. 1995), it has often taken a repressive and less facilitative stance in response to GJM actions. This approach can clearly be seen in the impressive policing apparatus deployed every year for the World Economic Forum (WEF) meetings in Davos—when both police forces and the army are engaged to secure the site of the meeting—or during the summit of the G8 held in Evian, when the Swiss government asked for the support of police forces from Germany to help local police, police forces from other cantons, and the army in ensuring that the summit went well. This repressive stance holds especially for the movement's early emergence, when authorities were probably taken by surprise by the level of disruption of the protest. More recently, the overreaction that characterized the early phases has been replaced by more targeted and differentiated measures.

In the next section, we outline the main focal points of the mobilization of the Swiss GJM (origins and turning points). We then address the other three aspects of the classic social movement agenda, which correspond at the same time to the three main components of the movement's definition mentioned earlier: organizational networks, movement identity and frames, and action repertoires. We illustrate our arguments by means of original data on organizations involved in the movement (organizational data) and on participants in activities promoted by the movement (survey data). In the conclusion, we try to put the main characteristics thus outlined into both national and international perspective.

Origins and Turning Points

The heritage of the NSMs has been very important for the emergence of the Swiss GJM. Although organizations and activists of the peace, ecology, and solidarity movements have contributed to its rise, the movement is not simply a continuation of the NSMs, but has emerged in a particular historical context. First, as in other countries, the international context of neoliberalism and its impact on the national level has brought new issues such as unemployment and neoliberalism into the public debate and created new opportunities for collective action, both at the national and transnational levels. In Switzerland, the discussion about neoliberalism moved from the extreme-left circles to the public space after the publication in 1995 of the *White Book* (De Pury et al. 1995), in which the authors advocate ultra neoliberal policies as a way to reduce state debt. As a response to this, the *Black Book of Neoliberalism* (VV. AA. 1996) was published one year later; it did not have the same impact on public opinion, but nevertheless opened the debate on neoliberalism in Switzerland.

The remobilization and radicalization that occurred in the social movement sector in Switzerland in the late 1990s can be linked to a large extent to the rise of the GJM. The most important event staged by the GJM in Switzerland during the 1990s is probably the demonstrations against the World Trade Organization (WTO) in Geneva that took place in May 1998 (Rossiaud 2001). These demonstrations have had both a symbolic and substantial impact on the further development of the movement. Incidentally, it is worth noting that this event occurred before what many see as the spurring event of the movement on the transnational stage, namely, the protest in Seattle in 1999 against the third ministerial meeting of the WTO.

In February 1998, activists from the Zapatista movement met in Geneva for the foundational conference of the Peoples' Global Action network. The welcoming committee was organized by Geneva squatters and composed of local urban autonomous groups, solidarity organizations, and labor unions. These actors reflect the composition of the GJM in Switzerland in the following years. This foundational conference also led to the organization of the demonstrations that took place during the WTO conference in Geneva in May 1998 (part of a global day of action across the world called by the Peoples' Global Action).

Although it is always difficult to precisely locate the beginning of a new movement or movement cycle in time, the four days of demonstrations that took place in Geneva in May 1998 can be seen as the starting point of the emergence of the GJM in the public domain in Switzerland and as the opening event of a cycle of protest spurred by the movement. These events marked a radicalization of the social movement sector, which had already started at the local level a few years earlier with a series of actions by the squatters and with a 1995 protest against a Swiss Army parade that witnessed some violence on the part of demonstrators. Forms of actions more common in the late 1960 and in the 1970s (especially perpetrated by the peace and antinuclear movements), such as direct actions and civil disobedience, were resumed after having been put on hold during the 1980s and early 1990s, at least at the national level. These forms of action were largely inspired by Reclaim the Streets, an important actor in the Peoples' Global Action network, which organized the 1998 demonstrations and "imported" these forms of action in Switzerland.

Unexpectedly, at least for those inclined to think that collective action in Switzerland takes mostly if not always a peaceful path, the 1998 demonstrations in Geneva turned violent. This turn has had important consequences for the future of the GJM in Switzerland, both positively and negatively. First, they had a symbolic impact, proving to opponents of globalization that the movement was indeed capable of mounting a significant challenge. Second, however, the turn to violence created the basis for an internal division of the movement, which would later deepen, precisely on the issue of violence. Third, the violent actions had large resonance in the Swiss media, largely overshadowing the peaceful direct actions. The impressive media campaign in the months before the demonstration against the 2003 summit of the G8 in Evian (a few kilometers from Geneva across the French-Swiss border) is perhaps the most striking example of this focus (Commission extraparlementaire d'enquête/G8 2004): Most of the attention of the press was directed at the threat of violence during the meetings. Fourth, they influenced the future reactions of the authorities and the repression that protests against the WEF in Davos and other GJM demonstrations would face in the following years.

In the years following the 1998 Geneva events, the stance of state authorities vis-à-vis the movement was characterized by overreaction, an attitude often shown by political authorities when they face a new challenge (Karstedt-Henke 1980). This can perhaps be best seen in the 2001 demonstrations against the annual WEF meeting in Davos. These events can be considered as another turning point, or at least a significant moment, of the Swiss GJM. Because the Davos authorities had declared a general demonstration ban in the town during the WEF meeting, demonstrators trying to reach the site were stopped by the police and the army in Landquart; only a few could reach the station. In reaction, some demonstrators blocked the highway in Landquart, while others left for Zurich, where violent demonstrations and confrontations with police forces were followed by many arrests. These demonstrations received great media attention, as the material damages were very high. But in addition, they opened the polemics about the militarization of the station (as not only the police but also the army were mobilized to protect Davos from demonstrations) and about the right to demonstrate and freedom of expression.

Another crucial event of the movement, at least in terms of popular participation, was the mass demonstration against the G8 meeting in Evian. This was the largest demonstration organized by the movement in Switzerland and perhaps the largest ever in this country. As mentioned earlier, media attention focused on the possible violence even before the summit began. The Geneva authorities called for a coordination of the demonstration with the Lemanic Social Forum, more or less created for the event. The main authorized demonstrations took place without major violence, but with the presence of police forces from other cantons and countries, in particular from Germany. According to the Lemanic Social Forum, about one hundred thousand people took part at the demonstration.

Participation in the demonstrations opposing the annual meetings of the WEF in Davos gives us a partial but significant indicator of the evolution of the movement's mobilization. Participation was at its highest in 2001. At the same time, this was also the year the protests took a more violent stance. Both participation and the level of violence then declined over the next four years. In January 2004, for example, no more than two thousand people took to the streets in Chur to protest against that year's meeting. To be sure, the anti-G8 demonstration held in Geneva in June 2003 gathered an impressive number of people, but this is largely because this event occurred only a few weeks after the U.S. intervention in Iraq, it captured much media attention, and it attracted a wider spectrum of demonstrators. In addition, protests against the G8 traditionally attract a higher number of participants.

In summary, although preceded by a phase of organization and consensus building, the Swiss GJM made its first striking appearance in the public domain in 1998 during the protest against the WTO in Geneva. From that moment and up to 2001–2002, the movement increased its activities, enlarged its public support (which has nevertheless remained quite limited in international perspective), and radicalized its action repertoire. After 2001–2002, participation began to decline (with the notable exception of the 2003 Geneva demonstration against the G8, which represented the highest moment in the movement's history in Switzerland), and the process of radicalization seemed to stop or at least to relent. Parallel to this evolution, however, the movement has remained stable in terms of mobilizing structures and less protest-oriented events such as social forums. We address this aspect in more detail in what follows.

Organizational Networks

As a result of the importance of the new cleavage that emerged with the NSMs and their strong mobilization throughout the 1970s and 1980s as well as the early 1990s, NSM organizations are very much present in the Swiss GJM. Among them, organizations of the ecology movement, such as Pro Natura, and of the solidarity movement, such as the Déclaration de Berne or Aktion Finanzplatz Schweiz, predominate. Of course, more recent organizations created during the emergence phase of the GJM are also very active. Among them, the most important (or at least the most active) are perhaps Attac, the anti-WTO Coordination, the Gipfelblockade, the Other Davos, and the two main social forums (the Swiss Social Forum and the Lemanic Social Forum). Traditional leftist organizations (parties and labor unions) are also involved, but to a lesser extent than in countries where the class cleavage is less pacified than in Switzerland. Nevertheless, the GJM has certainly contributed to remobilizing these actors.

The strong imprint of the NSMs provides the GJM with a strong presence of quite formalized and professionalized organizations of the environmental and solidarity movements. We have an indirect indicator of this if we look at the data on thirty-five organizations among those active within the movement that we gathered as part of the Demos project. Based on Web sites and internal documents of these organizations, we observe a higher presence of formal organizations in the movement. For example, on an additive index of formalization, nineteen organizations can be considered as formal, whereas only seven organizations are informal.[2] However, just as the NSMs include formalized and professionalized organizations (for example, in the environmental and solidarity movements), together with more informal and loosely structured organizations and groups (for example, in the peace and squatters' movements), the mobilizing structures of the GJM are made up of both formal organizations and informal networks. Furthermore, the organizations born during the emergence of the GJM are much less formalized and professionalized than certain organizations typical of the NSMs, especially those of the ecology and solidarity movements, which is not surprising as the former have been created only recently.

Although we do not have direct information on the relationships among the organizations involved in the movement (for example, about their collaboration or joint presence in protest events), we can try to assess the movement's organizational network indirectly. Figure 8.1 shows the network of hyperlinks found on the Web sites of the thirty-five organizations studied in the Demos project.[3] A network is made of nodes and ties. The nodes in the figure are organizations participating in the movement and having an Internet presence; the ties (arrows) represent references to other organizations made on an organization Web site. This gives us at the same time a

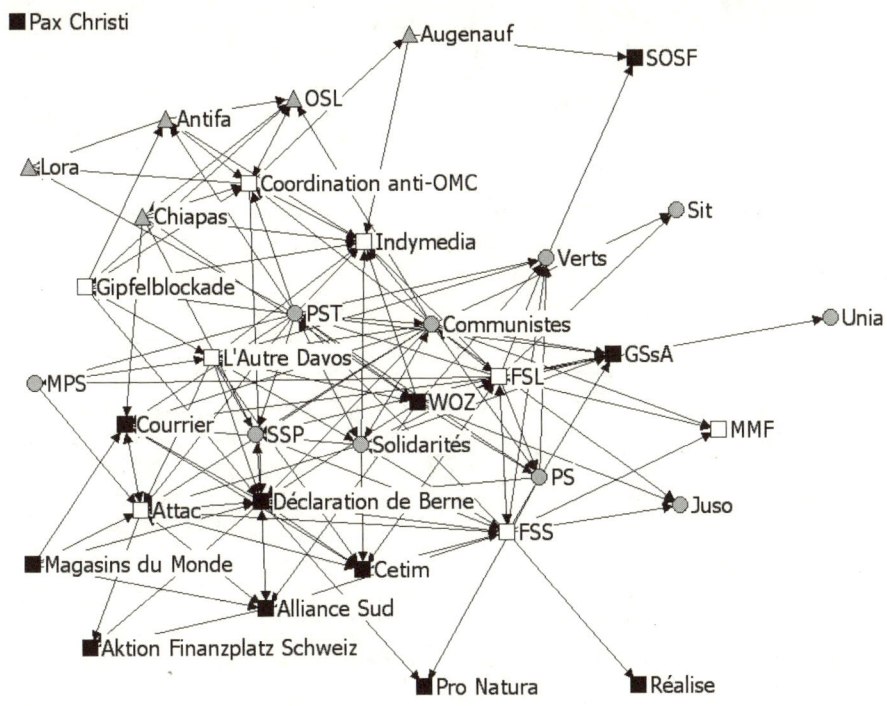

Figure 8.1 Hyperlinks Network of the Swiss GJM

Key to Figure 8-1:

Subnetworks		Organizations
⬤	Traditional left	Communistes, Juso, PS, PST, Sit, Solidarités, SSP, Unia, Verts
⬛	New social movements	Aktion Finanzplatz Schweiz, Alliance Sud, Cetim, Le Courrier, Déclaration de Berne, GSsA, Magasins du Monde, Pax Christi, Pro Natura, Réalise, SOSF, WOZ
△	Squatters/autonomous	Antifa, Chiapas, Augenauf, Gipfelblockade, Lora, MPS, OSL
☐	Global justice movement	Anti-WTO Coordination, Attac, FSL, FSS, Gipfelblockade, Indymedia, l'Autre Davos, MMF

Note: See the appendix to this chapter for a list of organizations.

Source: Data collected within the Democracy in Europe and the Mobilization of Society (Demos) project.

proxy of the centrality and the prestige of the organizations, not only of the degree of affinity among them (it is unlikely that an organization's Web site would mention another organization without some kind of affinity between them).

The picture provided by the network analysis of the hyperlinks in organizations' Web sites is quite straightforward. Three organizations receive the highest number of arrows and therefore of mentions: the Déclaration de Berne, Attac, and Indymedia.[4] Interestingly, they represent three different types of actors involved in the movement. The Déclaration de Berne is one of the most active organizations of the Swiss solidarity movement, that is, one of the most important NSMs in the Swiss context. Attac is the GJM organization almost par excellence, although it is much less developed in Switzerland than in other countries (most notably France and Germany). Indymedia, a very decentralized network, is perhaps the most well-known alternative media network active in the movement in many countries. Thus, at least as far as references to Web sites are concerned, one national organization of a traditionally strong NSM as well as two international organizations of the GJM seem to be central to the movement and have the most prestige. According to our data, organizations such as these seem to link the different branches of the highly divided Swiss GJM. This picture is to be taken with caution, as it is limited to the links between the organizations of our sample, taking into account only the hyperlinks among them. Nevertheless, it gives an indication of the credibility these organizations grant to each other and could be taken as an indicator of the collaboration potential among them.

The organizational network of the Swiss GJM can thus be divided into subnetworks. Two of these stem from the heritage of the NSM in Switzerland. We find on the one hand the environmental and solidarity movement organizations, which are very centralized and professionalized (for example, the traditional environmental organization Pro Natura or Alliance Sud). On the other hand, we find more loosely structured direct action networks, in particular the networks of informal groups mainly belonging to the squatters' and autonomous, anarchist, and New Left milieus, especially those active locally in the major cities (Zurich, Lausanne, Geneva, Bern, Basel). To these two subnetworks, we must add a third one, namely, actors from the more institutionalized arenas represented by left-wing parties and labor unions (especially the more radical ones). However, these actors are less important than in other countries, such as for example, France. Finally, also less important in the Swiss context in international perspective, there are the organizations created during the emergence of the GJM in the 1990s (for example, Attac, the Swiss Social Forum, or the Lemanic Social Forum).

The two main subnetworks work relatively independently from each other. In particular, they tend to participate in different types of events, or at least some organizations are more involved in certain events than others. The larger and more institutionalized organizations, such as those belonging to the NSMs, display a stronger presence in social forum types of events, whereas the most typical GJM organizations are more active in mass demonstrations and protest activities—although the former are not absent from this type of event either. In addition, there is hardly any permanent network. Instead, varying ad hoc coalitions are formed, depending on the place or event. On certain occasions, however, we observe a joint participation of organizations belonging to the two subnetworks. This occurs above all in the most important events, such as the 1998 anti-WTO and the 2003 anti-G8 demonstrations. On other occasions, such as the anti-WEF events in Davos, different organizations take part, but using different forms of actions (demonstrations, parallel forums, etc.).

The hyperlink network gives us some insights into the interrelationships among the four subnetworks of the Swiss GJM, as the organizations belonging to each subnetwork are represented with a different symbol (see the key to figure 8.1).[5] The type of organizations to which the three central actors (the Declaration de Berne, Attac, and Indymedia) are linked differ considerably. For example, Attac has no inbound or outbound tie to the groups or organizations from the squatters/autonomous milieus; it is only linked to the traditional left organizations and the NSMs. The same holds for the Swiss Social Forum, another GJM organization. Indymedia has links mainly with the squatters/autonomous and the GJM organizations, except for Solidarités and *WOZ*.[6] The third, more central actor in this network, the Declaration de Berne, is the only one of the three core actors with links to all types of organizations. It is therefore the only one linking all the subnetworks of the Swiss GJM, although the link with the squatters/autonomous organizations exists only through GJM organizations stemming from the squatters/autonomous milieus. Although we should be careful in extrapolating from this analysis, which is only based on hyperlinks, it nevertheless shows that the different subnetworks work quite independently. Indeed, if a hyperlink can be considered as an indicator of the potential collaboration between organizations, the fact that even this type of tie between the different subnetworks does not exist or is sporadic casts doubts on their actual collaboration.

Another way to grasp the weight of certain types of mobilizing structures within the Swiss GJM is to look at the individual level by means of survey data. Table 8.1 shows the distribution of organizational networks of participants in the GJM (regardless of their level of involvement in those networks). The data come from research conducted during two protest events against the WEF meeting in Davos in January 2004, following an approach similar to the one adopted in recent studies carried out in other countries (Andretta et al. 2002; della Porta 2003a, 2003b, and 2005a; della Porta and Mosca 2003;

Table 8.1 Organizational Networks of Participants in Two Protests against the WEF Meeting in Davos in 2004 (Percentages)

Organizational Networks	% Responses
Environmental Organizations	27
GJM Organizations	19
Parties	17
Humanitarian Organizations	16
Unions	15
Human Rights Organizations	14
Welfare Organizations	11
Antiracist/Promigrant Organizations	11
Peace Movement Organizations	10
Autonomous/Squatters' Movement Organizations	9
Youth Organizations	9
Tenants' Rights Organizations	5
Students' Organizations	5
Women's Organizations	3
Neighborhood Organizations	3
Consumers' Rights Organizations	2
Farmers' Organizations	2
Religious Organizations	2
Gay and Lesbian Organizations	1
Unemployed Rights Organizations	1
N	411

Note: Respondents were asked to mention the organizations/groups in which they participate or have participated. Percentages do not add up to 100 owing to multiple responses.

Source: Author's data.

della Porta et al. 2006; Fillieule et al. 2004; Passy and Bandler 2003), using a questionnaire distributed to participants in the two events.[7] Although these figures should be taken with some caution and cannot easily be generalized, because the survey is not based on standard random sampling and the sample is relatively small, they allow us to show the main patterns of the organizational networks in which participants in the GJM are embedded. Furthermore, although the sample cannot be seen as representative of the whole universe of participants, it gives us a picture of the most active participants, because some of the questionnaires were handed out en route to the meeting points.

Concerning the issue at hand, respondents were asked to mention organizations or groups in which they participate or have participated from a finite list of items. As we can see from the table, the largest proportion of participants in the two events are or have been members (or at least supporters) of environmental organizations (27 percent). Obviously, GJM organizations are also well represented, but they are ranked only second (19 percent). Many respondents also mentioned membership in humanitarian and human rights organizations. Together with antiracist/pro-migrant organizations, the latter can be considered as part of the solidarity movement (Passy 2001). If we add up the percentages for all three items, the solidarity movement clearly emerges as the most important organizational network of participants in the two events at hand (41 percent). In fact, perhaps stretching a bit the definition of this movement, we could add welfare organizations, making the solidarity movements even more central (52 percent). Also important for the participants in the two anti-WEF protests are more institutional actors such as parties (17 percent) and unions (15 percent). Among the former, quite understandably, leftist parties are virtually the only ones mentioned.

In spite of their limitations, these findings offer us a clue as to the organizations and networks underlying the mobilization of the GJM in Switzerland. First, the mobilizing structures of the Swiss GJM reflect the strength of a previous cycle of contention carried out by the NSM, hence largely reflecting the importance of the national traditions of contention. Second, more specifically, the organizations and networks of the environmental and solidarity movements play a central role. Third, at the same time, the presence of NSM organizations and networks is accompanied by that of more institutional actors such as left-wing parties and labor unions. However, these more institutionalized actors, although indeed present, are less important, reflecting the weakness of the class cleavage in Switzerland and, again, the national traditions of contention.

The impact of national traditions of contention on the structuring of the GJM in Switzerland can also be seen in a similar survey conducted by a team of French and Swiss social scientists (Fillieule et al. 2004) on participants in the protest against the G8 summit in Evian in June 2003. This survey, based on the same approach as the one mentioned earlier, was conducted on both sides of the French-Swiss border near Geneva, where the protest events took place over about one week. As a result, the sample includes the same number of French and Swiss participants (about 40 percent each), allowing for a direct comparison of the two groups. The survey shows that Swiss and French participants were embedded in different organizational networks—specifically, that GJM organizations were more present on the French side. This can be explained by the fact that France is one of the birthplaces of the GJM in Europe, as attested by the founding and strong development of Attac there. No equivalent social movement organization exists in Switzerland in terms of size, although environmental organizations, for example, are much larger in Switzerland than in France (Kriesi et al. 1995). Furthermore, NSM organizations (that is, environmental, humanitarian, human rights, and peace organizations) were much more present on the Swiss side. Again, here we see the impact of the national context. In particular, the mobilizing structures in the protest against the G8 in Evian reflect the strength of the NSM in Switzerland, as opposed to its weakness in France (Kriesi et al. 1995).

In summary, the mobilizing structures of the GJM in Switzerland consist of four main types of actors, or subnetworks: first, NSM organizations, especially those active in the environmental and solidarity movements (which have mobilized most often in the recent history of Swiss protest politics) and having a high degree of formalization and professionalization; second, a more informal and loosely structured network of organizations and groups belonging to the squatters' and autonomous, anarchist, and New Left milieus; third, but less important, the more institutionalized leftist sector made up of left-wing parties and labor unions; fourth, and perhaps even less important in the Swiss context, the organizations created during the emergence of the GJM in the 1990s. More generally speaking, the movement relies on previous organizations that have become involved in global justice issues in addition to their traditional and more specific issues (NSM organizations, but also unions and leftist parties), as well as on more recent organizations specifically created during the protest wave brought about by the movement.

Movement Identity and Frames

The framing perspective has taught us that a process of construction of the "problem" is necessary to activate the identities and motivations of actors to form a social movement (Snow 2004). However, this process is constrained and limited by previous mobilizations and ideas already expressed by previous social forces, most notably by previous social movements. Therefore, the collective action frames put forward by the GJM are likely to resemble in large part those of the cycle of contention that has preceded it, namely, that carried by the NSMs. Indeed, although there are certainly several novelties in the nature and mobilization of the GJM (in particular, concerning the scope of mobilization and the targets addressed), its claims are not entirely new and have been to a large extent brought about by the NSMs. This holds in general, as the NSMs have mobilized strongly all across Europe and beyond, but especially in Switzerland, where they have formed the major movement family during the past three decades or so (Giugni and Passy 1997; Kriesi et al. 1995).

Four aspects of the identity of the GJM in the Swiss context are of particular interest here: 1) the ideological cleavages as expressed in the issues and frames addressed by the movement, 2) the breadth of the movement's issues and frames (multi-issue versus single issue), 3) the territorial dimension

Table 8.2 Thematic Priorities of Selected Organizations Involved in the Swiss GJM (Percentages)

Principles	% Responses
Democracy	80
Another Globalization/Different Form of Globalization	77
Anti-Neoliberalism	77
Solidarity with Third World Countries	77
Social Justice/Defense of the Welfare State/Fighting Poverty/ Social Inclusion	74
Ecology	69
Workers' Rights	66
Human Rights	63
Sustainability	63
Critical Consumerism/Fair Trade	60
Ethical Finance	60
Immigrant Rights/Antiracism/Rights of Asylum Seekers	60
Global (Distributive) Justice	57
Peace	57
Nonviolence	54
Women's Rights	51
Anticapitalism	43
Alternative Knowledge	34
Gay and Lesbian Rights	23
Socialism	23
Autonomy and/or Antagonism (Disobedients)	14
Religious Principles	9
Communism	6
Animal Rights	6
Anarchism (Traditional Anarchism and/or Libertarian Anarchism)	3
Other	31
N	35

Note: The data refer to support for principles explicitly declared by the organizations. Percentages do not add up to 100 owing to multiple responses.
Source: Author's data.

of the movement's issues and frames, and 4) the identification of people to the movement. To get some purchase on the first three aspects, let us first look once again at our thirty-five organizations studied in the Demos project. Table 8.2 shows the thematic priorities of the selected organizations as stated in their internal documents and statutes.[8] Without going into all the details, we can see that issues typical of the NSMs have high priority. In particular, issues traditionally addressed by the ecology movement (ecology, sustainability, animal rights) and, above all, the solidarity movement (human rights, immigrant rights, antiracism and rights of asylum seekers, solidarity with Third World countries) are all ranked very high on the list of issues addressed by the organizations.[9] If we include peace issues and recalculate the percentages over the total responses (rather than the total cases, as in the figures shown in the table), they add up to about 30 percent of all issues. This amount becomes even higher if we include the other NSM-related issues such as women's rights or gay and lesbian rights.

The importance of NSM issues should not cause us to overlook that issues brought about specifically by the GJM, such as alternative views of globalization, global justice, and antineoliberalism and anticapitalism, have very high priority, perhaps even more than NSM issues. In addition, we observe the presence of issues belonging to the ideological repertoire of the traditional Left. In particular, social justice and the defense of the welfare state, but also workers' rights, are mentioned by many of the selected organizations. This is hardly surprising—first, because we are analyzing statements by organizations involved in this movement, and second, because these organizations include unions and leftist parties. What should be noted, however, is the importance of NSM issues over both issues typical of the GJM and issues of the traditional Left, which we expect to be higher, for example, in a country such as France in which the NSMs have mobilized less and in which the ideological cleavage structure keeps a strong class imprint.

Thus, the structure of social and political cleavages that characterize a given country, as well as its national traditions of contention, affect the ways in which global issues are framed in that country. In Switzerland, the pacification of the class cleavage that has historically occurred during the twentieth century, the strong degree of institutionalization of the system of industrial relations, and more generally the consensual character of the political system (reflected in neocorporatist arrangements in the administrative arena), together with the strength of the NSM sector, has produced a GJM more oriented toward claims typically made by the NSMs than toward claims of the traditional Left. At the same time, those relating specifically to the GJM are obviously among the central issues and frames addressed by organizations involved in this movement.

The second aspect relating to the movement's identity that we would like to address refers to the breadth of its thematic priorities. Perhaps in a somewhat too simplistic and reductive view, the NSMs have often been characterized in the literature as single-issue movements. The GJM, in contrast, is characterized by the breadth and heterogeneity of the actors involved. As we saw earlier, this holds for the Swiss GJM as well. Do we find a similar breadth and heterogeneity when it comes to the issues and frames addressed by the movement? To answer this question, we can refer to the same information that we just discussed, looking at the number of principles mentioned by the thirty-five selected organizations. In order to simplify the analysis, we have grouped them into four sets of five items.[10] The data suggest that the Swiss GJM is clearly not a single-issue movement, as most of the organizations (43 percent) address between sixteen and twenty different issues, and less than a fifth of them address fewer than five issues. Furthermore, the highest percentage (17 percent) is found for organizations addressing nineteen issues. Of course, these figures, like the others that we show concerning the organizations studied in the Demos project, acquire significance when compared with those referring to the other countries included in the project. However, even without a systematic cross-national comparison that would allow the singling out of Swiss peculiarities, our data suggest that the GJM in Switzerland has a strong multi-issue dimension.

We can strengthen our analysis of the movement's identity by referring once again to the research conducted on participants in two protest events against the 2004 meeting of the WEF. Table 8.3 shows the distribution of the most important claims as stated by participants in these events. Respondents were asked to mention the three most important claims from a finite list of items. The findings are very straightforward. Three claims clearly emerge as central for participants in the movement: suppress the Third World debt (61 percent), grant free access to drinking water (59 percent), and favor fair trade (45 percent). All other items are much less important, with the exception perhaps of generalizing freedom of speech (32 percent). However, when respondents were asked to say what they think should be done

Table 8.3 Most Important Claims for Participants in Two Protests against the WEF Meeting in Davos in 2004 (Percentages)

Claims	% Responses
Suppress Third World Debt	61
Grant Free Access to Drinking Water	59
Favor Fair Trade	45
Generalize Freedom of Speech	32
Make Bretton Woods Institutions (WTO, IMF, WB) Democratic	21
Create a Tax on Financial Transactions ("Tobin Tax")	21
Grant Unions Freedoms and Rights	18
Favor Access to Studies for Women in the South	17
Realize Demining	10
Acknowledge Adoption and Marriage for Homosexual Couples	2
N	411

Note: Respondents were asked to mention the three most important claims from a finite list of items. Percentages do not add up to 100 owing to multiple responses.
Source: Author's data.

to change society (again with three possible choices out of a finite list of items), the two principal items mentioned are establishing democratic forms alternative to the state and abolishing capitalism. These, indeed, are core issues of the GJM everywhere. Strengthening international law and breaking radically with current models of economic development come next in the priority ranking.

What do these figures tell us about the claims made by the GJM in Switzerland, with all the caution that should be used in interpreting them? They suggest, first, that participants in the GJM make a variety of claims. In other words, this is not a single-issue movement, but a heterogeneous one—not only in terms of the organizations and networks involved, but also with regard to the issues addressed. Second, the Swiss GJM seems to emphasize issues and frames traditionally put forward by the NSMs and, more specifically, by the environmental and solidarity movements (the two most important NSMs during the 1980s and 1990s). Taken together, these are issues relating to sustainable development, which can be seen as bridging the environmental and solidarity movements. Third, some of the central issues of the GJM worldwide (for example, fair trade) are also important, whereas others (for example, democratizing international institutions) are more marginal.

The third identity-related aspect considered here is the territorial dimension of the movement's issues and frames. We assess this aspect through the territorial level of the organizations, which we can take as a proxy for the territorial dimension concerning movement identity. Given that we are dealing with a "global" movement, one would expect the international level to be the most important. Our data on the two 2004 anti-WEF protest events, however, partly contradict this assumption, pointing again to the relevance of the national context even for the GJM. Although most of the thirty-five selected organizations are present on all four levels, most also have a local, regional, or national presence. Most important, contrary to expectations, the international level has the lowest score (63 percent, against a proportion ranging between 83 percent and 91 percent for the other levels).[11] This confirms what students of social movements have been warning us about, namely, that behind the fashionable labels of global activism, global civil society, and others, there is a reality made of nationally and even locally anchored actors and claims (Tarrow and della Porta 2005).

To be sure, the focus of the mobilization of the GJM is on transnational and global issues. However, the movement also deals with national issues, and the degree to which the latter enter the movement's agenda varies across countries. Given the relatively lower presence of unions in the mobilization of the GJM in Switzerland, national social issues seem less central than in other countries. Therefore, the movement tends to focus on global issues and to be less linked to the national situation and conflicts. Even national issues are often framed in global terms. For example, the issue of bank secrecy is framed in terms of global justice and the issue of immigration in terms of global migration.

The fourth and last aspect of movement identity that we would like to address concerns the degree to which participants identify with the movement. For an empirical grasp on this aspect, we can look once more at our data on the two protest events against the 2004 meeting of the WEF. Always with the necessary caution in interpreting them, the findings suggest that more than three-quarters of respondents identify either strongly (31 percent) or at least to some extent (49 percent) with the GJM; only a very small proportion (2 percent) do not identify with it at all (18 percent identify a little). These figures are very much in line with those found in the survey conducted among participants at the European Social Forum in Florence in 2002 (della Porta 2005a).[12] Thus, we can say that over a few years' time, people active in the movement have come to create important identity bonds in spite of the fact that they belong to organizations of other movements or that they make claims that preexisted the emergence of the GJM in the public domain. This could form a basis for the survival of the movement in times of lower mobilization due to more unfavorable political opportunities or other external and internal factors.

In summary, the framing processes within the Swiss GJM are characterized by the importance of NSM issues and frames, especially those previously made by the environmental and solidarity movements. Typical frames of both the Old and New Left, as well as frames that reflect core issues of the GJM everywhere, are also present, although to a lesser extent; they probably play a smaller role than in other countries. This can be seen both in the thematic priorities of organizations involved in the movement and in the claims of participants in activities promoted by the movement. The movement's issues and frames also keep strong national and even local roots. Finally, participants' strong identification with the movement should also be stressed.

Action Repertoires

Since the 1998 demonstrations against the WTO meeting in Geneva, an unprecedented police apparatus has been organized by the authorities at every event that could be the target of GJM protests, and confrontations with demonstrators have become more frequent than in the past. In particular, virtually all annual meetings of the WEF in Davos have witnessed a violent or at least a confrontational opposition (the first time in 1999), both near the site of the meeting and in other Swiss cities (even in 2002, when the WEF meeting was held in New York). Furthermore, the protests against the summit of the G8 in Geneva and Lausanne witnessed confrontations with the police (although they occurred before and after the main demonstrations, which went peacefully). The anti-WEF demonstrations of 2004, in contrast, were characterized by both lower participation and more peaceful behavior, perhaps marking a decline of the movement or at least a new phase more centered around consensus building (for example, through social forums and other reflexive events) than around overt protest activities.

The action repertoire of the GJM in Switzerland presents two main forms: mass demonstrations and protest activities addressed against major international governmental or private institutions or organizations, on the one hand, and parallel summits and social forums on the other. The former are protest oriented and have taken a radical or even violent turn when the more radical sectors of the movement have been involved (and also when the authorities have made use of repression). The latter are more self-reflexive and are aimed at identity formation, consensus mobilization, and public sensitization (Passy and Bandler 2003). Furthermore, to somewhat simplify a more complex picture, the latter see the involvement of the less institutionalized and more radical sectors of the movement (for example, the autonomous, anarchist, and New Left milieus more inclined to direct action and participatory democracy), whereas the former include the participation of institutional actors and more moderate sectors of the movement (left-wing parties, unions, and the more formalized organizations of the environmental and solidarity movements more inclined to conventional and media-oriented strategies).

The radical organizations and groups were more important and visible in the early phases of the Swiss GJM. They were very active and contributed, for example, to the creation of Peoples' Global Action and the organization of the anti-WTO protests in 1998; they were also actively involved in the first anti-WEF demonstrations. However, during the past few years, the moderate wing of the GJM seems to have gained in importance: Radical or violent actions have decreased as compared with the late 1990s and early 2000s, in particular in the anti-WEF demonstrations, but also during the protests against the G8 summit in 2003. Similarly to the evolution observed for the NSMs, the most radical sectors of the GSM are losing visibility and are increasingly criticized by the dominant, more institutionalized organizations. The Déclaration de Berne, for example, took an explicit position against violence in 2001 after the anti-WEF demonstrations, as did the Lemanic Social Forum before the anti-G8 demonstrations in Geneva. Although the attitudes toward violent repertoires have until recently been ambiguous within the movement, with some actors clearly condemning it from the beginning and others being less straightforward in this regard, most of the GJM organizations and those close to it are now more inclined to condemn the use of violence and to opt for more moderate and deliberative forms of action.

Social forums, as one of the principal characteristics of the GJM, can be considered as actors, but also as a particular form of action. Chronologically, this kind of activity came after the rise of protest in the streets.[13] The two principal social forums, the Swiss Social Forum and the Lemanic Social Forum, were set up more or less at the same time, in the early 2000s. The first Swiss Social Forum took place in 2003 and the second in 2005. The Lemanic Social Forum, a regional forum, was created in 2002, in the wake of the demonstration organized in November 2001 against the WTO ministerial conference and of the Porto Alegre appeal. It was particularly active in organizing the protest activities against the G8 summit in Evian. Like its national counterpart, however, its activities consist basically in informing the public about global issues and mobilizing consensus for the movement. Other forum-like events taking place more or less regularly in Switzerland include the yearly meeting of the Other Davos, the Summer University promoted by Attac, and the Public Eye on Davos. This parallel summit has been held every year in Davos since 1999 and is coordinated by the Déclaration de Berne and Pro Natura.

Social forums are an innovative and important aspect of the action repertoire of the GJM, not only because they facilitate the mobilization of consensus and the creation of organizational networks, but also insofar as they are vehicles for elaborating conceptions of democracy (della Porta 2005b). This function holds for any country in which the movement is active, but takes a particular meaning in Switzerland, where direct democracy forms one of the fundamental pillars of the country's political culture.

Another indicator of the action repertoire of the GJM is the forms of action used by the organizations involved in it (both those preexisting and those born during the rise of the movement). In order to address this aspect, we can take the sample of thirty-five organizations whose network of hyperlinks we analyzed earlier.[14] Table 8.4 shows the forms of action adopted by the selected organizations.[15] As we can see, nearly all the organizations (97 percent) have among their objectives spreading information, influencing the mass media, and raising public awareness. In this sense, the GJM does not differ very much from the NSMs, which also stress this kind of activity, at least in Switzerland (Giugni and Passy 1997; Kriesi et al. 1995). Yet perhaps the most significant finding for our present purpose is the importance of protest actions and tactics aimed at mobilizing the public (89 percent), as compared with the lower

Table 8.4 Forms of Action of Selected Organizations of the Swiss GJM (Percentages)

Forms of Action	% Responses
Spreading Information/Influencing Mass Media/Raising Awareness	97
Protest/Mobilization	89
Political Education of Citizens	60
Legal Protection and Denunciation of Repression	34
Representation of Specific Interests	31
Advocacy	26
Lobbying	26
Political Representation	20
Offer/Supply of Services to Constituents	17
Self-Awareness/Self-Help	11
Other	51
N	35

Note: The data refer to the functions/objectives explicitly mentioned by the organizations. Percentages do not add up to 100 owing to multiple responses.
Source: Data collected from the DEMOS project.

share of organizations using lobbying activities (26 percent) or political representation (20 percent).[16] This gives us a picture stressing social movement–like activities, all the more so if we note that included in our sample were six parties (including a party youth organization), three unions, and three media (see appendix to this chapter), which typically do not engage in protest or mobilization activities.

Finally, the repertoire of contention of the GJM can also be assessed at the individual level using the data from the survey of participants in two protest events against the 2004 meeting of the WEF described earlier (always keeping in mind the limitations of these data). Table 8.5 shows a selection of the unconventional forms of action that respondents have already used previous to their participation to these two events.[17] Demonstrative forms are quite predictably those that have been most often used. The most striking result, however, is the high proportion of respondents who have made use of confrontational actions and also the relatively important share of violent actions (as far as damaging goods is concerned). If we compare these findings with the action repertoire of social movements in Switzerland, which apart from some exceptions at the local level is typically quite moderate (Kriesi et al. 1995), we realize to what extent the GJM displays a repertoire of contention that significantly departs from the main trends of other movements. Furthermore, although the comparison is somewhat difficult, given the different types of events, participants in the 2004 anti-WEF protests in Switzerland seem even more prone to use violence for political purposes

Table 8.5 Unconventional Forms of Actions Previously Used by Participants in Two Protests against the WEF Meeting in Davos in 2004 (Percentages)

Forms of Action	% Responses	N
Demonstrative Actions		
Signing a Petition	87.0	368
Boycotting Certain Products, Stores, or Countries	87.4	373
Distributing Leaflets	73.3	374
Participating in Symbolic Actions	69.7	373
Participating in a Demonstration	96.3	381
Confrontational Actions		
Participating in a Building Occupation	34.7	369
Opposing Resistance to the Forces of Order	55.0	360
Participating in an Action Blocking Traffic	57.9	373
Violent Actions		
Damaging Goods or Property	23.7	367
Exerting Physical Pressure on Persons	7.6	369

Source: Author's data.

than participants in other events such as the demonstrations against the 2001 G8 summit in Genoa 2001 or the 2002 European Social Forum in Florence (della Porta et al. 2006).[18]

In summary, the repertoire of contention of the Swiss GJM presents two main forms not always linked to each other: mass demonstrations and protest activities (often taking a radical or even violent turn) addressed against major international governmental or private institutions or organizations, on the one hand, and parallel summits and social forums (more moderate and self-reflexive), on the other. However, the movement's radicalness, which at times has been particularly marked, seems to have declined over time.

Conclusion

Although the GJM, which emerged in the Swiss public domain in the late 1990s, certainly represents a new form of contention insofar as the scope of the conflict and its main targets are concerned (transnational or global rather than national), it did not come from nowhere. Quite to the contrary, it relies largely on previous movement families and traditions of contention. In a way, the central conflict on which this movement mobilizes combines those of the labor movement and of the NSMs. As a result, both new collective actors and actors that were formed during previous cycles of contention are present within the movement. Among the previously existing actors, those belonging to the NSM family and those of the more institutionalized Left (leftist parties and unions) predominate. Furthermore, the GJM combines new and preexisting issues and collective action frames. Among them, those put forward by the NSMs and the Left are particularly important.

Although this is true everywhere, each country presents a different mix of these elements, depending on the political opportunities for the movement's mobilization. More specifically, in each country, the GJM reflects the structure of social and political cleavages as well as the country's national traditions of contention. In the case of Switzerland, the main features of the national context that influence the emergence and mobilization of the GJM are a strong degree of pacification of the class cleavage (accompanied by the institutionalization of the system of industrial relations reflected in neo-corporatist arrangements in the administrative arena) and the imprint of the important NSM sector. The main characteristics of the Swiss GJM result in part from these features of the social and political context. In addition, the movement's political alliances with institutional actors and the state responses to the movement's mobilization determine its strength and action repertoires.

The characteristics of the GJM in Switzerland therefore owe much to the social and political context in which it has emerged. In particular, certain aspects of the political opportunity structure, such as state responses and the configuration of power, influence the levels and forms of the protest carried out by the movement. In international perspective, we can speak of a relatively weak and moderate GJM. In addition, the Swiss GJM reflects the conflict lines and traditions of contention that have characterized the country in recent decades, in particular the weakness of class-based mobilization and the strength of the NSMs. The picture that emerges is one of a particularly heterogeneous, if not divided, GJM. Two main branches, or subnetworks, coexist within the movement, each with its own strategies and means of action: a moderate, relatively institutionalized branch relying mostly upon organizations and activists of the ecology and solidarity movements as well as institutional actors such as small left-wing parties and unions, and a more radical and less institutionalized branch pivoting around the autonomous, anarchist, and squatters' milieus.

How can these characteristics be put in a broader international perspective? In other words, how can we expect the Swiss GJM to resemble or differ from its counterparts in other European countries? The heterogeneity of the GJM does not seem to be a Swiss characteristic, but more a characteristic of the movement. The distinctiveness of the Swiss GJM is to be found above all in its composition—that is, in the two main branches that coexist because of the pacification of the class cleavage and the strong heritage of the NSMs.

Appendix

Table 8.6 List of Selected Organizations

Organization Name	Organization Type
Aktion Finanzplatz Schweiz	Single organization (solidarity)
Alliance SUD	Network/federation (solidarity)
Antifa	Network/federation (solidarity)
Attac	Network/federation (global justice)
Augenauf	Network/federation (solidarity)
Centre Europe—Tiers Monde (Cetim)	Single organization (solidarity)
Solidarität mit Chiapas (Chiapas)	Single organization (solidarity)
Communistes	Single organization (party)
Coordination anti-OMC	Ad-hoc umbrella organization (global justice)
Courrier	Single organization (media)
Déclaration de Berne	Single organization (solidarity)
Forum Social Lémanique (FSL)	Ad-hoc umbrella organization (global justice)
Forum Social Suisse (FSS)	Ad-hoc umbrella organization (global justice)
Gipfelblockade	Ad-hoc umbrella organization (global justice)
Groupe pour une Suisse sans Armée (GSsA)	Single organization (peace)
Indymedia	Network/federation (media, global justice)
Jeunesse socialiste suisse (Juso)	Single organization (party youth)
L'Autre Davos	Ad-hoc umbrella organization (global justice)
Lora	Single organization (media, urban autonomous)
Magasins du Monde	Network/federation (solidarity)
Marche mondiale des femmes (MMF)	Ad-hoc umbrella organization (women)
Mouvement pour le socialisme (MPS)	Network/federation (global justice)
Organisation socialiste libertaire (OSL)	Single organization (anarchy, libertarian)
Parti Socialiste Suisse (PS)	Single organization (party)
Parti Suisse du Travail (PST)	Single organization (party)
Pax Christi	Network/federation (peace)
Pro Natura	Single organization (ecology)
Réalise	Single organization (welfare)
Solidarités	Network/federation (party)
Solidarité sans frontières (SOSF)	Single organization (solidarity)
Syndicat des services publics (SSP)	Network/federation (union)
Syndicat interprofessionnel de travailleuses et travailleurs (Sit)	Single organization (union)
Unia	Single organization (union)
Verts	Single organization (party)
WochenZeitung (WOZ)	Single organization (media)

Notes

1. We follow Kriesi et al. (1995) in considering the ecology and solidarity movements as part of the NSM family. Whereas this is quite clear and straightforward for
the ecology movements, the solidarity movement often has a strong religious component, and Switzerland is no exception to this rule. However, both movements rest
on new—rather than traditional—cleavages and share a similar social basis.

2. To create this index, we used the following variables: presence of a constitution, presence of a document of fundamental values, presence of a formally adopted
program, presence of formal membership, and presence of a fee-paying membership.
Organizations ranking from 0 to 0.4 are considered as informal, organizations ranking from 0.6 to 1 as formal. These results are to be taken with some caution, as the
organizations were selected also because of their Internet presence. As an Internet
presence requires a minimum of resources, the more formal the organization, the
higher the chance it will have a Web site. Many networks or organizations active in
the movement could not be selected because they have no Web site.

3. The objective of this part of the research is to draw a general picture of the
use of the Internet by GJM organizations in terms of quality of communication,
identity building, transparency, and offline as well as online mobilization in relation
to the formal character of the organizations, the presence of formal members in the
organizations, the territorial scope of the organizations, and the age of the Web sites.
The organizations were selected according to two criteria: the type of organization
and their importance within the movement. See the appendix to this chapter for the
complete list of organizations studied.

4. In the jargon of network analysis, these three organizations rank highest in
terms of in-degree. The network has a mean in-degree of 4.1, which is low given that
the network is composed of thirty-five actors. The in-degree of the three organizations equals eleven, which is largely above the mean.

5. The attribution of organizations to the four subnetworks is not always clear-cut.
For example, the Gipfelblockade and the Anti-WTO Coordination are here considered as GJM organizations, as they were established in the 1990s and mobilize on typical GJM issues, but these organizations stem directly from the squatters/autonomous
milieus. The two media organizations (*WOZ* and *Le Courrier*) are here considered as
NSM organizations. These two newspapers are now close to the GJM, but they were
created before its breakthrough into the public domain. For example, although *Le
Courrier* has strong religious roots (its original aim was to defend Catholics' interests
in Protestant Geneva), it was already close to the NSMs.

6. It should be stressed that Solidarités has a hybrid status. We define it here as
belonging to the traditional Left because it is a political party to the extent that it
competes for elections. However, this organization defines itself as a social movement.

7. The two events are a social forum–like event held in Zurich on January 17,
2004, and a protest demonstration that took place in Chur on January 24, 2004.

8. The data refer to support for principles explicitly declared by the organizations.
Each figure in the table represents the percentage of organizations mentioning a
given principle.

9. Ethical finance as well as critical consumerism and fair trade could perhaps be included in solidarity movement issues, although in this calculation we left them out in order to be on the conservative side.

10. The total number of principles equals 26.

11. Percentages do not add up to 100 because of multiple responses.

12. Although the distributions vary significantly depending on nationality, 63 percent of the participants in the 2002 European Social Forum in Florence displayed either a lot or some identification with the movement, although only 19 percent declared only a little or no identification (della Porta 2005a, table 8.5). The stronger identifiers were the British.

13. For example, on the world scale, the first World Social Forum took place in 2001, two years after the Seattle events.

14. In addition to examining the organizations' Web sites as described earlier, in another part of the Demos project we study their organizational ideology.

15. The data refer to the functions/objectives explicitly mentioned by the organizations.

16. Of the four organizations using protest or mobilization tactics, three are media (newspaper, radio, or alternative media). Of the nine organizations using lobbying tactics, two are unions and one is a party. Of the seven organizations using interest representation tactics, six are parties (including a party youth organization).

17. We have selected the forms of action that have most often been mentioned by participants and the most radical ones. Here we include signing a petition among the unconventional forms, although this can be debatable.

18. Both in the demonstrations against the 2001 G8 in Genoa and at the 2002 European Social Forum in Florence, the share of people who admit to having made use of violent forms (della Porta et al. 2006) are lower than among participants in the 2004 anti-WEF protest. This comparison, however, should be taken with some caution, as the events are not the same and the indicators are also partly different.

Chapter Nine

The Global Justice Movement in the United States since Seattle

Jennifer Hadden and Sidney Tarrow

Seattle, 1999 and Washington, D.C., 2001

In November 1999, when thousands of protesters shut down the WTO (World Trade Organization) Ministerial meeting in Seattle, Washington, something new was added to the global repertoire of contention. Although there had been "counter-summits" against major international organizations in the past (Pianta 2001b and Pianta et al. 2004), the Seattle campaign coordinated scores of protest events around the world (Lichbach and de Vries 2004, table 5). That campaign also employed a set of colorful and contentious public performances that would be remembered and imitated elsewhere under the label "the Seattle model" (Wood 2004) for years to come. Those tactics, and the clumsy and repressive reaction of Seattle's police and public authorities (Levi and Murphy 2004) in part inspired a cascade of transnationally organized events around the globe, from Genoa to Göteborg, from Prague to Cancún, from Porto Alegre to Mumbai.

The "Battle of Seattle" has gone down as a founding event in the history of transnational social movements. Though the global justice movement may have *preceded* Seattle in many places (in Germany and Switzerland, for example), it nevertheless attracted attention and sparked further transnational activism both in the United States and in Europe, as the chapters on

France and Spain in this volume suggest. It brought together trade unionists and ecologists, radicals and moderates, churchgoers and lay people, young and old, grassroots social movements and moderate nongovernmental organization (NGO) advocates.[1]

Less well known—but well documented—is the fact that the vast majority of protesters in Seattle came from within the United States. A smaller, but still significant proportion were from the Canadian northwest, and insignificant numbers traveled to Seattle from the global South (Lichbach and de Vries 2004, 43). But as the twentieth century drew to a close, it was mainly citizens in the heart of global capitalism who produced the most spectacular protest to date *against* global capitalism.

That leadership role was not to last. Only two years later, as summer was ending in Washington, D.C., a range of U.S. movement organizations tried to capitalize on the momentum of Seattle by planning a demonstration against the World Bank (WB) and the International Monetary Fund (IMF). Made up of a coalition of groups similar to those that had mounted the Seattle protest, they organized as the Mobilization for Global Justice (MGJ). As in Seattle, the coalition ranged from advocacy "insider" NGOs to radical action "outsiders." They too planned to use a combination of radical and conventional tactics, drawing heavily on the Seattle model. Their goal was to mount "the latest in a series of high-profile mass demonstrations since the Battle of Seattle had nearly brought the meetings of the World Trade Organization to a halt in 1999" (Gillham and Edwards 2003, 492). Events and opportunities seemed to conspire to promise the most vast, energetic, and potentially disruptive transnational protest of the year 2001.

But when, on September 11 of that year, three terrorist airplane-bombs crashed into the World Trade Center and the Pentagon, everything changed. In their careful reconstruction of the Washington protest, Patrick Gillham and Bob Edwards document the valiant efforts of the MGJ's organizers to salvage their carefully planned protest from the ruins of 9/11. One response was to cut back on their plans; of the roughly eighteen planned events, ten were canceled outright and four others were revised to respond to the new situation created by 9/11. The most theatrical and potentially disruptive events were canceled altogether, and several more conventional ones were put in their place.

Despite these changes, a number of groups that had been at the center of the coalition's planning either dropped out or scaled back their participation. In particular, the AFL-CIO—always leery of cooperating with grassroots radicals—pulled its forces out of the coalition and dedicated itself to disaster relief. Some groups wanted to cancel the demonstration altogether, others were determined to maintain it as planned, and still others urged that it be turned against the rapidly growing threat of war against al-Qaeda and the Taliban. Most of the media, which had publicized the Seattle demonstration, was already rallying around the drumbeat of war and gave little attention to the Washington demonstration. When, following the first World Social Forum in the winter of 2001, activists in the nation's capital tried to form a Washington social summit, little came of their efforts. September 11 was a historic hinge, not only for the United States and its international posture but also for a global justice movement that had effectively begun in that country. The activist dog that had barked loudly in 1999 had subsided to a whimper two years later.

From a Bark to a Whimper

What had transpired in the few years that separated the success of the Seattle WTO protest from the failure of the MGJ in Washington? Clearly, after 9/11, many activists who identified with the budding global justice movement were shocked into silence. But the failure of the 2001 Washington demonstration was not a short-term conjunctural effect of the national tragedy, nor did it lead to a decline in protest potential; in fact, in surveys Americans reported more positive attitudes to protest than they had in the 1990s. Nor have their voices been stilled by repression; in an interesting paired comparison, Lesley Wood has shown how global justice activists in one city—Toronto—have been more discouraged by repression than their counterparts in New York City (Wood 2006).

In this chapter, we cannot build on the kind of sustained database that our colleagues in this volume have used in the preceding chapters. Nor are we especially expert in the politics of the U.S. global justice movement. Instead, we have drawn on a variety of sources, interviewed activists and specialists, and we speculate about how the domestic conditions of the United States both before and after 9/11 have affected the fate of that movement. We will argue that three long-term factors conspired to lower the profile of U.S. activists and distinguish it from the robust European campaigns that have been reported in the preceding chapters:

- the ambivalence in the internationalism of U.S. public opinion;
- the frame-bridging success of the Bush administration's strategy of linking globalism to the threat of terrorism;
- and the overriding domestic preoccupations of U.S. social activists.

Compared with the other countries examined in this volume, U.S. social activists, who helped give life to the global justice movement (GJM) in Seattle, have subsided into largely domestic preoccupations.

Definitions and Differentiations

Before examining both the state of the GJM in the United States and the reasons for its fragility, it will be important to draw some definitional lines around it. In both academic and popular literature on resistance to globalization there is a disturbing tendency to draw the boundaries of the movement to include a range of protests and activities that can only be considered "global" by a very broad definition. Following the logic of an earlier paper by one of us (Tarrow 2002), we think there are serious disadvantages to such a "lumpy" definition. We argue that if we are going to measure the strength of the GJM in the United States against its vigorous growth in Europe, we will need to be precise in delimiting both its content and its boundaries. We need a definition that combines 1) *a constrained definition of social movements*, 2) *a specific conception of transnational activism*, and 3) *a precise notion of the nature of its claims:*

Social movements. In common parlance, the term *social movement* is used broadly to cover most or all of the overlap between contention and collective action, as well as extending it to the social background and consequences of contention and collective action. In this approach, for example, the women's movement could include all collective efforts past and present to advance women's rights and welfare, the entry of women into the workforce, the development of women's studies programs in universities, and the changes in cultural codes that have narrowed the gap between women and men (Tilly and Tarrow 2006, chap. 6). That extremely broad use of the term *social movement* has a pedigree: Leaders of social movements often rally their followers and taunt their opponents by referring to their glorious predecessors, to their solidarity with other struggles, and to the connection of movement actions with changing practices in everyday life.

For purposes of explanation, however, the expansion of the term *social movements* to most or all of contentious politics—as well as its background and consequences—has two serious drawbacks. First, it makes systematic comparison between forms of contentious politics more difficult. In order to describe and explain contentious politics adequately, we need to identify the special properties of revolutions, military coups, peasant revolts, industrial conflict, and social movements before discovering what they have in common. Second, it obscures a fundamental historical fact. As we know them, social movements only took shape about two centuries ago, and only became widely available as a means of popular claim making during the twentieth century.

In our narrower sense of the term, the social movement that emerged in the early nineteenth century and eventually became a staple of popular politics during the twentieth century involved sustained challenges to power holders in the name of a population living under the jurisdiction of those power holders by means of public displays of that population's worthiness, unity, numbers, and commitment. Our definition of a social movement is *a sustained campaign of claim making, using repeated performances that advertise the claim, based on organizations, networks, traditions, and solidarities that sustain these activities.*

Social movements differ from other forms of contentious politics by combining 1) sustained campaigns of claim making, 2) an array of public performances including marches, rallies, demonstrations, creation of specialized associations, public meetings, public statements, petitions, letter writing, and lobbying, 3) repeated public displays of worthiness, unity, numbers, in commitment by such means as wearing colors, marching in disciplined ranks, displaying signs, chanting slogans, and picketing public buildings. This combination clearly distinguishes social movements from other forms of contention such as revolutions and individual protest campaigns. The former is a conflict between two groups of contenders for control of a state, each of which enjoys substantial support from societal groups, and the latter is a short-term campaign that might include movements, political parties, unaffiliated participants, and even state officials. For us, a social movement is a particular form of contentious politics—and not *all* of contentious politics.

Transnational social movements. Our conception of a transnational social movement is broad but equally constrained. We define transnational movements as "*socially mobilized groups with constituencies in at least two states, engaged in sustained contentious interactions with power holders in at least one state other than their own, or against international institution, or a multinational economic actor*" (Tarrow 2005, 11).

Here, too, there has been a tendency to stretch the boundaries of a concept beyond all reasonable scope. Were the New York gardeners who attended the Seattle demonstrations transnational activists? Hardly. Are Korean workers who protest the closure of their plant by a multinational corporation transnational activists? Only when they go to Canada to lodge a complaint with the Canadian NAALC. Are Indian farmers who protest against—or in favor of—GM seeds transnational activists? Only if their actions are coordinated with the actions of others like themselves in other parts of the world.

What makes transnational activists different from domestic activists is their ability to shift their activities among levels, taking advantage of the expanded nodes of opportunity in an increasingly complex international society. Some transnational activists behave as "insiders," lobbying and collaborating with international elites and institutions to a point approaching co-optation, whereas others challenge states' and international institutions' policies and—in some cases—challenge their existence. The line between insiders and outsiders is difficult to draw consistently, and coalitions between the two families of activists are increasingly common.

Our definition is not limited to full-time international activists but includes a variety of groups and individuals whose activism is both domestic and transnational. It contains immigrant activists who are in touch with politics in their home countries, but not all immigrants (Portes 2001); labor activists from the South who forge ties with foreign unions and NGOs, but not all workers (Anner 2004); ecologists who gravitate around international institutions but not all ecologists (Dalton and Rohrschneider 2002); members of transnational advocacy networks, but not all NGO advocates (Keck and Sikkink 1998); transnational Islamist terrorist networks, but not all Islamist militants (Sageman 2004); and domestic activists who are part of the sustained campaign against neoliberalism that we call the global justice movement.

Global justice. For purposes of this analysis, we define the GJM as *a sustained, transnational movement of grassroots activists and organized advocacy groups working for global justice (economic, social, political, and environmental) and against the neoliberal model of international development and the policies of the states and international institutions that advance it, and in favor of a model of development aimed at combating the gross inequalities that that model implies.* This is a broad definition, but it is far less expansive than the tendency we find in the literature to make a mechanical leap from opposition to globalization to transnational activism. That equation between globalization and transnational activism says both too much and too little. It says too much because some of the most successful transnational movements have little to do with globalization. Consider the campaign to end the production and use of antipersonnel landmines, the global opposition to militarism, and the human rights campaigns in authoritarian states: These are all vital transnational movements but have a relationship to globalization that is at best highly mediated.

The broad equation of globalization with transnational activism also says too little. It ignores the fact that concern with globalization often leads to passivity (e.g., "What can we do if the Chinese produce the same products as we do but at one-tenth the cost?"). And it leaves out the intervening processes of consensus mobilization and action mobilization across borders that are necessary to lead people to engage in transnational contention. As we will see, many Americans are concerned about globalization, but relatively few of them identify with the GJM.

In summary, if we want to assess whether a global justice movement is alive and well in the United States (or in Western Europe, for that matter), we need to define that movement in clear and unshifting terms. We cannot, for example, expand it to include activism against the Iraq war on the grounds that the primary exponent of that war is also the dominant economic power in the world. Other transnational movements—like the movement against the Iraq war—might be *related to* the GJM; they might i*nherit* activists, forms of activism, and collective action frames from the earlier cycle of protest (Fisher 2006). They might also make heroic attempts to frame their opposition in similar terms to the opposition to global neoliberalism, but, as Rootes and Saunders write of Great Britain in this volume, "it is a mistake simply to assimilate the antiwar movement to the global justice movement" (Rootes and Saunders, chapter 6 this volume).

There is also a methodological reason for our insistence on a constrained definitional strategy: Conflating a movement against global neoliberalism with campaigns against U.S. militarism or anything else that crosses borders is not only conceptually foggy; it makes impossible the examination of the *transitions* between different areas of contention and the potential "social movement spillover" of activists from one movement to the other (Meyer and Whittier 1994). Or so we are prepared to argue.

Americans, Europeans, and Globalization

We begin at the most general level. Americans think and talk a great deal about globalization. Consider the elite public opinion surveys carried out by James Rosenau and his collaborators. In 1998 they carried out a first survey of elite opinion, dividing their sample of elites into "cutting-edgers" (e.g., elites involved in transnational activities) and "non-cutting edgers." They carried out a near-identical survey with the same elites after 9/11. Globalization is certainly a term that elites recognize and support; in both waves of interviews, Rosenau and his collaborators found that more than 70 percent say it enhances the creation of jobs, increases economic integration, and enhances capitalism in general (Rosenau and Earnest 2004, 4).

But do U.S. elites engaged in transnational activities "think globally"? The majority of the elites interviewed by Rosenau and his collaborators think of themselves primarily as citizens of the United States, including those on the "cutting edge of globalization." They do believe that international institutions are important, even after the Iraq war showed how little official Washington thought of the UN (Rosenau et al. 2006, chap. 3). But there were few statistically significant differences in this respect between the attitudes of the "cutting-edgers" and the other elites interviewed by Rosenau and his collaborators.

Many members of the U.S. mass public worry a lot about globalization. According to the Pew Global Attitudes 2002 Survey, 62 percent of Americans think globalization is "very good" or "somewhat good" in comparison with

69 percent of Canadians, 68 percent of British, and 67 percent of German respondents. Only the French and Italians had lower levels of support for globalization (60 and 51 percent, respectively).[2] Strikingly, when the Chicago Council for Foreign Relations asked Americans to translate these views into policy prescriptions, their support for globalization seemed to be of a rather passive variety. Only 14 percent said the United States should actively promote globalization, and 35 percent thought the United States should allow it to continue; 24 percent would have liked to try to slow it down, and 15 percent wanted to try to reverse it.[3] Americans in general are far from activist cheerleaders for globalization.

What of younger Americans—the most plausible source of support for the GJM? Surprisingly, eighteen- to twenty-nine-year-olds were far more likely to respond that globalization was "very good" than any other age group (43 percent of 18-to-29-year-olds vs. 35 percent of respondents in the 30 to 49 and 50 to 64 age categories and 27 percent of respondents over 65). The Pew data also show that American youth are more favorably disposed toward globalization than youth in Western Europe.[4] But these are rather abstract orientations that could well be triggered by the survey instruments used: Are young Americans more or less likely than Europeans to identify themselves with collectivities larger than the nation-state? To the extent that they think globalization is a good thing, we might expect them to have more "global" identity attachments. But to the extent that such attachments might imply a lack of patriotism in this highly nationalistic country, they might be less likely to identify with collectivities beyond the nation-state. A question in the World Values Study (WVS) on the level of people's primary attachments (local, national, or supranational) provides some insight into this issue.[5] When asked what their most important level of attachment is, Europeans and Americans from different age cohorts claimed to have primarily global attachments in the proportions listed in table 9.1.

As is often the case with international survey data, the findings are ambiguous. At the most general level, the data show that older American age cohorts are *more* likely to have global attachments than Europeans of the same age; but younger Americans are *less* likely to have global attachments than corresponding Europeans, with the exception of the post-1977 age cohort in the 2001 survey, where 24 percent of the youngest Americans claimed a first global attachment, compared with only 16 percent of the youngest Europeans. The differences are small, but they are nevertheless statistically significant (F (19.88, 23397.65) = 2.1879, P = 0.0017) and suggest that younger Americans are now more global in their attachments than they were in the past or than younger Europeans are today. Whatever "global attachments" might mean, the youngest Americans interviewed during the year preceding September 11 had not retreated into parochial nationalism.

Table 9.1 Global Attachment by Age Group in the United States versus Europe (First Attachment Only)

Age Cohort		Pre-1936	1937–1946	1947–1956	1957–1966	1967–1976	1977–1986	N
2001 WVS	United States	8.08%	13.62%	18.94%	19.84%	15.69%	23.83%	230
	Europe	8.74%	8.42%	15.41%	22.41%	28.83%	16.19%	990

Note: Global identifiers account for 7.74% of the total U.S. respondents (*N* = 2,041) in 1981 WVS, 16.62% in 1990 WVS (*N* = 1,775), and 19.52% in 2001 WVS (*N* = 1,178). They also account for 7.11% of the total European respondents (*N* = 13,284) in 1981 WVS, 7.44% in 1990 WVS (*N* = 17,777), and 6.7% in 2001 WVS (*N* = 14,779). Out of the seventeen-country sample, "Europe" includes eleven countries: the United Kingdom, France, West Germany, Italy, Spain, Belgium, the Netherlands, Denmark, Sweden, Iceland, and Ireland.

Source: World Values Study, 2001; data provided by Jai Kwan Jung.

Global Thinking; Local Inaction

How do Americans' concern with globalization and younger Americans' global attachments translate into participation in the GJM? We can examine that participation in three ways:

- First, from the few public opinion surveys that ask people about "globalization," we can look for evidence of Americans' tendency to transfer their concerns about globalization to support for the goal of global justice;
- Second, we can examine data on Americans' participation in transnationally organized counter-summits like the World Social Forum;
- Third, we can examine the extent to which the social forum process has been internalized through the creation of national, regional, and local counterparts to the WSF.

Public Opinion and the GJM

The GJM is so new, and U.S. social survey researchers so inclined to ask the same questions of respondents year after year to facilitate time-series analyses, that we have few sources of evidence about how Americans have responded to that movement. Comparative surveys are somewhat more helpful, but the most global survey, the World Values Study, has not been administered recently enough or often enough to provide much purchase on this question. From that survey, we know that the U.S. propensity to protest in general has increased, and from the National Election Study, we also know that Americans were dramatically more interested in the 2004 presidential campaign than they were in any previous campaign.[6]

But the increased U.S. interest in politics and their increased propensity to protest do not translate into sympathy for the GJM; fewer Americans sympathized with it than citizens of most other Western democracies. When samples of citizens in forty-four countries were asked, "What kind of influence [antiglobalization protesters] are having on the way things are going in [surveyed country]," only 30 percent of Americans answered "very good" or "somewhat good," compared with 39 percent of Canadians, 44 percent of the French, and 34 percent of Germans. (Only Italians, with 27 percent answering "very good" or "somewhat good" had an equivalently low level of support.)[7] The Americans were also most likely to either refuse to answer the question or to reply "don't know" (21 percent), compared with 11 percent of Canadians, 10 percent of Germans, and 5 percent of French respondents (with only Italy and Great Britain having comparable scores with 20 percent and 19 percent, respectively).

Youth in America *do* seem to have been somewhat impacted by the global justice movement. The 2002 National Civic Engagement Survey indicates that almost a third (28 percent) of 15- to 25-year-olds (e.g., those in the United States who are most likely to protest) claimed that the wave of protests against globalization have made them more likely to participate in politics and to vote. Only 19 percent thought the protests would make them less likely to participate, and 39 percent indicated their propensity to participate had been unchanged.

However, the protests against globalization exerted a much lower impact on young Americans' attitudes than the war on terrorism, which 70 percent of respondents answered would make them more likely to participate in politics and to vote. Other domestic political events, such as the attacks of September 11 (67 percent said they were "more likely to participate"), the 2000 election (41 percent), the recession (43 percent), and the Bush and Clinton presidencies (50 percent and 45 percent, respectively) all exerted a greater impact on young American's political attitudes than the protests against globalization.[8]

Participation in Parallel and Counter-Summits

U.S. activists can take pride in the fact that the Seattle protest against the WTO helped launch the movement that today has spread across the world in the name of global justice. That movement takes many different forms, but it has generally followed the pattern of "counter-summits" organized in parallel to, or in criticism of official summits. Seattle did not invent that form; it first emerged in Scandanavia in the 1970s and in Berlin in 1988 against an IMF–World Bank meeting (Gerhards and Rucht 1992), and became almost a routine accompaniment to international meetings during the 1990s (Pianta 2001b and Pianta et al. 2004).

In part because so many international organizations have their offices in the United States, Americans have hosted a significant number of parallel or counter-summits, beginning in 1990, with a summit organized in parallel to an IMF–World Bank meeting in Washington, D.C. Mario Pianta and his collaborators have identified twenty-eight such parallel summits in the United States between 1990 and the end of 2005.[9] But most of these were mounted in conjunction with major summits of international organizations and at the sites of those meetings; almost none were independent "civil society" events or social forums.[10] As we can see from table 9.2, more than 35 percent of the European events identified by Pianta and his team were coded as either social forums or independent civil society events; none of those identified in the United States fit this independent profile.

Do not mistake what we mean: These events were not insignificant; although some were modest in size, others attracted more than ten thousand

Table 9.2 Countersummits in Europe and North America, 1990–2005, by Type of Event

| | TYPE OF EVENT | | | | | | |
CONTINENTS	UN Summits	IMF/WB/WTO Summits	G7/G8 Summits	Regional Summits	Social Fora	Civil Society Events	TOTAL
Europe	15.1%	5.5%	13.7%	30.1%	5.5%	30.1%	100.0%
North America	17.9%	39.3%	17.9%	25.0%	—	—	100.0%
TOTAL	15.8%	14.9%	14.9%	28.7%	4.0%	21.8%	100.0%

Note: Data Provided by Mario Pianta and Duccio Zola (2005).

participants. But the largest events in the United States were organized in response to summits of major international organizations: the WTO protests in Seattle in 1999, the IMF–World Bank protests in Washington, D.C., in 2000, 2002, and 2005, and the Miami FTAA protests in 2003. In contrast, European events attracted a larger number of participants, with 71.2 percent of events having attendance of more than a thousand people as compared with 57.1 percent of North American events, and were more frequently independent of official international institutional summits.

No international meeting—whether in Europe or in North America—has had anything like the success of the World Social Forum that has been variously organized in Porto Alegre, Mumbai, or in the three cities of the global South where the WSF was held in 2005. Data on the Porto Alegre forums in 2001, 2002, and 2003 suggests that the United States sent an increased number of participants there each year, with a big jump in 2003, to 547 participants, making the United States the third-largest participating country after Brazil and France.[11] By 2005, Americans' participation had increased to 1,753, a growth of more than 300 percent since 2003.

But when we control these figures by population size, Americans' participation in the WSF has to be redimensioned. Despite the growth in North American participation, European participation in Porto Alegre in 2005 was 2.4 times stronger in per capita terms than the United States and Canada. Table 9.3 combines data on WSF participation in 2003 and 2005 (the only two years for which we were able to find complete data for all these countries) for the United States, Canada, France, and four Latin American countries (Argentina, Chile, Paraguay, and Uruguay). Table 9.3 records these participation data and their changes over time.

We should note that, in addition to the increased participation of U.S. activists in the WSF, the forum itself has tended to become more "American" in its preoccupations. Especially since the invasion and occupation of Iraq, we find an increasing preoccupation with U.S. militarism in the themes and

Table 9.3 Participation in the World Social Forum by Nationality

Country	Number of Participants[1] 2003	Number of Participants[1] 2005	Participants per 1,000,000 Inhabitants[2] 2003	Participants per 1,000,000 Inhabitants[2] 2005	Growth Rate per Capita
United States	547	1,753	1.884	6.038	320%
Canada	250[3]	623	7.762	19.344	249%
France	597	873	9.920	14.506	146%
Latin America[4]	2,526	5,240	39.579	82.103	207%

Note: Participation Data from Ibase (The Institute for Brazilian Social and Economic Analyses) and Conway 2006.

[1] Ibase Survey on the World Social Forum 2003 and 2005. Available at www.ibase.br/fsm2003/ingles.htm and www.ibase.br/userimages/relatorio_fsm2005_INGLES2.pdf (Accessed June 22, 2006). Participants in the 2003 World Social Forum measured as a sum of the number of delegates and nondelegate participants (excluding campers).

[2] U.S. Census Bureau. www.census.gov (Accessed June 2006). International Database www.census.gov/ipc/www/idbnew.html (Accessed June 2006).

[3] Estimated 2003 Canadian participation from Janet Conway "La difusión global del Foro Social Mundial: La política de lugar y escala vista desde Canada," trans. Daina Greene. *El Foro Social Mundial: Camino a un mundo nuevo.* Ed. Frank Bracho. Caracas: Fondo Editorial Question, 2006, 77–89.

[4] "Latin America" here includes only Argentina, Chile, Paraguay, and Uruguay.

discussion groups of the forum. This "mission creep" has given an increasingly visible role to U.S. activists and could go far in explaining the increased willingness of Americans to travel great distances to participate in the forum.

Internalization and Downward Scale Shift

The major payoff for domestic politics in both Latin America and Western Europe of the World Social Forum has been the creation of local, national, and regional forums in great numbers around the world since 2001. But there has been no equivalent internalization of the social forum process in the United States to the one that our coauthors in this volume have identified in Western Europe. Whereas outgoing American participation in the WSF has grown geometrically, the same cannot be said for the internalization and downward scale shift of the forum process that has been examined in the other chapters of this book.

By "internalization" we mean *the migration of international pressures and conflicts into domestic politics.* By "downward scale shift" we mean *the tendency of domestic activists to shift the scale of transnational mobilizations to the local, national, or regional level* (Tarrow 2005, chaps. 5 and 7). While Europeans have been organizing a series of well-attended social fora in Paris, Florence, London, and Athens and creating networks of local social forums throughout their societies, U.S. activists have been unable to coalesce around a similar process.

Using a Web-based search using the term *social forum* in July 2006, we have been able to identify the following events and organizations since the first World Social Forum in 2001:

- Boston Social Forum (2004)
- Chicago Social Forum (2005, 2006)
- Houston Social Forum (2006)
- Maine Social Forum (2006)
- Midwest Social Forum (2004, 2005, 2006)
- Southeast Social Forum (2006)
- The Border Social Forum (held in Ciudad Juarez in October 2006)
- U.S. Social Forum (rescheduled for 2007)

This list is not exhaustive, as Web sites for social forums in the United States are often either pulled down or not maintained after their organizational collapse. The New York Social Forum, for example, held two successful events in 2003 before its dissolution and does not currently maintain a Web site. Similar stories can be told for other local forums, such as that of Ithaca, New York, where a social forum was held in 2002,[12] or in Washington, D.C., where planning for a local social forum that would have been of national importance never reached fruition, to the best of our knowledge.

U.S. social forums seem to differ significantly in character from European forums. For example, social forums in the United States rarely have formal ties with labor unions or political parties, though members of these organizations may attend as individual participants. As one activist describes the difference, North American social forums tend to come from "the independent left, not the organized left."[13] Lack of financial and other resources remains a great organizational challenge.

One good example of the social forum process in the United States is the Midwest Social Forum. The Midwest Forum was founded at the Havens Center for the Study of Social Structure and Social Change at the University of Wisconsin–Madison in 1983 and was later called "Radfest." The event changed its name and location in 2003, adopting the title "Midwest Social Forum" and convening in Milwaukee (www.nigd.org/docs/MidwestSocialForumMarcBecker2006). The Midwest Social Forum has been organizationally active for many years and has been able to attract about 1,000 participants to its most recent event.

However, in contrast to the European experience, both the participants in and the issues dealt with by the Midwest Social Forum have been overwhelmingly domestic in nature. For example, the 2006 forum focused on immigration rights, as well as racism, water, and issues of police brutality. One activist interviewed described his puzzlement that a group from Africa had expressed interest in attending the Midwest Forum, reflecting to what extent the forum is intended to be a local event. Rather than seeing this local focus as a lacuna, many U.S. activists see the U.S. forum process as more fully embodying a critique of the Porto Alegre World Social Forum itself: Keep it local, keep it decentralized, keep it small.[14]

As for higher-level meetings along the lines of the European model, U.S. activists were urged by the International Council of the WSF in 2003 to organize a national social forum.[15] A U.S. social forum, which was originally scheduled for the summer of 2006, is now scheduled for the summer of 2007.[16] Although the official reason for the delay is the aftermath of Hurricane Katrina in the southern United States, an activist interviewed identified the real cause of the postponement to be a shortage of resources, and more important, a lack of political will.[17] A U.S.-Mexico border forum, originally scheduled for May 2006, was rescheduled after many organizations petitioned organizers for a delay so that they could participate in the May 1 rallies for immigrants' rights.[18] There was further discussion of a North American forum in Caracas in 2006, though no progress toward planning seems to have been made there.

The debates that U.S. activists have had about the prospects for such events are as revealing as its failure to materialize. At a panel on North American Social Forums at the 2005 World Social Forum, it was lamented that social forums in the United States face a number of difficult challenges: a lack of concrete proposals, a failure to integrate and involve grassroots organizations and unorganized people, difficulty interacting with local political structures, and struggles to involve the youth who were so active in the antiwar and anti-WTO protests in the social forum process.[19] At a similar meeting at the Caracas summit in 2006, U.S. activists worried about the near total absence of the working class from the radical Left and the lack of gender inclusiveness among participants (www.nigd.org/docs/USSFMarcBecker). Although local social forums report significant improvement in attracting these constituencies, there remains a recognition of "the significant barriers that we need to overcome in order to realized visions of alternative worlds in the United States."[20]

In summary, the social forum process in the United States has faced a variety of organizational challenges and setbacks. Public opinion in the United States indicates that Americans are less favorably disposed toward antiglobalization protestors, and that those most likely to protest are primarily motivated by domestic concerns. Although outgoing American participation in the WSF has grown geometrically, the same cannot be said for the internalization and downward scale shift of the forum process that has been examined in the other chapters of this book.

Why That Dog Won't Hunt

These summary observations only scratch the surface of the state of the "global" U.S. Left in the post–9/11 era. A more profound investigation would need to examine at least the following issues:

- Did Global Forum international organizers (perhaps because they are so deeply instilled with a "South versus North" specification of globalization) fail to reach out effectively to U.S. activists?
- What has been the impact on U.S. activists of the repressive climate in the United States since the "War on Terror" began?[21]
- Are there differences among the social forum experiments in different parts of the country?

In the absence of the sustained research that would be required to examine these questions, we close our chapter with some observations that in our minds help to explain why the "dog that barked" in Seattle has been stilled to a whimper since then. We think that although the shock of 9/11 and the repressive climate that followed it certainly played a role in turning U.S. public opinion against the nascent movement against neoliberal globalization, it was not responsible for stilling the voices of activism. On the contrary, the tendency of Americans to protest has *increased* in the new century, and U.S. activists participated strongly in the anti-Iraq war campaign in 2003. We think it was primarily the shift of the domestic opportunity structure to a concern with domestic security that has disarmed the internationalist U.S. Left.

The logic of our argument is the following:

First, the war against the Taliban and the war in Iraq enabled the already unilateralist Bush administration to change the subject of public debate from domestic issues like the environment and the economy to the self-proclaimed "War on Terror." This move awakened Americans' instinctive patriotism and at least temporarily neutralized the opposition's capacity to criticize Bush's expansionist ambitions—especially after troops were on the ground in Afghanistan and Iraq. Second, the Bush/Cheney foreign strategy activated a sharpened cognitive and cultural boundary between most Americans and the rest of the world. For example, the well-orchestrated attacks on France from Washington met with a spontaneous increase of revulsion in middle America against an ally that dared to have its own view of international affairs. Third, these factors produced a shrinking of the constituency for internationalism in moderate U.S. opinion and a "social movement spillover" from the budding global justice movement to opposition to the war, and then to the Dean campaign in the 2004 presidential election.

Three specifications of this argument are necessary, regarding U.S. internationalism, the "frame-bridging" strategy of the Bush administration, and the overwhelmingly domestic orientation of the progressive U.S. Left:

Table 9.4 European and North American Countersummits by Type of Relationship to Official Summit, 1990–2005

CONTINENTS	RELATION TO THE OFFICIAL SUMMIT				
	Strong Conflict	Criticism of Policies	Active Dialogue	Integration in the Official Summit	TOTAL
Europe	27.7%	53.2%	14.9%	4.3%	100.0%
North America	28.6%	53.6%	3.6%	14.3%	100.0%
Total	28.0%	53.3%	10.7%	8.0%	100.0%

Note: Data Provided by Mario Pianta and Duccio Zola (2005).

The limits and nature of U.S. internationalism. It is sometimes forgotten that the United States went through an internationalist decade during the 1990s. Despite obstruction from Congress and influential right-wing lobbies, the Clinton administration entered into more international agreements than its predecessors, supported multilateral actions, and looked with much greater favor on the growth of non-state NGO activity abroad. Although the growth rate for NGO formation was greater during this decade in the South than in the North (largely because southern countries started from such a low level in the first place), both the number and size of U.S.-based NGOs continued to expand during the decade of the 1990s.

But U.S. internationalism has always been a double-edged sword; the same internationalist impulse that supported the growth of NGO activity during the Clinton years also supported U.S. intervention in foreign countries in the name of democracy and human rights. Americans' internationalism is *liberal*—both in its instinct to support pluralist democracy and in its support for U.S. interests abroad (Huntington 1973).

Moreover, U.S. NGOs also tend to be more integrated with the international institutions whose activities they monitor than European activists. When Mario Pianta and his group analyzed the relationship of U.S. parallel summits to the institutions whose summits they were organized around, they found them to be far less conflictual and more cooperative in nature than those in Europe. As we can see in table 9.4, 14.3 percent of all North American events were characterized as "integrated into the official summit" in comparison with only 4.3 percent of European events.

Frame bridging and boundary creation. The Bush/Cheney foreign policy drew on muscular militarism and the desire to clamp down on the claimed military threat of Saddam Hussein. But when that justification proved unsustainable and as the number of body bags of U.S. troops arriving home began to grow, Bush turned to the more traditional "liberal" policy of intervention in the name of democracy. That justification might have left opponents of the war cold, but it was intended to reach out to moderate opinion—including opponents of globalization, like the unions—leaving the radical Left without potential allies in its attempt to characterize the war as an expression of imperial expansion.

In the language of contentious politics, the Bush administration was not simply reaching out for new justifications for a war and an occupation that were going badly: They were bridging the ever-popular domestic frame of democracy with the post–9/11 frame of protecting Americans from harm. In doing so, they hardened the boundary between "good" U.S. support for democracy abroad and "foreign" pusillanimity and self-centeredness. The attempts to characterize John Kerry as "French" in the 2004 presidential campaign were surface hints of how deeply this raising of boundaries was felt. The 2006 determination of the House of Representatives to penalize illegal immigrants and those Americans who offer them support were more lethal political expressions of the same instinct.

Domestic politics and the forum process. This reinforcement of the United States's "liberal" imperial mission and the reinforcement of the boundaries between "us" and "them" internationally created a profound dilemma for the newly born global justice movement. It was not just that the domestic political agenda had shifted away from issues—like jobs and the environment—that could be linked to global justice; it was also the case that the war, the atmosphere of muscular nationalism that sustained it, and the us/them framing of relations with foreigners made it difficult for U.S. activists to engage in transnational activism.

This was nothing new in U.S. activism. The "freeze" movement of the 1980s was isolated from the parallel movement in favor of disarmament in Western Europe at the same time. U.S. activists were constrained from too close an embrace of that movement by their opportunities for cooperation with the liberal wing of the Democratic Party and the primacy of domestic politics (Meyer 1990; Tarrow and McAdam 2005).

From the beginning, the forum process in the United States was heavily imbricated with domestic politics. As we have seen, it was domestic issues that were most responsible for the rise in protest potential among Americans and the one surviving forum—in the Midwest—is almost wholly preoccupied with domestic issues. The one domestic movement that was strongly supportive of the process—the Green Party—created resentment among activists when it tried to control the New York Social Forum. Eventually, that process imploded as activists began to fight over who would control the organization. In Boston, a forum process surged around the nomination of John Kerry as the Democratic Party's presidential candidate in 2004, but did not continue after Kerry lost the election.

The paradox is that the "international" crisis set off by 9/11, the ensuing War on Terror, and the Iraq war and occupation turned U.S. activists' attention inexorably inward to U.S. politics, where their cooperation with the vigorous Latin American and European branches of the global justice movement finds little purchase.

Conclusion

The findings of this rapid survey are easy to summarize but not so easy to interpret. Americans tend to hold more favorable attitudes toward globalization and less favorable attitudes toward global justice protesters than citizens in Western Europe. Further, while the youngest Americans are more likely to have global attachments and to participate in politics than in the past, the direction of this participation has been largely determined by the domestic events of the last decade. Our analysis of surveys of participants at the 2003 and 2005 World Social Forums indicated that U.S. participation in these events is increasing dramatically, although it is still low on a per capita basis. And finally, the internalization of the social forum process in the United States has been indifferent, marked by organizational fragility and internal conflict, and is domestically oriented.

Some readers might find it surprising that we should paint so bleak a picture of the movement for global justice in the United States. After all, isn't this the country whose activists mounted the Battle of Seattle, and which provided large numbers of participants for the protest against the invasion of Iraq in 2003? On single issues, like landmines and help for HIV/AIDS victims in Africa, didn't Americans and U.S.-based NGOs play a crucial role?[22] And doesn't the tremendous success of the immigrant rights movement of 2006 speak volumes about the potential for contentious politics among people who have crossed borders to live in the same country?

These tendencies are real, but they do not create either the transnational links or the transposition of international frames into domestic politics that would make U.S. activists a central part of the global justice movement. Many Americans supported the insurgency in Chiapas, applauded or participated in the Battle of Seattle, and rose up in protest against the U.S. imperial adventure in the Middle East. Many of these are still active in political activism. But the shift toward elected authoritarianism in U.S. politics has proven both frightening and irresistible to thousands who were socialized into politics in the name of fighting global neoliberalism. That has produced a paradoxical inversion of the expected relationship between transnational and domestic activism.

We often think of transnational activists as people who are socialized into politics at home and who take their activism abroad as they become aware of the international nature of the issues with which they identify. We can call this process externalization (della Porta and Tarrow 2005; Tarrow 2005). In particular, the globalization of the world's economy is often thought to have drawn domestic labor and other activists into transnational ties and coalitions (Anner 2004; Tarrow 2005, chap. 8).

The two stories at the beginning of this chapter tell a different story—one that might actually offer some hope to the progressive Left in the United States. True, 9/11 and its aftermath show how national involvements can weaken a budding transnational movement; but if we are correct, in the transposition of the U.S. global justice movement from Seattle, Washington, to Washington, D.C., we might be seeing a process of internalization of transnational protest into domestic activism. If that helped to reverse the slide of U.S. politics toward elective authoritarianism, then this shift could one day offer an example to the more highly developed European global justice movement.

Notes

We wish to thank Mark Becker, Donatella della Porta, Jai Kwan Jung, Mario Pianta, Ruth Reitan, Jackie Smith, Lesley Wood, and Duccio Zola for their precious advice and for data analyses carried out on our behalf.

1. Jackie Smith illustrates both the range of the coalition and its internal division of labor when she writes that "groups with the least routinized and formalized transnational ties were more likely to be engaged in the important work of grassroots level education and mobilization," while "groups with more routine transnational ties and formal transnational structures were better able to monitor developments in international policy and to help people make connections between locally experiences grievances and local processes" (Smith, forthcoming: 147).

2. The Pew Global Attitudes Project. "44-Nation Major Survey." Pew Research Center. http://pewglobal.org/reports/pdf/185topline.pdf, p. 41 (Accessed June 2006).

3. Chicago Council on Foreign Relations. "World Views 2002" Chicago Council on Foreign Relations and the German Marshall Fund. http://www.worldviews.org/detailreports/compreport.pdf, p. 25 (Accessed June 2006).

4. The Pew Global Attitudes Project. "Views of Changing World: Summer 2002 44-Nation Survey [dataset]." http://pewglobal.org/datasets/ Pew Research Center, 2003.

5. We are extremely grateful to Jai Kwan Jung for analyzing these data from the WVS on our behalf, and helping us to interpret them. See his "Growing Supranational Identities in a Globalizing World? A Multilevel Analysis of the World Values Survey," unpublished paper, for a more elaborate analysis of the relationship between affective globalization and age cohort.

6. World Values Survey and European Values Survey 1981–1984, 1980–1993,

1989–1993, and 1999–2004 [Integrated Data Set] http://www.worldvaluessurvey. org/ (Accessed June 2006). The American National Election Studies (www.election-studies.org). THE 1948–2004 ANES CUMULATIVE DATA FILE [dataset]. Stanford University and the University of Michigan [producers and distributors], 2005.

7. The Pew Global Attitudes Project. "44-Nation Major Survey." Pew Research Center. http://pewglobal.org/reports/pdf/185topline.pdf, p. 51 (Accessed June 2006).

8. National Civic Engagement Survey 2002. http://www.civicyouth.org/research/products/YouthVote2002survey/youthvote_national_survey_june_2002_toplines.pdf, p. 9 (Accessed June 2006).

9. We would like to express our warm gratitude to Mario Pianta and Duccio Zola for sharing these data and their reflections on them with us.

10. Pianta's data is gathered from a survey that reports on the nature of the parallel summit, the events that occurred, their forms of organization, and their impact. His questionnaire was distributed to hundreds of organizations; researchers also monitored newspapers, journals, and Web sites. More information can be found in Mario Pianta. "Parallel Summits of Global Civil Society," in Helmut Anheier, Marlies Glasius, and Mary Kaldor. 2001. *Global Civil Society 2001*. New York: Oxford University Press.

11. The World Social Forum. "Numbers." http://www.forumsocialmundial.org.br/dinamic.php?pagina=memoria_numeros_ing Updated 06/26/06 (Accessed June 2006).

12. The Ithaca Social Forum was held November 22–23, 2002. Its sponsors included the Cornell Forum for Justice and Peace, the Ithaca Coalition for Global Justice, the Citizens' Planning Alliance, and the Public Service Center at Cornell. Ravishankar, Priya. "Social Forum Focuses on Global, Local Connections." *Cornell Daily Sun*, Monday, November 25, 2002. http://cornellsun.com/node/7374 (Accessed July 14, 2006).

13. Judy Rebick. Interview with Jennifer Hadden (June 28, 2006).

14. Marc Becker. Interview with Jennifer Hadden (July 13, 2006).

15. UE Vermont. "Promoting the Social Forum Process in the United States: WSF International Council Statement," July 14, 2003. www.uevermont.org/politicalaction/wsf_ussf.html. (Accessed June 2006).

16. For a report on the Caracas meeting, go to www.nigd.org/docs; for the planning of the USSF in Atlanta, go to www/ussf2007.org.

17. Marc Becker. Interview with Jennifer Hadden (July 13, 2006).

18. Foro Social Fronterizo Weblog. http://forosocialfronterizo.blogspot.com/ (Accessed June 2006).

19. Marc Becker and Thomas Ponniah. "Toward North American Social Forums: A panel discussion at WSF 2005," May 20, 2005. http://www.forumsocialmundial.org.br/dinamic.php?pagina=bal_ponniah_2005_ing (Accessed June 2006).

20. Ibid., p. 2. A major problem seems to have been a lack of financial support. Activists have had difficulty generating "buy-ins" from domestic community and labor organizations to support the forum process (uevermont.org/political action/wsf_ussf. html).

21. But see Lesley Wood (2006), who finds evidence that repression has had a more

negative effect upon Torontonian, than on New York City, activists. We are grateful to Lesley Wood for allowing us to cite her unpublished paper and for her comments on our work.

22. Donatella della Porta emphasizes this point in her comments on an earlier version of this chapter. We hope to take up her suggestion later.

Chapter Ten

The Global Justice Movement in Context

Donatella della Porta

The Global Justice Movement in Context: Cross-National Similarities and Differences

In all of the analyzed countries, the global justice movement (GJM) has brought about a wave of mobilization, linking local and global issues. As with previous waves of protest, this one has innovated the repertoires of collective action. Common characteristics of the GJM in our countries are the development of transnational and cross-issue networks, the bridging of various frames around concerns for global justice and "democracy from below," the combination of old and new forms of action in common protest campaigns. Owing to the very nature of this movement—networked, transnational, heterogeneous—research on the GJM must address organizations and issues that were once treated separately, by specialized areas of social movement studies. Since local and transnational campaigns on global issues involve ecologists and unionists, feminists and communists, religious groups and autonomous squatted centers, large NGOs and affinity groups, our accounts also had to address and link all of these various streams. In this sense, the chapters of this book can be read as a dense description of some emergent trends in contentious politics. We can add that these trends seem to be here to stay. All of our chapters stressed the vitality (at least in

Europe) of a movement that, notwithstanding rapid ups and downs, is still active, consolidating and expanding transnational networks and multiplying protest campaigns.

In this concluding chapter, I discuss some explanations for the development of this wave of protest at the turn of the millennium and its emerging forms, by looking at the social, political, and cultural context in which this mobilization developed. In doing so, I address the similarities, but also some cross-country differences, that the national accounts have made evident. They converge in singling out the presence of the global justice movement—with (1) well (and increasingly) networked groups, (2) common meta-frames on global justice and radical democracy, and (3) mobilization in common campaigns. At the risk of some simplification, we can single out the presence of two different constellations of GJMs:

- In the first, disruptive protest dynamics appear as more dominant; networks are more dense and decentralized, with participation of both informal groups and formal associations; and the issue of global justice is linked with a struggle against neoliberalism at home (framing the struggle against neoliberalism at home) within a global discourse and a conception of radical participatory democracy. In Italy, the meta-frame of global justice contributed to bringing together a dense network of rank-and-file unions (and later more traditional unions as well), religious groups, squatted youth centers, ecologists, and peace activists. This is the case in Spain, where a frame of radical democracy spread together with appeals for direct action. Also in France, social issues— represented by radical unions, farmers' organizations, and the "mouvement de sans" but also by the strongly rooted Attac—play a central role. In all these cases, although more traditional NGOs are also present, the GJM network developed as activist based and protest oriented.
- In the second, collective action relies to a larger extent on lobbying and media campaigns; strong associations and NGOs are more visible, although not unchallenged; solidarity with the South of the world is a master frame (global justice issues are framed especially, although not exclusively, in terms of solidarity with the South); and associational conceptions of democracy prevail. In Germany as well as in Britain, the GJM is supported by well-endowed NGOs, which confront the frustrating results of more moderate techniques. Similarly in Switzerland, notwithstanding the presence of a more radical wing around the PGA and a remobilization of the unions, the GJM relies heavily on the already existing, resource-rich, and well-structured organizations from the 1970s New Social Movements (especially on environmental and solidarity issues), while the weakness of the class cleavage reduces the support of the Old Left.

In the first constellation, unions are (more) present in the GJM, both in the form of the "critical unions" that emerged in an already fragmented system of industrial relations and in the left-wing component of the traditional unions. Especially in Italy and France, rank-and-file unions have been involved in the transnational wave of protest since its very beginning. Political opportunities appear as closed in terms of access to government but open in terms of potential allies; and the GJM is stronger in terms of its capacity to mobilize in the street. In Spain, the socialists of the PSOE are more open toward the GJM when opposing a right-wing Partido Popular (PP) government; in Italy, the movement gained enormous mobilization capacity during Berlusconi's government, but also developed from a critique of the party system in general.

In the second constellation, with more institutionalized systems of industrial relations, critical unions are weak or nonexistent, and traditional unions, involved in neo-corporatist agreements, remain more distant from the GJM (with the exception of public-sector and metalworkers' unions). With more open political opportunities at home (with the Red-Green coalition in power in Germany, the New Labour in the UK, and the all-party coalition in Switzerland), the GJM tends to rely less on street mobilization and more on lobbying and information campaigns. However, the movement does often take to the streets in these countries: In fact, the mobilization capacity of the movement derives from the availability of moderate NGOs to voice their claims though transnational protest campaigns.

In comparison with these European cases, the United States presents some peculiarities. Similar to the Northern European constellation in terms of the presence of large and well-endowed NGOs, the U.S. protest in Seattle and beyond did not meet with the same neo-corporatist, inclusive political opportunities. Although occasionally enjoying the alliance of community-oriented rank-and-file unions and of the reformed AFL-CIO federation (more sensitive to basis-oriented strategies),[1] the movement seemed unable to consolidate the unity of action between the "turtles and teamsters" (quoted in the Seattle slogan as "united in the struggle"). In contrast with the Southern European constellation, in the United States the strong confrontation with a right-wing government has only occasionally spurred mass demonstrations; when it has, they have focused especially on single issues such as the war in Iraq or migrants' rights. Especially since September 11, attention in the United States has focused much more on home affairs.

The wave of transnational protest impacted both constellations. In a process of downward scale shift (Tarrow and McAdam 2005), cosmopolitan activists who had been involved in transnational counter-summits and protest campaigns contributed to bringing the conflict back home. However, the global justice movement was also fed by upward scale shift as global concerns were developed during local and national protest campaigns (della Porta and Piazza forthcoming). In what follows, I discuss how the main trends in social movement research can help to explain the general characteristics of the GJM and the cross-national differences. At the same time, I suggest that, as previous movements have done, the GJM challenges some concepts and hypotheses developed on previous waves of protest. First, focusing on the concept of social cleavages, I will discuss to what extent the GJM can be seen as a form of revitalization of the "old" class cleavage. Second, addressing the political opportunities available for the GJM, I will focus on the uneasy relations between movements and parties and the transformations of both. Third, looking at the resources the GJM has mobilized, I will suggest the relevance of previous movement networks and will discuss the different effects on movement configuration of the mix of associational versus experiential social capital available in the different countries.

Social Movements and Social Cleavages: The GJM as the Revitalization of the Class Cleavage?

Although most scholars would agree that social movements do express conflicts, attention to the sources of protest has been scattered. The valuable idea that grievances alone do not produce mobilization had the (negative) side effect of moving the focus away from reflection on the structural foundation of social movements. Additionally, the European sociologists who had paid more attention to this level of analysis had focused especially on new social movements, building on the assumption of the institutionalization of the working class and the emergence of new post-industrial conflicts (e.g., Touraine 1977). Especially in the 1970s, environmental, women's, and even peace and ethnoregionalist movements were considered as midwives of a new type of society that succeeded the industrial, materialistic, Fordist, and/or modern one. More modestly, since the 1980s, those very movements were considered as more and more institutionalized actors (richer in material resources and channels of access to decision makers), active on single issues. The "social movement society" (Meyer and Tarrow 1998) was, all in all, a pragmatic one; the "normalization" of protest (Piven and Cloward 1992) had contributed to moderate contention. Social movement organizations seemed to evolve (or degenerate) into hierarchical nongovernmental organizations (NGOs), well-structured public interest groups, commercial enterprises (even if of alternative goods), charities (although with strong advocacy aims) (della Porta 2003c; Kriesi 1996).

This normalized image was shaken in the 1990s and broke down after the year 2000. As stressed by Mario Pianta and Raffaele Marchetti in their chapter

(chapter 2, this volume) on the transnational dimension of the GJM, cross-border protest events have multiplied in the last two decades, pointing at a "scale shift" toward a more cross-issue perspective. Since the last decade, in fact, reactions to what activists refer to as "hegemonic neoliberalism" have brought about a resurgence of social issues, although blended with "new social movement" issues. In this sense, the GJM refocuses attention on the structural nature of social conflicts, dismissing the hypothesis of a definitive institutionalization of the "class cleavage" (Rokkan 1982). At least some of the various streams of protest that, as the contributions to this volume demonstrate, converged in the formation of the GJM can be interpreted as a reaction to the retrenchment of the welfare state and the increasing inequalities, revitalizing a social cleavage that had appeared as tamed, if not pacified.

Globalization—in its different meanings and understandings—has also produced increasing conflicts at both the local and the transnational levels. Economic globalization has raised specific problems that mobilize actors, both old and new. Signs of emerging political opposition to the consequences of a forced convergence of socioeconomic models of development were noted as developing already in the first part of the 1990s (Berger 1998, 37). Globalization tends to favor if not a homogeneous and self-conscious global working class, at least growing contacts among workers in different states (Silver 2003, 10). In the North of the world, the increase in unemployment and especially in job insecurity and unprotected working conditions brought about frequent mobilizations of both industrial and agricultural workers.

In the South, unions seemed capable of taking advantage of globalization, with labor conflict developing in at least some of the countries where capital was now invested—as Beverly Silver (2003, 164) observes, "the deep crisis into which the core labor movement fell in the 1980s was not immediately replicated elsewhere. On the contrary, in the late 1980a and 1990s, major waves of labor militancy hit 'showcases' of rapid industrialization in the Second and Third Worlds." The unions have since the 1980s been the main protesters in some Southern countries against the negative social effects of the substantial cuts in social spending imposed by the major international economic organizations. Urban movements and groups of unemployed have joined with them in Latin America as well as in Asian and African countries (Walton and Seddon 1994; Bennani-Chaïbi and Fillieule 2003).

In the North and in the South, social concerns have been linked with other issues. In Latin America as well as in Asia, local populations have often mobilized against the destruction of their physical habitats through the private exploitation of natural resources, and against development projects with major environmental impact sponsored by international governmental organizations (Passy 1998). Similarly, in the industrialized world, local struggles against "Locally Unwanted Land Use" (from the construction of roads to high-speed trains or airports) have been increasingly framed as opposition to the global exploitation of resources (see, among others, della Porta and Piazza forthcoming). Moreover, solidarity-based movements have mobilized proactively on "distant" issues not directly connected with their own national contexts. Increased perception of issues as global also heightens people's willingness to mobilize at the transnational level. Transnational networks of ethnocultural communities help in the readaptation of local traditions to new contexts (Thompson 1995).

The GJM we have analyzed in this volume represents just one of the multiple reactions to globalization and, more generally, to the sociopolitical transformations that followed the fall of the Berlin wall. It also coincided with (contributed to and was favored by) a shift in the Zeitgeist, or spirit of the time (Brand 1990), with growing concern for the social consequences of the trend toward market deregulation but also a tendency to locate causes and solutions for social problems at the supranational level. Neoliberal ideas have been dominant in the last two decades: The GJM accompanied an inversion in the trend toward acceptance of the prevalence of the market over the state and of private over public institutions. If the free market was considered in the 1990s as a solution to public deficits and unemployment, since the year 2000 the negative consequences of economic globalization have come into public light. The GJM was successful in singling out neoliberalism, as well as large corporations and international financial institutions, as at the root of various single-issue concerns. The resonant movement "master frame" is the critique of the negative effects of globalization (as stressed by Christopher Rootes and Clare Saunders in their chapter[chapter 6, this volume]) as well as the identification of "neoliberalism as a key evil and central target" (as Dieter Rucht, Simon Teune, and Mundo Yang put it in chapter 7). Transnational campaigns converged—as Mario Pianta and Raffaele Marchetti wrote in chapter 2—"in protesting the injustice of neoliberal globalization."

The GJM was in fact able to sensitize public opinion on some main socioeconomic issues. Significantly, the recent European Social Survey (2002/2003) confirms that concerns expressed by the global justice movement are shared by a large majority of the national public opinions, at least on the Old Continent. Against the neoliberal frame of a reduction of state intervention, between 60 percent (in Germany, Switzerland, and the UK) and 80 percent (in Italy, France, and Spain) of the respondents believe that their governments should reduce differences in income levels; about 70 percent agree that "employees need strong trade unions to protect work conditions/wages"; and, finally, a substantial fraction (above 30 percent in Germany, Switzerland, and the UK; well above 50 percent in Italy, Spain,

Table 10.1 Degree of Agreement on Different Claims, 2002–2003 (Percent Agree or Agree Strongly)

Country	Government Should Reduce Differences in Income Levels	Employees Need Strong Trade Unions to Protect Work Conditions/ Wages	Economic Growth Always Ends Up Harming Environment	The Less Government Intervenes in Economy, the Better for the Country
France	83.3	77.5	55.2	25.0
Italy	79.6	71.6	52.6	28.4
Germany	58.2	66.2	39.7	44.3
Spain	79.7	74.6	55.5	27.1
United Kingdom	62.5	65.8	32.7	30.5
Switzerland	63.6	75.6	43.9	38.8

Source: Our elaboration from European Social Survey, www.europeansocialsurvey.org

and France) thinks that "economic growth always ends up harming environment." Only a minority (larger in Germany and Switzerland) agrees instead with the sentence "the less government intervenes in economy, the better for the country" (see table 10.1).

In national public opinion, these concerns are linked to a perception of globalization as a threat and of the need to develop institutions to control it. Recent data from a "Flash Eurobarometer" focused on "Globalisation" (2003) indicate substantial awareness of the process of globalization (ranging from 62% in the UK to 88% in Italy), considered as a threat by a large part of the population (from 32% in Italy to 58% in France) and, especially, seen as a

Table 10.2 Opinions on Regulation of Globalization, 2003

Country	Would you say that more regulation or less regulation is needed, or that the current regulation is sufficient in order to monitor the development of globalization?			
	More Regulation	Less Regulation	Current Regulation Sufficient	Don't Know/ No Answer
France	66%	11%	18%	5%
Italy	72%	9%	17%	3%
Germany	47%	27%	21%	5%
Spain	59%	6%	21%	14%
United Kingdom	53%	21%	16%	10%

Source: Adapted from "Flash Eurobarometer" on "Globalization" (2003).

Table 10.3 Opinions on Globalization Actors

Country	Could you tell me if in your opinion financial markets benefit from globalization (% yes)	Could you tell me if multinationals have too much influence, not enough influence or just the right level of influence on the process of globalization (too much %)	Could you tell me if you trust multinationals for ensuring that globalization goes in the right direction (% do not trust)
France	85%	61%	66%
Italy	80%	75%	63%
Germany	82%	60%	70%
Spain	78%	78%	65%
United Kingdom	79%	45%	59%

Source: Adapted from "Flash Eurobarometer" on "Globalization" (2003).

phenomenon that requires more regulation (especially in Italy and France, where about two-thirds of the citizens agree with this statement) (see table 10.2). The majority of citizens in each country agree that regulating the process of globalization is not only desirable but also possible.

Mistrust of multinational corporations, financial circles, and international institutions voiced by the GJM also seems to resonate with widespread concerns (see table 10.3). Over three-quarters of citizens in our European countries believe that multinational corporations and financial markets benefit from the process of globalization. At the same time, large majorities in each country (except Britain) consider that multinationals have too much influence on the process of globalization, and a clear majority of citizens do not trust multinationals to ensure that globalization goes in the right direction.

A general trend of growing concern with social issues and globalization processes therefore emerges in all of our cases, contributing to our understanding of the capacity of the GJM to involve different actors, bridging "old" and "new" conflicts within a global framing of identities and grievances. This emerging critique of globalization as a "discursive opportunity" for the GJM also helps to explain the observed cross-national differences. Although in the analysis of the "new social movements" the pacification of the "old" cleavage was considered as propitious to the mobilization of "new" issues (Kriesi et al. 1995), the GJM has used more disruptive (and visible) repertoires of mass protest where labor issues were less institutionalized and unions weaker in terms of numbers, but richer in the resources of militancy. In this sense, we could interpret our cross-national differences as indeed linked to the degree of institutionalization of the class cleavage.

An indicator of these cross-national differences in the degree of institutionalization of the class cleavage is in the number of strikes and lockouts, as well as the number of workers involved: Whereas Italy, France, and Spain express high levels of labor conflict, Germany, Switzerland, and (to a certain extent) the UK show a less mobilized labor force (see table 10.4).[2] In general, the data indicate that in Southern European countries, public opinion seems more convinced than in Northern ones of the need to strengthen public intervention in order to reduce inequalities, as well as favoring more political regulation.

Class conflict has in fact remained more visible in France, Italy, and Spain—countries characterized by more exclusive traditions of dealing with the labor movement—and this is reflected in the language and alliance structures of their respective GJMs. In Southern Europe, the GJM emerged in fact as more heterogeneous, frequently combining labor and Catholic groups, squatted social centers, and "new social movements" in common activities (as stressed in chapter 3 discussing Italy). Not only the critical unions, but also the mainstream ones became interested in the movement's concerns—often sensitized to them by their own rank and files, through the mechanism of social reappropriation. In Germany and Switzerland, with social-democratic parties in power for long periods, modern systems of industrial relations have institutionalized the role of unions, reducing the salience of class conflicts (Kriesi et al. 1995) and therefore the unions' propensity to ally with left-libertarian movements. Similarly, in the UK a long period of economic growth and New Labour in power has contributed to marginalizing "class discourse." The GJM emerged here especially from the disillusionment of more pragmatic NGOs and well-structured "new social movement" organizations with "insider" strategies. Moreover, in Southern Europe the GJM more clearly "positions itself to the Left," as stressed by Isabelle Sommier and Hélène Combes in their chapter (chapter 5) on France, whereas in the North a traditional left-wing ideology is less dominant.

Whereas the "new social movements" have therefore been considered stronger in countries where traditional cleavages were more pacified (Kriesi et al. 1995), the GJM, with its involvement of unions and "Old Left" issues, emerges as more visible in Southern Europe. In contrast, in the Northern countries a (somewhat less visible) GJM is more influenced by "new social movements" (see chapters on Germany [7] and Switzerland [8]) or large NGOs (see chapter 6 on Britain), with weaker links to trade unions. Here as well, the United States appears to be a different case. Similar to the Northern European countries in terms of the lack of an open class cleavage to which the GJM can link, the United States does not, on the other hand,

Table 10.4 Statistics on Strikes and Lockouts in Selected Countries per 10,000 Paid Employees in 2000–2003

Country	Number of Strikes and Lockouts				Number of Workers Involved in Strikes and Lockouts				Number of Days Not Worked for Strikes and Lockouts			
	2000	2001	2002	2003	2000	2001	2002	2003	2000	2001	2002	2003
France*	12.6	9.6			0.9	0.5			36.9	31.0		
Italy	6.3	4.8	3.9	4.4	45.0	72.0	341.4	158.9	57.9	65.6	304.9	121.7
Germany					0.2	1.9	13.2	1.2	0.3	0.8	9.6	5.1
Spain	6.1	5.8	5.2	5.0	168.3	97.3	345.0	53.6	294.4	150.5	376.3	58.25
United Kingdom	0.8	0.8	0.6	0.5	7.2	7.0	36.6	5.8	19.5	20.3	51.3	19.2
Switzerland	0.3	0.1	0.1	0.3	1.3	6.5	7.12	2.1	1.6	6.6	7.0	1.9

Note: excluded agriculture and public administration

Source: Adapted from International Labour Organization (ILO) data: http://laborsta.ilo.org.

share with those countries the experience of a strong New Social Movement sector, rooted in left-libertarian tradition; instead, it is characterized more by a fragmented, although rich panorama of single-issue social movement organizations.

Social Movements and Political Opportunities: The Revitalization of the Left?

The structure of social cleavages has an impact on their political representation (Rokkan 1982). In the past, old and new movements tended to align along the lines of existing party families or to form new ones. In either case, especially in Europe, not only the labor movement but also the "new social movements" tended to ally with left-wing parties. During the protest cycle of the late 1960s and early 1970s, if the emerging New Left criticized the institutional Left for its alleged betrayal of their original "revolutionary" values (Pizzorno 1996), the traditional left-wing parties channeled many of the emerging social movements' demands into representative institutions. Social movements of the 1970s produced strong Green parties (especially in Northern Europe), but also contributed to revitalizing the social-democratic parties, providing new members and a new sensitivity to ecological as well as gender issues. Since the 1980s, a de facto division of tasks has developed: Although social movements "retreated" to the social sphere, left-wing political parties represented (some of) their claims in political institutions.

If sociological research has pointed to the tensions between the traditional Left emphasis on equality and the New Social Movements' stress on individual freedom (Kitschelt 1993), the reemergence of social issues as a central concern in the recent wave of protest has not helped to maintain the alliance between the GJM and center-left parties. On the contrary, as our national narratives indicate, the protests against neoliberal globalization have been met with various levels of distrust by center-left parties that had undergone (more or less profound) changes in their ideological standing and organizational structure.

This paradox can be explained by the structural and behavioral changes in political parties often emphasized by social science literature in the field. The recent acceleration of the evolution from mass parties to "baseless," "professionalized" parties (more dramatic in the Italian case) has in fact reduced the potential for contacts and alliances between social movements and left-wing parties (Katz and Mair 1992; della Porta 2001). Party membership underwent a general decline, especially visible in absolute numbers in Italy and in France but also in the UK (the only exception being Spain, which in 1980 had just started its process of democratization) (see table 10.5). In addition, the political parties developed a strong mistrust toward their own

Table 10.5 Changes in Party Membership between 1980 and 2000

Country*	Members as % of Voters in 1980	Members as % of Voters in 2000	Changes in %	Changes in Absolute Numbers	Membership Decline in %
France	5.05	1.57	-3.48	-1,122,128	-64.59
Italy	9.66	4.05	-5.61	-2,091,887	-51.54
Germany	4.52	2.93	-1.59	-174,967	-8.95
Spain	1.20	3.42	+2.22	+808,705	+250.73
United Kingdom	4.12	1.92	-2.20	-853,156	-50.39
Switzerland	10.40	6.50	-3.90	-90,800	-50.39

Note: *The first elections oscillate between 1977 and 1980, the final one between 1997 and 2000.

Source: Adapted from Mair and van Biezen 2001 (except for Switzerland, Ladner 2001).

bases. Considering activists as too radical vis-à-vis their potential electorate, they tended to focus their energies on mass-mediatic campaigns oriented toward capturing the sympathy of the so-called median voter (who, being ideologically moderate—or "in the middle"—is considered more likely to shift his/her electoral preferences) (Crouch 2003; della Porta 2001). Opinion polls substitute for party sections in the "bottom up" communication of grievances and concerns; professional public relations specialists play a more and more pivotal role in electoral campaigns. The development of the GJM must be seen against this background of profound changes—although not always involving the "collapse of the traditional party system" outlined in Herbert Reiter's chapter (chapter 3) for the Italian case.

Not just structural, but also attitudinal changes hamper the alliances between the GJM and the main parties of the Left. The crisis of Left support for Keynesian economic policies and the mentioned hegemony of neoliberal ideology have reduced the room for mutual understanding between the movement and the mainstream left-wing parties, at least in the Western democracies. Analyses of party manifestos have in fact confirmed that the mainstream left-wing parties of Western society have become more moderate, moving toward the center of the political spectrum (Budge et al. 2001; Bell and Shaw 2003). The movement's claims against privatization, flexibility of the labor market, and liberalization of financial flows are perceived as an attack against the reforms of the welfare state that the social-democratic parties have championed when in government and failed to oppose when in opposition. Not only Tony Blair's New Labour but also Zapateros' Partido Socialista Obrero Espanol (PSOE) indicate that some Libertarian, New Social Movement concerns are easier to accommodate within the party line than are the more traditional demands for social equality and state intervention.

These reduced opportunities for institutional alliances have not, however, jeopardized the mobilization capacity of the GJM. To the contrary, our national narratives point at consistent waves of protest, involving not only the invention of new forms of collective action, but also the return of large masses of people to the streets. Among the varied repertoires used by the GJM, direct action has been accompanied by massive marches—especially in Italy, Spain, and France, but also occasionally in Germany, Switzerland, and Britain. Even where the mobilizations targeted right-wing governments, they also expressed a strong criticism of the perceived neoliberal turn of the main parties of the Left. In all countries, as the previous chapters indicate, the GJM has criticized not only policy choices, but also a conception of politics as a specialized activity for professional politicians, voicing a conception of politics from below. In this sense, the GJM has catalyzed energies and resources once committed to political parties. As Herbert Reiter put it in chapter 3, changes in party politics in Italy "liberated large sectors of communist and Catholic-inspired voluntary organizations from their traditional party allegiance." Similarly in France, a growing autonomy of the left-wing associations from partisan links has been observed (see Sommier and Combes, chapter 5 this volume).

The GJM has also been influenced by another evolution of left-wing party politics. Although moderate-left parties mistrust the global justice movement, "critical" left-wing parties (especially the Communists but also the Greens) perceive it as an unexpected occasion for interrupting the downward (especially for the Communist parties) trend of the last decades. In fact, to varying extents, the GJM has been supported by these parties and contributed to their revitalization (Andretta, della Porta, Mosca, and Reiter 2002 and 2003; della Porta, Andretta, Mosca, and Reiter 2006). Interactions between the GJM and Communist parties has been quite intense in Italy, where Rifondazione Comunista, which supported the GJM from its very beginning, grew from 5.0 to 8.5 percent of votes in the lower Chamber between 2001 and 2006. The national Communist parties have also sponsored some movement claims in Spain, with Izquierda Unida; in France, with the French Communist Party; and in Germany, with the PDS. Trotskyite groups have also aligned with the movement: In France, where the Trotskyite candidate achieved 10 percent of votes in the 2003 presidential election, LCR in particular makes frequent references to the GJM; in the UK, the Socialist Workers' Party, and its network, Globalise Resistance, are, though small, very visible. Although with some internal tensions and less enthusiasm, Green parties have also participated in the activities of the GJM. Especially in Southern Europe, an attempt to revitalize—or "regenerate the Left," as Sommier and Combes put it—is relevant for the evolution of the GJM.

Here as well, we have to point at cross-country differences. Research on the new social movements in Europe stresses the role of the division in the Left in orienting the availability of movement allies. In that case, a unified (and reformed) Left was said to be more keen toward New Social Movement concerns than a split one, where more parties competed for the votes of the traditional workers' electorate (Kriesi et al. 1995). Within the same logic, but with opposite results, the GJM seems to have been able to exert more pressure on the main left-wing parties in Southern Europe, where the Left was divided. Splinter Communist and Trotskyite parties were in fact electoral competitors for the left-wing vote. With its bi-party system and the weakness of a left-wing discourse, the U.S. GJM has inherited from previous social movement organizations a tendency toward pragmatic, single-issue discourse. Although supporting the Democrats against an aggressive Republican government, U.S. activists are far from enjoying steady sympathies from within the party system. Relationships with the Democratic Party, in fact, remain sporadic.

This evolution in the (left-wing) parties seems to have expanded the networking capacity of the GJM and focused on movement politics those resources of activism that it had freed. Although not hampering the movement's mobilization of resources, it does leave open the efficacy question (debated also within the movement): How are the movement's claims to be channeled inside the institutions? The Communist parties remain in fact small (oscillating between the 5 percent of the French PCF and the Spanish IU and the more than 8 percent of the Italian RC and the German PDS), as are the Greens (whose support ranged in the last national elections somewhere between 2.5 percent in Italy and 8.6 percent in Germany). As for the main European socialist parties, the GJM seems to have affected them, either by sensitizing their members to the social consequences of the policies of deregulation, privatization, and market flexibility that had became hegemonic even in the center-left, or by instrumental considerations linked to the risk of losing electoral support to their Left. Confirming previous studies (della Porta and Diani 1999, 202–207), the parties opening to the movement's concerns has been more frequent when the socialist parties were in opposition—especially in Italy, France, and Spain (until 2004) against right-wing governments. Even in these cases, however, they have for the moment produced more of a change in those parties' language than in their attitudes and behaviors. Moreover, the shift from center-right to center-left governments (for example in Spain and, more recently, in Italy) seems also to have reduced the mobilization capacity of the GJM.

The development of the GJM therefore coincides with some transformations in social movements' traditional allies: the parties of the Left. At least in part, it can be seen as a sign of the reaction to a process of organizational weakening and ideological moderation and a demand of what the French call "*gauche gauche.*" This explains the capacity of the movement to go beyond single issues and its aiming at a global vision of "another possible world." The characteristics of the institutional Left in different countries also explain the different mobilization capacities of the GJM: its propensity to take itself into the street in countries characterized by a divided Left (as in Italy, France, and Spain) and to remain less visibly contentious elsewhere; the somewhat easier relationships where the main socialist parties have maintained more of a left-wing profile (as in France, Italy, and even Spain) than where they stressed a new "Third Way" image (as in Britain with New Labour and, in part, in Germany). The weakness of the endowment with left-wing ideology in the United States might also contribute to explaining the difficulties experienced by the social forums in that country and more in general the retreat of mass mobilizations after Seattle.

Mobilizing Resources: Back into the Street?

Notwithstanding the tensions with the institutional Left, the development of the GJM has been facilitated by its capacity for networking. As mentioned in the various chapters, the mobilizations since the year 2000 are the outcome of a long-lasting process of creation of ties and intensification of solidarities during transnational campaigns: To quote Rucht, Teune, and Yang's chapter (chapter 7), the GJM is "strongly rooted in diverse strands of earlier progressive movements." Transnational counter-summits and social forums—as described in Pianta and Marchetti's chapter (chapter 2)—are part and parcel of this process of mobilization. From this viewpoint, the GJM confirms the importance of the availability of resources for mobilization that social movement studies have strongly stressed since the 1970s. At the same time, as Rootes and Saunders emphasize in chapter 6, part of the novelty of the GJM is in its capacity to involve people and groups (especially NGOs) that were—as they say—"little if at all involved in earlier waves of social movement action."

As the data quoted in various chapters on the multiorganizational memberships of the activists indicate, the GJM has reactivated already existing social movement organizations and networks of activism and also more formal associations and NGOs active in different fields. In this, it was helped by the spread of sympathy for various types of civil society organizations. In the last two decades, in fact, while support for political parties has been declining, membership in voluntary associations has grown steadily, with especially sharp trends for international NGOs (see table 10.6). Various sources confirm the strength of associational membership in countries such as Switzerland, the UK, and Germany and its contrasting weakness in Mediterranean countries

Table 10.6 Organizational Density, Membership Density, International Nongovernmental Meetings, and Number of Paid Workers and Unpaid Volunteers of Nonprofit Section

Country	NGOs: Organizational Density per Million Population		Only International NGOs: Membership Density per Million Population		Number of International Nongovernmental Meetings According to the Country in Which the Event Was Held			Number of Paid Workers and of Volunteers of Total Nonprofit Section in 1995–1996	
	1991	2001	1991	2001	1999	2000	2001	Paid Workers	Volunteers
France	29.4	25.6	73.7	110.4	857	963	723	959,821	1,021,655
Italy	8.2	10.4	67.0	102.7	462	549	443	597,655	565,310
Germany	9.3	11.4	51.5	78.5	715	656	502	1,440,850	978,074
Spain	4.2	7.5	87.1	139.4	366	421	356	475,179	253,599
United Kingdom	25.3	31.6	68.1	105.8	754	765	510	1,415,743	1,120,283
Switzerland	98.6	96.1	477.9	726.5	286	365	301	—	—

Source: Union of International Associations, *Yearbook of International Organizations: Guide to Civil Society Networks*, Brussels 1991 and 2001. For data on numbers of paid workers and volunteers of total nonprofit section: The Johns Hopkins Comparative Nonprofit Sector Project 1999; Istituto Nazionale di Statistica 1999.

such as Italy and Spain, often defined in terms of the former's strong social capital and the latter's "incivility." Additionally, neocorporatist countries (such as Germany and Switzerland) have traditionally offered more institutional resources to social movement organizations, often co-opting them as public interest groups or service-oriented associations. These differences have been referred to in order to explain the creation of a strong and professionalized movement sector in the former, and, in contrast, the organizational weakness of social movements in the latter (on the environmental movement, see della Porta and Diani 2004a).

The cross-national data on organizational membership confirm the image of richer associations in Northern and Central Europe, and instead a "Mediterranean syndrome" with lower membership rates, in Southern Europe. The idea that social capital (as associational membership) increases the capacity for collective action would predict a lower capacity to mobilize where (as in Southern Europe) fewer organizational resources are available. Our national narratives, however, do not confirm this prediction for the GJM, indicating instead that different movement configurations tend to reflect different types of propensity toward collective action. In particular, the GJM seems to have been in all countries a by-product of a remobilization of once institutionalized NGOs and social movement organizations. If this is a general trend, it is more visible in the Northern European constellation than in the Southern one. Even where large and well-established NGOs do exist and collaborate with the GJM, they do not dominate the scene. As the chapters on Switzerland, Britain, and Germany indicate, in fact, the tensions between "horizontal" and "vertical" actors, or between direct action and lobbying strategies, are actually more divisive. In contrast, in the Southern countries, grassroots, decentralized, and informal protest structures tend to prevail (as in Spain), or at least to find an easier (although not tension-free) relationship with better-structured movement organizations and trade unions. In fact, the deeper divisions within the movement stressed in the chapters on Britain and Germany (the latter stressing the plurality of movements focusing on global justice) are linked to the presence of specific group identities, with loyalties to feminism, environmentalism, or unionism prevailing over the emerging common concern for global justice. Organizationally stronger movement sectors reduce the space for innovation. In contrast, mass campaigns develop where associations such as the unions are weaker in terms of members; as Sommier and Combes stress for France, social conflicts spread "in spite of—or perhaps because of—the weakness of traditional interest groups." Here the movement remains more decentralized and horizontal, stressing frames of "radical democracy" (as Jiménez and Calle [chapter 4 this volume] point out for Spain and Reiter [chapter 3 this volume] for Italy).

Additionally, the weakness of associational membership is not reflected in our data in less dense networks of activists. In fact, a social capital of a different type seems to counteract the (relative) weakness of the associational tradition: an *experiential* social capital, that is, the experience in collective action, even of a more disruptive type. Movement activists share wide experiences in various protests, where solidarity ties, commitment, and skills for mobilization are formed. In fact, the greater visibility of the GJM in Italy, France, and Spain seems to reflect the greater propensity toward unconventional forms of collective action in those countries. Recent data confirm that although conventional actions such as signing a petition are widespread in all countries (except for Spain), Germans, Italians, Spaniards, and French are more keen to participate in lawful demonstrations and more prone to join official strikes, and Italians and French (followed by Spaniards) to occupying buildings (see table 10.7).

The different experiences with more radical forms of protest are reflected in the protest repertoire of the GJM, with more visible direct action in the Southern European constellation and more insider strategies in the Northern European ones. Even in the latter, forms of direct action are far from absent, but remain more confined within a part of the movement, whereas in Southern Europe they seem to spread more easily.

Table 10.7 Extent to Which People Have Taken Different Political Action for or against a Particular Cause

Country	1990–1993					2000				
In Percentage of all Respondents	Signed Petition	Joined Boycott	Attended Lawful Demonstration	Joined Official Strikes	Occupied Building	Signed Petition	Joined Boycott	Attended Lawful Demonstration	Joined Official Strikes	Occupied Building
France	53.7	12.5	32.7	10.1	7.9	68.3	13.2	39.7	12.6	9.0
Italy	48.1	10.9	36.0	6.1	7.6	54.6	10.3	34.8	5.4	8.0
Germany*	56.5	10.0	20.5	2.3	1.1	54.5	8.5	34.1	1.8	0.8
Spain	20.4	5.6	23.5	6.9	2.9	28.6	5.6	26.9	8.7	3.1
United Kingdom*	75.4	14.7	13.6	8.5	2.3	69.9	15.2	17.6	9.6	2.3
Switzerland	62.9	0.0	15.4	2.1	0.0	63.6	12.2	16.9	1.9	1.1

* 1990–1993 data West Germany only.

** UK excluding Northern Ireland for 1990–1993 data.

Source: Anheier, Glasius, and Kaldor 2002.

249

Conclusion

Our analysis of the GJM has confirmed the usefulness of the "tool-kit" of concepts developed in previous waves of protest and upon previous social movements: Social cleavages, political opportunities, and mobilizable resources still seem relevant to explaining the movement's collective identities, organizational models, and repertoires of action. However, the GJM does challenge some previous hypotheses, such as the steady decline of class cleavages, the prevalence of libertarian over left-wing frames, the growing single-issue nature of movement politics, the institutionalization of protest repertoires with a move from the street into the lobby, and the bureaucratization of movement organizations. It also pushes toward a rethinking of the relationship between social movements and parties and a focus on changing conceptions of democracies. If the movements of the 1970s and 1980s had seemed somehow more "advanced" in the "more developed" countries of the North (including Northern Europe), the GJM shows instead the presence of different models of movement mobilization, with more visible mobilization in the southern constellation.

More in general, the chapters presented in this volume have contributed, if not to respond to, at least to articulate relevant questions for further research not only on the GJM but on contemporary movements in general. First, they have pointed at continuous shifts from the local to the global and vice versa, which might be interpreted as a fusion between the different geographical levels into multilevel mobilization. If previous waves of protest had opened a debate on the normalization of social movements, the participation in the global campaigns of institutionalized actors (from charities to unions and parties) focus attention on a sort of internalization of former allies into protest politics.

In addition, the debate on the development of a new movement focusing on global justice remains open. Some of our authors have stressed the important function of domestic as well as transnational events in building a common identity, but others seemed more doubtful about the capacity for consolidation of temporary coalitions into long-term movement networks. Along the same lines, although some of us have preferred to use the concept Global Justice Movement in singular, stressing a certain degree of reticularity and common identification, others have instead used it in the plural in order to underline the larger degree of heterogeneity in the ideas and strategies on global justice as well as the difficulties in sustaining dense networks among such diverse actors. If the mobilization into transnational campaigns is able to steer stable networking or whether it will limit itself to the construction of temporary coalitions is still an open question that addresses the single- versus multi-issue nature of mobilization as well as the tension between externalization and internalization of protest.

Further, in-depth research is needed in order to improve our knowledge on all of these pivotal questions.

Notes

I gratefully acknowledge the assistance of Massimiliano Andretta in collecting the comparative data referred to in this chapter.

1. On recent changes in U.S. trade unions, see, among others, Piven and Cloward 2000; Fantasia and Stepan-Norris 2004.
2. It is worth noting, however, that protest on labor issues still accounts for a very high percentage of unconventional participation even in countries where the class cleavage has been considered to be tamed (for Germany, see Neidhardt and Rucht 2001).

References

Adell, Ramón. 2004. Mani-Fiesta-Acción: la contestación okupa en la calle. In R. Adell and M. Martínez (eds.), *¿Dónde están las llaves? El movimiento okupa: prácticas y contextos sociales.* Madrid: Catarata, pp. 89–114.

AG Widerstand der Gruppe felS. 2003. Berlin umsonst—koste es, was es wolle! Die Kampagne Berlin umsonst! eröffnet Debatte um Aneignung. *Analyse and Kritik,* p. 13.

Agnoletto, Vittorio. 2003. *Prima persone. Le nostre ragioni contro questa globalizzazione.* Roma-Bari: Laterza.

Agrikoliansky, Eric. 2005. Du tiers-monde à l'altermondialisme. In E. Agrikoliansky, O. Fillieule, and N. Mayer (eds.), *L'altermondialisme en France. La longue histoire d'une nouvelle cause.* Paris: Flammarion, pp. 43–73.

Agrikoliansky, Eric, Olivier Fillieule, and Nonna Mayer (eds.). 2005. *L'altermondialisme en France. La longue histoire d'une nouvelle cause.* Paris: Flammarion.

Agrikoliansky, Eric, and Isabelle Sommier (eds.). 2005. *Radiographie du mouvement altermondialiste français: le FSE de Paris Saint-Denis.* Paris: La Dispute.

Agrikoliansky, Eric, and Isabelle Sommier (with Ilhame Hajji). 2005. Formes et publics de l'altermondialisme. In E. Agrikoliansky and I. Sommier (eds.), *Radiographie du mouvement altermondialiste français: le FSE de Paris Saint-Denis.* Paris: La Dispute, pp. 287–304.

Ajangiz, Rafael. 2000. Movimiento pacifista: una crisis que no es tal. In E. Grau and P. Ibarra (eds.), *Anuario movimientos sociales. Una mirada sobre la Red.* Barcelona: Icaria, pp. 165–194.

Álvarez, José. 1975. El anarquismo en España. In I. L. Horowitz (ed.), *Los anarquistas* (Vol. II). Madrid: Alianza Editorial, pp. 220–234.

———. 1995. *Movimientos sociales en España: del modelo tradicional a la modernidad postfranquista.* Madrid: Instituto Universitario Ortega y Gasset.

Amin, Samir, and François Houtart (eds.). 2002. *Mondialisation des Résistance. L'Etat des luttes 2002.* Paris: L'Harmattan.

Andretta, Massimiliano. 2005. Il framing del movimento contro la globalizzazione neoliberista. *Rassegna Italiana di sociologia* 46: 249–274.

Andretta, Massimiliano, Donatella della Porta, Lorenzo Mosca, and Herbert Reiter. 2002. *Global, noglobal, new global. La protesta contro il G8 a Genova.* Roma: Laterza.

————. 2003. *Global—new global. Identität und Strategien der Antiglobalisierungsbeweung.* Frankfurt am Main: Campus Verlag.

Anheier, Helmut, Marlies Glasius, and Mary Kaldor. 2001a. Introducing Global Civil Society. In H. Anheier, M. Glasius, and M. Kaldor (eds.), *Global Civil Society 2001.* Oxford: Oxford University Press, pp. 3–19.

———— (eds.). 2001b. *Global Civil Society 2001.* Oxford: Oxford University Press.

———— (eds.). 2002. *Global Civil Society 2002.* Oxford: Oxford University Press.

———— (eds.). 2003. *Global Civil Society 2003.* Oxford: Oxford University Press.

Anheier, Helmut, and Nuno Themudo. 2002. Organisational Forms of Global Civil Society: Implications of Going Global. In M. Kaldor (ed.), *Global Civil Society 2002.* Oxford: Oxford University Press, pp. 191–216.

Anner, Mark. 2004. Between Solidarity and Fragmentation: Labor Responses to Globalization in the Americas. Ph.D. dissertation, Cornell University, Dept. of Government, 1999.

Archibugi, Daniele. 2003. Cosmopolitan Democracy and Its Critics. In B. Morrison (ed.), *Transnational Democracy in Critical and Comparative Perspectives.* Aldershot: Ashgate, pp. 191–214.

Arrighi, Giovanni, Terence K. Hopkins, and Immanuel Wallerstein. 1989. *Antisystemic Movements.* London: Verso.

Atton, Chris. 2003. Reshaping Social Movement Media for a New Millennium. *Social Movement Studies* 2(1): 3–15.

Barthélémy, Martine. 2000. *Associations: un nouvel âge de la participation?* Paris: Presses de Sciences Po.

Becucci, Stefano. 2003. Disobbedienti e centri sociali fra democrazia e rappresentanza. In P. Ceri (ed.), *La democrazia dei movimenti. Come decidono i noglobal.* Soveria Mannelli: Rubbettino, pp. 75–93.

Bell, David, and Eric Shaw. 2003. Introduction. *Parliamentary Affairs* 56: 1–5.

Bennani-Chaïbri, Mounia, and Olivier Fillieule (eds.). 2003. *Résistances et protestations dans les sociétés musulmanes.* Paris: Presses de Sciences Po.

Bennett, Lance. 2005. Social Movements beyond Borders: Understanding Two Eras of Transnational Activism. In D. della Porta and S. Tarrow (eds.), *Transnational Protest and Global Activism.* Lanham, MD: Rowman and Littlefield, pp. 203–226.

Berger, Suzanne. 1998. Introduzione. In S. Berger and R. Dore (eds.), *Differenze nazionali e capitalismo globale.* Bologna: il Mulino, pp. 9–40.

Bergstedt, Jörg. 2004. *Mythos Attac. Hintergründe, Hoffnungen, Handlungsmöglichkeiten.* Frankfurt am Main: Brandes und Apsel.

Béroud, Sophie, and Georges Ubbiali. 2005. La CGT, entre soutien distancié et refondation de l'activité internationale. In E. Agrikoliansky, O. Fillieule, and N. Mayer (eds.), *L'altermondialisme en France. La longue histoire d'une nouvelle cause.* Paris: Flammarion, pp. 291–316.

Berzano, Luigi, and Renzo Gallini. 2000. Centri sociali autogestiti a Torino. *Quaderni di Sociologia* 22: 50–79.

Berzano, Luigi, Renzo Gallini, and Carlo Genova. 2002. *Liberi tutti. Centri sociali e case occupate a Torino.* Torino: Ananke.

Black, Maggie. 1992. *A Cause for Our Times: Oxfam, the First Fifty Years.* Oxford: Oxford University Press.

Bobbio, Norberto. 1976. *Gramsci e la concezione della società civile.* Milan: Feltrinelli.

Boli, John, and George M. Thomas. 1999. *Constructing the World Culture: International Nongovernmental Organizations since 1875.* Palo Alto, CA: Stanford University Press.

Boltanski, Luc, and Eve Chiapello. 1999. *Le nouvel esprit du capitalisme.* Paris: Gallimard.

Brand, Karl-Werner. 1990. Cyclical Aspects of New Social Movements: Waves of Cultural Criticism and Mobilization Cycles of New Middle-Class Radicalism. In R. Dalton and M. Kuechler (eds.), *Challenging the Political Order.* Cambridge: Polity Press, pp. 23–42.

Brand, Ulrich. 2002. Fragend geht'sgeht's voran. Wie die Bewegung auf den Begriff kommt. In *Wo steht die Bewegung? Eine Zwischenbilanz der Globalisierungskritik,* ed. BUKO-Arbeitsschwerpunkt Weltwirtschaft und Informationszentrum 3. Freiburg: Welt, pp. 54–57.

———. 2005. *Gegen-Hegemonie. Perspektiven globalisierungskritischer Strategien.* Hamburg: VSA.

Brand, Ulrich, and Markus Wissen. 2002. Ambivalenzen praktischer Globalisierungskritik: Das Beispiel Attac. *Kurswechsel* 2: 102–113.

Bray, John. 1998. Web Wars: NGOs, Companies, and Governments in an Internet-Connected World. *Green Management International* 24: 115–129.

Brecher, Jeremy, Tim Costello, and Brendan Smith. 2000. *Globalization from Below. The Power of Solidarity.* Cambridge: South End Press.

Broad, Robin, and Zahara Heckscher. 2003. Before Seattle: The Historical Roots of the Current Movement against Corporate-Led Globalization. *Third World Quarterly Journal of Emerging Areas* 4: 713–728.

Bromley, Catherine, John Curtice, and Ben Seyd. 2001. Political Engagement, Trust, and Constitutional Reform. In A. Park et al. (eds.), *British Social Attitudes: The 18th Report.* London: Sage, pp. 199–225.

Brooks, Christopher. 2004. Faction in Movement: The Impact of Inclusivity on the Anti-Globalization Movement. *Social Science Quarterly* 85(3): 559–577.

Bruneau, Ivan. 2004. La Confédération paysanne et le mouvement altermondialisaiton. *Politix* 68: 111–134.

Budge, Ian, Hans-Dieter Klingemann, et al. 2001. *Mapping Policy Preferences.* Oxford: Oxford University Press.

Calle, Ángel. 2000. *Ciudadanía y solidaridad: las ONG de solidaridad internacional como movimiento social.* Madrid: IEPALA.

———. 2002. La Red Ciudadana por la Abolición de la Deuda Externa. *Documentación Social* 126: 179–188.

———. 2004. Okupaciones. Un movimiento contra las desigualdades materiales y expresivas. In F. Tezanos (ed.), *Tendencias en desigualdad y exclusión social.* Madrid: Sistema, pp. 459–502.

———. 2005a. *Nuevos Movimientos Globales. Hacia la radicalidad democrática.* Madrid: Editorial Popular.

———. 2005b. Nuevos Movimientos Globales: sedimentando e impactando. In E. Grau and P. Ibarra (eds.), *Anuario de movimientos sociales 2004. Nuevos escenarios, nuevos retos en la red.* Barcelona: Icaria/Betiko Fundazioa, pp. 156–164.

Campanya contra l'Europa del Capital. 2002. Assembly's minutes, March, www.pangea. org/campanyaUE/documents/index.php. (Accessed December 12, 2006.)

Ceri, Paolo (ed). 2003. *La democrazia dei movimenti. Come decidono i noglobal.* Cosenza: Rubbettino.

Chabanet, Didier. 2002. Les marches européennes contre le chômage, la précarité et les exclusions. In R. Balme and D. Chabanet (eds.), *L'action collective en Europe.* Paris: Presses de Sciences Po, pp. 461–494.

Chandhoke, Neera. 2003. The Limits of Global Civil Society. In M. Kaldor (ed.), *Global Civil Society 2003.* Oxford: Oxford University Press, pp. 35–53.

Charnovitz, Steve. 1997. Two Centuries of Participation: NGOs and International Governance. *Michigan Journal of International Law* 18(2): 183–286.

Chen, M. A. 1995. Engendering World Conferences: The International Women's Movement and the United Nations. *Third World Quarterly* 16(3): 477–493.

Chesters, Graeme. 1999. Resist to Exist? Radical Environmentalism at the End of the Millennium. *ECOS* 20(2): 19–25. Available online at www.shiftingground.freeuk. com/ecos1.htm, accessed 12/2/04.

———. 2000. The New Intemperance: Protest, Imagination and Carnival. *ECOS* 21(1): 2–9. Available online at www.shiftingground.freeuk.com.ecos2.htm, accessed 12/2/04.

Chesters, Graeme, and Ian Welsh. 2004. Rebel Colours: Framing in Global Social Movements. *Sociological Review* 52(3): 314–335.

CIRCA. 2004. About the Army. Available online at www.clownarmy.org/about.htm, accessed 1/5/05.

CIS. 2002. *Ciudadanía, participación y democracia.* Estudio 2450 (www.cis.es).

Clark, John. 1991. *Democratizing Development: The Role of Voluntary Organizations.* London: Earthscan.

——— (ed.). 2003a. *Globalizing Civic Engagement. Civil Society and Transnational Action.* London: Earthscan Publications.

———. 2003b. Introduction: Civil Society and Transnational Action. In J. Clark (ed.), *Globalizing Civic Engagement. Civil Society and Transnational Action.* London: Earthscan Publications, pp. 1–28.

Clemens, Elisabeth S., and Debra Minkoff. 2004. Beyond the Iron Law: Rethinking the Place of Organisations in Social Movements Research. In D. A. Snow et al. (eds.), *The Blackwell Companion to Social Movements.* Oxford: Blackwell, pp. 155–170.

Cohen, Jean L. 1985. Strategy or Identity: New Theoretical Paradigms and Contemporary Social Movements. *Social Research* 52(4): 663–716.

Cohen, Jean L., and Andrew Arato. 1992. *Civil Society and Political Theory.* Cambridge, MA: MIT Press.

Cohen, Robin, and Shirin M. Rai (eds.). 2000. *Global Social Movements.* London: Athlone Press.

Colomer, Josep M. 1997. Las instituciones de la crispación política. *Claves de Razón Práctica* 74: 44–47.

Comisión de Comunicación y Prensa, FSS. 2002. Autovaloración de la comisión de comunicación y prensa del foro social de Sevilla. Internal report, July 10. www. forosocialsevilla.org. (Accessed December 12, 2006.)

Commins, Steven. 1997. World Vision International and Donors: Too Close for

Comfort? In D. Hulme and M. Edwards (eds.), *NGOs, States and Donors: Too Close for Comfort?* Basingstoke: MacMillan, pp. 140–155.

Commission on Global Governance. 1995. *Our Global Neighbourhood.* Oxford: Oxford University Press.

Conca, Ken. 1995. Greening the United Nations: Environmental Organisations and the UN System. *Third World Quarterly* 16(3): 441–447.

Contamin, Jean-Gabriel. 2005. Les grèves de décembre 1995: un moment fondateur? In E. Agrikoliansky et al. (eds.), *L'altermondialisme en France. La longue histoire d'une nouvelle cause.* Paris: Flammarion, pp. 233–263.

Coulouarn, Tangui, and Ariane Jossin. 2005. Représentations et présentations de soi des militants alermondialistes. In E. Agrikoliansky and I. Sommier (eds.), *Radiographie du mouvement altermondialiste français: le FSE de Paris Saint-Denis.* Paris: La Dispute, pp. 127–156.

Crettiez, Xavier, and Isabelle Sommier (eds.). 2006. *La France rebelle.* 2nd ed. Paris: Michalon.

Crossley, Nick. 2003. From Reproduction to Transformation: Social Movement Fields and the Radical Habitus. *Theory Culture Society* 20(6): 43–68.

Crouch, Colin. 2001. *Sociologia dell'Europa occidentale.* Bologna: Il Mulino.

———. 2003. *Postdemocrazia.* Roma-Bari: Laterza.

Curtice, John, and Roger Jowell. 1995. The Sceptical Electorate. In R. Jowell (ed.), *British Social Attitudes: The Twelfth Report.* Aldershot: Dartmouth, pp. 141–172.

Dalton, Russell J., and Robert Rohrschneider. 2002. A Global Network? Transnational Cooperation among Environmental Groups. *Journal of Politics* 64 (May): 510.

De Pury, David, et al. 1995. *Le Livre Blanc: Courage pour le renouveau.* Zurich: Orell Füssli.

de Sousa Santos, Boaventura. 2003. The World Social Forum: Towards a Counter-Hegemonic Globalization. www.ces.fe.uc.pt/documentos/wsf.pdf. Last accessed 2004.

Del Giorgio, Elena. 2004. I Social Forum in Toscana. Funzionamento e rapporto con il contesto locale di arene deliberative in costruzione. In E. Diodato (ed.), *La Toscana e la globalizzazione dal basso.* Florence: Chiari, pp. 155–176.

della Porta, Donatella. 2001. *I partiti politici.* Bologna: Il Mulino.

———. 2003a. *I New Global.* Bologna: Il Mulino.

———. 2003b. Politics, Anti-Politics, Other Politics: Conceptions of Democracy and the Movement for a Globalization from Below. Paper for the ECPR General Conference, Marburg (Germany).

———. 2003c. Social Movements and Democracy at the Turn of the Millennium. In P. Ibarra (ed.), *Social Movements and Democracy.* New York: Palgrave Macmillan, pp. 105–136.

———. 2005a. Multiple Belongings, Tolerant Identities, and the Construction of "Another Politics." In D. della Porta and S. Tarrow (eds.), *Transnational Protest and Global Activism.* Oxford: Rowman and Littlefield, pp. 175–202.

———. 2005b. Making the Polis: Social Forums and Democracy in the Global Justice Movement. *Mobilization* 10: 73–94.

———. 2005c. Sociologia dei movimenti sociali globali. Introduction to the special issue of *Rassegna Italiana di Sociologia* 46: 215–220.

della Porta, Donatella, Massimiliano Andretta, Lorenzo Mosca, and Herbert Reiter. 2006. *Globalization from Below: Transnational Activists and Protest Networks.* Minneapolis: University of Minnesota Press.

della Porta, Donatella, and Mario Diani. 1999. *Social Movements: An Introduction.* Oxford: Blackwell.

———. 2004a. *Movimenti senza protesta? L'ambientalismo in Italia.* Bologna: Il Mulino.

———. 2004b. No to the War with No Ifs or Buts: Protest against the War in Iraq. In V. Della Sala and S. Fabbrini (eds.), *Italian Politics.* Oxford: Berghahn Books, pp. 200–218.

———. 2006. *Social Movements.* 2nd ed. Oxford: Blackwell.

della Porta, Donatella, and Olivier Fillieule. 2004. Policing Social Movements. In D. A. Snow et al. (eds.), *The Blackwell Companion on Social Movements.* Oxford: Blackwell, pp. 217–241.

della Porta, Donatella, Hanspeter Kriesi, and Dieter Rucht (eds.). 1999. *Social Movements in a Globalizing World.* London: Macmillan.

della Porta, Donatella, and Lorenzo Mosca (eds.). 2003. *Globalizzazione e movimenti sociali.* Roma: Manifestolibri.

———. 2005a. Global-Net for Global Movements? A Network of Networks for a Movement of Movements. *Journal of Public Policy* 25(1): 165–190.

———. 2005b. In movimento. Organizational dynamics in the emergence of the global justice movement. Paper prepared for presentation at the ACI conference on the Origins of the Global Movement, Paris, September.

della Porta, Donatella, Abby Peterson, and Herbert Reiter (eds.). 2006. *Policing Transnational Protest.* Aldershot: Ashgate.

della Porta, Donatella, and Gianni Piazza (forthcoming). *Voci dalla Valle, voci dallo stretto. Proteste e "grandi opere."* Milan: Feltrinelli.

della Porta, Donatella, and Herbert Reiter (eds.). 1998a. *Policing Protest: The Control of Mass Demonstrations in Western Democracies.* Minneapolis: University of Minnesota Press.

———. 1998b. The Policing of Mass Demonstrations in Western Democracies. In D. della Porta and H. Reiter (eds.), *Policing Protest: The Control of Mass Demonstration in Western Democracies.* Minneapolis: University of Minnesota Press.

——— (eds.). 2004. *La protesta e il controllo. Movimenti e forze dell'ordine nell'era della globalizzazione.* Milano and Piacenza: Altraeconomia/Ed. Berti.

della Porta, Donatella, and Sidney Tarrow (eds.). 2005. *Transnational Protest and Global Activism.* Lanham, MD: Rowman and Littlefield.

Denis, Jean-Michel. 2005. La constitution d'un front antilibéral: l'Union syndicale Groupe des Dix Solidaires et Attac. In E. Agrikoliansky et al. (eds.), *L'altermondialisme en France. La longue histoire d'une nouvelle cause.* Paris: Flammarion, pp. 265–290.

Diani, Mario. 1992a. Analysing Social Movement Networks. In M. Diani and R. Eyerman (eds.), *Studying Collective Action.* London: Sage, pp. 107–135.

———. 1992b. The Concept of Social Movement. *Sociological Review* 40: 1–25.

———. 1995. *Green Networks: A Structural Analysis of the Italian Environmental Movement.* Edinburgh: Edinburgh University Press.

———. 2003a. Introduction. In M. Diani and D. McAdam (eds.), *Social Movements and Networks: Relational Approaches to Collective Action*. Oxford: Oxford University Press, pp. 1–18.

———. 2003b. "Leaders" or "Brokers"? Positions and Influence in Social Movement Networks. In M. Diani and D. McAdam (eds.), *Social Movements and Networks*. Oxford: Oxford University Press, pp. 105–122.

———. 2003c. Networks and Social Movements: A Research Programme. In M. Diani and D. McAdam (eds.), *Social Movements and Networks: Relational Approaches to Collective Action*. Oxford: Oxford University Press, pp. 299–319.

———. 2005. Cities in the World: Local Civil Society and Global Issues in Britain. In D. della Porta and S. Tarrow (eds.), *Transnational Protest and Global Activism*. Lanham, MD: Rowman and Littlefield, pp. 45–67.

Díaz-Salazar, Rafael. 1996. *Redes de Solidaridad Internacional: Para derribar el muro Norte-Sur*. Madrid: Ediciones HOAC.

———. 1998. *La Izquierda y el Cristianismo*. Madrid: Taurus.

Dines, Nicholas. 1999. Centri sociali: occupazioni autogestite a Napoli negli anni novanta. *Quaderni di Sociologia* 21: 90–111.

Doherty, Brian. 2004. Studying Local Activist Communities over Time: Direct Action in Manchester, Oxford and North Wales 1970–2001. Unpublished paper, School of Politics, International Relations and the Environment, Keele University.

Donson, Fiona, Graham Chesters, Ian Welsh, and Andrew Tickle. 2004. Rebels with a Cause, Folk Devils without a Panic. *Internet Journal of Criminology*. Available online at www.internetjournalofcriminology.com/ijcarticles.html, accessed 5/4/06.

Dryzek, John S. 2004. Handle with Care: The Deadly Hermeneutics of Deliberative Democracy. Paper presented at the conference on Empirical Approaches to Deliberative Politics, European University Institute, Florence, May 22–23.

Dubourg, Auguste, Sylvain Bachelier, José Bové, Gabe Cohn-Bendit, Annick Coupé, Camille Guillot, Charles Piaget, Malika Zediri, and Guy Robert. 2001. *La subversion démocratique*. Paris: Le temps des cerises.

Eberlei, Walter. 2002. Entwicklungspolitische Nicht-Regierungsorganisationen in Deutschland. Euphorie, Ernüchterung, Erneuerung. *Aus Politik und Zeitgeschichte* 6–7: 23–28.

Echart, Enara, Sara López, and Kamala Orozco. 2005. *Origen, protestas y propuestas del movimiento antiglobalización*. Madrid: Catarata.

Edwards, Michael. 1999. *Future Positive, International Cooperation in the 21st Century*. London: Earthscan.

Edwards, Michael, and John Gaventa (eds.). 2001. *Global Citizen Action*. Boulder, CO: Lynne Rienner.

Ekins, Paul. 1992. *A New World Order: Grassroots Movements for Global Change*. London and New York: Routledge.

Falk, Richard. 1999. *Predatory Globalization: A Critique*. Malden, MA: Polity Press.

Fantasia, Rick, and Judith Stepan-Norris. 2004. The Labour Movement in Motion. In D. A. Snow et al. (eds.), *The Blackwell Companion to Social Movements*. Oxford: Blackwell, pp. 555–575.

Farnsworth, Kevin. 2004. Anti-globalization, Anti-capitalism, and the Democratic State. In M. J. Todd and G. Taylor (eds.), *Democracy and Participation: Popular Protest and New Social Movements*. London: Merlin, pp. 28–54.

Favre, Pierre, Olivier Fillieule, and Nonna Mayer. 1997. La fin d'une étrange lacune de la sociologie des mobilisations. L'étude par sondage de manifestants: fondements théoriques et solutions technique. *Revue francaise de science politique* 1: 3–28.

Fillieule, Olivier, and Philippe Blanchard. 2005. Carrières militantes et engagements contre la globalisation. In E. Agrikoliansky and I. Sommier (eds.), *Radiographie du mouvement altermondialiste français: le FSE de Paris Saint-Denis.* Paris: La Dispute, pp. 157–186.

Fillieule, Olivier, Philippe Blanchard, Eric Agrikoliansky, Marko Bandler, Florence Passy, and Isabelle Sommier. 2004. L'altermondialisme en réseaux. *Politix* 17: 13–48.

Finelli, Pietro. 2003a. Un'idea partecipativa della politica. Strutture organizzative e modelli di democrazia in Attac Italia. In P. Ceri (ed.), *La democrazia dei movimenti. Come decidono i noglobal.* Soveria Mannelli: Rubbettino, pp. 31–56.

———. 2003b. Un granello di sabbia negli ingranaggi della globalizzazione. Per un profilo di Attac-Italia. *Quaderni di Sociologia* 33(47): 45–58.

Fisher, Dana R. 2006. Taking Cover beneath the Anti-Bush Umbrella: Cycles of Protest and Movement-to-Movement Transmission in an Era of Repressive Politics. *Research in Political Sociology* 15: 27–56.

Flash Eurobarometre on Globalisation. 2003. EOS Gallup Europe, http://europa.eu.int/comm/public_opinion/flash/FL151bGlobalisationreport.pd.

Florini, Ann M. (ed.). 2000. *The Third Force: The Rise of Transnational Civil Society.* Tokyo and Washington: JCIE and CEIP.

Follesdal, Andreas. 2004. Political Consumerism as Chance and Challenge. In M. Micheletti et al. (eds.), *Politics, Products and Markets. Exploring Political Consumerism Past and Present.* New Brunswick, NJ: Transaction Publishers, pp. 3–20.

Ford, Peter, and Alexandra Poolos. 2000. Protesters Speed up Debt Relief. *Christian Science Monitor* 92: 215.

Fox, Jonathan A., and L. David Brown (eds.). 1998. *The Struggle for Accountability: The World Bank, NGOs, and Grassroots Movements.* Cambridge: MIT Press.

Fréour, Nadège. 2005. Le répertoire d'action collective comme répertoire d'offre d'engagement: un éclairage sur les contraintes liées aux processus de mobilisation contemporains. Paper presented at the Congress of Political Science French association, Lyon, September 16.

Friends of the Earth (FoE). 2002a. *Strategic Plan 2003–8.* Friends of the Earth.

———. 2002b. *GATS Gotta Go.* Briefing, Friends of the Earth.

———. 2003. Blair Challenged over WTO. Friends of the Earth Press Release, 04/09/03, at www.foe.co.uk/resource/press_releases/blair_challenged_over_wto.html, accessed 1/19/05.

Fritz, Thomas. 2002. Kapital bewegt. Attac, die Finanzmärkte und das Elend linker Kritik. *iz3w* 258: 22–24.

Fruci, Gian Luca. 2003. La nuova agorà. I social forum tra spazio pubblico e dinamiche organizzative. In P. Ceri (ed.), *La democrazia dei movimenti.* Soveria Mannelli: Rubettino, pp. 169–200.

Fuchs, Dieter. 1991. The Normalization of the Unconventional. Forms of Political Action and New Social Movements. In G. Meyer and F. Ryszka (eds.), *Political*

Participation and Democracy in Poland and West Germany. Varsovie: Wydawca, pp. 148–169.

Gadner, Gary. 2002. Religion and Spirituality in the Quest for a Sustainable World. *WorldWatch Paper* 164 (www.worldwatch.org/pubs/paper/164). (Accessed December 12, 2006.)

Gamson, William A. 1992. The Social Psychology of Collective Action. In A. D. Morris and C. M. Mueller (eds.), *Frontiers in Social Movement Theory.* New Haven, CT: Yale University Press, pp. 53–76.

Gaxie, Daniel. 1978. *Le cens cache.* Paris: Le Seuil.

Gebauer, Thomas. 1998. Die NGOs und die Perspektiven internationaler Solidarität. Das Beispiel der internationalen Minenkampagne. In Roth Görg Christoph (ed.), *Kein Staat zu machen. Zur Kritik der Sozialwissenschaften.* Münster: Roland, pp. 484–502.

Gerhards, Jürgen, and Dieter Rucht. 1992. Mesomobilization: Organizing and Framing in Two Protest Campaigns in West Germany. *American Journal of Sociology* 98(3): 555–596.

Gerlach, Luther. 1976. Movements of Revolutionary Change. Some Structural Characteristics. *American Behavioral Scientist* 43: 813–836.

———. 2001. The Structures of Social Movements: Environmental Activism and Its Opponents. In J. Arquila and D. Ronfeldt (eds.), *Networks and Netwars: The Future of Terror, Crime and Militancy.* Santa Monica: Rand, pp. 289–309.

Gillan, Kevin. 2006a. Meaning in Movement: An Ideational Analysis of Sheffield-Based Protest Networks Contesting Globalisation and War. Ph.D. thesis, Department of Politics, University of Sheffield.

———. 2006b. Another Ideology? Novelty and Familiarity in the Belief Structures of Social Forum Participants. Paper presented at Alternative Futures conference, Manchester Metropolitan University.

Gillham, Patrick, and Bob Edwards. 2003. Global Justice Protesters Respond to the September 11 Terrorist Attacks: The Impact of an Intentional Disaster on Demonstrations in Washington, D.C. In *Beyond September 11: An Account of Post-Disaster Research.* Boulder, CO: Natural Hazards Research and Information Center, University of Colorado, pp. 483–520.

Giugni, Marco, and Florence Passy. 1997. *Histoires de mobilisation politique en Suisse.* Paris: L'Harmattan.

———. 2002. Le champ politique de l'immigration en Europe: opportunités, mobilisations et héritage de l'État national. In R. Balme et al. (eds.), *L'action collective en Europe.* Paris: Presses De Science Po, pp. 433–460.

Glasius, M. 2001. Chronologies. In H. Anheier, M. Glasius, and M. Kaldor (eds.), *Global Civil Society 2001.* Oxford: Oxford University Press, pp. 323–337. Available online at http://www.lse.ac.uk/Depts/global/Publications/Yearbooks/2001/2001chapter911.pdf. (Accessed December 12, 2006.)

———. 2005. *The International Criminal Court: A Global Civil Society Achievement.* London: Routledge.

Gobille, Boris, and Aysen Uysal. 2005. Cosmopolites et enracinés. In E. Agrikoliansky and I. Sommier (eds.), *Radiographie du mouvement altermondialiste français: le FSE de Paris Saint-Denis.* Paris: La Dispute, pp. 105–126.

Gomà, Ricard, Eva Alfama, Robert González, Lluc Peláez, and Guiomar Vargas. 2004.

La red crítica global en Cataluña en los albores del siglo XXI. Paper presented at the VIII Congreso Español de Sociología, Alicante.

Gomà, Ricard, and Joan Subirats (eds.). 1998. *Políticas públicas en España. Contenidos, redes de actores y niveles de gobierno.* Barcelona: Editorial Ariel.

González, Luis. 2003. Movimiento antiglobalización 2003: otro punto de inflexión es necesario. *El Ecologista* 36: 43–45.

Gordenker, Leon, and Thomas G. Weiss. 1995. Pluralising Global Governance: Analytical Approaches and Dimensions. *Third World Quarterly* 16: 357–387.

Gramsci, Antonio. 1971. *Selections from the Prison Notebook of Antonio Gramsci.* New York: International Publishers.

Grazioli, Marco, and Giovanni Lodi. 1984. Giovani sul territorio urbano: l'integrazione minimale. In A. Melucci (ed.), *Altri codici. Aree di movimento nella metropoli.* Bologna: Il Mulino, pp. 63–126.

Greven, Thomas, and Thomas Grumke (eds.). 2006. *Globalisierter Rechtsextremismus? Die extremistische Rechte in der Ara der Globalisierung.* Wiesbaden: VS Verlag.

Grothe, Nicole. 2005. *InnenStadtAktion—Kunst oder Politik? Künstlerische Praxis in der neoliberalen Stadt.* Bielefeld: Transcript.

Grzybowski, Cândido. 2000. We NGOs: A Controversial Way of Being and Acting. *Development in Practice* 10(3): 436–444.

Gubitosa, Carlo. 2003. *Genova nome per nome. Le violenze, i responsabili, le ragioni. Inchiesta sui giorni e i fatti del G8.* Milano and Piacenza: Altra Economia/Ed. Berti.

Guiraudon, Virginie. 2002. Weak Weapons of the Weak? Transnational Mobilization around Migration in the European Union. In D. Imig and S. Tarrow (eds.), *Contentious Europeans. Protest and Politics in an Emerging Polity.* Lanham, MD: Rowman and Littlefield, pp. 163–183.

Hanloser, Gerhard (ed.). 2004. *Sie war'nwar'n die Antideutschesten der Linken. Zur Geschichte, Kritik und Zukunft antideutscher Politik.* Münster: Unrast.

Haug, Christoph, Simon Teune, and Mundo Yang. 2005. Von Porto Alegre nach Berlin. Lokale Sozialforen in Deutschland. *Forschungsjournal Neue Soziale Bewegungen* 18(3): 84–90.

Held, David, and Anthony G. McGrew. 2002. *Globalization/Anti-Globalization.* Cambridge: Polity.

Herreros, Tomás. 2001. El estado actual de la apuesta del Moviment de Resistència Global. *Emergències* 1 (www.pangea.org/mrg/emergencies).

Hierlmeier, Josef. 2002. *Internationalismus. Eine Einführung in die Ideengeschichte des Internationalismus—von Vietnam bis Genua.* Stuttgart: Schmetterling Verlag.

Holmes Cooper, Alice. 1996. *Paradoxes of Peace. German Peace Movements since 1945.* Ann Arbor: University of Michigan Press.

Holzapfel, Miriam, and Karin König. 2001. Chronik der Globalisierungsproteste. *Mittelweg* 36(6): 24–34.

Houtart, François, and François Polet (eds.). 1999. *L'autre Davos. Mondialisation des résistances e des luttes.* Paris: L'Harmattan.

Huntington, Samuel P. 1973. Transnational Organizations in World Politics. *World Politics* 25: 333–368.

Iglesias, Pablo. 2002. Desobediencia civil y movimiento antiglobalización. Una herramienta de intervención política. (www.filosofiayderecho.com/rtfd/numero5/desobediencia3.htm.) (Accessed December 12, 2006.)

Imig, Doug, and Sidney Tarrow (eds.). 2002. *Contentious Europeans. Protest and Politics in an Emerging Polity.* Lanham, MD: Rowman and Littlefield.

Inglehart, Ronald. 1977. *The Silent Revolution. Changing Values and Political Styles among Western Publics.* Princeton, NJ: Princeton University Press.

Jaime-Jiménez, Oscar, and Fernando Reinares. 1998. The Policing of Mass Demonstration in Spain: From Dictatorship to Democracy. In D. della Porta and H. Reiter (eds.), *Policing Protest: The Control of Mass Demonstration in Western Democracies.* Minneapolis: University of Minnesota Press.

Jasper, James M. 1997. *The Art of Moral Protest.* Chicago: University of Chicago Press.

JDC. 2001a. *Jubilee Debt Campaign Founding Document,* 03/24/01.

———. 2001b. *Memorandum and Articles of Association of Jubilee Debt Coalition,* 12/6/01.

Jerez, Ariel, and Victor Sampedro. 2001. Visibilidad y tratamiento informativo del movimiento de cooperación al desarrollo. Paper presented at VII Spanish Congress of Sociology, September, Salamanca.

Jiménez, Manuel. 2003. Public Identity and Coalition Building Process: The Antiglobalization Movement in Spain. Paper presented at the conference Transnational Processes and Social Movements, Bellagio, Italy.

———. 2005. *El impacto político de los movimientos sociales. Un estudio de la protesta ambiental en España.* Colección Monografías, 214. Madrid: CIS-Siglo XXI.

———. 2006. Cuando la protesta importa electoralmente. El perfil sociodemográfico y político de los manifestantes contra la guerra de Irak." *Papers. Revista de Sociología* 81.

Jiménez, Manuel, and Javier Alcalde. 2002. La Construcción de la identidad del movimiento antiglobalización en España. *Revista Internacional de Sociología* 33: 211–235.

Jordan, Grant, and William Maloney. 1997. *The Protest Business? Mobilizing Campaign Groups.* Manchester and New York: Manchester University Press.

Jowell, Richard, Alison Park, Lindsay Brook, Katrina Thompson, and Roger Jowell (eds.). 1997. *British Social Attitudes: The 14th Report.* Aldershot: Ashgate.

Jowell, Richard, Alison Park, Katrina Thomson, and Roger Jowell (eds.). 1999. *British Social Attitudes: The 16th Report.* Aldershot: Ashgate.

Jung, Jai Kwan. 2006. Growing Supranational Identities in a Globalizing World? A Multilevel Analysis of the World Values Survey. Unpublished paper, Cornell University Department of Government, Ithaca, NY.

Kaldor, Mary. 2000. "Civilizing" Globalization? The Implication of the "Battle in Seattle." *Millennium* 29: 100–114.

———. 2003. *Global Civil Society. An Answer to War.* Cambridge: Polity Press.

Karl, Terry L. 1990. Dilemmas of Democratization in Latin America. *Comparative Politics* 23(1): 1–21.

Karstedt-Henke, Sabine. 1980. Theorien zur Erklärung terroristischer Bewegungen. In E. Blankenberg (ed.), *Politik der inneren Sicherheit.* Frankfurt: Suhrkamp, pp. 198–234.

Katz, Hagai, and Helmut Anheier. 2005. Global Connectedness: The Structure of Transnational NGO Networks. In M. Glasius et al. (eds.), *Global Civil Society 2005/6.* London: Sage, pp. 240–265.

Katz, Robert, and Peter Mair (eds.). 1992. *How Parties Organize: Change and Adaptation in Party Organizations in Western Democracies 1960–1990*. London: Sage.

Keck, Margaret, and Kathryn Sikkink. 1998. *Activists Beyond Borders*. Ithaca, NY: Cornell University Press.

Khagram, Sanjeev, James V. Riker, and Kathryn Sikkink (eds.). 2002. *Reconstructing World Politics: Transnational Social Movements, Networks and Norms*. Minneapolis: University of Minnesota Press.

Kitschelt, Herbert. 1993. Social Movements, Political Parties, and Democratic Theory. *The Annals of the AAPSS* 528: 13–29.

Klandermans, Bert, and Jackie Smith. 2002. Survey Research: A Case for Comparative Design. In B. Klandermans and S. Staggenborg (eds.), *Methods of Social Movement Research*. Minneapolis: University of Minnesota Press, pp. 3–31.

Klein, Naomi. 2000. *No Logo*. London: Flamingo.

Klingeman, Hans D., Richard Hoffenbert, and Ian Budge. 1994. *Parties, Policies and Democracies*. Boulder, CO: Westview Press.

Kolb, Felix. 2003. The Impact of Transnational Protest on Social Movement Organizations: Mass Media and the Making of ATTAC Germany. Unpublished manuscript, Bellagio.

———. 2005. The Impact of Transnational Protest on Social Movement Organizations: Mass Media and the Making of *Attac* Germany. In D. della Porta and S. Tarrow (eds.), *Transnational Protest and Global Activism*. Lanham, MD: Rowman and Littlefield, pp. 95–120.

Koopmans, Ruud. 1995. *Democracy from Below: New Social Movements and the Political System in West Germany*. Boulder, CO: Westview Press.

Koopmans, Ruud, and Ann Zimmerman. 2003. Internet: A New Potential for European Political Communication? *Wissenschaftszentrum Berlin fuer Sozialforschung* 4: 402.

Kriesi, Hanspeter. 1996. The Organizational Structure of New Social Movements in a Political Context. In D. McAdam, J. McCarthy, and M. N. Zald (eds.), *Comparative Perspectives on Social Movements*. Cambridge, NY: Cambridge University Press, pp. 152–184.

Kriesi, Hanspeter, Ruud Koopmans, Jan Willem Duyvendak, and Marco Giugni. 1995. *New Social Movements in Western Europe*. Minneapolis: University of Minnesota Press.

Ladner, Andreas. 2001. Swiss Political Parties: Between Persistence and Change. *West European Politics* 24: 123–143.

Lancaster J18 Collective. 1999. If I Can Dance It's Not My Revolution. Available online at www.flag.blackened.net/af/online/j18/reflec1.html, accessed 12/7/04.

Leggewie, Claus. 2001. Nach dem Fall. Globalisierungskritik und ihre Kritik. *Aus Politik und Zeitgeschichte* (B 52–53): 18–22.

———. 2003. Rechts gegen Globalisierung. *Internationale Politik* 58(4): 33–40.

Lent, Adam. 2001. *British Social Movements Since 1945: Sex, Colour, Peace and Power*. Basingstoke: Palgrave.

Levi, Margaret, and Gillian Murphy. 2004. Coalitions of Contention: The Case of the WTO Protests in Seattle. Manuscript, Department of Political Science, University of Washington.

Lichbach, Mark Irving, and Helma G. E. de Vries. 2004. Global Justice and Antiwar Movements: From Local Resistance to Globalized Protests. Manuscript, Department of Government and Politics, University of Maryland.

Lipschutz, Ronnie D. 1992. Reconstructing World Politics: The Emergence of Global Civil Society. *Millennium: Journal of International Studies* 21: 389–420.

Livezey, Lowell. 1989. U.S. Religious Organizations and the International Human Rights Movement. *Human Rights Quarterly* 11(1): 14–81.

Lotti, Flavio, and Nicola Giandomenico (eds.). 1996. *L'Onu dei popoli.* Turin: Edizioni Gruppo Abele.

Macdonald, Stephen. 1972. *Action for World Development: The World Development Movement in the 1970s.* London: The World Development Movement.

Mair, Peter, and Ingrid van Biezen. 2001. Party Membership in Twenty European Democracies, 1980–2000. *Party Politics* 7: 5–21.

Marchetti, Raffaele, and Duccio Zola. 2005. Visions of Democracy/Movement Discourse on Democracy. The Transnational Case. DEMOS WP3 report. Urbino: University of Urbino—DEMOS project.

Marcon, Giulio. 2004. *Le utopie del ben fare. Persorsi di solidarietà: dal mutualismo al terzo settore, ai movimenti.* Napoli: Ancora del Mediterraneo.

Marradi, Claudio, and Enrico Ratto. 2001. *Da Seattle a Genova. Gli 8 non valgono una moltitudine.* Genoa: Fratelli Frilli Editori.

Martínez, Miguel. 2002. *Okupaciones de viviendas y centros sociales. Autogestión, contracultura y conflictos urbanos.* Barcelona: Virus.

Mathieu, Lilian. 2004. Notes provisoires sur l'espace des mouvements sociaux. *ContreTemps* 11: 51–59.

McAdam, Doug, John D. McCarthy, and Mayer N. Zald (eds.). 1996a. *Comparative Perspectives on Social Movements: Political Opportunities, Mobilizing Structures, and Cultural Framings.* Cambridge: Cambridge University Press.

———. 1996b. Introduction: Opportunities, Mobilizing Structures, and Framing Processes—Toward a Synthetic, Comparative Perspective on Social Movements. In D. McAdam, J. D. McCarthy, and M. N. Zald (eds.), *Comparative Perspectives on Social Movements.* Cambridge: Cambridge University Press, pp. 1–20.

McAdam, Doug, Sidney Tarrow, and Charles Tilly. 2001. *Dynamics of Contention.* Cambridge. Cambridge University Press.

McCarthy, John D., and Mayer N. Zald. 1977. Resource Mobilization and Social Movements: A Partial Theory. *American Journal of Sociology* 82(6): 1212–1241.

Meloni, Maurizio, and Giacomo Schettini. 1994. Le ragioni del controvertice. *Onde Lunghe* 2 (supplement): 3.

Melucci, Alberto. 1996. *Challenging Codes.* Cambridge and New York: Cambridge University Press.

Meyer, David S. 1990. *A Winter of Discontent: The Nuclear Freeze and American Politics.* New York: Praeger.

Meyer, David S., and Sidney Tarrow (eds.). 1998. *The Social Movement Society.* New York: Rowman and Littlefield.

Meyer, David S., and Nancy Whittier. 1994. Social Movement Spillover. *Social Problems* 41 (2): 277–298.

Micheletti, Michele. 2003. *Political Virtue and Shopping. Individuals, Consumerism, and Collective Action.* London: Palgrave Macmillan.

Misereor and BUND. 1996. *Zukunftsfähiges Deutschland. Ein Beitrag zu einer global nachhaltigen Entwicklung.* Berlin: Birkhäuser Verlag.

Moody, Kim. 1997. *Workers in a Lean World. Unions in the International Economy.* London: Verso.

Morland, Dave, and John Carter. 2004. Anarchy and Democracy. In M. J. Todd and G. Taylor (eds.), *Democracy and Participation: Popular Protest and New Social Movements.* London: Merlin, pp. 78–95.

Mouchard, Daniel. 2002. Les mobilisations des "sans" dans la France contemporaine: l'émergence d'un "radicalisme autolimité." *Revue française de science politique* 52(4): 425–447.

MPH. 2004. *Founding 2005 Mobilisation Statement,* July 2004.

———. 2005. *Manifesto,* January 2005.

MRG. 2003. *El MRG ha muerto ... ¡comienza la fiesta!* Public report, January, www.lahaine.org/articulo.php?p=254&more=1&c=1. (Accessed December 12, 2006.)

Neidhardt, Friedhelm, and Dieter Rucht. 2001. Protestgeschichte der Bundesrepublik Deutschland 1950–1994: Ereignisse, Themen, Akteure. In D. Rucht (ed.), *Protest in der Bundesrepublik. Strukturen und Entwicklungen.* Frankfurt/Main and New York: Campus, pp. 27–70.

NGO Millennium Forum. 2000. *We the Peoples. Strengthening the United Nations for the 21st Century. Final Declaration.* New York: NGO Millennium Forum.

Notes from Nowhere (eds.). 2003. *We Are Everywhere, the Irresistible Rise of Global Anti-Capitalism.* London: Verso.

O'Brien, Robert, Anne Marie Goetz, Jaan Aart Scholte, and Marc Williams. 2000. *Contesting Global Governance. Multilateral Economic Institutions and Global Social Movements.* Cambridge: Cambridge University Press.

Offerlé, Michel. 1994. *Sociologie des groupes d'intérêts.* Paris: Montchrestien.

Olejniczak, Claudia. 1999. *Die Dritte Welt Bewegung.* Leverkusen: Deutscher Universitätsverlag.

Olesen, Thomas. 2003. *International Zapatismo: The Construction of Solidarity in the Age of Globalization.* London: ZED Books.

———. 2004. The Transnational Zapatistas Solidarity Network: An Infrastructure Analysis. *Global Networks* 4(1): 89–107.

Ollitrault, Sylvie. 1996. Science et militantisme: les transformations d'un échange circulaire. Le cas de l'écologie française. *Politix,* 36: 141–162.

Otto, Dianne. 1996. Nongovernmental Organizations in the United Nations System: The Emerging Role of International Civil Society. *Human Rights Quarterly* 18: 107–141.

Passy, Florence. 1998. *L'Action altruiste: Contraintes et opportunités de l'engagement dans les mouvements sociaux.* Geneva: Droz.

———. 2001. Political Altruism and the Solidarity Movement: An Introduction. In M. Giugni and F. Passy (eds.), *Political Altruism.* Lanham, MD: Rowman and Littlefield, pp. 3–25.

Passy, Florence, and Marko Bandler. 2003. Protestation altermondialiste: une nouvelle vague de contestation? Une analyse des cadres narratifs et des réseaux d'action. Paper presented at the annual Congress of the Swiss, German, and Austrian political science associations. Berne, November 14–15.

Péchu, Cécile. 1996. Quand les exclus passent à l'action. *Politix,* 34: 114–133.

———. 2001. Les générations militantes à Droit Au Logement. *Revue française de science politique,* 1–2 (February–April): 73–103.

———. 2005. *The Autonomisation of a Militant Field: Analysis and Discussion of a Concept Starting from the Example of the "Committee of People with Poor Lodging" ("Comité des Mal Logés").* Paper presented at the Third ECPR Conference, September 8–10, Budapest.

Petchesky, Rosalind. 2000. Reproductive and Sexual Rights: Charting the Course of Transnational Women's NGOs (Occasional Paper 8). Geneva: UNRISD.

Peters, Bill. 2000. Jubilee 2000. *Journal of Modern African Studies* 32(4): 699–700.

Pettifor, Anne. 1998. The Economic Bondage of Debt, and the Birth of a New Movement. *New Left Review* 230 (July/August): 115–122.

———. 2001. Debt. In E. Bircham and J. Charlton (eds.). *Anti-Capitalism, a Guide to the Movement.* London: Bookmarks, pp. 43–56.

Pianta, Mario. 1998. Imagination without Power. Notes on Contemporary Social Movements in Italy. *Soundings. A Journal of Politics and Culture* 10: 40–50.

———. 2001a. *Globalizzazione dal basso. Economia mondiale e movimenti sociali.* Roma: Manifestolibri.

———. 2001b. Parallel Summits of Global Civil Society. In H. Anheier et al. (eds.), *Global Civil Society 2001.* Oxford: Oxford University Press, pp. 169–194.

———. 2002. Parallel Summits: An Update. In H. Anheier et al. (eds.), *Global Civil Society.* Oxford: Oxford University Press, pp. 371–377.

———. 2003. Democracy vs. Globalization. The Growth of Parallel Summits and Global Movements. In D. Archibugi (ed.), *Debating Cosmopolitics.* London: Verso, pp. 232–256.

———. 2005. UN World Summits and Civil Society. The State of the Art. Geneva: UNRISD Programme-Working Paper.

Pianta, Mario, and Federico Silva. 2003. *Globalisers from Below. A Survey on Global Civil Society Organisations.* Roma: Globi Research Report.

Pianta, Mario, Federico Silva, and Duccio Zola. 2004. Global Civil Society Events: Parallel Summits, Social Fora, Global Days of Action. http://www.lse.ac.uk/Depts/global/yearbook04chapters.htm. (Accessed December 12, 2006.)

Pianta, Mario, and Duccio Zola. 2005. The Rise of Global Movements, 1970–2005. Unpublished manuscript, Paris.

Piazza, Gianni, and Marco Barbagallo. 2003. Tra globale e locale. L'articolazione territoriale del movimento per una globalizzazione dal basso: i social forum in Sicilia. Paper presented at the annual congress of the Società Italiana di Scienza Politica, Trento, September.

Piven, Frances F., and Richard Cloward. 1992. Normalizing Collective Protest. In A. Morris and C. McClurg Mueller (eds.), *Frontiers in Social Movement Theory.* New Haven, CT: Yale University Press, pp. 301–325.

———. 2000. Power Repertoires and Globalization. *Politics and Society* 28: 413–430.

Pizzorno, Alessandro. 1996. Mutamenti istituzioni e sviluppo dei partiti. In *La storia dell'Europa Contemporanea.* Torino: Einaudi, pp. 961–1031.

Plows, Alexandra. 2004. Activist Networks in the UK: Mapping the Build Up to the Anti-Globalization Movement. In D. Morland and J. Carter (eds.), *Anti-Capitalist Britain.* Cheltenham: New Clarion Press, pp. 93–113.

Portes, Alejandro. 2001. Introduction: The Debates and Significance of Immigrant Transnationalism. *Global Networks: A Journal of Trasnational Affairs* 1(3): 181–194.

Purseigle, François. 2005. Le monde paysan et les sources chrétiennes de la solidarité internationale. In E. Agrikoliansky et al. (eds.), *L'altermondialisme en France. La longue histoire d'une nouvelle cause*. Paris: Flammarion, pp. 75–106.

Raghu, Krishnan, and B. Skanthakumar. 2001. Anti-Globalization and Its Discontents. *Canadian Dimension* 35(2): 16–18.

Rajagopal, Balakrishnan. 2003. *International Law from Below. Development, Social Movements and Third World Resistance*. Cambridge: Cambridge University Press.

Risse-Kappen, Thomas (ed.). 1995. *Bringing Transnational Relations Back in: Non-State Actors, Domestic Structure and International Institutions*. Ithaca, NY: Cornell University Press.

Rodríguez, Gregorio (ed.). 2003. *Las entidades voluntarias de acción social. Informe general*. Madrid: Fundación FOESSA/Cáritas Española.

Rokkan, Stein. 1982. *Cittadini, elezioni, partiti*. Bologna: Il Mulino (original edition 1970).

Rootes, Christopher. 1980. Student Radicalism: Politics of Moral Protest and Legitimation Problems of the Modern Capitalist State. *Theory and Society* 9(3): 473–502.

———. 1995. A New Class? The Higher Educated and the New Politics. In L. Maheu (ed.), *Social Movements and Social Classes: The Future of Collective Action*. London: Sage, pp. 220–235.

——— (ed.). 2003a. *Environmental Protest in Western Europe*. Oxford and New York: Oxford University Press.

———. 2003b. Britain. In C. Rootes (ed.), *Environmental Protest in Western Europe*. Oxford and New York: Oxford University Press, pp. 20–58.

———. 2003c. Conclusion: Environmental Protest Transformed? In C. Rootes (ed.), *Environmental Protest in Western Europe*. Oxford and New York: Oxford University Press, pp. 234–257.

———. 2003d. The Resurgence of Protest and the Revitalisation of British Democracy. In P. Ibarra (ed.), *Social Movements and Democracy*. New York: Palgrave Macmillan, pp. 137–186.

———. 2004. Is There a European Environmental Movement? In J. Barry, B. Baxter, and R. Dunphy (eds.), *Europe, Globalization, Sustainable Development*. London and New York: Routledge, pp. 47–72.

———. 2005. A Limited Transnationalization?: The British Environmental Movement. In D. della Porta and S. Tarrow (eds.), *Transnational Protest and Global Activism*. Lanham, MD: Rowman and Littlefield, pp. 21–43.

Rootes, Christopher, and Clare Saunders. 2005. Social Movements in Britain since the 1960s. DEMOS Working Paper no. 1/2005. Canterbury: Centre for the Study of Social and Political Movements, University of Kent.

Rosanvallon, Pierre. 2005. Démocratie participative: perspective historique. Paper presented at the seminar Démocratie participative, délibération et mouvements sociaux, Iresco, Paris, September 5.

Rosenau, James N., and David C. Earnest. 2004. On the Cutting Edge of Globalization, Before and After 9/11. Paper presented to the annual meeting of the American Sociological Association, San Francisco.

Rosenau, James N., David C. Earnest, Yale H. Ferguson, and Ole R. Holsti. 2006. *On the Cutting Edge of Globalization: An Inquiry Into American Elites.* Lanham, MD: Rowman and Littlefield.

Rosi, Marco. 1992. Master Frames and Cycles of Protest. In A. Morris and C. Mueller (eds.), *Frontiers in Social Movement Theory.* New Haven, CT: Yale University Press, pp. 133–155.

———. 2003. Etica e pratica: il modello di protesta del movimento del Commercio Equo e Solidale in Italia. *Quaderni di Sociologia* 33(47): 71–83.

Rossiaud, Jean. 2001. *Mobillisations globales, manifestations locales.* Geneva: University of Geneva.

Roth, Roland. 1994. *Demokratie von unten: neue soziale Bewegungen auf dem Wege zur politischen Institution.* Köln: Bund-Verlag.

Rucht, Dieter. 1988. Themes, Logics and Arenas of Social Movements. A Structural Approach. *International Social Movement Research* 1: 305–328.

———. 1994. *Modernizierung und Soziale Bewegungen.* Frankfurt am Main: Campus.

———. 2002a. The EU as Target of Political Mobilization: Is There a Europeanization of Conflict? In R. Balme et al. (eds.), *L'action collective en Europe.* Paris: Presses De Science Po, pp. 163–194.

———. 2002b. Social Movements Challenging Neo-liberal Globalization. In P. Ibarra (ed.), *Social Movements and Democracy.* New York: Palgrave, pp. 211–328.

———. 2003. Die Friedensdemonstranten—wer sind sie, wofür stehen sie?" *Forschungsjournal NSB, Sonderdruck: Konturen der Zivilgesellschaft, Zur Profilierung eines Begriffs*: 1610–1613.

———. 2004. The Quadruple "A": Media Strategies of Protest Movements since the 1960s. In W. van de Donk et al. (eds.), *Cyber Protest: New Media, Citizens and Social Movements.* London: Routledge, pp. 29–56.

———. 2005. Un movimento di movimenti? Unità e diversità fra le organizzazioni per una giustizia globale (Übersetzung: Manlio Cinalli). *Rassegna Italiana di Sociologia* 46(2): 1–31.

Sageman, Marc. 2004. *Understanding Terror Networks.* Philadelphia: University of Pennsylvania Press.

Sampedro, Victor. 1997. *Debates sin mordaza: desobediencia civil y servicio militar, 1970–1996.* Madrid: Boletín Oficial del Estado; Centro de Estudios Constitucionales.

Sampedro, Víctor (ed.). 2005. *13–M Multitudes on line.* Madrid: La Catarata.

Saunders, Clare. 2004. Collaboration, Competition and Conflict: Social Movement and Interaction Dynamics in London's Environmental Movement. Ph.D. thesis, School of Social Policy, Sociology and Social Research, University of Kent at Canterbury.

———. 2005. The Configuration of the Global Justice Movement in Britain: Exploring Networks of Concern, Collective Action and Overlapping Memberships of Make Poverty History March participants, Edinburgh, July 2, 2005. Paper presented to the ACI conference on "Genealogies of the Global Justice Movement," Paris, September 30–October 1.

Saunders, Clare, and Christopher Rootes. 2005. The Global Justice Movement in Britain. DEMOS Working Paper no. 2/2005. Canterbury: Centre for the Study of Social and Political Movements, University of Kent.

Schnews. 2004. Away Fixture: Brits Mobilise to Prague. In Justice? (ed.), *Schnews at Ten.* London: Calverts Press, pp. 197–199.

Schulz, M. S. 1998. Collective Action across Borders: Opportunity Structures, Network Capacities, and Communicative Praxis in the Age of Advanced Globalization. *Sociological Perspectives* 41(3): 587–616.

Schwarzmeier, Jan. 2001. *Die Autonomen zwischen Subkultur und sozialer Bewegung.* Books on Demand.

Sen, Jai, Anita Anand, Arturo Escobar, and Peter Waterman (eds.). 2004. *World Social Forum. Challenging Empires.* New Delhi: The Viveka Foundation.

Seoane, José, and Emilio Taddei (eds.). 2001. *Resistencias Mundiales. De Seattle a Porto Alegre.* Buenos Aires: Clacso.

Sikkink, Kathryn. 2005. Patterns of Dynamic Multilevel Governance and the Insider-Outsider Coalition. In D. della Porta and S. Tarrow (eds.), *Transnational Protest and Global Activism.* Lanham, MD: Rowman and Littlefield, pp. 151–174.

Sikkink, Kathryn, and Jackie Smith. 2002. Infrastructures for Change: Transnational Organizations 1953–1993. In S. Khagram et al. (eds.), *Reconstructing World Politics: Transnational Social Movements, Networks and Norms.* Minneapolis: University of Minnesota Press, pp. 24–44.

Silver, Beverly J. 2003. *Forces of Labor: Workers' Movements and Globalization since 1870.* New York: Cambridge University Press.

Smelser, Neil J. 1962. *Theory of Collective Behavior.* New York: Free Press.

Smith, Jackie. 2004. The World Social Forum and the Challenges of Democracy. *Global Networks* 4(4): 413–421.

———. Forthcoming. *Changing the World: Struggles for Global Democracy.* University of Notre Dame.

Smith, Jackie, and Hank Johnston (eds.). 2002. *Globalization and Resistance: Transnational Dimensions of Social Movements.* Lanham, MD: Rowman and Littlefield.

Smith, Jackie, Ron Pagnucco, and George Lopez. 1998. Globalizing Human Rights: The Work of Transnational Human Rights NGOs in the 1990s. *Human Rights Quarterly* 20: 379–412.

Snow, David A. 2004. Framing Processes, Ideology, and Discursive Fields. In D. A. Snow et al. (eds.), *The Blackwell Companion to Social Movements.* Oxford: Blackwell, pp. 380–412.

Snow, David A., and Robert Benford. 1992. Master Frames and Cycles of Protest. In A. Morris and C. McClurg Mueller (eds.), *Frontiers in Social Movement Theories.* New Haven, CT: Yale University Press, pp. 133–155.

Social del Deute Extern a Catalunya. Barcelona: Editorial Mediterrània.

Some Members of the London May Day Collective. 2004. May Day Cancelled! Available online at http://www.ourmayday.org.uk, accessed 1/6/04.

Sommier, Isabelle. 2003. *Le renouveau des mouvements contestataires à l'heure de la mondialisation.* Paris: Flammarion.

Space Hijackers. 2004. Web site at www.spacehijackers.co.uk, accessed 1/11/04.

Stop the War Coalition. 2005. Web site at www.stopwar.org.uk/iraqfeb15demo.asp, accessed 1/17/05.

Stützle, Ingo, and Boris Kanzleiter. 2002. Dabei sein ist alles —Attac: politisch nahe der Fernsehkameras. *ak—analyse and kritik* 459: 26.

Subirats, Joan, and Ricard Gomà. 1998. Democratización, dimensiones de conflicto y políticas públicas en España. In R. Gomà and J. Subirats (eds.), *Políticas públicas en España*. Barcelona: Editorial Ariel.

Tarrow, Sidney. 1989. *Democracy and Disorder. Protest and Politics in Italy, 1965–1975*. Oxford and New York: Oxford University Press.

———. 1996. States and Opportunities: The Political Structuring of Social Movements. In D. McAdam et al. (eds.), *Comparative Perspectives on Social Movements*. Cambridge: Cambridge University Press, pp. 41–61.

———. 2001. Transnational Politics: Contention and Institutions in International Politics. *Annual Review of Political Science* 4: 1–20.

———. 2002. From Lumping to Splitting: Specifying Globalization and Resistance. In J. Smith and H. Johnston (eds.), *Globalization and Resistance: Transnational Dimensions of Social Movements*. Lanham, MD: Rowman and Littlefield, pp. 229–249.

———. 2005. *The New Transnational Activism*. Cambridge: Cambridge University Press.

Tarrow, Sidney, and Donatella della Porta. 2005. Conclusion: "Globalization," Complex Internationalism, and Transnational Contention. In D. della Porta and S. Tarrow (eds.), *Transnational Protest and Global Activism*. Lanham, MD: Rowman and Littlefield, pp. 227–246.

Tarrow, Sidney, and Doug McAdam. 2005. Scale Shift in Transnational Contention. In D. della Porta and S. Tarrow (eds.), *Transnational Protest and Global Activism*. New York: Rowman and Littlefield, pp. 121–149.

Taylor, Verta. 1989. Social Movement Continuity: The Women's Movement in Abeyance. *American Sociological Review* 54: 761–775.

Teivainen, Teivo. 2002. The World Social Forum and Global Democratisation: Learning from Porto Alegre. *Third World Quarterly* 23(4): 621–632.

Tejerina, Benjamín; Iñaki Martínez de Albéniz, Beatriz Cavia, Andrés Gómez, and Amaia Iraola. 2005. *Encuesta sobre El movimiento por una justicia global en España*. Bilbao: Universidad del País Vasco.

Tempest, Matthew. 2002. Operation Overhype. *Guardian*, 4/30/02. Available online at http://www.guardian.co.uk/mayday/story.0,,707752,00.html, accessed 12/7/04.

Thompson, Edward P. 1980. *The Making of the English Working Class*. London: Penguin Books.

Thompson, John B. 1995. *The Media and Modernity*. Cambridge: Cambridge University Press.

Tilly, Charles. 1995. Contentious Repertoires in Great Britain, 1758–1834. In M. Traugott (ed.), *Repertoires and Cycles of Collective Action*. Durham, NC, and London: Duke University Press, pp. 15–42.

Tilly, Charles, and Sidney Tarrow. 2006. *Contentious Politics*. Boulder, CO: Paradigm.

TJM. 2004. *Standing Orders and Regulations*, April 2004.

———. 2005. *Articles of Association of the Trade Justice Movement*, 4/29/05.

Touraine, Alain. 1977. *The Self-Production of Society*. Chicago: University of Chicago Press.

———. 1997. *Eguaglianza e diversità. I nuovi compiti della democrazia*. Bari and Roma: Laterza.

Trapese. 2005. Web site at http://network23.nologic.org/trapese/, accessed 1/13/05.

Tyler, Wat. 2003. Dancing at the Edge of Chaos: A Spanner in the Works of Global Capitalism. In Notes from Nowhere (ed.), *We Are Everywhere: The Irresistible Rise of Global Anti-Capitalism.* London: Verso, pp. 188–195.

Uehlinger, Hans-Martin. 1988. *Politische Partizipation in der Bundesrepublik.* Opladen: Westdeutscher Verlag.

Un ponte per. 2005. *XXV Assemblea nazionale di Un Ponte per . . . Relazione introduttiva a nome del comitato nazionale uscente.*

UNDP. 2003. *Human Development Report 2003—The Millennium Development Goals.* Oxford: Oxford University Press.

UNRISD. 2003. UN World Summits and Civil Society Engagement: Report on Project Planning Workshop. UNRISD Working Paper. Geneva: UNRISD.

Uvin, Peter. 1995. Scaling Up the Grass Roots and Scaling Down the Summit: The Relations between Third World Non Governmental Organisations and the United Nations. *Third World Quarterly* 16(3): 495–551.

Van Aelst, Peter, and Stefaan Walgrave. 2001. Who Is That (Wo)man on the Street? From the Normalization of Protest to the Normalization of Protesters. *European Journal of Political Research* 39: 461–486.

Van Rooy, Alison. 1997. The Frontiers of Influence: NGO Lobbying at the 1974 World Food Conference, the 1992 Earth Summit and Beyond. *World Development* 25(1): 93–114.

Veltri, Francesca. 2003a. "Non si chiama delega, si chiama fiducia." La sfida organizzativa della Rete di Lilliput. In P. Ceri (ed.), *La democrazia dei movimenti. Come decidono i noglobal.* Soveria Mannelli: Rubbettino, pp. 3–30.

———. 2003b. La Rete di Lilliput: identità, lotte, progetti. *Quaderni di Sociologia* 33(47): 85–99.

Voices from Ecological Resistance (VER). 2000a. November 30th 1999, a Global Day of Action, Resistance and Carnival. *Do or Die* 9: 112–113.

———. 2000b. On the Attack in Prague! Against the IMF and World Bank. *Do or Die* 9: 1–8.

———. 2000c. Here Comes the Barmy Army, Pink and Silver on the War Path. *Do or Die* 9: 12–14.

———. 2000d. May Day; Guerrilla Gardening? *Do or Die* 9: 69–81.

VV. AA. 1996. *Le livre noir du néolibéralisme.* Vevey: Editions de l'Aire.

Walgrave, Stefaan, and Dieter Rucht (eds.). Forthcoming. *Protest Politics: Antiwar Mobilization in Western Democracies.* Minneapolis: University of Minnesota Press.

Walton, John, and David Seddon. 1994. *Free Markets and Food Riots. The Politics of Global Adjustment.* Oxford: Blackwell.

Waterman, Peter. 1998. *Globalisation, Social Movements and the New Internationalism.* London: Mansell.

Waterman, Peter, and Jill Timms. 2005. Trade Union Internationalism and a Global Civil Society in the Making. In H. Anheier et al. (eds.), *Global Civil Society 2004/5.* London: Sage, pp. 175–205.

Wilkinson, Michael D. 1996. Lobbying for Fair Trade: Northern NGDOs, the European Community and the GATT Uruguay Round. *Third World Quarterly* 17(2): 251–267.

Wissen, Markus. 2002. Die Fesselungskünstler. Attac, die Finanzmärkte und die Notwendigkeit linker Kritik. *iz3w* 258: 25–26.

Wood, Lesley. 2004. The Diffusion of Direct Action Tactics: From Seattle to Toronto and New York. Unpublished Ph.D. Thesis, Columbia University, New York.

———. 2006. Stopping Seattle: The Effect of Repression on the Spread of the Anti-Globalization Movement. Unpublished paper, York University, Toronto, Canada.

XCADE (Xarxa Ciutadana per l'Ábolició del Deute Extern). 2001. *La Consulta.*

Yanacopulos, Helen. 2005. The Strategies that Bind: NGO Coalitions and their Influence. *Global Networks* 5(1): 93–110.

Yang, Mundo. 2005. Der Nord-Süd-Konflikt im Umfeld der internationalen Jubilee 2000–Kampagne. *Forschungsjournal Neue Soziale Bewegungen* 18(1): 72–79.

Ysmal, Colette. 1994. Transformations du militantisme et déclin des parties. In P. Perrineau (ed.), *L'engagement politique. Déclin ou mutation?* Paris: Presses de la Fondation nationale des sciences politiques, pp. 41–66.

Zwei Seelen in einer Brust. Streitgespräch zwischen Attac Deutschland und dem BUKO-Arbeitsschwerpunkt Weltwirtschaft. 2004. *iz3w* Sonderheft 63–66.

Index

affiliation. *See* memberships
affinity groups, 136, 137
aid, trade, and development
  organizations (ATDOs), 130–133, 146,
  154
alliance building, 19–20. *See also*
  coalition building
alliance structure, 240
allies of movements. *See* parties, political;
  religious groups; unions
Amnesty International, 91, 114, 146, 152,
  167
antagonist groups, 110, 115, 118,
  168–169, 177, 182 n. 6
anticapitalist movement, 56, 84, 143, 149,
  170
antiglobalization movement. *See* global
  justice movement
antinuclear movement, 34, 114, 139, 188
antiracist movement, 105, 114, 169
antiwar movement. *See* peace movement
Attac, 57; in Britain, 154; in France, 108;
  in Germany, 157–158, 170–171, 175,
  178–179; in Italy, 57, 61, 62–63; in
  Spain, 98, 101 n. 23; in Switzerland,
  192, 193. *See also* media strategies
attachment, global, 216–218

Benford, Robert, 67
Black Bloc, 12, 57, 95, 135
Bourdieu, Pierre, 115–116, 182 n. 5
Bové, José, 109, 112–113, 100 n. 21, 125
boycott, 13, 59, 75
Brand, Ulrich, 177
BUND, 167, 177

Bundeskongress entwicklungspolitischer
  Gruppen (BUKO), 161, 167, 169, 175,
  179
Bush administration, 50 n. 9, 225,
  226–227

Cassen, Bernard, 108, 109
Centre de recherché et d'information
  pour le développement (CRID), 114
charities, 130–133, 138, 155 n. 1, 167, 177
Charnovitz, Steve, 32
civil disobedience, 60, 93, 95, 121, 164,
  188
class, 21, 90
class cleavage, 185, 195, 198, 206,
  235–241, 251 n. 2
class conflict, 213, 240
cleavages, GJM, 58, 102 n. 35, 188, 190
Clinton administration, 226
coalition building, 55, 153; in
  transnational networks, 44–45
Cohen, Jean, 118
collective identity. *See* identity, collective
communication, 13; and the use of new
  technologies, 9, 83, 90, 95, 98, 178,
  179. *See also* Internet
communist parties. *See* parties,
  communist
comparison, cross-national, 22–28, 181,
  186, 199, 206, 232–235
Confédération paysanne, 107, 109,
  112–113, 119
configuration of power, 81–82, 206
consensus. *See* decision making, methods
  of

About the Contributors

Massimiliano Andretta, Political and Social Sciences Department, European University Institute, Florence, mandrett@iue.it

Ángel Calle, Institute for Advanced Social Studies of Andalusia, Córdoba, angel.calle@nodo50.org

Hélène Combes, Centre de recherches politiques de la Sorbonne, Paris, combeshvc@yahoo.com

Donatella della Porta, Political and Social Sciences Department, European University Institute, Florence, donatella.dellaporta@iue.it

Nina Eggert, University of Geneva, nina.eggert@politic.unige.ch

Marco Giugni, Laboratoire de recherches sociales et politiques appliquées (Resop), University of Geneva, marco.giugni@politic.unige.ch

Jennifer Hadden, Government Department, Cornell University, jlh242@cornell.edu

Manuel Jiménez, Institute for Advanced Social Studies of Andalusia, Córdoba, mjimsan@upo.es

Raffaele Marchetti, University of Urbino, r.marchetti@uniurb.it

Lorenzo Mosca, SPS Department, European University Institute, Florence, lmosca@iue.it

Mario Pianta, University of Urbino, m.pianta@uniurb.it

Herbert Reiter, Political and Social Sciences Department, European University Institute, Florence, herbert.reiter@iue.it

Christopher Rootes, Centre for the Study of Social and Political Movements, University of Kent at Canterbury, c.a.rootes@kent.ac.uk

Dieter Rucht, Social Science Research Center, Berlin, rucht@wz-berlin.de

Clare Saunders, Centre for the Study of Social and Political Movements, University of Kent at Canterbury, c.e.saunders@kent.ac.uk

Isabelle Sommier, Centre de recherches politiques de la Sorbonne, Paris, isabelle.sommier@univ-paris1.fr

Sidney Tarrow, Government Department, Cornell University, sgt2@cornell.edu

Simon Teune, Social Science Research Center, Berlin, teune@wz-berlin.de

Mundo Yang, Social Science Research Center, Berlin, munco@wz-berlin.de